The Factory-Free Economy

Studies of Policy Reform

Series Editors:

Daniel Cohen and Claudia Senik

This series brings new and innovative policy research to the forefront of academic and policy debates.

It addresses the widest range of policies, from macroeconomics to welfare, public finance, trade, migration, and the environment. It hosts collaborative work under the auspices of CEPR and CEPREMAP.

Titles Published in the Series

The Economics of Clusters
Gilles Duranton, Philippe Martin, Thierry Mayer, and Florian Mayneris

Cultural Integration of Immigrants in Europe
Edited by Yann Algan, Alberto Bisin, Alan Manning, and Thierry Verdier

Happiness and Economic Growth: Lessons from Developing Countries
Edited by Andrew Clark and Claudia Senik

Charitable Giving and Tax Policy: A Historical and Comparative Perspective
Edited by Gabrielle Fack and Camille Landais

Productivity Puzzles Across Europe
Edited by Philippe Askenazy, Lutz Bellmann, Alex Bryson, and Eva Moreno Galbis

Labour Market and Retirement Interactions
Edited by Jean-Olivier Hairault and François Langot

The Factory-Free Economy

Outsourcing, Servitization, and the Future of Industry

Edited by
Lionel Fontagné and Ann Harrison

OXFORD
UNIVERSITY PRESS

OXFORD
UNIVERSITY PRESS

Great Clarendon Street, Oxford, OX2 6DP,
United Kingdom

Oxford University Press is a department of the University of Oxford.
It furthers the University's objective of excellence in research, scholarship,
and education by publishing worldwide. Oxford is a registered trade mark of
Oxford University Press in the UK and in certain other countries

© CEPREMAP 2017

The moral rights of the authors have been asserted

First Edition published in 2017
Impression: 1

Published in the United States of America by Oxford University Press
198 Madison Avenue, New York, NY 10016, United States of America

British Library Cataloguing in Publication Data
Data available

Library of Congress Control Number: 2016950096

ISBN 978-0-19-877916-2

Printed in Great Britain by
Clays Ltd, St Ives plc

Preface

Each industrial revolution produces its own organization of labour. The first one created the factory system. The second invented mass production and the assembly line. The third, the digital revolution, is creating, in turn, something entirely new: a 'factory-free' economy.

The term is purposely ambivalent. It describes an economy in which manufacturing, as we knew it, is vanishing. Firms, in advanced economies, tend to specialize upstream and downstream: they innovate, imagine new goods on the one hand, and try to sell them, make them reach the customer on the other hand. The middle step, producing the good itself, becomes the least important part of the process. Pharmaceuticals are a good example of what is at stake. Huge amounts of R&D allow firms to discover new molecules, while doctors, in a face-to-face relationship to their patients, prescribe them. Producing the drug is secondary. Richard Baldwin, in the opening chapter of this volume, calls it the 'smile curve' economy. Value is high at both extremes and low in between.

But the factory-free term also refers to a wider process that goes beyond the end of manufacturing. It echoes a line of Serge Tchuruk, former CEO of Alcatel-Lucent, heralding a world where firms would have no factories and factories no workers. The old Taylorist system, in which a hierarchical production process assigned to every worker a task designed to be as repetitive as possible, is ending. Firms now try to outsource as many tasks as they can. The old question raised by economists: 'why not just one firm' has become: 'why any firm at all?' Offshoring is part of a broader question: which tasks require 'arms-length' supervision and which can be outsourced? A new dividing line, coined in the literature as routine vs non-routine tasks, is now organizing labour worldwide.

These complementary dimensions of the 'factory-free' economy, the 'servitization' of the economy on the one hand and the new 'division of tasks' on the other, are superbly knit together in this volume. I'm very grateful to Lionel Fontagné and Ann Harrison for having brought together this brilliant collection of papers in a volume which will certainly become a reference in the field.

Daniel Cohen
Director of CEPREMAP

Acknowledgements

The initial idea of a book addressing such a challenging economic policy issue is the outcome of stimulating discussions with Daniel Cohen (PSE and CEPREMAP) on the future of advanced economies' industry. The conference held to discuss initial versions of the chapters received support from the CEPREMAP, the Wharton School (University of Pennsylvania), the Centre d'Economie de la Sorbonne (University Paris 1 and CNRS), the Paris School of Economics, and Labex OSE. We also acknowledge financial support from the CEPREMAP and the Wharton School for the preparation of this book. Philippe Aghion (Harvard and Collège de France), Joseph Francois (World Trade Institute), Nicholas Sly (Federal Reserve Bank of Kansas City), and Thierry Verdier (PSE) attended the workshop and challenged our ideas. Lionel Fontagné acknowledges long-standing support from the CEPII for studying countries' specializations and world economy transformations. Anna Ray and Elsa Leromain provided excellent support in the preparation of the final manuscript. Aimée Wright has been a patient and efficient correspondent between us and our editor.

Contents

Contents

List of Figures

List of Figures

List of Tables

List of Contributors

Richard Baldwin, Graduate Institute, Geneva and Oxford University

Andrew B. Bernard, Tuck School of Business at Dartmouth, CEPR and NBER

Rosario Crinò, Catholic University of Milan and CEPR

Matthieu Crozet, Chinese University of Hong Kong

Aurélien D'Isanto, INSEE, Paris

Avraham Ebenstein, Hebrew University of Jerusalem

Paolo Epifani, University of Nottingham (UK and Ningbo, China)

Matteo Fiorini, European University Institute

Lionel Fontagné, Paris School of Economics-Université Paris 1 Panthéon Sorbonne and CEPII

Teresa C. Fort, Tuck School of Business at Dartmouth, CEPR, and NBER

Ann Harrison, The Wharton School, University of Pennsylvania and NBER

Jean Imbs, Paris School of Economics (CNRS) and CEPR

Marion Jansen, International Trade Center (UNCTAD-WTO)

Francis Kramarz, CREST, ENSAE, Paris-Saclay University

Margaret McMillan, Tufts University and NBER

Philippe Martin, Sciences-Po and CEPR

Thierry Mayer, Sciences-Po, Banque de France, CEPII and CEPR

Florian Mayneris, Université catholique de Louvain, IRES and CORE

Emmanuel Milet, University of Geneva

Michael J. Ryan, Western Michigan University, USA

Farid Toubal, Ecole Normale Supérieure de Cachan and CEPII, France

Weisi Xie, Antai College of Economics and Management at Shanghai Jiao Tong University, China

Introduction

Lionel Fontagné and Ann Harrison

De-industrialization was accelerated by the 2008–2009 crisis in most high-income countries. Yet the trend began decades earlier, as comparative advantage of emerging economies shifted towards more advanced goods and their growing populations commanded an increasing share in global demand. This shift towards a *factory-free economy* in high-income countries has drawn the attention of policy makers in North America and Europe. Some politicians have articulated alarming views, initiating mercantilist or beggar thy neighbour cost-competitiveness policies. Yet companies like Apple, which concentrates research and design innovations at home but no longer has any factories in the USA, may be the norm in the future.

This ongoing transformation of the industrial economies may be consistent with evolving comparative advantage, but has significant short-run costs and requires far-sighted investments. These include the costs to workers who are caught in the shift from an industrial to a service economy, and the need to invest in new infrastructure and education to prepare coming generations for their changing roles. A conference held in Paris aimed to provide an economic analysis of this phenomenon. A selection of the papers presented has been chosen as a starting point for this book. Since then, authors have revised their papers, prolonged their research, refined their conclusions, and drafted stimulating chapters summarized here.

Richard Baldwin starts off the volume by dividing global forces for trade and industrialization into two historical periods. In the first period, which he refers to as 'globalization's first unbundling', falling transport costs and freer trade allowed the industrial countries to rapidly industrialize and dominate manufacturing. From the industrial revolution to the early 1980s, rich countries benefited from a virtuous cycle of innovation, agglomeration, and increasing competitiveness in manufacturing. Manufacturing wage increases were more than offset by productivity increases, and G7 nations saw their share of world gross domestic product (GDP) soar from a fifth in 1920 to two-thirds by 1990. Baldwin attributes most of the impetus for globalization during this period to improvements in transport, which radically lowered transport costs and allowed countries to exploit scale economies and comparative advantage. With agglomeration, cities grew in size and the North industrialized while the South de-industrialized.

Beginning sometime between 1985 and 1995, according to Baldwin, this trend reversed. This is the so-called 'second unbundling', when the nature of globalization changed and led to the upheaval which is the focus of our book. Baldwin zeroes in on the information and communication technologies (ICT) revolution as the driver of this change, as telecommunications became cheaper and more reliable. The ICT revolution was accompanied by the increasing integration into the global economy of a small number of developing countries, which rapidly increased their share of global manufacturing as well as global GDP. While the first unbundling made it easier to buy and sell goods internationally, according to Baldwin 'the ICT revolution changed this. High-tech firms found it profitable to combine their firm-specific know-how with low-wage labour in developing nations'. European firms could now combine their manufacturing technology with labour outside of Europe.

Baldwin describes the changing nature of globalization as shifting the drivers from lower transport costs and tariffs which made it possible to concentrate production and exports in the North, to ICT innovations which allow manufacturing to be dispersed and sent to the South. He also introduces the concept of 'smile curve economics', first proposed by Acer founder Stan Shih, whereby the share of who appropriates value added follows a so-called smile: high at the design phase, lower during the manufacturing phase, and high again in the distribution phase. He points out that the smile 'deepened' during the second unbundling, as manufacturing's share in value added fell with industrialization in the South.

What does all this imply for manufacturing jobs in Europe? Baldwin paradoxically concludes that while industrial country manufacturing firms are likely to retain a leading role, manufacturing *jobs* in the North will continue to decline. Industrial country firms will continue to extract a large share of value added through their role in product design and research and development (R&D), as well as sales, marketing, and after sales services, and will contract out or oversee manufacturing in the 'South'. While some manufacturing jobs will remain at home, they will more likely be the high-skill intensive jobs. While value added may remain in industrial countries, it is unlikely that this will bring more factory jobs. These shifts will support the ever-increasing importance of cities, which Baldwin concludes 'are to the twenty-first century what factories were to the twentieth century. Urban policy will be the new industrial policy'.

The bottom line is that there is nothing like a traditional factory in the twenty-first century. Tasks have been split according to Adam Smith's view of the pin factory, but thanks to digitization at the global level. This has led to a dramatic reshaping of tasks maintained in the high income economies. Growth is now fuelled by talents and their agglomeration. Services and industry are one and the same thing, and if there is something like a factory, this is now the big city where talents, ideas, and services can be combined. Hence the economic competition between agglomerations and the related policies to support their development. The big challenge, from a macroeconomic perspective is the induced disconnection between the creation of value added and the creation of jobs. Although the other face of this coin is productivity gains, distributional issues will become increasingly relevant in advanced economies as value is now shaped by intangible assets.

Japan is certainly one of the most affected of the advanced economies: specialization in electronic equipment, scarcity of resources, and offshoring to low-cost locations for most industrial tasks combine here in a large shock to the domestic industry. Japan's hollowing out is the focus of the second chapter of the book, co-authored by Michael Ryan and Farid Toubal. Ryan and Toubal analyse a unique dataset following Japanese firms between 1982 and 2001. Their data allow them to identify whether Japanese multinational firms were responsible for the hollowing out of the economy in shifting manufacturing jobs abroad.

Ryan and Toubal focus on the so-called lost decade which followed Japan's economic collapse in 1991. They begin by documenting that an enormous expansion in Japanese multinational activity began around that time. The number of Japanese multinationals jumped by 290 per cent between 1985 and 1992, and continued to rise at a slower pace after that. While Japanese overseas production was just over 3 per cent in 1982, it increased by five fold over the next twenty years to reach 17 percent in 2002. Ryan and Toubal also document that over these decades Japanese multinational firms reallocated their networks from North America to Asia and Europe. The share of Japanese vertical affiliates (located in a different business line than their parents) more than doubled in these two regions while it halved in North America.

The aggregate employment data for Japanese multinationals are strongly suggestive of a hollowing out. Between 1997 and 2012, for the manufacturing sector as a whole Japanese parents reduced domestic employment by almost 3 per cent. While employment in Japan shrank in most sectors, Japanese multinationals expanded employment abroad. Econometric evidence confirms that Japanese multinationals contracted domestic employment post-1991, although over the entire two decades the effect is surprisingly small and insignificant. This is partly because other Japanese companies also experienced employment stagnation, so that in comparison Japanese multinationals do not appear to engage in significant hollowing out. Compared to non-multinationals, Japanese multinational companies (MNCs) reduced domestic employment by 0.17 per cent per year from 1992 to 2001, mostly in vertically organized firms.

Ryan and Toubal conclude that there is only limited evidence of hollowing out of the Japanese economy by Japanese multinational enterprises (MNEs) moving production abroad. They hypothesize that the limited effect on domestic employment of outward Japanese MNE activity could be due to the well-known lifetime employment policies adopted by many Japanese firms. Since their formal analysis stops in 2001, it is also possible that the negative effects accelerated after that period.

An alternative way to think about the de-industrialization in rich countries documented in Chapters 1 and 2 is through the concept of structural transformation. Recent databases on trade in value added show that goods trade cannot easily be distinguished from services trade, and this is more so for advanced economies. This mirrors the shift from manufacture to services which has been documented by Hollis Chenery and Moises Syrquin, among others. As income per capita increases, there is a shift in the sectoral structure of the value added, employment and consumption patterns. All in all, the shift in value terms is magnified, compared to evolutions of value added in volume. But the implied reduction in the labour share (as labour shifts towards less productive sectors) is at odds with a balanced growth path combining a constant growth rate of real per capita output, a constant capital–output ratio and a constant labour income share over time.

Jean Imbs in his chapter describes this structural transformation taking place in countries of the Organisation for Economic Co-operation and Development (OECD). He documents that de-industrialization of rich economies is accelerating, as labour moves away from industrial sectors. Imbs notes that 'this reallocation is taking centre stage in political circles, where calls for industrial policy, rising regulation or protectionism are heard increasingly loudly'.

Imbs documents the main features of structural change in fifteen OECD countries since 1970. He identifies that de-industrialization began in the OECD in the 1980s, but only in terms of changes in the allocation of labour, not the allocation of value added. Beginning in the mid-1980s, employment shares decreased in manufacturing, and increased in services. Imbs measures the changes in sectoral shares over four decades. He finds that on average, employment shares in manufacturing have declined by 1.7 per cent per year since 1970, whereas employment shares in services have increased by 1.3 per cent per year. Measured in terms of employment per se, manufacturing employment fell by 1.23 per cent per year while services employment increased by 1.82 per cent. But the same is not true of the sectoral allocation of value added. In particular, between 1970 and 2011, the share of manufacturing in value added does not display any significant trend. As labour productivity rose more quickly than elsewhere, this actually also translated into higher wage growth for manufacturing than for services. The reallocation of employment away from manufacturing is consistent with Baumol's (1967) view that sectors with relatively high productivity growth lose employment.

Imbs finds that for the OECD countries, the share of the manufacturing sector in value added exhibited no clear downward trend between 1970 and 2011, whereas the share of services increased. This is quite different from the conventional view going back to Chenery, Robinson, and Syrquin (1986), where the reallocation goes from manufacturing to services. Falling employment in manufacturing but stable value-added shares are associated with rising productivity and wages in the manufacturing sector. As Imbs points out, 'de-industrialization would not be apparent just on output data', which 'suggests quite some resilience in industrial production'.

Imbs also unpacks the trends within both manufacturing and services. While light industries fell precipitously, the share of heavy industries (including metals, metal products, machinery, equipment, and transport equipment) actually increased as a share of value added. In services, the number one recipient of employment was administrative services, and the star in terms of output gains was ICT—where employment, value added, and productivity growth all increased.

Examining changes in structural transformation between 1970 and 2011, Imbs makes three additional observations. First, de-industrialization did not begin until the mid-1980s, and the share of manufacturing value added remained roughly constant until the year 2000, when de-industrialization accelerated. We comment in passing that the precipitious decline in manufacturing around this period has been noted by others, particularly Justin Pierce and Peter Schott, who associate it with China's entry into the World Trade Organization (WTO) in late 2001.

Second, Imbs notes that the share of construction in value added contracted somewhat in the 1990s but accelerated following the 2007–2008 financial crisis. Finally, services has both accelerated its share in gross domestic product (GDP) and its share in employment, with the result that employment is being drawn to the lowest productivity sector. Imbs concludes his chapter by noting that one reason why 'structural change is back with a vengeance in policy conversations' is that post-2000 output shares of manufacturing in value added in the OECD finally declined. In the last six years of his sample, both labour and output shares collapsed simultaneously in heavy manufacturing. It was not until the 2000s, and the great recession, that manufacturing output shares collapsed across all sectors in the OECD.

Whatever the mechanisms at play, Chapter 4 suggests that the shift from industry to services is to some extent a matter of definition. In the words of Matthieu Crozet and Emmanuel Milet, 'the frontier between manufacturing and services is quite blurry'. How do we define an industry? Does one refer to large-scale production, increasing returns, new consumption items that are increasingly affordable to the consumer? Taking such a broad view, many services could compare with industries. And even within manufacturing industry in the usual sense, services represent an increasing share of value added. The shift towards services within the manufacturing sector is known as the 'servitization' of the manufacturing sector.

Crozet and Milet document the importance of the servitization of French manufacturing firms over the 1997–2007 period. They define servitization as the increase in the share of services in firms' production sales. They have a database of about 635,000 French manufacturing firms, which allows them to identify trends in the percentage of services produced and sold within manufacturing firms during that time period.

While most of the literature on de-industrialization focuses on the types of shifts from industry to services documented in Chapter 3 by Jean Imbs, Chapter 1 by Richard Baldwin and Chapter 4 by Crozet and Milet show that these same trends are very much present within French firms themselves. They document a moderate, but significant and steady increase in servitization over the period. They also decompose the trend into between and within firm changes, and find that servitization is mainly driven by changes that occur within firms. By the end of their sample period, in 2007, they document that 83 per cent of manufacturing firms sold some services, 40 per cent sold more services than goods, and 26 per cent did not even produce goods.

There are both positive and negative implications of Chapter 4 by Crozet and Milet. On the one hand, taking servitization into account provides a harsher diagnosis for de-industrialization of the French economy. Crozet and Milet estimate that the decline in the proportion of workers involved in the production of goods has been up to 8 per cent higher than the usual measures of de-industrialization based on the proportion of workers employed in manufacturing firms. On the other hand, Crozet and Milet argue that this kind of within firm shift towards services has a much more benign and likely beneficial impact on workers than the intersectoral shifts occurring at the macro level. While job losses in manufacturing and job creation in services sectors in the aggregate industrial economies are creating large social costs, the services provided by manufacturing firms are quite different. These services—think of an Apple or a Rolls Royce—are typically strongly linked to the product they sell. Crozet and Milet optimistically conclude that 'this strong complementarity is likely to support the sales of manufacturing products and to defend manufacturing employment and enhance productivity'.

From a statistical point of view, a redefinition of sectors and activities is needed as soon as manufacturing firms perform services. In contrast, some firms are outside the manufacturing sector according to official government statistics but nonetheless are heavily involved in the production of manufactured goods. Although not actually *producing* such goods, how do we classify firms like Apple designing and selling products without factories? In Chapter 5, Bernard and Fort refer to these firms as 'Factoryless Goods Producers' and document their importance using US census data.

Bernard and Fort shift the focus outside of manufacturing to examine the importance of factoryless goods producers, or FGPs for short, defined as firms classified as part of the wholesale trade sector but that 'design the goods they sell and coordinate the production activities'. In their words, these FGPs are 'manufacturing-like' in the sense that they might take a product from the concept through production and delivery but do not actually engage in the production themselves. Examples of such companies include Apple, Mindspeed Technologies (a fabless semiconductor company), and the British appliance firm

Dyson, which designs and sells innovative vacuum cleaners but does not manufacture them itself.

The chapter by Bernard and Fort is an important contribution to this book insofar as there exists little evidence to date about the importance of these kinds of enterprises. The chapter is also particularly timely as beginning in 2017 the US Census Bureau will move FGP establishments to manufacturing. Bernard and Fort estimate that this reclassification of FGPs would have increased the number of manufacturing employees in the USA in 2007 by a minimum of 431,000 to a maximum of 1,934,000, an increase of between 3 and 14 per cent.

While the servitization of firms implies an overly optimistic estimate for manufacturing employment according to Crozet and Milet, the significance of factoryless goods producers suggests the opposite in that many wholesalers are engaging in important aspects of the manufacturing process. Indeed, according to Baldwin, the highest value-added aspects of manufacturing are captured by these FGPs, with possible benefits for firm productivity, innovation, and wage compensation.

Using the US Census Bureau Census of Wholesale Trade, Bernard and Fort estimate that FGPs accounted for 37 per cent of these establishments in 2002. Bernard and Fort suggest that 'these results challenge the stereotype of a wholesale establishment that simply intermediates between producer and consumers. The wholesale sector is a heterogeneous mix of traditional resellers and plants that are actively involved in production activities.'

The two chapters by Crozet and Milet and Bernard and Fort present contrasting phenomena: manufacturing firms increasingly engage in services—which represents 'hidden de-industrialization'—while part of the observed de-industrialization is due to sourcing and design activities performed by factoryless goods producers whose activities were once done within manufacturing. There is indeed no contradiction here: the boundaries of the firm—and even more so for multinational companies—are permanently adjusted to focus on core competencies (catering is not a core competence for a car maker, but designing new software might be). Thus the question is what should be internalized, what can be performed arms-length (Antras 2003), and how productivity is shaped by this choice (Defever and Toubal 2013). Making a decision on outsourcing is even more difficult in an international context: in the presence of incomplete contracts, only the largest and most efficient firms will benefit from offshoring (Antras and Helpman 2004). All in all, there is nothing like a one-size-fits-all strategy: different firms, with different productivity levels, working in industries resorting differently to intangible assets, will make different choices. Some firms may even contemplate offshoring, but eventually decide against it.

Chapter 6 by Lionel Fontagné and D'Isanto focuses explicitly on this critical question of what to retain within the firm and what to outsource or offshore. The chapter presents results from the 2012 survey of global value chains in fifteen European countries to uncover the main determinants of international sourcing choices. They focus on a survey of 28,000 firms located in France, with more than fifty employees at the end of 2008, belonging to industry, trade, and non-financial services sectors.

This survey, carried out by the French National Institute of Statistics and Economic Studies (INSEE) in 2012, is innovative in many aspects. The questionnaire aimed to uncover the strategic choices made by firms to either perform activities themselves inside the firm, sourcing in France, or abroad. One may criticize the joint treatment of domestic and offshore sourcing, but presenting the questionnaire in that way avoided focusing on the always sensitive question of offshoring. Offshoring of an activity was defined as total or partial transfer of this activity to another firm located abroad, which may, or may not, be part of the parent's group.

The survey makes a useful distinction between the core business activity and the support business activities of the respondents. A core business activity is usually the firm's main activity, while support business activities are carried out by the firm to allow or facilitate the production of goods or services for the market or for third parties. Six segments of the value chain were considered beyond the core business of the surveyed firm: distribution and marketing, sales and after sales services, ICT services, administrative and management functions from legal services or accounting to corporate financial and insurance services, research and development, and a residual category.

Fontagné and D'Isanto identify reasons why leading firms decide not to offshore certain activities, and tentatively assess the direct consequences for employment of French firms' offshoring strategies. The survey covered the decision to offshore over a three-year period between 2009 and 2011. Only 4 per cent of French firms, representing 6.5 per cent of employees in the firms within the scope of the survey, reported at least one decision to offshore. An additional 3 per cent of the firms contemplated offshoring, but eventually decided not to. Firms that chose not to offshore cited as reasons uncertainty about the quality of goods and services produced in the offshore location, the need for close interaction with clients, or legal and administrative barriers in the host country and union problems in the home country.

Reasons for offshoring, as reported by respondents, are very much in line with the usual predictions of theories addressing the boundaries of the multinational firms. Distance (a proxy for transaction and information costs, beyond transport) is an important barrier to offshoring. Also the strategic segments of the value chain, when offshored, are kept within the firm's boundaries pointing to the potential for problems related to incomplete contracts. Offshoring firms are shown to be different: the larger the firm's employment, the larger the proportion of firms that offshored parts of their activity. Similarly, the proportion of firms that offshore is increasing with the share of exports in their turnover. For a given sector, size, and firm type, exporters offshored on average four times more often than non-exporting firms. Larger firms source to more remote places, where enforcement of contracts can be more difficult, confirming that in the presence of incomplete contracts, only the largest and most efficient firms will benefit from offshoring. Finally, firms that offshore are not only bigger, they are also members of international groups.

Lastly, Fontagné and D'Isanto estimate that 20,000 jobs (or 0.3 per cent of employment in the surveyed firms in 2011) were offshored between 2009 and 2011. This figure, however, takes no account of general equilibrium effects, and is not based on a proper counterfactual. This is where surveys, although very informative on certain decisions (like not offshoring), are intrinsically an incomplete source of information. Another, less obvious, limitation is worth mentioning: given the design of the survey performed on behalf of EUROSTAT, the definition of offshoring used excludes situations where relocations of activity abroad goes hand-in-hand with an expansion of the activity at home. Although defining international sourcing as a substitute to domestic production is restrictive enough to avoid misinterpretation of the questions by respondents, it neglects more complex strategies where outsourcing and domestic activity are complements. The measure of job losses provided in this chapter must accordingly be considered as indicative, as it excludes by assumption all offshoring activity that could be complementary with domestic activity.

Fontagné and D'Isanto provide a transition in Chapter 6 from documenting de-industrialization in the North to measuring the implications for labour markets. The next part of the book shows that de-industrialization has been accompanied by real costs for industrial country workers. Those costs take the form of a lower demand for less skilled workers, rising inequality, negative effects on real wages and the declining power of unions. It is evident from the chapters in this volume that the transition from industrial to factory-free or primarily service economies is painful for many segments of the population.

The chapter by Rosario Crinò and Paolo Epifani, Chapter 7, suggests that large and rising global imbalances—illustrated by China's trade surpluses and US trade deficits—have directly led to rising inequality in industrial countries. They show, using a model which allows for a continuum of intermediate trade goods, that trade deficits in industrial countries and surpluses in lower-skilled countries can explain increases in demand for skill in both regions. In their empirical work, they show using US data that the results are consistent with their theory. They also rule out other explanations for increasing skill intensity, such as skill-biased technical change (SBTC).

The model developed by Crinò and Epifani builds on the insights of Gordon Hanson and Robert Feenstra who showed that capital flowing from a skill-intensive Northern country to the South could result in greater inequality in both countries. The intuition comes from the fact that more capital in the South leads to a fall in the return to capital there, allowing the South to produce a greater set of skill-intensive goods which can be traded and at the same time narrowing the set of skill-intensive goods in which the North has a comparative advantage. Crinò and Epifani apply the same intuition to a trade surplus in the South (and resulting in a trade deficit in the North) and show that in their model this also leads to greater demand for skill in both regions.

In their empirical section Crinò and Epifani present estimates consistent with their theory and take into account other competing explanations for the rising demand for skill, including the role of offshoring as well as SBTC. They focus on within-industry changes in the US manufacturing sector, and use as their measure of skill bias the share of non-production workers in value added at the disaggregated industry level. They begin by documenting at the aggregate level a positive correlation between skill upgrading and the trade deficit, which holds strong even after controlling for standard proxies for offshoring, trade openness, and technical change.

Next, using a panel of 380 6-digit US manufacturing industries for the 1977 through 2005 period, they test whether sector-level trade deficits are associated with a systematic within-industry increase in the relative demand for skills. Consistent with their aggregate results, they find a strong association between sector level trade deficits and skill upgrading within US industries. They also find that this effect is statistically larger than the effects of offshoring, trade liberalization, and SBTC.

Between 1983 and 2008, US manufacturing employment declined from 22 to 16 million workers. After the 2008 financial crisis, the manufacturing sector lost an additional 2 million jobs. Today, millions of Americans of working age are either unemployed or out of the labour force entirely. In Chapter 8, Ebenstein, Harrison, and McMillan evaluate claims by critics of globalization that 'good' manufacturing jobs have been shipped overseas, and that China is to blame.

Ebenstein, Harrison, and McMillan identify shortcomings of research that is restricted to analysing workers within the manufacturing sector. The effect of import competition on wages is typically identified by exploiting variation in the prices (or quantities) of imported goods across different manufacturing industries. Insofar as globalization affects the US labour market by pushing workers out of manufacturing and into services, a better measure of globalization's impact is found by focusing on occupational exposure to globalization, as workers can more easily switch industries than occupations, and so the wage declines will be felt by workers who are forced to leave manufacturing or their occupation entirely.

In their previous work, Ebenstein, Harrison, and McMillan (2014) presented evidence that an occupation-based analysis is more effective at uncovering the impact on worker wages of global competition. In this chapter, they extend their previous analysis up to 2008, which allows them to include a period characterized by rapid increases in offshoring, especially to China.

Their chapter also disaggregates the impact of geographically distinct sources of offshore employment changes on domestic US wages. In particular, Ebenstein, Harrison, and McMillan measure the impact of offshore employment by US parents in China, Mexico, India, and other low-income locations. They also compare the effects of import competition from China and offshore employment in China on US worker wages.

Consistent with their earlier work, they find that offshoring to low-wage countries is associated with wage declines for US workers, and the workers most affected are those performing routine tasks. Their results indicate that a 10 per cent increase in occupational exposure to import competition is associated with a 2.7 per cent decline in real wages for workers who perform routine tasks. They also find substantial wage effects of offshoring to low wage countries: a 10 percentage point increase in occupation-specific exposure to overseas employment in low-wage countries is associated with a 0.27 per cent decline in real wages for workers performing routine tasks for our entire sample, and nearly a 1 per cent decline for 2000 through 2008.

The downward pressure from trade and offshoring on US wages using occupational (but not industry-level) measures of globalization explains the puzzling results found by Autor, Dorn, and Hanson (2013). David Autor and his co-authors find a positive but insignificant impact of import competition on local wages, leading them to conclude that 'manufacturing plants react to import competition by accelerating technological and organizational innovations that increase productivity and may raise wages'. Ebenstein, Harrison, and McMillan in Chapter 8 suggest that occupational exposure to globalization puts significant downward pressure on wages because such a measure captures the movement of workers out of manufacturing and into lower wage services. Using a subset of the Current Population Surveys (CPS) data where they are able to follow the same worker over time, they measure what happens to workers' wages when they switch industries or occupations. They find evidence that while the wage impacts of switches within manufacturing are mild, leaving manufacturing for services is associated with an appreciable loss in wages, and larger losses still for workers who are forced to switch occupation upon leaving manufacturing. This highlights the importance of examining the impact of globalization by looking beyond workers only employed directly in manufacturing.

Ebenstein and colleagues then turn to a more in-depth analysis of competition from China, the US's second largest trading partner and second most popular destination for offshoring (after Mexico) in 2008. They present evidence that both imports from China and offshoring to China are associated with lower US worker wages. Increasing occupational import penetration from China by a 10 percentage point share of a market is associated with a 5.6 per cent wage decline, and increasing occupational offshore exposure to China is associated with a further 1.6 per cent decline in wages. They compare for the first time the impact of both import competition from China and offshore activities by US multinationals in China. The results suggest that focusing on imports alone (as Autor, Dorn, and Hanson do) understates the role of globalization in contributing to falling US wages.

Lastly, they examine the role played by trade and offshoring in explaining US labour force participation. In the wake of the global financial crisis, the US suffered persistently high rates of unemployment relative to historical averages, and generational lows in labour force participation rates. Ebenstein, Harrison, and McMillan show that neither offshoring nor international trade are associated with a significant reduction in labour force participation. Their results indicate that the most important factors associated with a reduction in US labour force participation during the sample period were computer use rates or increasing capital intensity, and that offshore activities to China or elsewhere played a very small role. These last set of results suggest that declining labor force participation in the United States is better explained by technical change as computers have replaced routine jobs, than by globalization.

Francis Kramarz also focuses on the costs to the labour market of increasing international competition. He examines the impact of globalization on the labour market in France. The Single Market Program (SMP), an attempt to implement the European Community's internal market, was conceived in 1985, launched in 1988, with the hope of being achieved around 1992. It entailed decreased tariffs and barriers within the EC, leading to a rapid increase in import competition in France during the second half of the 1980s. Kramarz addresses two questions in his chapter: with increased competitive pressures and expanded opportunities due to the SMP, was foreign outsourcing a possible response to the high wages and strong unions? Second, he asks what was the impact of increased outsourcing on wages and employment.

Kramarz begins his chapter with a formal theoretical model that shows how the threat of offshoring forces workers in firms with strong unions to accept a lower share of the profits. Offshoring creates a threat point that reduces the size of the rent to be shared after bargaining. This pushes firms facing strong unions to outsource. Through these changes in the quasi-rent, this effect depresses wages. One important contribution of this chapter is to trace out the mechanism from offshoring to its (negative) impact on worker wages, which occurs as firms with stronger union activity are able to bargain more effectively with their workers.

Kramarz is able to use a unique French dataset that has firm level information on outsourcing decisions, imports, and union strength. He combines that data with matched employer and employee data that allows him to measure the impact of globalization on wages at the disaggregate level. He uses the exogenous shock of the SMP to trace out first its effect on the bargaining strength of unions at the firm level, and consequently the impact on firm level decisions to outsource employment. Outsourcing and import competition at the firm level in turn affected domestic wages and employment.

Kramarz shows, both theoretically and empirically, that in France there are essentially two types of firms: firms facing strong unions in which workers capture half of the rents and firms facing weaker unions where workers are paid their opportunity wage. Kramarz first identifies the exercise of union power with firm size, in particular with firms having at least fifty employees. The fifty employee cutoff is associated with the Auroux Laws in France, which stipulate that bargaining should take place every year in an establishment or a firm with more than fifty employees. Kramarz then goes beyond the firm size cutoff and uses firm level information on union activity to confirm the extent of union strength.

Kramarz finds that large firms decrease employment when their offshoring increases. At the same time, rent sharing declines. In terms of magnitudes, he finds that a 10 percentage point increase in the share of offshoring in sales is associated with a 1.3 percentage point decrease in employment. Kramarz concludes that firms facing strong unions increased offshoring and decreased employment while other firms increased relative employment and used outsourcing much less intensively. As he points out, 'Union strength may well have backfired'.

Fiorini, Jansen, and Xie summarize the trends documented in the first nine chapters of this book, documenting increasing globalization, structural change in all economies, and employment losses in manufacturing. One issue that remains unresolved is the relative importance of offshoring, labour saving technological change, and finally the natural shift of economies towards services in explaining these global trends. Such shifts are not independent: offshoring is one consequence of the shifting comparative advantage of industrialized economies, and technical change is partly a response to competition from low-wage countries. If structural change observed in industrialized countries goes hand-in-hand with offshoring, it should also have a mirror image: structural change in the developing world.

Fiorini, Jansen, and Xie take a comprehensive view of structural change in Chapter 10 by comparing and contrasting trends in both developing and industrialized countries. Two questions are the focus of the research presented in their chapter: (1) has structural change accelerated in recent years, and (2) has the movement of factories to the developing world been systematic and global?

On the first question, focusing in particular on the relative role of the manufacturing sector in the USA, the chapter suggests that changes in recent years are not dramatic. The decline in manufacturing employment has been steady over the past three decades. A somewhat different picture arises in terms of value added, as a result of changes in relative prices and productivity differentials: the sector's role in terms of (the volume of) value added declined less than employment.

On the second question, they find that in most industrialized countries the decline of the manufacturing sector has occurred in conjunction with increased imports from the developing world. While such a trend might imply causality between the two, changes observed in the sectoral composition of economic activity are far more complex than what would be expected from this pure offshoring story. Interestingly, even China, the so-called 'world's factory' experienced a decline in the relative weight of manufacturing employment in the 1990s. They also find that Japan, Germany, and Korea went through significant labour shedding in manufacturing in the 1990s and now have trade surpluses with China. Such structural transformation in China suggests that the gradual decline in employment shares of manufacturing cannot be attributed primarily to emerging market competition but are part of a global and perhaps universal process of structural transformation.

In the light of this inconclusive prima facie evidence, Fiorini, Jansen, and Xie seek to properly measure structural change. They develop a structural change index which reflects the share of a given economy that has shifted sectoral allocation over a certain period of time. This index does not indicate the direction of change (it does not say whether economic activity has moved away from manufacturing towards services or vice versa) but the intensity of change. This measure can easily be compared across countries and can be calculated using sectoral value added or employment data.

Structural change in terms of value added has not accelerated over the past three decades for the USA, whereas it has in terms of employment. The authors find that this acceleration does not necessarily hold for other developed countries and one should refrain from drawing general conclusions based on the US example only.

Finally, Fiorini, Jansen, and Xie explore the relationship between growth and structural change, but find that no general pattern arises. In most advanced economies, the values of their structural change indices are comparable across decades while decade-level growth rates have declined. In Asia, growth rates have remained relatively stable across the decades, while most of the reshuffling took place in the 1980s. Finally, for Latin America there may be a negative relationship between growth and structural change. All in all, they conclude that there is no clear link between growth and structural change. Structural change can take place in a context of positive, no, or negative growth.

These inconclusive findings, which refute the popular view of a direct relationship between growth in developing countries and de-industrialization in the developed world, lead Fiorini, Jansen, and Xie to conclude that structural change is not automatically associated with productivity increases or growth. Episodes of large structural changes in economies at different levels of development do not necessarily coincide. Microeconomic evidence, ideally using matched employer–employee data, is needed to precisely assess what are the ultimate consequences of offshoring and de-industrialization on the labour market.

The last chapter of the volume is by Philippe Martin, Thierry Mayer, and Florian Mayneris. They explore why some firms were able to weather the 2008–09 crisis better. In particular, they focus on the role of cluster policies in allowing some exporters to survive the collapse of international trade in 2009 better than others. The authors address whether cluster policies are one solution to de-industrialization and worker dislocation, which is a theme of this entire book.

Martin, Mayer, and Mayneris are specifically interested in French cluster policies, the pôles de compétitivité (competitiveness clusters) which were launched in 2005. Their results show that the agglomeration of exporters positively affects the survival probability of firms on export markets, and conditioning on survival, the growth rate of their exports. However, these spillover effects were not stronger during the crisis; if anything, the opposite is true. They then show that this weaker resilience of firms in clusters is probably due to the fact that firms in clusters are more dependent on the fate of the largest exporter in the cluster.

As Martin and his co-authors point out, 'clusters are popular among policy makers. There are good reasons for this: geographical concentration of firms operating in the same industry has been extensively shown to favour firm-level economic performance.' In contrast, previous literature shows modest gains from public policies that provide incentives for more clustering. This is because agglomeration gains are already partly internalized by firms in their location choices.

The authors of Chapter 11 fill the gap in the business cycle literature by investigating whether firms in clusters are better able to resist economic shocks than others. They highlight an interesting feature of clusters that has been ignored so far: by reinforcing the relationships and the interdependencies between firms, clusters might amplify the transmission of shocks, and thus increase the volatility of activity at the local level. Policy makers interested in promoting clusters may want to consider this amplification of shocks when evaluating the costs and benefits of implementing a cluster policy.

This book addresses the new role for technology, which makes it possible to handle complexity and to exchange an unprecedented amount of information on a global scale instantaneously. Recent developments in the literature on global value chains (see Baldwin, Chapter 1) give a better understanding of the extent to which trade in intermediate goods changes the overall picture of traded value added. Such changes may lead researchers to compute adjusted revealed comparative advantage indicators (Koopman, Wang, and Wei 2014).

Choices made by firms clearly affect their total employment, conditional on the complementarity or substitutability of the offshored tasks. But beyond the volume of hours worked, choices regarding the boundaries of the firm affect the nature of tasks performed within the firm. In a factory-free economy, the content of tasks performed in the industrial sector has little to do with the physical transformation of materials into products. The two main activities are designing new products, or new bundles of products and services (iPhone and iTunes), and supervising the global value and logistic chains leading to the physical product delivered to the final consumer. Most of the tasks are focused on research and development, and treatment of complex batches of information. Associated tasks being skill-intensive, the skill content of tasks performed within the factory-free company is likely to increase.

We know since Feenstra and Hanson (1996) that the vertical fragmentation of production at the international level contributed to rising wage inequality in the United States. What is different in the case of 'factory-China' is the size of the country where physical production activities are offshored. In such a case, trade imbalances (only partially compensated by services income, e.g. royalties) may well reinforce the mechanisms at stake on industrial country labour markets. International trade is no longer about products, but tasks (Grossman and Rossi-Hansberg 2008). Low-wage countries tend to specialize in offshorable tasks, while advanced countries specialize in the less offshorable segments of sequential value chains handling complexity, while unskilled non-offshorable tasks may be maintained as well.

Ebenstein, Harrison, and McMillan in this volume show that reorganization of production on a global scale is leading to the reallocation of workers away from high-wage manufacturing jobs into other sectors or other occupations within industry. Trade in tasks can affect a wider class of workers than those directly affected in handling physical products. Displaced workers will face a reduction in their earnings as they shift industries (even from manufacturing to services), but continue performing tasks that are routine and offshorable. Indeed, Kramarz in Chapter 9 shows that unions can paradoxically reinforce the desirability of offshoring for firms confronted by competition, but could also limit the ultimate recourse to offshoring as well.

If the distinction between industry and services is no longer relevant, if tasks performed are the relevant prism to analyse transformations in the labour market, and if cities are the twenty-first century 'factories', how should public policies adjust? One likely outcome is that public policies will be redesigned to target individuals, rather than industries (manufacturing or services), when addressing employment issues. The other dimension is about the promotion of cities. How do we interpret the evidence presented in the last chapter of this book that productivity gains are associated with clusters? Denser areas are more productive. This can be due to selection, as only the most productive firms can survive in more competitive environments. This can also be due to agglomeration economies, associated with better access to a variety of inputs, or the circulation of ideas (Duranton and Puga 2004). If such difference in the efficiency of big cities is mainly the outcome of a selection issue, and if firms internalize agglomeration economies in their location decisions, the gains to be expected from policies reinforcing clustering might be limited. Fortunately, selection is only part of the answer. The comparison of the empirical firm productivity distribution across high- and low-density locations confirms that there is a substantial efficiency premium associated with city size, and that it is even higher for highly productive firms (Combes et al. 2012). Fontagné and Santoni (2015) explain this outcome of firm optimization in terms of hiring and displacing inputs. Resource misallocation and the associated effect on productivity is not only related to firm characteristics but also to the environment in which firms operate. Denser locations offer a better match between employers and employees, hence higher overall productivity, beyond individual firm characteristics.

This book presents contributions from leading researchers studying the process of de-industrialization. These researchers, based in Europe and the USA, present a daunting picture of a new, factory-free world. Richard Baldwin begins the volume with a broad sweep of history showing that de-industrialization is happening in all the industrial countries. Jean Imbs reinforces the picture. Our authors then show that the macro level trends away from manufacturing are reinforced by micro firm data for Japan, the USA, and countries in Europe.

The three chapters by Richard Baldwin, Jean Imbs, and Fiorini, Jansen, and Xie all concur that structural transformation towards a factory-free economy has been happening in industrial countries for many decades. The evidence in this book suggests that de-industrialization is a process that happens over time in all countries, even in China today. One implication is that the current vogue of China-bashing is not likely to provide a solution to these long-term trends. Another implication is that the distinction between manufacturing and services is likely to become increasingly blurry.

More manufacturing firms are engaging in services activities, and more wholesale firms are engaging in manufacturing. One optimistic perspective suggests that industrial country firms may be able to exploit the high value-added and skill-intensive activities associated with design and innovation, as well as distribution, all components of the global value chain for manufacturing.

A less optimistic picture emerges when we turn to an evaluation of the impact of these trends on industrial country labour markets. While over the longer term economies may adjust to the shift towards a factory-free economy, in the medium term the personal and political costs are significant. The most painful adjustment is for workers who do routine jobs, who are older and less educated, and cannot easily adjust to the demands of this factory-free world.

These findings raise challenges for economic policy. If workers do not benefit from globalization, they will cease to support it. While the goal of this book is primarily to document the trends in industrial economies and impact on labour markets, as editors we would like to offer some suggestions. A first issue relates to the statistical definition of manufacturing and services. We have shown in this book that there is no longer a boundary between the two: services increasingly rely on immobilized capital and technology as exemplified by data centres, cloud computing, and exploitation of big data; manufactured goods are increasingly bound to services to the client; factoryless producers develop and market new products without any single tangible intervention on goods or materials.

Second, a clear challenge is how to design public policies that address the structural changes documented in this book. In a situation where the value chain is long and highly fragmented, policy makers should consider promoting the creation, design, and marketing of attractive bundles of products and services. These are areas of innovation, economies of scale, and high productivity. Industrial policy, be it horizontal or more targeted, is likely to become dedicated to innovation across all sectors, not only manufacturing.

Funding declining activities with public money and raising obstacles to the development of new activities will not stop the movement described in these pages. These changes are global, rapid, and result from a combination of technical progress and raising capabilities of the new players in the world economy. However, promoting new activities across all economic sectors and combining that promotion with greater competition could be highly effective (see Aghion et al. 2015). A side effect of the new organization of the world economy is the rising importance of big cities as clustering talents; nations are less relevant with globalization, while cities gain in importance.

The third issue highlighted in this volume is the cost to displaced workers and the consequences for educational policies and social safety nets. We have shown that certain occupations are particularly hit by the ongoing process. Policies like safety nets or vocational training should be targeted at individuals, rather than positions. In the USA, legislation passed in 2015 extends assistance to workers hurt by trade to the service sectors. However, research shows that only half of the US workers who could benefit from trade adjustment assistance actually apply for it. Particularly in the USA, educational opportunities are skewed towards the better off. A more globalized world requires significantly greater investments in education, infrastructure, and social safety nets.

Current policies were been designed in a era very different from the evolution described in this book. Ultimately, the disconnection between value added and physical production is a big challenge for public budgets: the tax base is highly mobile and the value added is increasingly associated with intangibles.

The last issue goes beyond this book and beyond the economic analysis. There is now good evidence that locations particularly exposed to the changes that we describe elect more extremist members of the traditional political parties (in the US) or even vote for extremist parties (in Europe). This is the big challenge for our democracies: creating the policies and the political dialogue to make the structural transformations acceptable for citizens.

While international economists for many years downplayed the transitional costs associated with structural changes, it is increasingly evident that globalization imposes significant adjustment costs. Those costs are borne disproportionately by less skilled workers. One of the great challenges of the twenty-first century will be how to improve the lives and opportunities for those left behind.

Bibliography

Acemoglu, Daron and Veronica Guerrieri (2008). Capital Deepening and Non-Balanced Economic Growth, *Journal of Political Economy*, 116(3): 467–97.

Aghion, Philippe, Jing Cai, Mathias Dewatripont, Luosha Du, Ann Harrison, and Patrick Legros (2015). Industrial Policy and Competition, *American Economic Journal: Macroeconomics*, 7(4): 1–32.

Antras Pol (2003). Firms, Contracts and Trade Structure, *Quarterly Journal of Economics*, 118(4): 1375–418.

Antras, Pol and Elhanan Helpman (2004). Global Sourcing, *Journal of Political Economy*, 112(3): 552–80.

Antras, Pol and Esteban Rossi-Hansberg (2009). Organizations and Trade, *Annual Review of Economics*, 1: 43–64.

Autor, David H., David Dorn, and Gordon H. Hanson (2013). The China Syndrome: Local Labor Market Effects of Import Competition in the United States, *American Economic Review*, 103(6): 2121–68.

Baldwin, Richard (2012). Global Supply Chains: Why They Emerged, Why They Matter, and Where They are Going. CEPR discussion papers 9103.

Baumol, William J. (1967). Macroeconomics of Unbalanced Growth: The Anatomy of Urban Crisis, *American Economic Review*, 57(3): 415–26.

Boppart, Timo (2014). Structural Change and the Kaldor Facts in a Growth Model With Relative Price Effects and Non-Gorman Preferences, *Econometrica*, 82(6): 2167–96.

Bryan, Jon L. (2013). Offshore Outsourcing: Will the Robust Growth Continue? mimeo, Bridgewater State University.

Chenery, Hollis B., Sherman Robinson, and Moshe Syrquin (1986). *Industrialization and Growth*. Washington, DC: World Bank.

Combes, Pierre-Philippe, Gilles Duranton, Laurent Gobillon, Diego Puga, and Sébastien Roux, S. (2012). The Productivity Advantages of Large Cities: Distinguishing Agglomeration From Firm Selection, *Econometrica*, 80(6): 2543–94.

Costinot, Arnaud, Vogel Jonathan, and Su Wang (2013). An Elementary Theory of Global Supply Chains, *Review of Economic Studies*, (80): 109–44.

Defever, Fabrice and Farid Toubal (2013). Productivity, Relationship-specific Inputs and the Sourcing Modes of Multinationals, *Journal of Economic Behavior & Organization*, 94, 345–57.

Dixit, Avinash K. and Gene M. Grossman (1982). Trade and Protection with Multistage Production, *Review of Economic Studies*, 49: 583–94.

Duranton, Gilles and Diego Puga (2004). Micro-foundations of urban agglomeration economies. In J. V. Henderson and J. F. Thisse (eds), Volume 4 of *Handbook of Regional and Urban Economics*, Amsterdam: Elsevier, 2063–117.

Feenstra, Robert C. and Gordon Hanson (1996). Foreign investment, outsourcing and relative wages. In R. C. Feenstra et al. (eds), *The Political Economy of Trade Policy: Papers in Honor of Jagdish Bhagwati*, Cambridge, MA: MIT Press, 89–127.

Fontagné, Lionel and Gianluca Santoni (2015). Firm Level Allocative Inefficiency: Evidence from France, CEPII working paper, 2015–12.

Fort, Teresa C. (2013). Breaking up is Hard to do: Why Firms Fragment Production across Locations, working paper, Tuck School of Business, 1, 3.

Grossman, Gene M. and Esteban Rossi-Hansberg (2008). Trading Tasks: A Simple Theory of Offshoring, *American Economic Review*, 98(5): 1978–97.

Harrison, Ann and Margaret McMillan (2011). Offshoring Jobs? Multinational and U.S. Manufacturing Employment, *Review of Economics and Statistics*, 93(3): 857–75.

Head, Keith, Mayer Thierry, and John Ries (2009). How Remote is the Offshoring Threat? *European Economic Review*, 53(4): 429–44.

Helpman Elhanan, Melitz Marc J. and Stephen R. Yeaple (2004). Export Versus FDI with Heterogeneous Firms, *American Economic Review*, 94(1): 300–16.

Hijzen, Alexander, Jean Sébastien, and Thierry Mayer (2011). The Effects at Home of Initiating Production Abroad: Evidence from Matched French Firms, *Review of World Economics*, 147(3): 457–83.

Hummels, David, Ishii Jun, and Kei-Mu Yi (2001). The Nature and Growth of Vertical Specialization in World Trade, *Journal of International Economics*, 54(1): 75–96.

Johnson, Robert C. and Guillermo Noguera (2012). Accounting for Intermediates: Production sharing and trade in value added, *Journal of International Economics*, 86(2): 224–36.

Koopman, Robert, Wang, Zhi, and Shang-Jin Wei (2014). Tracing Value Added and Double Counting in Gross Exports, *American Economic Review*, 104(2): 459–94.

Melitz, Marc J. (2003). The Impact of Trade on Intra-industry Reallocations and Aggregate Industry Productivity, *Econometrica*, 71(6): 1695–725.

Miroudot, Sébastien, Rainer Lanz, and Alexandros Ragoussis (2009). Trade in Intermediate Goods and Services, OECD, TAD/TC/WP(2009)1/Final.

Ngai, Rachel and Christopher A. Pissarides (2004). Structural Change in a Multi-sector Model of Growth, CEPR discussion paper, No. 627.

Nunn, Nathan (2007). Relationship-specificity, Incomplete Contracts and the Pattern of Trade, *Quarterly Journal of Economics*, 122: 569–600.

Rowthorn, Robert and Ramana Ramaswamy (1998). Growth, Trade an Deindustrialization, IMF working paper, WP/98/60.

Sanyal, Kalyan K. and Ronald W. Jones (1982). The Theory of Trade in Middle Products, *The American Economic Review*, 72(1): 16–31.

Stehrer, Robert (2012). Trade in Value Added and Value Added in Trade, WIIW working papers 81, The Vienna Institute for International Economics.

Thoenig Mathias and Thierry Verdier (2003). A Theory of Defensive Skill-biased Innovation and Globalization, *The American Economic Review*, 93(3): 709–28.

Yeaple, Stephen R. (2006). Offshoring, Foreign Direct Investment and the Structure of US Trade, *Journal of the European Economic Association*, 4(2–3): 602–11.

1

Factory-free Europe? A Two Unbundlings Perspective on Europe's Twentieth-century Manufacturing Miracle and Twenty-first-century Manufacturing Malaise

Richard Baldwin

1.1 Introduction

For a century, textile mills were abundant in the US state of South Carolina. Jobs were plentiful for high- and low-skilled workers alike. This is no longer true (Davidson 2012). South Carolina low-skill workers are fighting robots at home and China abroad. The battle is not going well. Digitally-assisted manufacturing transformed South Carolina textile mills into nearly autonomous, computer-run machines. The telling local joke is that a modern textile mill employs only a man and a dog. The man is there to feed the dog, and the dog is there to keep people away from the machines.

Manufacturing is bifurcating. Stages of production that stay in the USA employ a few high-skilled workers and lots of technology. Low-skill occupations are packed up into stages and offshored to low-wage nations, or automatized. Things have not yet gone so far in Europe, but the trend is clear. Europe's post-war manufacturing miracle has turned into the twenty-first-century manufacturing malaise.

This malaise evokes an understandable nostalgia from policy makers, social activists, and analysts. In 1950, a fifth of Europeans worked on farms, incomes were low, and social services were meagre. By the 1973 oil shock, Europe was transformed. Postwar hunger, dislocation, and destruction were replaced by mass consumerism and middle-class affluence. Europe's cradle-to-grave social policy was the envy of the world. All this was closely correlated with Europe's manufacturing miracle. Industrial output rose faster than national incomes and industrial exports grew faster than either (Crafts and Toniolo 1996).

Many take this manufacturing–prosperity correlation as causal and seem determined to fight Europe's current malaise by fostering European manufacturing. It worked for the post-war generation, why can't it work for the post-Crisis generation?

This chapter suggests a stark answer: manufacturing cannot play the role today that it did in the post-war years for one simple reason. The nature of globalization changed.

1.1.1 Globalization and Manufacturing Changed

For a century and a half, globalization was driven by lower trade costs that separated production and consumption internationally while clustering it locally into factories. I call this globalization's first unbundling.[1]

Freer trade allowed Europe to exploit its comparative advantage in high-end manufacturing. Europe's industrial wages were high, but it was globally competitive since the technology gap more than offset the wage gap. Growing production fostered innovation and agglomeration which boosted European competitiveness thus feeding a virtuous helix of production, innovation, and employment. The opposite happened in poor nations. This is why the first unbundling saw the 'North' industrialize and the 'South' de-industrialize with most of the action coming before the First World War (Table 1.1).

This changed from the late 1980s, when globalization began to be driven by the ICT revolution rather than lower trade costs (Baldwin 2006). Cheaper, surer, and more ubiquitous communication made it feasible to organize complex manufacturing processes at a distance. Globalization's 'second unbundling' involves the unbundling of Europe's factories in two ways: fractionalization and dispersion. Manufacturing processes fractionalized off into finer stages of production—many of which had more extreme factor-intensities. Given vast wage differences, many of the unbundled stages shifted to low-wage nations—along with generous doses of European technology. This explains why the second unbundling saw Northern de-industrialization and Southern industrialization—just the reverse of the first unbundling.

---

[1] See Baldwin (2008) for the original presentation of the two-unbundlings view of globalization.

Table 1.1 Per capita industrialization levels, 1759–1913

(UK in 1900 = 100)	1750	1800	1830	1860	1880	1900	1913
Developed countries	8	8	11	16	24	35	55
Europe	8	8	11	17	23	33	45
Europe (ex-UK)	7	8	9	14	21	36	57
Austria-Hungary	7	7	8	11	15	23	32
Belgium	9	10	14	28	43	56	88
France	9	9	12	20	28	39	59
Germany	8	8	9	15	25	52	85
Italy	8	8	8	10	12	17	26
Russia	6	6	7	8	10	15	20
Spain	7	7	8	11	14	19	22
Sweden	7	8	9	15	24	41	67
Switzerland	7	10	16	26	39	67	87
UK	10	16	25	64	87	100	115
Outside Europe	7	7	11	17	33	63	116
Canada		5	6	7	10	24	46
USA	4	9	14	21	38	69	126
Japan	7	7	8	7	9	12	20
Third World	7	6	6	4	3	2	2
China	8	6	6	4	4	3	3
India-Pakistan	7	6	6	3	2	1	2
Brazil				4	4	5	7
Mexico				5	4	5	7
World	7	6	7	7	9	14	21

Source: Bairoch (1982, table 9).

The deep economic fundamentals of this tectonic shift are twofold:

- the heightened international mobility of European technical, managerial, and marketing know-how; and
- the fact that know-how is firm-specific rather than nation-specific.

During the first unbundling, European workers and European technology were on the same team. Globalization's second unbundling split up the European labour-technology team.

Before the ICT revolution, high European wages were more than offset by high productivity in skill-intensive stages. While productivity did not offset high wages in low-skill stages, the team as a whole was competitive globally. The ICT revolution made it feasible to spatially unbundle the team. It gave European manufacturers the option of leveraging their firm-specific know-how with high-wage labour at home for some stages and low-wage labour abroad for others.

- In this sense, European manufacturing continues to flourish—at least when one defines 'European' in terms of know-how rather than the location of factories and passports of the workers.

Recombining European technology with low-wage labour is the key. European policy choices mean that low-skill labour cannot move to the technology, so the technology moves to the labour. This outcome has many monikers—offshoring, fragmentation, vertical specialization, production unbundling, production sharing, global value chains, etc. A similar phenomenon happened during the pre-war phase of globalization's first unbundling but then the recombination involved European labour going to New World land.

1.1.2 Prima Facie Evidence of the Changes

Globalization's second unbundling had radically different effects compared to the first, as Figure 1.1 shows. During the first unbundling, G7 nations saw their share of world GDP soar from a fifth in 1820 to two-thirds by 1990. From about 1990, the G7's shares dropped to under 50 per cent—about where it was 110 years ago.

As Figure 1.2 shows, the absolute number of manufacturing jobs has fallen in developed economies since globalization's second unbundling (Figure 1.2, left panel) and manufacturing's share of jobs has fallen steadily since 1970. Globalization has been only part of the reason for this job loss. Debande (2006) notes that expenditure shifts towards

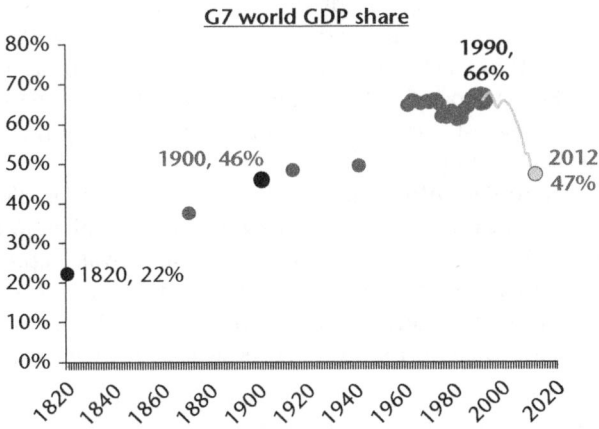

Figure 1.1 Globalization: one paradigm or two?
Source: Maddison's database and WTO database.

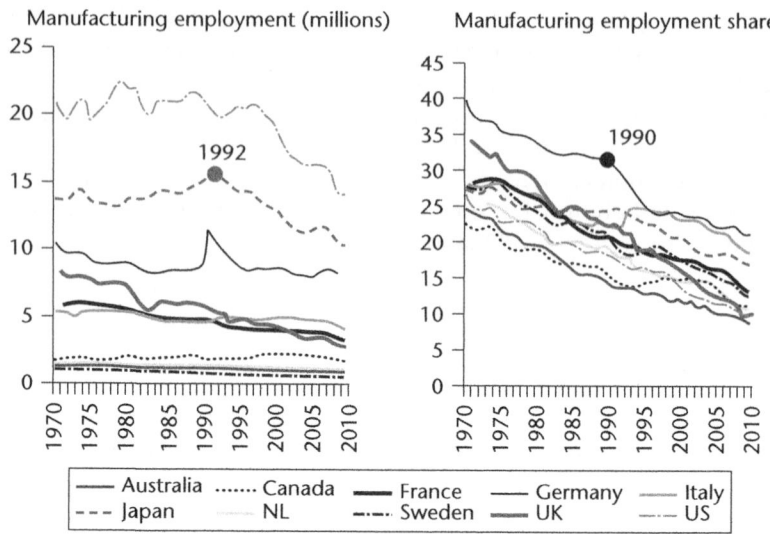

Figure 1.2 Number and share of employment in manufacturing, rich nations, 1970–2010

Source: US Bureaus of Labor Statistics online data.

services have pulled labour out of manufacturing[2] just as rapid productivity growth reduced the need for workers at any given level of output.

European manufacturers' position has also slipped—gradually during the first unbundling and rapidly since the second (Figure 1.3, left panel). Europe lost five percentage points in the two decades following 1970, but more than twice that during the two decades following 1990. Figure 1.3 also shows that the trend is shared by the G7 nations as a whole—this is not a Europe-specific phenomenon. The right-hand panel zooms in on the five biggest European manufacturers, showing how all have lost global market share.

Europe's manufacturing malaise is not universal as Figure 1.4 shows. Poland has seen a very important industrialization during the second unbundling as have the Czech and Slovak Republics and Ireland. Sweden and Finland have also managed to counter the general advanced nation de-industrialization trend. For all of these apart from Turkey, an inflection point of sorts seems to occur around 1990.

---

[2] Being non-traded, prices and wages adjust until enough local labour is pulled into these sectors to meet local demand. Given that there is so little labour left in agriculture, the shift to services necessarily comes at the expense of industry.

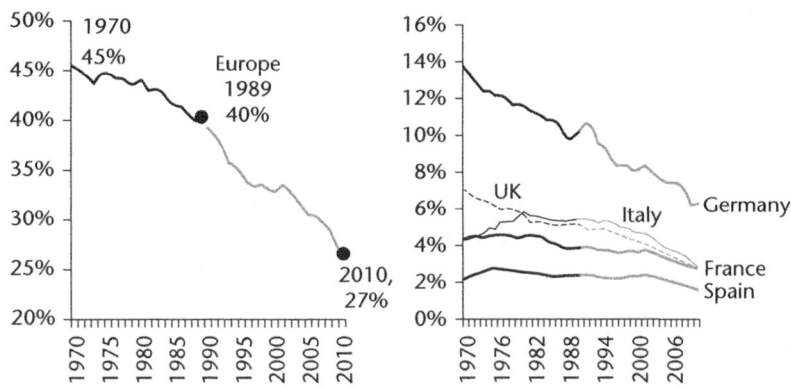

Figure 1.3 European shares of global manufacturing, 1970–2010
Source: unstats.un.org

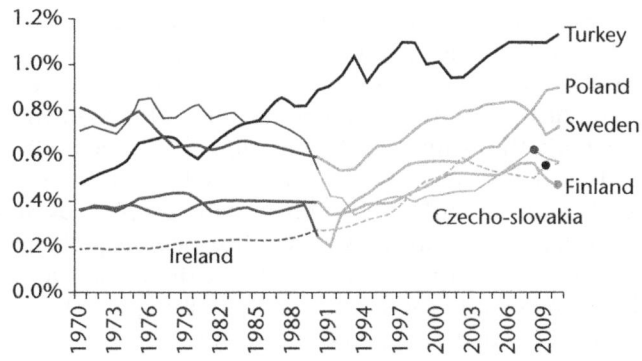

Figure 1.4 European share winners in manufacturing, 1970–2010
Source: unstats.un.org

Note that all these nations are part of the German supply chain (as we document later) except Ireland, which is heavily involved in the British and US supply chains.

1.1.3 *Plan of the Chapter*

Sections 1.2 and 1.3 look at the first and second unbundlings in more detail to explain how the first fostered the European manufacturing miracle while the second fostered manufacturing malaise. The subsequent section looks ahead with conjectures on how on-going globalization is likely to impact European manufacturing. Finally, Section 1.5 presents my concluding remarks.

1.2 Globalization's First Unbundling

Before turning to details of globalization's first and second unbundlings and their economic logic, we briefly set the stage by considering the pre-globalized world.

1.2.1 The Pre-globalization World

Since the rise of agriculture, the costs of moving goods, ideas, and people forced a geographic 'bundling' of production and consumption. Long distance trade did exist, but it was only for exotic items with high value to weight ratios. Every village made almost everything it consumed. Since most humans were engaged in subsistence agriculture, the world's economic geography was quite homogenous. The world really was 'flat' from an economic perspective, apart from a few cities.

The pre-industrialized world had no factories. This dampened innovation on both the demand side and supply side. A brilliant idea meant little if it was only applied on a very local scale, so demand was modest. Innovation flourishes when many people look at similar problems from dissimilar angles, so spatially separating problem solvers hinders the supply of innovations. In the pre-industrial world, there was little technological progress—certainly nothing like the sustained rise in productivity that drives modern growth.

As Figure 1.5 shows, there was virtually zero per capita income growth until the second millennium (West European annual growth rates shown above bars in left panel). Growth started only in Western Europe—basically after the Black Plague (Findlay and O'Rourke 2007). Until the Industrial Revolution, growth remained at zero in most of the world and a pitiful tenth of a percent even in Western Europe. Up until the late nineteenth century, Asia was by far the largest economic mass given its population. In the pre-globalized world, however, the size of the market was almost immaterial as so little of it was accessible to all but the most local producers.

1.2.2 Production and Consumption Unbundle Spatially

Improvements in shipping technology, especially steam power, released the world from the shackles of 'village economics'. Railroads

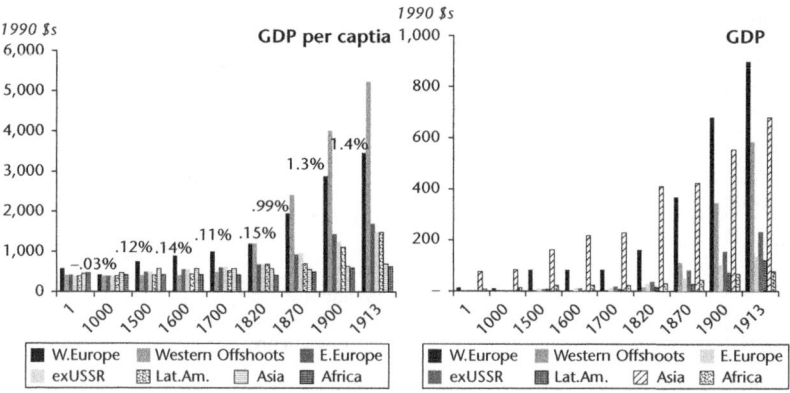

Figure 1.5 GDP and GDP per capita from year 1 to 1913, various regions

and steamships radically lowered transport costs thus making it feasible to spatially separate production and consumption (O'Rourke and Williamson 1999 Ch. 3). Scale economies and comparative advantage made separation profitable. International trade boomed as production shifted internationally towards the most cost-effective locations. As production dispersed internationally, it concentrated locally into large-scale factories with these gathering in industrial districts. Consumption clustered into ever-larger cities. This was globalization's first unbundling.

Baldwin and Martin (1999) list the five central outcomes of globalization's first bundling: (1) industrialization/de-industrialization—the 'North' (Western Europe, Japan, the USA, etc.) industrialized while the South (especially India and China) de-industrialized (Bairoch 1982; Findlay and O'Rourke 2007); (2) international income divergence—North and South incomes diverged massively (Prichett 1997) as Figure 1.5 shows; (3) international trade boomed (Jacks et al. 2011); (4) growth take-offs occurred (Rostow 1960); and (5) urbanization accelerated in the North.

NORTHERN INDUSTRIALIZATION AND SOUTHERN DE-INDUSTRIALIZATION

The Industrial Revolution was revolutionary but came from a century of incremental technical, organizational, social, and institutional changes. The starting date of 1776 provides as good a landmark, as Crafts (1995) finds a structural break in the growth of British industrial production in 1776. Belgium was next—industrializing rapidly between 1820 and 1870 with France, Switzerland, Prussia, and the USA following

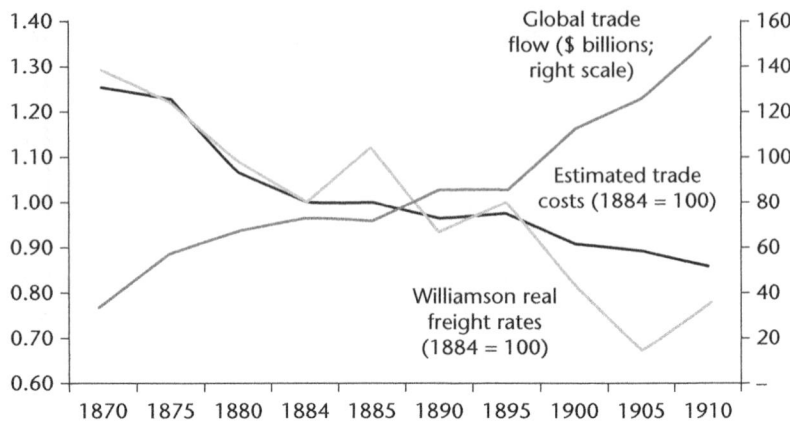

Figure 1.6 Trade costs and trade volumes, 1870–1910

Source: Jacks et al. (2011), and Williamson and Mohammed (2004).

in the 1830s and 1840s. Russia, the Austria-Hungarian Empire, Italy, Sweden, Canada, and much of the rest of Europe came along during the end of the 1800s.

As the nineteenth century reached into its second half, new industries and production methods emerged. Thus began the so-called second industrial revolution. In sectors such as steel, chemicals, electrical goods, and engineering products based on internal combustion engines, Germany and the USA leapfrogged the UK. As Europe industrialized, the South de-industrialized (Kuznets 1965, p.20; Chaudhuri 1966; Braudel 1984).

The rise of global trade during the Industrial Revolution has been widely documented (Findlay and O'Rourke 2007). Figure 1.6 shows the facts from 1870 onwards along with two measures of the impact of the steam revolution on trade costs. The volume of trade expanded by 328 per cent over the whole period, with a noticeable acceleration from around 1895. On average, trade grew at about 4 per cent per year. Trade costs came down from between 40 and 60 per cent; this was enough to open up vast swathes of the world's land masses to international trade.

URBANIZATION

While large cities had arisen at various times in history, up until the Industrial Revolution no city grew larger than Rome was when the first millennium started. As Table 1.2 shows, western cities saw declining populations until the eighteenth century. Eastern cities reached their peak around the turn of the first millennium and then declined. They

Table 1.2 City sizes from year 1 to 1900 (populations in hundreds of thousands)

Year	Largest Western	Population	Largest Eastern	Population
1	Rome	1,000	Chang'an	500
200	Rome	800	Luoyang	120
400	Rome	500	Luoyang	150
600	Constantinople	125	Daxingcheng	250
800	Damascus	175	Chang'an	1,000
1000	Cordoba	200	Kaifeng	1,000
1200	Baghdad	250	Hangzhou	800
1100	Cairo	125	Nanjing	500
1000	Constantinople	100	Beijing	600
900	Constantinople	400	Beijing	700
1700	London	600	Beijing	650
1800	London	900	Beijing	1,100
1900	London	6,600	Tokyo	1,750

Source: Morris (2010), table A.2.

re-attained the year 1000 populations only in the nineteenth century. The key fact for our purposes is that the population in all cities began to rise with the first unbundling—not only those in rapidly industrializing nations.

1.2.3 Economics of the First Unbundling

The economic logic of the globalization's first unbundling is best understood with a combination of the new economic geography (Krugman 1991; Venables 1996) and endogenous growth theory (Romer 1986, 1990; Lucas 1988; Aghion and Howitts 1992).

To describe the fundamental economic logic as cleanly as possible, we explain the economics as a highly simplified economy. There are two nations—North and South—that are identical ex ante, that is, in the pre-globalized, pre-industrial era. The first task is to consider the 'new economic geography' of the Industrial Revolution and its association with trade costs. The basic argument is from Krugman and Venables (1995).

NEG FORCES: AGGLOMERATION AND DISPERSION
The focus of the new economic geography (NEG) is on firms' location decisions. These decisions rest on the balance of two sets of forces— dispersion forces and agglomeration forces.

Dispersion forces favour geographic dispersion to avoid some sort of congestion broadly defined. The key, global-level dispersion force is local competition, that is, firms would, ceteris paribus, prefer to put trade costs between them and the bulk of their competitors. Agglomeration forces favour spatial clustering. While there are many such forces most only operate on a very local scale (like the knowledge spillovers) and are thus not relevant to explaining the first unbundling's global pattern of industrialization and de-industrialization.

Note that, in a somewhat dated terminology, demand and supply linkages are called 'backward and forward linkages'. The two key agglomeration forces are supply-side and demand-side circular causality. Demand-linked circular causality is driven by market size. Firms want to locate where they have good access to customers to reduce selling costs. But since firms buy inputs from other firms and attract workers who spend locally, firm relocation feeds back into market size. The causality is thus circular. The second agglomeration force involves 'supply linkages'. Firms operating at industrial scales buy many inputs from other firms, so locating near an industrial cluster reduces the cost of inputs (avoids transportation costs). The causality becomes circular since each new firm offers its supply and thus lowers the production cost of the location.

Starting from very high, pre-steam power trade costs, a gradual reduction of transportation costs erodes both the agglomeration forces and the dispersion forces—place begins to matter less. In a wide class of models, dispersion forces start out stronger than agglomeration forces, so the symmetric equilibrium is stable, but improved transportation erodes the dispersion forces faster. As a result, there is a threshold level of trade costs below which all industry moves to one region or the other. As history would have it, this was the North, even though the South was larger economically when taken as a whole (Figure 1.5). Of course, the NEG framework leaves out many, many important factors for the sake of clarity, but for particular instances, the omitted factors may be critical. For a broader view, see Scott and Storper (1986).

This explains three of our facts: industrialization of the North, de-industrialization of the South, and the boom in trade as the South focuses on exporting primary goods and the North on manufacturing. Within each region this sort of 'punctuated equilibrium' time path would appear as a sweeping inter-sectoral resource shift not unlike the observed one during the Industrial Revolution.

GROWTH TAKE-OFF WITH ENDOGENOUS GROWTH THEORY

This agglomeration of industry surely localized knowledge spillovers. As per the endogenous growth literature, what extenuates such spillovers is pro-growth.

Virtually all endogenous growth models posit technological externalities that prevent the return to further investments from falling as the human, physical, and/or knowledge capital stocks rise. Indeed, Rosenberg (1994) and Crafts (1995) explicitly stress the importance of localized cumulative learning processes in their accounts of the Industrial Revolution.

Baldwin, Martin, and Ottaviano (2001) show how combining these two sets of lessons can produce a two-region model in which the gradual, exogenous lowering of trade costs driven by lower transportation and communication costs as well as by market opening initiatives can produce three stages of growth.

- In the first stage with high trade costs, gradual improvements in transportation technology boost trade gradually. Growth may be positive in a 'village economy' setting but low since the geographical dispersion of industry hinders the externalities essential to innovation.

- In the middle stage when trade costs have just entered the 'catastrophic' region, industrial agglomeration occurs very rapidly. This industrialization triggers a take-off in the North and stagnation in the South. The agglomeration of industry and growth bifurcation produces a massive income divergence that continues until the industrial saturation point is reached in the North.

- In the third stage, high growth becomes stable and self-sustaining in both regions, but income divergence persists.

The Baldwin–Martin–Ottaviano model captures elements of the classic analyses by Kuznets and Rostow. Kuznets (1966) divides growth into two types: traditional growth (pre-1750) and modern economic growth (post-1750). The distinctive feature of modern growth, according to Kuznets, is the rapidity of the shifts in industrial structure (he talks of sweeping structural changes) and their magnitude when cumulated over decades. Rostow (1960) goes further, identifying five stages in economic growth: the traditional society, the preconditions for take-off, the take-off, the drive to maturity, and the age of high mass consumption. The take-off can be traced to a sharp stimulus, Rostow asserts, and he lists a number of these, including one that hinges on lower trade costs. The take-off 'may come about through a technological (including transport) innovation which sets in motion a chain of secondary expansion in modern sectors and has powerful potential external economy effects which the society exploits.' (Rostow 1960, p.36). Rostow also lists three conditions for a take-off: a rising investment rate, rapid expansion of one or more industrial sectors marked by external economies, and rapid emergence of structures that are necessary for self-sustaining growth.

1.3 The Second Unbundling

The ICT revolution was the exogenous shock that changed globalization. It began sometime between 1985 and 1995. Starting in the mid-1980s, telecommunications became cheaper and more reliable. The price of telephone calls plummeted, faxes became standard, cellular phone usage exploded, and the telecommunication network became denser, more reliable, and cheaper. Two other trends interacted with cheaper communication costs—the spectacular fall in the price of computing power (Moore's Law) and the equally spectacular rise in fibre optic transmission rates (Gilder's Law). Long-distance information sharing was revolutionized as these developments in telecoms were complemented by the rise of the internet—first email and then web-based platforms.

The telecom and internet revolutions triggered a suite of information-management innovations that made it easier, cheaper, faster, and safer to coordinate complex activities at distance. Email, editable files (*.xls, *.doc, etc.), and more specialized web-based coordination software packages revolutionized peoples' ability to manage multifaceted procedures across great distances. Working methods and product designs also shifted to make production more modular and thus easier to coordinate at a distance. Stages of production that previously had to be performed in close proximity—within walking distance to facilitate face-to-face coordination of innumerable small glitches—could now be dispersed without an enormous drop in efficiency or timeliness. Collectively, this is known as the ICT revolution.

Figure 1.7, which displays several ICT, indicators, shows that there was an inflection point in the growth of internet hosts in 1985 and in telephone subscribers in 1995. This suggests that the coordination glue began to weaken sometime between 1985 and 1995.

1.3.1 Globalization's Second Unbundling is Different: Stylized Facts

At about the same time as the G7's share of global income tanked, international commerce changed. While supply-chain trade among rich nations has long been important (US–Canada and intra-EU), from the late 1980s it boomed between high-tech and low-wage nations.

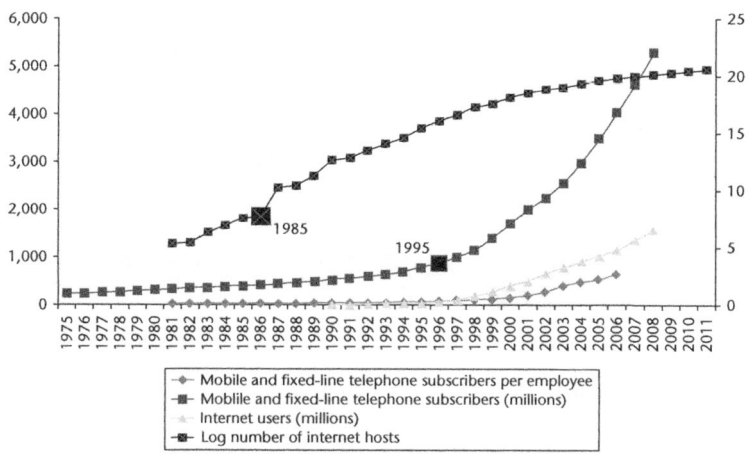

Figure 1.7 Growth of global internet hosts and phone lines, 1975–2011

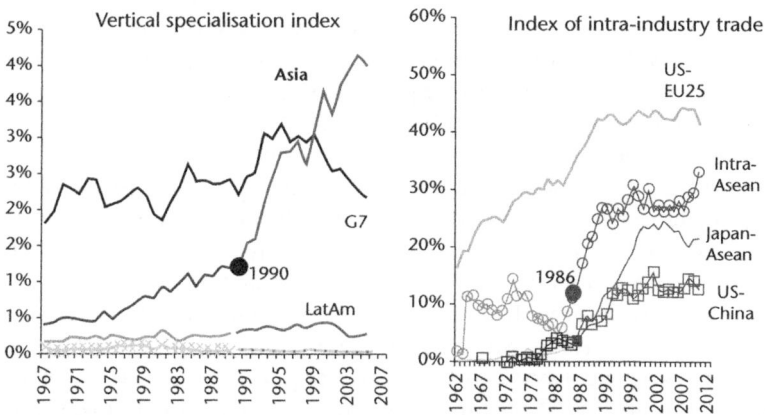

Figure 1.8 Indirect measures of supply-chain trade from the 1960s

Source: left: Amador and Cabral (2006); right: Brülhart (2009); adapted from Baldwin and Lopez-Gonzales (2012).

Figure 1.8 illustrates the timing with two proxies for supply-chain trade—a vertical specialization index and partner-wise intra-industry trade indices. These changes have been widely noted.[3]

---

[3] The mid-1980s structural break has been demonstrated by many (Feenstra and Hanson 1996; Dallas Fed 2002; Fukao, Ishito, and Ito 2003; Ando and Kimura 2005) and the trade changes by many others (Hummels, Ishii, and Yi 1999; Yi 2003; Bems, Johnson, and Yi 2010; Koopman, Powers, Wang, and Wei 2011; Johnson and Noguera 2012a, 2012b).

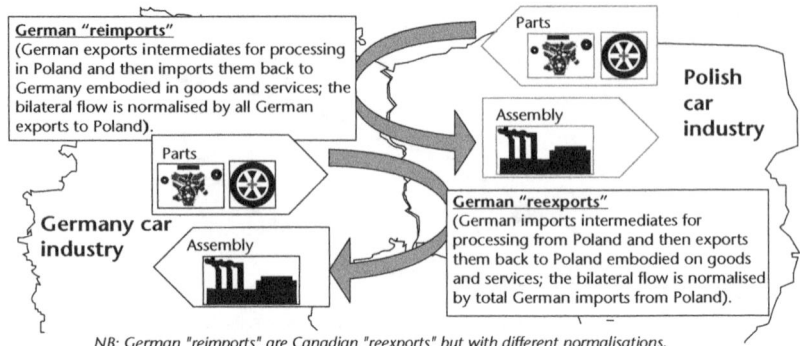

German "reimports"
(German exports intermediates for processing in Poland and then imports them back to Germany embodied in goods and services; the bilateral flow is normalised by all German exports to Poland).

Parts

Polish car industry

Assembly

Parts

Germany car industry

Assembly

German "reexports"
(German imports intermediates for processing from Poland and then exports them back to Poland embodied on goods and services; the bilateral flow is normalised by total German imports from Poland).

NB: German "reimports" are Canadian "reexports" but with different normalisations.

Figure 1.9 Schematic illustration of reimporting and reexporting supply chain trade

Source: Adapted from Baldwin and Lopez-Gonzales (2012).

A more direct measure of supply-chain trade is so-called reimport/ reexports. This measures the back-and-forth trade that is common in offshoring relationships where one nation is sending parts to another for processing and then bringing them back for further processing or consumption as illustrated by Figure 1.9.

The offshoring revolution has also created what could be called Factory Europe—mostly around Germany. The pattern is of re-importing/re-exporting between a high-tech hub and low-wage spoke nations. Figure 1.10 shows the re-import and re-export pattern around Germany. The top left panel shows that Germany does a great deal of supply-chain trade with its low-wage neighbours. But it also engages in this sort of trade with high-wage nations such as Austria, the Netherlands, and France (Baldwin and Lopez-Gonzales 2012). Notice the asymmetric relationships between Germany and its lower-wage neighbours. Germany re-imports from a wide range of nations, but Poland and the Czech Republic are mainly working with Germany.

In addition to Germany, which is one of the four global manufacturing giants (the others being China, the USA, and Japan), Europe has three other high-technology nations with large manufacturing sectors: Britain, France, and Italy. Figure 1.11 shows their patterns drawn to the same scale as Germany's. We see immediately that these three nations have re-importing and re-exporting patterns that clearly place them in the headquarter category—that is, much more re-importing than re-exporting—although Italy is a borderline case. The three re-importing patterns are not as diverse as Germany's. Moreover the overall importance of these with at least one partner

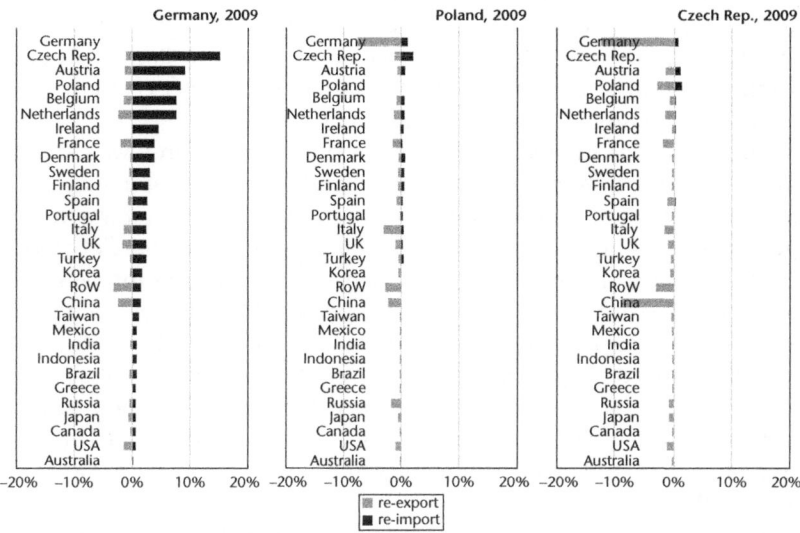

Figure 1.10 Factory Europe: Germany and low-wage factory economies, 2009
Source: Baldwin and Lopez-Gonzales (2012).

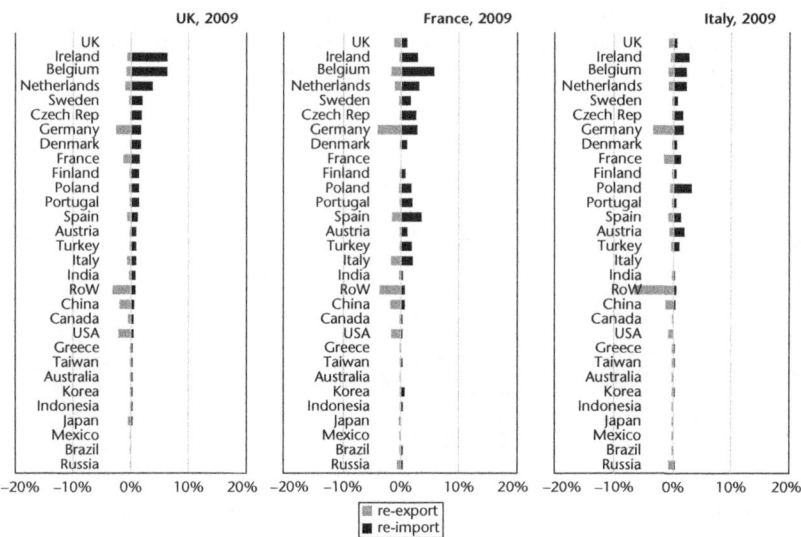

Figure 1.11 Re-exporting/re-importing flows for UK, France, and Italy, 2009
Source: Baldwin and Lopez-Gonzales (2012).

is smaller in magnitude. It is also worth stressing that these three do some processing for Germany, but very little for each other. This suggests that there is a hub-and-spoke arrangement in Europe around Germany and the system includes the other headquarter economies as well as the factory economies (Lejour et al. 2012).

Turning to the broader pattern of global manufacturing, we see that as the second unbundling started, a handful of developing nations saw their share of global manufacturing output soar. This was not a general trend—only seven developing nations saw their share of global manufacturing rise by more than half a percentage point between 1990 and 2010. Most developing nations saw their shares decline or stagnate. Figure 1.12 (left panel) shows the nations whose share of global manufacturing GDP rose or fell by at least one percentage point. All the G7 nations have lost shares since 1990 (middle panel) and all 'seven risers' saw their shares rise (right panel). Note that all the risers, except perhaps India, are near enough to join US, Japanese, or German supply chains.

The second unbundling was also accompanied by radical changes in developing nation trade and investment policies. From the early post-war days right up to the late 1980s, most developing nations eschewed trade liberalization and viewed foreign investment as a ruse. They viewed the protection of industry as just that—protecting industry. For most of them, this changed in the early 1990s. The openness that facilitated international production sharing was suddenly embraced by developing nations. As Figure 1.13 shows, they:

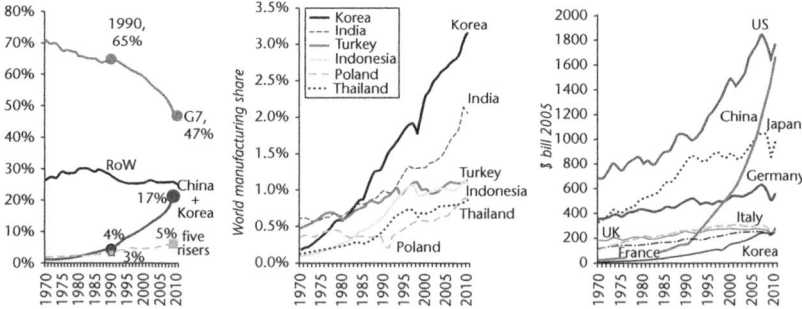

Figure 1.12 Seven risers and seven losers: manufacturing reversal of fortunes

Source: UNSTAT.org. Note: Left panel shows share of world manufacturing GDP, the seven risers are China, Korea, India, Turkey, Indonesia, Thailand, and Poland; the seven losers are the G7; middle panel plots global shares of six of the seven risers; right panel shows manufacturing GDP (2005 USDs) of China and the G7.

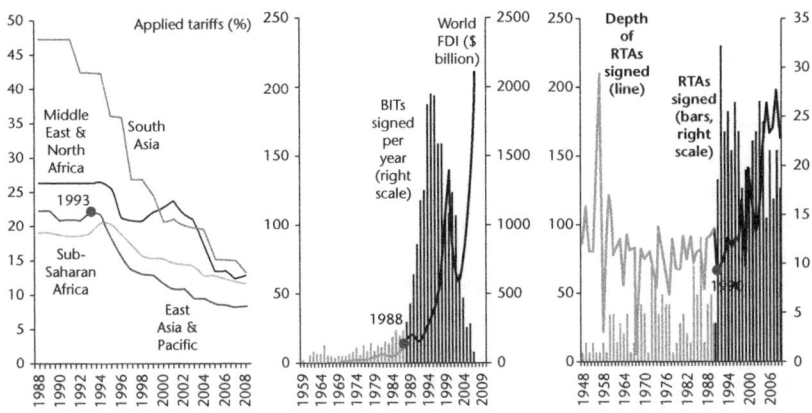

Figure 1.13 Take-off in BITs, FDI, unilateralism, and deep RTAs

Sources: Tariffs from World databank, WTO; BITs from ICSID; RTAs and depth from Baccini et al. (2011); adapted from Baldwin and Lopez-Gonzales (2012).

- slashed tariffs unilaterally (left panel);
- signed Bilateral Investment Treaties (BITs), which are mostly unilateral concessions to rich-nation firms seeking to invest (middle panel); and
- signed a massive wave of Regional Trade Agreements (RTAs) with 'deep' provisions that are pro-supply-chain, e.g. assurances for intellectual property, capital movements, competition policy, business visas, etc. (right panel).

Importantly, this is not the 1970s and 1980s view of trade openness embraced by Singapore, Hong Kong, and Taipei (lower tariffs, fewer quotas, etc.). This liberalization wave included many measures traditionally viewed as purely domestic, since joining a supply chain meant a much more thorough integration of a developing nation's economy with that of the headquarter nation directing the supply chain.

1.3.2 *Economics of the Second Unbundling*

Traditional trade economics focuses on simple, made-here-sold-there goods. The producing nation accounts for 100 per cent of the export's value added, so exports can be thought of as a bundle of national technology and factors of production. There are two key points here as far as Europe's manufacturing miracle and malaise are concerned. During the first unbundling:

- Comparative advantage is conceptualized as a purely national concept.

- Trade costs reductions allow nations to specialize in producing what they make best while importing the rest.

To put it differently, the first unbundling made it easier to buy and sell goods internationally. These two facts go a long way to explaining Europe's manufacturing miracle in the nineteenth and twentieth centuries—at least if one adds in the agglomeration forces favouring Europe as a location for manufacturing.

The ICT revolution changed this. High-tech firms found it profitable to combine their firm-specific know-how with low-wage labour in developing nations. Simplifying to illustrate the point clearly, this is what turned Europe's manufacturing miracle into malaise. The malaise was not caused by problems with European manufacturing technology. It was caused by the way the second unbundling allowed European firms to combine it with labour outside of Europe.

The fundamental change is that comparative advantage has become a multinational concept. The competitiveness of a nation's exports depends upon the combination of several nations' technology, labour, capital, etc. Moreover, the location of 'comparative advantage' is under the control of the firms that own the know-how. Know-how was always the property of firms but, before the ICT revolution, it was hard to take it abroad. Observe that this is not technology transfer in the traditional sense. Firms go to great lengths to avoid transferring their firm-specific know-how to other firms be they domestic or foreign. Nevertheless, from the macro perspective it was as if some of the advanced nations' technology was moving to developing nations.

For the purposes of this chapter, there are two main implications: (i) for the location of manufacturing jobs, and (ii) for developing nation growth. The economics of these are addressed in turn.

IMPLICATIONS FOR MANUFACTURING JOBS AND LOCATION OF VALUE ADDED

The recombination of technology and factors across nations comes in two forms.

- In its most direct form, twenty-first-century trade involves high-tech firms from high-wage nations combining their managerial, marketing, and technical know-how with low-wage labour in developing nations.

There are many names for this 'technology lending': foreign affiliates, joint ventures, contract manufacturing, offshoring, reimporting, export platforms, etc. A more indirect form of twenty-first-century trade involves imported intermediates that embody foreign technology and productive factors.

• Here the recombination technology and factors across nations happens via the foreign know-how and factors embodied in imported parts and components (Jones 1990; Deardorff 2005).

In both the direct and indirect cases, comparative advantage becomes a multinational concept.

We can more precisely illustrate the two aspects of production unbundling with two partial equilibrium diagrams. We start with the direct recombination and to set the stage, we show how the basic diagram can be used to elucidate how different the notion of comparative advantage is in the first and second unbundlings.

To keep the analysis simple, consider a world where 'North' has better technology but higher wages than 'South'. The North's technology edge, however, outweighs its high-wage disadvantage, so North has a comparative advantage in the industry under study. We think of this as a generic manufacturing sector. The point of departure is the first unbundling where globalization means relaxation of the transportation constraint.

Figure 1.14 helps organize the economic logic. The left and right panels show South's and North's supply and demand curves using obvious notation. The middle panel shows world export supply and import demand curves (XS and MD). The initial situation with high trade costs is shown by the grey lines. The initial trade cost of T drives a wedge between the price that the importing South pays—namely P'— and the price exporting North receives ($P' - T$).

The first unbundling eliminates T, resulting in a convergence of prices on the free trade level shown as P^{FT}. This trade cost reduction allowed Northern firms to better exploit their comparative advantage by producing more and selling more of it to South. In aggregate, this would look like an industrialization of the North and a de-industrialization of the South. While this diagram does not admit such effects, the tendency was strengthened by agglomeration forces and knowledge spillovers as discussed already.

Now consider the impact of the second unbundling starting from free trade in goods. The change we focus on is how the ICT revolution gives high-tech Northern firms the confidence to deploy their firm-specific know-how abroad. As it is now safe, high-tech firms combine

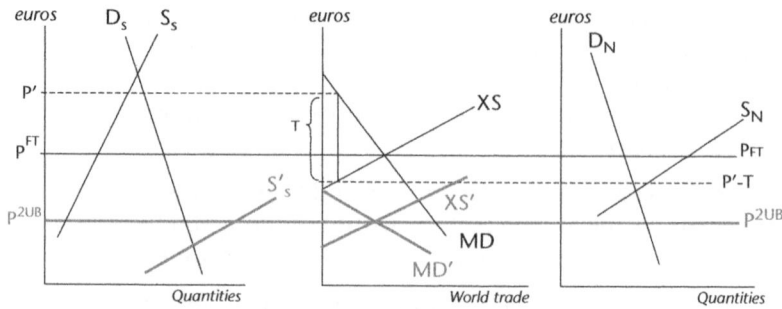

Figure 1.14 Comparative advantage in the first and second unbundlings
Source: Author's elaboration.

their know-how with low-wage labour in South. The impact of this is a massive downward shift in South's supply curve.[4] The new Southern supply curve is shown as S_S'. Nothing happens to the North's supply curve as Northern production still uses North technology and North labour.

The main changes are:

• 'National' comparative advantages appear to flip.

The world price of manufactures drops to P^{2UB} and at this price North is an importer of manufactured goods rather than an exporter.

• North appears to de-industrialize while South industrializes, but Northern firms' share of global production is maintained or increased, but with more of it in the South.

Next we turn to more indirect combinations of comparative advantage.

In the previous example, trade is only allowed in final goods. In the real world, production unbundling typically involves intermediate goods (Ando and Kimura 2005).[5] Here we present an illustration that allows for such considerations. To spotlight the indirect recombination, we revert to assuming that technology is immobile while trade in goods is perfectly free.

In the pre-RTA world, all stages of production in both nations are bundled spatially into factories or industrial district to economize on communication and coordination costs. Exports have 100 per cent

---

[4] Recall that neoclassical supply curves are marginal cost curves, so high-tech plus low wages shifts S_S down massively.

[5] Also see Gereffi (2001) for early examples and the website http://www.globalvaluechains.org/ for abundant recent case studies.

local value added. The second unbundling makes possible the two-way flows of goods, ideas, and the people needed to support international production unbundling. When the various stages of production are performed in different nations, the downstream good becomes a multination combination of technology and factors.

To illustrate simply, we allow for an upstream or intermediate good, Y, and a downstream good, Z (the mnemonic is that as Y comes before Z, so Y is upstream of Z). The linked diagrams (Figure 1.15) show the equilibrium in South for the upstream goods Y (left panel) and downstream good Z (right panel). Supply and demand curves are marked with S and D respectively with subscripts indicating the good. The input–output linkage is simple; one unit of Y is required for each unit of Z. In addition to the cost of the input Y, there is a marginal cost producing Z shown as MS_Z in the right diagram. The supply curve for Z is the vertical sum of MC_Z and the price of Y.

Before the second unbundling, South must make its own Y locally since it is prohibitively expensive to undertake the production of Y and Z in separate nations (even though trade in goods is perfectly free). The idea here is that producing Y and Z requires continuous coordination in the form of two-way flows of goods, ideas, and people. Before the RTA, it is too expensive or too risky to attempt this coordination internationally. Some of the things we have in mind are unreliable supply-chain logistics (express mail, air cargo), telecommunications, and business mobility (key managers and technicians moving to coordinate Y and Z production). In short, firms cannot count on

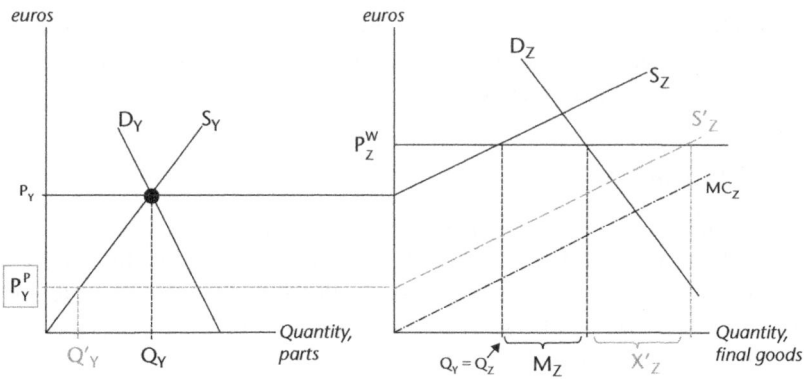

Figure 1.15 Supply-chain trade with intermediate goods and no technology lending

Source: Author's elaboration.

cheap and quick exchanges that are necessary to allow a Z factory in one nation to source its Y in another nation. As a result, the supply curve in Z is MC_Z plus the equilibrium price of P_Y. Note that South is producing Y and Z; however, given S_Z, South imports Z in an amount indicated as M_Z (right panel).

After the second unbundling, supply-chain linkages become costless and perfectly reliable, so South can import Y from North at the price, P_Y^P. South starts to import Y, reducing its own Y production to Q'_Y. The lower price for Y lowers S_Z to S'_Z. The key effects are:

• South switches from importing Z to exporting it, and it starts to import Z.

Importantly, this new trade did not stem from trade liberalization per se; there were no trade barriers before or after. The switch came from a relaxation of the coordination constraint, not the transportation constraint.

Although we have not shown North explicitly, it would be easy to draw a case where:

• North exports Z before the second unbundling, but afterwards imports Z and exports Y.

This is a clear example of how foreign technology and factors embodied in the imported component can transform South's comparative advantage. New trade in Y is created and South's pattern of trade in Z is reversed.

There is no mystery in this outcome. Before the second unbundling, South had a latent comparative advantage in Z, but a latent comparative disadvantage in Y. The second unbundling allows South to specialize in its comparative advantage sector.

1.3.3 *Reshoring?*

Anecdotal evidence, and some rough calculations by the US consulting firm BCG (BCG 2011) have provoked some discussion of the concept of 'reshoring', that is, the reversal of production offshoring. There are two salient points with respect to reshoring to be made. The first is that some reshoring is perfectly in line with the forces that lead to offshoring in the first place. As has been pointed out in the theoretical literature, when deciding how many stages to offshore, firms balance the cost of separating stages spatially against the gains of lower wages. At the level of separation, costs—everything from transportation to tariffs and loss of timeliness—are the key. The key point, however, is that regardless of the level of separation costs that triggers offshoring, too many stages will be offshored. This has been called offshoring 'overshooting' (Baldwin and Venables 2013). That is, once firms offshore any stage, they will offshore some stages that do not naturally belong abroad in order to economize on separation costs. Then as the separation costs continue to fall with advancing globalization, the overshooting is reversed and some stages return home.

The second point is that although there is some evidence that manufacturing activities are returning to G7 nations, the manufacturing jobs are not. As Forbes writer Bill Conerly has put it: 'The brightest prospects for factories here in the United States involve those that use a lot of natural gas, not much labour, and need flexibility in production to meet changing customer needs' (Conerly 2014). In any case, the facts are quite clear. The number of manufacturing workers continues to decline. Reshoring may mean more 'jobs' for US-based robots, but not for US-based factory workers.

SOUTHERN GROWTH TAKE-OFF

A key feature of the first unbundling was the take-off in Northern growth that was driven by the agglomeration of industry in the North and the resulting knowledge spillovers that accelerated technology innovation. The central pillar in this take-off story was the localized nation of knowledge spillovers. The second unbundling—with its emphasis on the heightented international mobility of know-how—almost surely affects the extent to which pro-innovation knowledge spillovers are localized in the North. As per the endogenous growth theory, this should have growth implications.

When it comes to Southern growth, the second unbundling has two conflicting effects. The dispersion of manufacturing reduces the localization of spillovers that sparked the nineteenth-century growth take-offs. This effect would tend to lower the global steady state growth rate. The application of Northern technology in the South would directly boost Southern growth during the transition, and it is also likely to increase pro-innovation, and pro-imitation knowledge spillovers in the South. This effect would tend to boost Southern grow rates in transition.

Overall, the ICT revolution is clearly pro-growth for the South, at least in the medium term, but the dispersion of manufacturing globally might lower global growth in the long run. The key is whether the reduced localization of spillovers is sufficient to offset the anti-growth effects of the dispersion of manufacturing.

As Baldwin and Forslid (2000) show, lowering the barriers to the spatial diffusion of public knowledge is a powerful dispersion force when it comes to the location of manufacturing. To see this, we can draw a parameter space that allows for trade costs and knowledge spillovers to vary independently (Figure 1.16).

The diagram works with two ex ante symmetric regions (North and South as usual) and it plots the 'freeness' of goods trade on the horizontal axis, and the freeness of knowledge spillovers on the vertical axis. The dashed curve shows the combinations of the two forms of freeness where a symmetric division of industry is a stable equilibrium. The dashed line is upwards sloped since freer spillovers favour dispersion while free trade favours a concentration of industry. The solid curve shows the 'sustain' points, that is, the level of freeness where full agglomeration is the stable outcome. The northwest corner has dispersed industry; the southeast corner has clustered industry. To be concrete, the clustering occurs in the North if it is stable.

The idea here is that the first unbundling was dominated by the lowering of trade costs via better transportation technology (before the First World War) and lower tariffs (after the Second World War) even though the development of international postal services, subsea telegraph cables, telephones, and radios also freed up the flow of knowledge by making international communication cheaper. This pushes the world from a situation where dispersion was stable to one where clustering was stable. The second unbundling saw the reverse emphasis, with communication costs falling much faster than trade costs. In Figure 1.16, this is shown as taking the world back into the range of parameters of dispersed industry.

URBANIZATION AND TRADE VOLUMES

The last bit of economics concerns the rising volume of trade and urbanization. Both of these features are among the key elements of the first unbundling and continue to be features of the second.

There is no mystery when it comes to urbanization. The Glaeser-forces that encouraged urbanization during the nineteenth and twentieth centuries continue to apply in the twenty-first century. Cities are still places where people meet and the fall in the cost of messages has not replaced the need for meetings. Indeed, there is a very close analogy with the income and substitution effects of canonical consumer theory. While the ICT revolution radically shifted the relative price of messages versus meetings, the rise in business activity that resulted increased the overall need for meetings (Gaspar and Glaesner 1998). Moreover, good communication technology actually allowed greater specialization

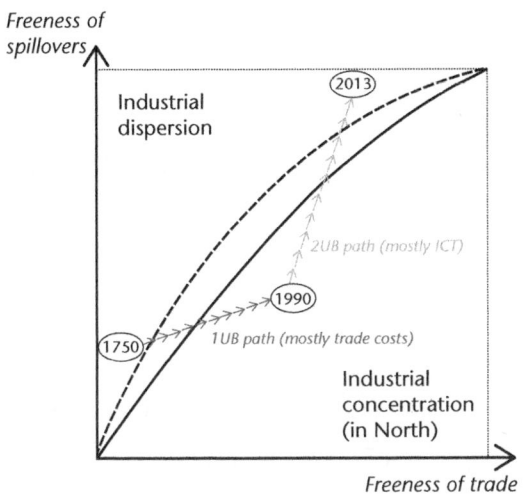

Figure 1.16 Stabilizing and destabilizing integration: first and second unbundlings

in service provision and thus raised the need for occasional face-to-face meetings. Empirical evidence is provided by De la Roca and Puga (2012).

The rise in trade is very naturally boosted by the second unbundling as noted by Yi (2003).

1.4 Factory-free Europe?

This section looks ahead to make some conjectures about the future of manufacturing in Europe. Two analytic tools are useful in this context—the TOSP (Task; Occupation; Stage; Product) framework for thinking about the implications of future ICT advances, and the 'smile curve' that helps integrate the likely outcomes with developments to date.

1.4.1 The TOSP Framework

As ICT improves, the unbundling of European factories will continue. But what will this mean for manufacturing jobs and value added in Europe?

The economics of this change is best considered by decomposing the second unbundling into two phenomena: fractionalization of production into stages and international dispersion of stages.

The TOSP framework

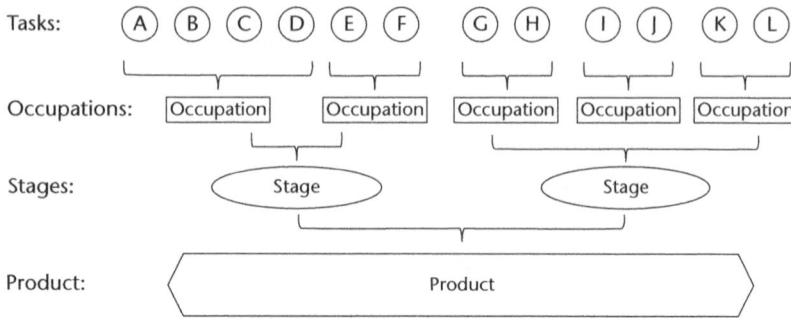

Figure 1.17 Tasks, occupations, stages, and product—the TOSP framework

Notes: The circles represent individual tasks, the rectangles represent individual occupations, and the ovals represent individual stages of production.

Source: Baldwin (2012a).

FRACTIONALIZATION OF THE MANUFACTURING PROCESS

Think of the supply chain at four levels of aggregation (Figure 1.17). At the base is the full list of everything that must be done to get the product into consumers' hands and provide them with associated after sales services. Following Grossman and Rossi-Hansberg (2008), and recent important contributions by Acemoglu and Autor (2010) and others, we refer to these as 'tasks'. Individual workers undertake specific tasks so the next natural aggregation is 'occupations'. Some sets of occupations are typically performed in tight proximity and we refer to these sets as 'stages of production'. Typically stages are the small unit that is offshored. The top level is the product. Consider the economics of the optimal tasks per occupation and occupations per stage.

The key trade-off in the TOSP framework (Baldwin 2012a) is between efficiency and coordination. Greater specialization improves efficiency but raises coordination costs. As ICT improves, the effects on the specialization-versus-coordination trade-off are not straightforward, as Bloom et al. (2009) show. Some ICT improvements reduce the benefits of specialization while others reduce the cost of specialization.

ICT affects the optimal division of labour via two channels:

* Communication and organizational technologies—call them coordination technologies, or CT, for short—facilitate transmission of ideas, instructions, and information. CT favours specialization by reducing the cost of coordination.

- Information technology, or IT for short, makes it easier for individual workers to master more tasks. IT disfavours specialization by reducing the cost, grouping many tasks into a single occupation.

This happens in several ways. Computer Integrated Manufacturing (CIM) and Computer Aided Design/Computer Aided Manufacturing (CAD/CAM) started with numerically controlled machine tools in the 1950s, but today many factories can be thought of as computer systems where the peripherals are industrial robots, computerized machine tools, automated guided vehicles, and so on. This has moved manufacturing from a situation where machines helped workers make things to one where workers help machines make things. Perhaps in the future it will be called 'compufacturing'. In terms of the TOSP framework, this is an advance in information technology that brings many routine tasks within the ambit of a single machine operator.

The integration and automation of tasks, however, does not stop at the factory gate. Many design, engineering, and management tasks have been computerized (Alavudeen and Venkateshwaran 2010). Computers have greatly boosted the productivity and speed of product design as well as greatly reduced the need for prototyping. Once designed, the production process can be outlined using computer-aided process planning systems and design programmes can create instructions for numerically controlled machines. Models of the manufacturing system can be simulated before they are built. The basic manufacturing functions—machining, forming, joining, assembly, and inspection—are supported and integrated by CAM systems and automated materials-handling systems. Inventory control is automated, tracking inventory movement, forecasting requirements, and even initiating procurement orders.

A recent special report by *The Economist* extrapolates these trends even further (*Economist* 2012). It notes that manufacturing may be going through a new industrial revolution due to the advent of additive manufacturing. This bundles virtually all stages of manufacturing into a single machine. While this is an important trend, it is not new; *Automation, the Advent of the Automatic Factory* was the title of a 1956 book and indeed the Luddite movement was about the same thing.

Bloom et al. (2009) develop a similar result by focusing on a hierarchy model where the key trade-off is between the cost of training workers to deal with problems and the cost of hiring managers to help workers with problems that they cannot solve. This Bloom et al. insight has recently received some empirical support from Lanz et al. (2012). They find that offshoring of business services complements manufacturing activities, in the sense that increased import penetration in business services is associated with a shift in local task content from information and communication related tasks towards tasks related to handling machinery and equipment. Offshoring of other services complements local information-intensive tasks in that it shifts local task composition towards ICT-related tasks.

Box 1.1 EXAMPLE OF IT AND TASK REGROUPING

The principal example in Davidson (2012) contrasts workers in a Greenville factory making fuel injectors. One type of worker does manual tasks that require little training or education. Her real competitors are not Chinese workers, but American-designed robots. Earning $13 an hour, she is still cheaper than the robot but many of her co-workers have already been replaced.

The second type is a $30-an-hour skilled machinist who got his job after three years studying machine tooling, five years of on-the-job experience in another factory, and a month of training on his particular piece of the digitized manufacturing revolution—a half-million-dollar turning contraption which machines valves to a tolerance of a quarter micron. For the machinist, manufacturing is basically applied engineering. To maintain such extreme precision, he tests parts every few minutes with sophisticated testing tools and makes the necessary adjustments—about twenty per shift—by entering them into the machine's computer.

This polarization of the shop floor has many implications but for the low-education worker, the worst aspect is that there is no longer a gradual path of skill accumulation between the $13 and $30 jobs. The in-between-skilled jobs have all been bundled into the machine.

The digitization of manufacturing is changing the nature of the stages not offshored in a way that is important for policy makers. Many of the manufacturing jobs being 'reshored' are of the $13 type, not the $30 manufacturing jobs that still come to mind when people speak glowingly of manufacturing.

An instructive example of this can be found in the recent BCG study (BCG 2011). This shows that faster wage growth in China brings US job competitiveness close to the 'tipping point', that is, the point where making things in the USA will be cheaper than in China. 'By around 2015', the report notes, 'the total labour-cost savings of manufacturing many goods in China will be only about 10 to 15 percent when actual labour content is factored in'. But new manufacturing jobs created here will be low-skill/low-wage jobs.

The fact that low-skilled Americans are almost competitive with low-skilled Chinese is not an unmitigated blessing. Chinese wages rose by almost 20 per cent per year while US manufacturing wages have actually fallen (Moretti 2012, p. 25). For example, as part of the deal that let it survive the recent global economic crisis, Ford now pay new hires only $15 to $16 per hour—about half what the legacy workers receive.

SPATIAL DISPERSION: OFFSHORING
The TOSP framework as hereto presented does not directly address the impact of the second unbundling on manufacturing in Europe. The missing piece of the puzzle involves the process of moving some stages abroad—especially to low-wage nations. Plainly this has radical implications for manufacturing jobs in the high-wage nations.

Before the ICT revolution, Northern firms had to exploit their firm-specific assets by manufacturing in the North. After the ICT revolution, they have the option of offshoring labour intensive stages. There are three subtle points in this line of reasoning: one involving better IT, one involving better CT, and one involving the development of intensive advanced manufacturing technologies that require high levels of skill and technology.

First, IT makes it easier to wrap labour-intensive tasks into occupations that involve higher degrees of skill. Thus IT tends to:

• make the stages that remain in Europe more skill intensive;

• reduce the number of workers needed to complete the tasks; and

• allow firms to group remaining unskilled tasks into stages that can be offshored.

Second, the rapid advance of CT tends to increase the range of stages that can be profitably offshored.

Third, the rapid evolution on advanced manufacturing technology is likely keep some manufacturing in Europe, but this value added with be associated with few jobs, most of which are for high-skilled workers. There will be no 'jobs for yobs' in the factories of the future. There will be jobs for applied engineers and jobs for robots.

The key Dispersion forces favouring the geographic dispersion of stages are wage gaps and firm-level excellence. Wages gaps determine 'vertical specialization'; firm-level specialization and excellence determine 'horizontal specialization'.

Two wage gaps matter: low-skilled and high-skilled. 'Headquarter economies', like the UK, have sent labour-intensive stages to nearby low-wage neighbours—what might be called 'factory economies' (Figure 1.18). Highly-skilled labour, however, remains relatively abundant and thus relatively cheap in headquarter economies (Figure 1.19).

Wages gaps are not the only motive for supply chain internationalization. International supply chains existed among high-wage economies long before the second unbundling (Figure 1.8). The dispersion here is driven by a much more micro gain from specialization.

Hourly labour costs, manufactures

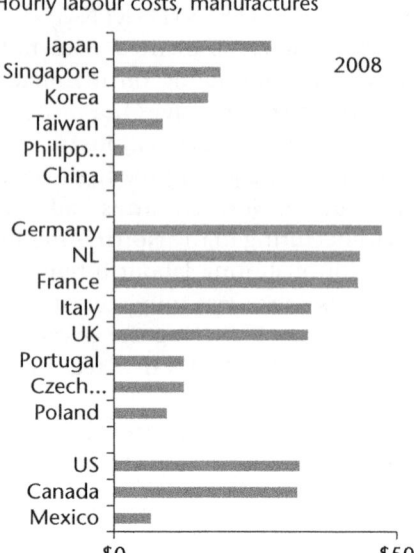

Figure 1.18 Wage differences in Factory Asia, Factory North American, and Factory Europe

Source: Baldwin and Evenett (2012).

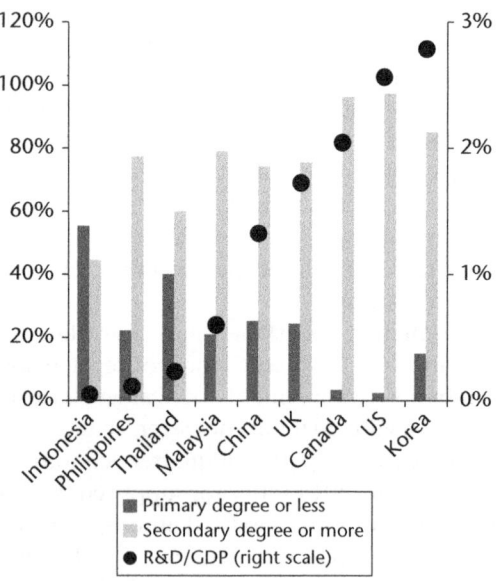

Figure 1.19 Education and R&D: ASEANs, China, Korea, US, Japan, and Canada, 2005

For example, when it comes to automobile air conditioners, the French company Valeo competes in the European market through excellence—not low wages. While each European carmaker could make their own air conditioners, scale economies mean that it is cheaper for Italian and German car manufacturers to source them from France. Given the systemic importance of learning-by-doing and the growing role of scale economies in an ever more fractionalized supply chain, it is natural that regional champions will emerge in particular parts and components.

This firm-level excellence is the key to the 'horizontal' internationalization of value chains among high-wage nations.

1.4.2 *Smile Curve Economics*

The second unbundling made it feasible to offshore stages of production. Some stages moved; others did not. Curiously, value added along the value chain seemed to shift away from the offshored stages. This observation is known as the 'smile curve', which shows the value added at each stage of production (Figure 1.20).

The smile curve concept, which was first proposed around 1992 by the founder of Acer computers, Stan Shih, asserts that fabrication involves less value creation today than it did before the second unbundling. Putting it differently, the smile deepened, so to speak.

An example of the allocation of value added along a value chain can be seen in the decomposition of the total retail sales price of the

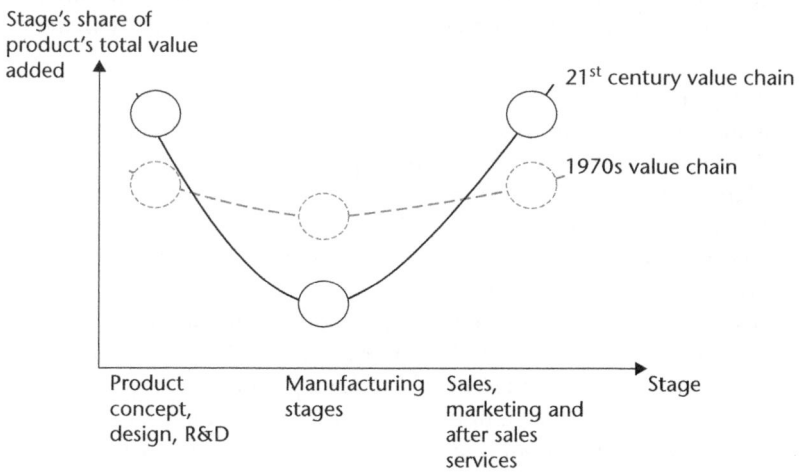

Figure 1.20 The smile curve: good and bad stages in the value chain
Source: Baldwin (2012a).

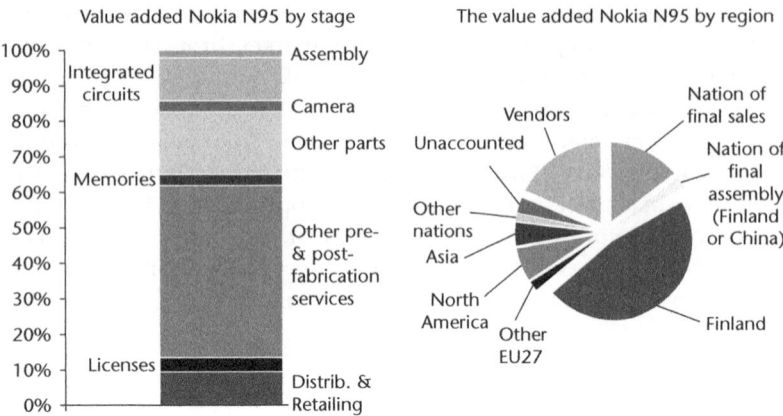

Figure 1.21 Breakdown of the Nokia N95's €546 pre-tax retail price circa 2007
Source: Ali-Yrkkö et al. (2011).

Nokia N95 phone (Ali-Yrkkö et al. 2011). Although the phone is mostly 'made' in Asia, Figure 1.21 shows that most of the value added accrues in Europe. The total value added in Europe depends on where the phone is sold (retail margin) and assembled (China or Finland). In the worst of cases—an N95 assembled in China and sold in the USA—more than half the value added is in Europe; the high end figure is 68 per cent.

The smile curve is the basic concept behind the thought that Europe might soon be 'factory-free' so it is important to explore it empirically and theoretically. Unfortunately, neither has been done convincingly.

WHY DID THE SMILE DEEPEN?

A definitive answer to this question awaits detailed empirical research. Simple economics and cost accounting, however, suggest an obvious explanation. When a stage's cost is reduced by offshoring, its share in value added falls since a stage's value added is based on costs. Even if the cost saving is fully passed on to consumers, the offshored stage's share of value added will fall.

Baldwin (2012a) conjectures that the reduced cost share of offshored stages derives from three distinct mechanisms. The first is the usual cost reduction that comes from better exploitation of comparative advantage (low-skill stage undertaken in low-skill abundant nations). The second is the recombination of high-tech with low-wages. The third is market power of the offshoring firms. Offshored tasks tend to be things that can be done in many emerging nations—most of them eager to attract such stages. The non-offshored stages, by contrast, tend to involve things where firms naturally have market power due to product differentiation, branding, etc. In short, offshored tasks become commoditized; the onshore tasks do not.

1.5 Concluding Remarks: The New Landscape of Work

The changed nature of globalization and the digitization of manufacturing mean that European manufacturing firms are likely to retain a leading global role. This does not mean, however, that manufacturing as traditionally conceived will flourish in Europe.

European technical, managerial, and marketing know-how are increasingly combined with labour abroad. Just as the surfeit of labour and shortage of land led European labour to flow to New World land in the nineteenth century, European manufacturing technology is now flowing to emerging market labour. This is not traditional tech transfer since it is under the control of European firms, but the impact on the economic landscape in Europe and emerging markets has been dramatic.

The upshot is plain. European manufacturing will never again be a source of high paying jobs for the 'common man'.

- The total number of manufacturing production jobs will almost surely continue to decline.
- The remaining jobs will increasingly resemble applied engineering positions that require post-secondary education.
- Progress in 'advanced manufacturing' techniques may keep more manufacturing value added in Europe, but it will not bring more factory jobs with it.

European policy makers must adjust to this new reality. There may be good reasons for promoting manufacturing, but mass employment is not one of them. These labour market outcomes are as much a consequence of technological advance as they are of globalization. Even if the clock was somehow turned on by globalization, the trend of 'manu-facturing' turning into 'compu-facturing' would continue.

The smile curve concept points the way forward. Good jobs will continue to be associated with manufacturing, but they will be in the pre-fabrication and post-fabrication stages rather than in fabrication. Most of them will be in services and located in cities.

One very attractive idea that flows from this is the Dutch thinking on the future of Europe's economy as elucidated by Bas ter Weel, Albert van der Horst, and George Gelauff (CPB 2010) in a publication strongly influenced by the thinking of Ed Glaeser (e.g. Glaeser 2011). It has also been reflected more recently in the US setting by Moretti (2012).

1.5.1 *Cities as Twenty-first-century Factories*

Since talented people gather in cities and make each other more productive, human capital and cities are likely to be the foundations of the twenty-first-century landscape of work.[6] This logic is straightforward. Cities are where people meet—in a sense cites are a 'technology' for reducing the cost of face-to-face interactions. Cities also optimize the matching between workers and firms, and between suppliers and customers. In this sense, cities become skill-clusters—or as Moretti (2012) calls them, 'brain hubs'. The link between city success and human capital is a close one. One of the most persistent predictors of urban growth over the last century is the skill level of a city (Glaeser and Resseger 2009).

Important thinking in CPB (2010) and a book by Enrico Moretti (2012) suggests that ICT advances are leading to a spikier landscape of work. The reason is that high-skilled jobs in the tradable sector tend to be subject to agglomeration economies. One type is highly localized knowledge spillovers where workers and firms implicitly benefit from each other's knowledge creation. Another type is the chicken-and-egg aspect of labour-pooling; firms locate near wide and deep local labour markets that are in turn supported by the presence of many firms. The City of London is a classic example of this.

In writing about the USA, Moretti (2012, p.5) says: 'More than traditional industries, the knowledge economy has an inherent tendency towards geographical agglomeration. ...The success of a city fosters more success as communities that can attract skilled workers and goods jobs tend to attract even more. Communities that fail to attract skilled workers lose further ground.'

Of course, most Europeans will never work in innovation activities. But just as good factory jobs created multiplier effects in communities, high-tech jobs can create/attract many more jobs. Approximately two-thirds of jobs are in local service sectors, such as government administration, health, education, retail, leisure, and hospitality. For

---

[6] There is symmetry here. In the first unbundling workers clustered in factories, and factories clustered in industrial districts—in part to reduce coordination costs and in part to benefit from knowledge spillovers. A standard story was that they were jointly working out how best to exploit two 'general purpose technologies' that were new at the time—electric motors and chemical processes. Cities are now playing a similar role when it comes to today's new general purpose technology, ICT.

the most part, these are sheltered from international competition by the dictates of proximity. But their location is very sensitive to 'anchor' jobs. Moretti estimates, for example, that each new high-tech job creates an additional five jobs in the local economy.

The agglomeration economies mentioned create another important fact: 'sticky' jobs tend to be good jobs and vice versa. As Moretti (2012, p.15) writes: 'In innovation, a company's success depends on the entire ecosystem that surrounds it . . . it is harder to delocalise innovation than traditional manufacturing . . . you would have to move not just one company but an entire ecosystem.'

Cities should not be thought of as mere collections of people, but rather as complex work spaces that generate new ideas and new ways of doing things. In a nutshell, cities are to the twenty-first century what factories were to the twentieth century. Urban policy will be the new industrial policy.

1.5.2 Policy Implications

As this chapter has illustrated, globalization has been transformational for almost two centuries, but it changed dramatically around 1990. This section considers a few policy implications of the second unbundling way of thinking about recent globalization.

European governments have long been fixated on manufacturing jobs, especially factory jobs. The economic logic was that manufacturing was a driver of productivity growth. Factory workers were only part of the story since productivity growth came from product and process innovations. The number of factory jobs, however, served as a convenient yardstick for the productivity gains since all the various stages were bundled spatially. Unbundling and offshoring changed this. Labour-intensive fabrication stages—including many factory jobs— were offshored along with the G7 know-how necessary to bring the offshored fabrication up to G7 standards. This high-tech low-wage combination radically lowered the cost of fabrication and thus lowered its value added. As a result, fabrication (and factory jobs) were commoditized while the pre- and post-fabrication service stages were not. This suggests that future governments should look more to service jobs related to manufacturing and less to factory jobs.

Moreover, due to servitization, whether manufacturing competitiveness increases depends upon national service sectors. Diversity and high quality design, coordination, engineering, and marketing services are increasing the 'industrial base' that matters. Consequently, G7 industrial policy shouldn't just be about industry, or at least not about industry in the factory sense of the word. It should also be about fostering manufacturing-linked services. Moreover, when it comes to value creation in G7 nations, good jobs—even those connected to manufacturing—will increasingly be service jobs. European factory workers are competing with robots at home and with China abroad. European designers and engineers are competing most with G7 designers and engineers.

LOSE SOME JOBS OR LOSE THEM ALL?
The second unbundling suggests that comparative advantage is operating at a finer degree of resolution on the European economy. Effort to resist this may lead to a loss of even more jobs. Consider the example of Dyson, maker of high-tech vacuum cleaners, etc. Dyson moved its production to Malaysia with the direct loss of 800 jobs. But the company's head, James Dyson, argued that this offshoring saved jobs and indeed would create jobs. The undeniable reality is that other leading manufacturing nations are mixing and matching different nations' sources of comparative advantage. The nations that strive to keep all stages at home are likely to continue to lose competitiveness.

In a nutshell, European policy makers should stop thinking manufacturing exports and start thinking service inputs into manufactured exports. They should stop thinking good sectors, start thinking good (service) jobs. And they should stop thinking of domestic factories as the industrial base and start thinking of the service sector as the twenty-first-century industrial base.

Bibliography

Acemoglu, Daron and David Autor (2010). Skills, Tasks and Technologies: Implications for Employment and Earnings. NBER WP NBER Working Paper 16082.
Aghion, Philippe and Peter Howitt (1992). A Model of Growth Through Creative Destruction, *Econometrica* 60(2): 323–51.
Alavudeen, A. and N. Venkateshwaran (2010). *Computer Integrated Manufacturing*. Delhi: PHI Learning.
Ali-Yrkko, Jyrki, Petri Rouvinen, Timo Seppala, and PekkaYla-Anttila (2011). Who Captures Value in Global Supply Chains? Case Nokia N95 Smartphone, *Journal of Industry, Competition and Trade*, 11(3): 263–78.
Amador, Joao and Sonia Cabral (2009). Vertical Specialization across the World: A Relative Measure, *The North American Journal of Economics and Finance*, 20(3): 267–80.
Ando, M. and F. Kimura (2005). The formation of international production and distribution networks in East Asia. In T. Ito and A. Rose (eds), *International Trade*

(NBER-East Asia seminar on economics, volume 14), Chicago: The University of Chicago Press.

Autor, David, Frank Levy, and Richard Murnane (2003). The Skill Content of Recent Technological Change: An Empirical Exploration. *Quarterly Journal of Economics*, 118(4): 1279–333.

Baccini, L., A. Duer, M. Elsig, and K. Milewicz (2011). The Design of Preferential Trade Agreements. World Trade Organization, World Trade Report: 'Preferential Trade Agreements and the WTO: A New Era'.

Bairoch, Paul (1974). Geographical Structure and Trade Balance of European Foreign Trade from 1800 to 1970, *Journal of European Economic History*, 3(3): 557–608.

Bairoch, Paul (1982). International Industrialization Levels from 1750 to 1980, *Journal of European Economic History*, 2: 269–333.

Bairoch, Paul (1989). European trade policy, 1815–1914. In P. Mathias and S. Pollard (eds), *Cambridge Economic History of Europe Volume VII*. Cambridge: Cambridge University Press.

Bairoch, Paul (1993). *Economics and World History: Myths and Paradoxes*. London: Harvester-Wheatsheaf.

Bairoch, Paul and Randy Kozul-Wright (1996). Globalisation Myths: Some Historical Reflections on Integration, Industrialization and Growth in the World Economy. UNCTAD Discussion Paper 113.

Baldwin, Richard (1997). Agglomeration and Endogenous Capital. GIIS manuscript.

Baldwin, Richard and Rikard Forslid (1997a). Trade liberalization and endogenous growth: A q-theory approach. Revised version of NBER Working Paper 5549.

Baldwin, Richard (2006). Globalisation: the great unbundling(s). In *Globalisation Challenges for Europe*, edited by Secretariat of the Economic Council, Helsinki: Finnish Prime Minister's Office.

Baldwin, Richard (2010). Unilateral Tariff Liberalisation. NBER Working Paper 16600.

Baldwin, Richard (2011a). 21st Century Regionalism: Filling the Gap between 21st Century Trade and 20th Century Trade Rules. *CEPR Policy Insight*, 56.

Baldwin, Richard (2011b). Trade and Industrialization after Globalisation's 2nd Unbundling: How Building and Joining a Supply Chain are Different and Why it Matters. NBER Working Paper 17716.

Baldwin, Richard (2012a). Global Supply Chains: Why They Emerged, Why They Matter, and Where They are Going. CEPR DP 9103.

Baldwin, Richard (2012b). WTO 2.0: Global Governance of Supply-chain Trade. *CEPR Policy Insight*, 64.

Baldwin, Richard (2013). Multilateralising 21st Century Regionalism. CEPR DP.

Baldwin, Richard and A. Venables (2013). Spiders and Snakes: Offshoring and Agglomeration in the Global Econom, *Journal of International Economics* 90(2): 245–54.

Baldwin, Richard and Rikard Forslid (2000). The Core–Periphery Model and Endogenous Growth: Stabilizing and Destabilizing Integration, *Economica* 67(267): 307–24.

Baldwin, Richard and Simon Evenett (2012). Value creation and trade in 21st century manufacturing: what policies for UK manufacturing? In David Greenaway (ed.), *The UK in a Global World: How can the UK focus on steps in global value chains that really add value?* London: CEPR.

Baldwin, R. and J. Lopez-Gonzalez (2012). Supply–chain Trade: A Portrait of Global Patterns and Several Testable Hypotheses, *The World Economy*, 38(11): 1682–721.

Baldwin, Richard and Philippe Martin (1999). Two Waves of Globalisation: Superficial Similarities, Fundamental Differences (No. w6904), National Bureau of Economic Research.

Baldwin, Richard, Philippe Martin, and Gianmarco I.P. Ottaviano (2001). Global Income Divergence, Trade, and Industrialization: The Geography of Growth Take-Offs, *Journal of Economic Growth*, 6(1): 5–37.

Barro, Robert and Xavier Sala-i-Martin (1992). Convergence, *Journal of Political Economy* 100(2): 223–51.

Baumol, William (1994). Multivariate growth patterns: contagion and common forces as possible sources of convergence. In W. Baumol, R. Nelson, and E. Wolf (eds), *Convergence of Productivity, Cross National Studies and Historical Evidence*, New York: Oxford University Press.

BCG (2011). Made in America, Again: Why Manufacturing Will Return to the U.S.

Bloom, Nicholas. Luis Garicano, Raffaella Sadun, and John Michael van Reenen (2009). The Distinct Effects of Information Technology and Communication Technology on Firm Organization. NBER Working Paper 14975.

Braudel, Fernand (1984). *Civilization and Capitalism, 15th–18th Century, The Perspective of the World Vol 3*. New York: Harper and Row.

Brulhart, Marius (2001). Evolving Geographical Concentration of European manufacturing Industries, *Weltwirtschaftliches Archiv*, 137(2): 215–43.

Brülhart, Marius (2009). An Account of Global Intra-Industry Trade, 1962–2006. *The World Economy*, 32(3): 401–59.

Caballero, Ricardo J. and Adam B. Jaffe (1993). How High are the Giants' Shoulders: An Empirical Assessment of Knowledge Spillovers and Creative Destruction in a Model of Economic Growth. In *NBER Macroeconomics Annual 1993*, Cambridge, MA: MIT Press.

Chaudhuri, K. N. (1966). India's Foreign Trade and the Cessation of the East India Company's Trading Activities, 1828–40, *Economic History Review*, 19(2): 345–63.

Cohen, Daniel (1997). *Richesse du Monde, Pauvretes des Nations*. Paris: Flammarion.

Conerly, Bill (2014). Reshoring or Offshoring: U.S. Manufacturing Forecast 2015–2016. Forbes.com.

CPB (2010). The Netherlands of 2040 by Bas ter Weel, Albert van der Horst, and George Gelauff. CPB Special Publication 88, Netherlands Bureau for Economic Policy Analysis.

Crafts, Nicholas and Gianni Toniolo (1996). *Economic Growth in Europe since 1945*. Cambridge: Cambridge University Press.

Crafts, Nicholas F. R. (1995). Exogenous or Endogenous Growth? The Industrial Revolution Reconsidered, *The Journal of Economic History* 55(4): 745–72.

Crafts, Nicholas F. R. and C. Harley (1992). Output Growth and the British Industrial Revolution: a Restatement of the Crafts-Harley View, *Economic History Review*, 45(4): 703–30.

Crafts, Nicholas F. R. (1989). British Industrialization in an International Context, *Journal of Interdisiplinary History*, 29(3): 415–28.

Crafts, Nicholas F. R. (1984). Patterns of Development in Nineteeth Century Europe, *Oxford Economic Papers*, XXXVI: 438–58.

Crafts, N. and Toniolo, G. (eds) (1996). Economic Growth in Europe since 1945. Available at: https://www.cambridge.org/core/books/economic-growth-in-europe-since-1945/29329FABFE383589DA45DFA55319607D.

Dallas, F. (2002). Maquiladora Industry: Past, Present and Future. Federal Reserve Bank of Dallas, El Paso Branch, Issue 2.

Davidson, Adam (2012). Making It in America, *Atlantic Magazine*, January/February.

De la Roca, Jorge and Diego Puga (2012). Learning by Working in Big Cities. CEPR DP 9243.

Deane, Phyllis (1979). *The First Industrial Revolution*. Cambridge: Cambridge University Press.

Deardorff, A. V. (2005). A Trade Theorist's Take on Skilled-labor Outsourcing, *International Review of Economics & Finance*, 14(3): 259–71.

Debande, Olivier (2009). De-industrialisation, No 3/2006, EIB Papers, European Investment Bank, Economics Department.

Eaton, J. and S. Kortum (1996). Trade in Ideas: Productivity and Patenting in the OECD, *Journal of International Economics*, 40(3): 251–78.

Economist, The (2012). A Third Industrial Revolution, *Economist Magazine Special Report*, 21 April 2012.

Engerman, Stanley (1996). *Trade and the Industrial Revolution, 1700–1850*. Brookfield: Edward Elgar Publishing Limited.

Faini, Ricardo (1984). Increasing Returns, Nontraded Inputs and Regional Developments, *Economic Journal*, 94: 308–23.

Feenstra, R. C. and G. H. Hanson (1996). Globalization, Outsourcing, and Wage Inequality, *American Economic Review*, 86: 240–4.

Findlay, Ronald and Kevin O'Rourke (2007). *Power and Plenty*. Princeton: Princeton University Press.

Fujita, M., Paul Krugman, and Anthony Venables (1999). *The Spatial Economy: Cities, Regions and International Trade*. Cambridge, MA: MIT Press.

Gaspar, Jess and Edward L. Glaeser (1998). Information Technology and the Future of Cities, *Journal of Urban Economics*, 43(1): 136–56.

Glaeser, Edward (2009). Why-Has-Globalization-Led-to-Bigger-Cities? Blog entry, Today's Economist.

Glaeser, Edward (2011). *Triumph of the City: How Our Greatest Invention Makes Us Richer, Smarter, Greener, Healthier, and Happier*. Harmondsworth: Penguin Books.

Glaeser, Edward and Matthew G. Resseger (2009). The Complementarity between Cities and Skills, NBER Working Paper 15103.

Gonzalez, Javier Lopez (2012). Vertical Specialisation and New Regionalism. Thesis PhD thesis, University of Sussex.

Grossman, Gene M. and Helpman, Elhanan (1991). *Innovation and Growth in the World Economy*. Cambridge, MA: MIT Press.

Grossman, G.M. and E. Rossi-Hansberg (2008). Trading tasks: a simple theory of offshoring, *American Economic Review*, 98: 1978–97.

Horn, Henrik, Petros C. Mavroidis, and Andre Sapir (2009). Beyond the WTO? An Anatomy of EU and US Preferential Trade Agreements. CEPR DP 7317.

Hummels, D., J. Ishii, and K-M. Yi (1999). The Nature and Growth of Vertical Specialization in World Trade, *Federal Reserve Bank of New York Staff Reports* 72.

Jacks, David S., Christopher M. Meissner, and Dennis Novy (2011). Trade Booms, Trade Busts, and Trade Costs. *Journal of International Economics*, 83(2): 185–201.

Jaffe A., Trajtenberg and R. Henderson (1993). Geographic Localization of Knowledge Spillovers as Evidenced by Patent Citations, *Quarterly Journal of Economics*, 108(3): 577–98.

Johnson R.C. and G. Noguera (2012). Accounting for Intermediates: Production Sharing and Trade in Value Added, *Journal of International Economics*, 86(2): 224–36.

Johnson, R. C. and G. Noguera (2012). Fragmentation and Trade in Value Added Over Four Decades, NBER Working Paper 18186.

Jones, Ronald W. and Henryk Kierzkowski (1990). The role of services in production and international trade: a theoretical framework. In Ronald Jones and Anne Krueger (eds), *The Political Economy of International Trade*, Oxford: Basil Blackwell.

Kelly, Morgan (1997). The Dynamics of Smithian Growth, *Quarterly Journal of Economics*, 108(3): 939–64.

Kind, H. J. (1997). Trade Liberalization, Innovation and Imitation, *NHH mimeo*, Bergen Norway.

Koopman, R., Z. Wang, and S. J. Wei (2008). Give Credit where Credit is Due: Tracing Value Added in Global Production Chains, NBER Working Paper 16426.

Krugman, Paul, and Anthony Venables (1995). Globalization and the Inequality of Nations, *Quarterly Journal of Economics*, 110(4): 857–80.

Krugman, Paul (1981). Trade, Accumulation and Uneven Development, *Journal of Development Economics*, 8(2): 149–61.

Krugman, Paul (1989). *Geography and Trade*. Cambridge, MA: MIT Press.

Krugman, Paul (1991a). Increasing Returns and Economic Geography, *Journal of Political Economy*, 99(2): 483–99.

Krugman, Paul (1991b). History versus Expectations, *Quarterly Journal of Economics*, 106(2): 651–67.

Kuznets, Simon (1965). *Economic Growth and Structure: Selected Essays*. London: Heinemann Educational Books limited.

Kuznets, Simon (1966). *Modern Economic Growth, Rate Structure and Spread*. New Haven: Yale University Press.

Landes, David S. (1969). *The Unbound Promotheus, Technological Change and Industrial Development in Western Europe from 1750 to the Present*. Cambridge, MA: Cambridge University Press.

Lanz, Rainer, Sebastien Miroudot, and Hildegunn Kyvik Nordis (2012). Does Fragmentation of Production Imply Fragmentation of Jobs? OECD Trade and Agriculture Directorate Working Paper.

Lejour, A., H. Rojas-Romagosa, and P. Veenendaal (2012). The Origins of Value in Global Production Chains. Paper financed by DG Trade of the European Commission under the contract 'EU trade in value added' as part of implementing Framework Contract No TRADE/07 A, 2.

Lucas, Robert (1988). On the Process of Economic Development, *Journal of Monetary Economics*, 22(1): 3–42.

Lucas, Robert (1993). Making a Miracle, *Econometrica*, 61(2): 251–72.

Maddison, Angus (1971). *Class Structure and Economic Growth: India and Pakistan since the Moghuls*, London: Taylor & Francis.

Maddison, Angus (1983). A Comparison of Levels of GDP Per Capita in Developed and Developing Countries, 1700–1980, *Journal of Economic History*, 43(1): 27–41.

Maddison, Angus (1991). *Dynamic Forces in Capitalistic Development: A Long Run Comparative View*. New York: Oxford University Press.

Martin, Philippe and Gianmarco Ottaviano (1996a). Growing Locations: Industry Location in a Model of Endogenous Growth, *European Economic Review*, 43(1999): 281–302.

Martin, Philippe and Gianmarco Ottaviano (1996b). Growth and Agglomeration, CEPR DP 1529.

Matsuyama, Kiminori (1991). Increasing Returns, Industrialization, and Indeterminacy of Equilibrium, *Quarterly Journal of Economics*, 106(2): 617–50.

Mokyr, Joel (1993). Introduction: the new economic history and the industrial revolution. In Joel Mokyr (ed.), *The British Industrial Revolution: An Economic Perspective*. Oxford: Westview Press.

Moretti, E. (2012). *The New Geography of Jobs*, Boston: Houghton Mifflin Harcourt.

Morris, Ian (2010). *Why the West Rules for Now*. New York: Profile Books.

Murphy, Kevin M., Andrei Shleifer, and Robert W. Vishny (1989a). Industrialization and the Big Push, *Journal of Political Economy*, 97(5): 1023–26.

Murphy, Kevin M., Andrei Shleifer, and Robert W. Vishny (1989b). Income Distribution, Market Size and Industrialization, *Quarterly Journal of Economics*, 104(3): 537–64.

Niepmann, F. and G. Felbermayr (2010). Globalisation and the Spatial Concentration of Production, *World Economy*, 33(5): 680–709.

North, Douglass (1968). Sources of Productivity Change in Ocean Shipping, 1600–1850, *Journal of Political Economy*, 76(5): 953–70.

O'Brien, Patrick and Stanley Engerman (1991). Exports and the growth of the British economy from the Glorious Revolution to the Peace of Amiens. In Barbara Solow (ed.), *Slavery and the Rise of the Atlantic System*, Cambridge: Cambridge University Press.

O'Rourke, Kevin and Jeffery Williamson (1999). *Globalization and History*, Cambridge, MA: MIT Press.

Patterson, Gardner (1966). *Discrimination in International Trade: The Policy Issues 1945–1965*. Princeton: Princeton University Press.

Porter, M.E. (1985). *Competitive Advantage*. New York: Free Press.

Prichett, Lant (1997). Divergence, Big Time, *Journal of Economic Perspectives*, 11(3): 3–17.

Puga, Diego and Anthony Venables (1996). The Spread of Industry: Spatial Agglomeration in Economic Development, *Journal of the Japanese and International Economies*, 10(4): 440–64.

Rivera-Batiz, Luis and Paul Romer (1991). Economic Integration and Endogenous Growth, *Quarterly Journal of Economics*, 106(2): 531–55.

Rodrick, Dani (1995). Getting Interventions Right: How South Korea and Taiwan Grew Rich, *Economic Policy*, 10(20): 53–107.

Romer, Paul (1986). Increasing Returns and Long Term Growth, *Journal of Political Economy*, 94(5): 1002–37.

Romer, Paul (1990). Endogenous Technological Change, *Journal of Political Economy*, 98(5) part II: S71–S102.

Rosenberg, Nathan (1994). *Exploring the Black Box: Technology, Economics and History*. Cambridge: Cambridge University Press.

Rostow, W.W. (1960). *The Stages of Economic Growth: A Non-Communist Manifesto*. Cambridge: Cambridge University Press.

Scott, A.J. and Storper, M. (1986). *Production, Work, Territory: The Geographical Anatomy of Industrial Capitalism*. New York: HarperCollins Publishers Ltd.

Simchi-Levi, David (2010). Impact of Crude Oil Volatility on Network Design. Power Point.

Simchi-Levi, David, James Paul Peruvankal, Narendra Mulani, Bill Read, and John Ferreira (2011). Made in America: Rethinking the Future of US Manufacturing, Accenture, available at: www.accenture.com/SiteCollection Documents/PDF/ Accenture-Made-in-America.pdf.

Spitz, A. (2004). Are Skill Requirements in the Workplace Rising? Stylized Facts and Evidence on Skill-Biased Technological Change, ZEW DP 04–33.

Sullivan, Richard (1989). England's Age of Invention: The Acceleration of Patents and Patentable Invention during the Industrial Revolution, *Explorations in Economic History*, 26(4): 424–52.

Venables Anthony (1987). Customs Union, Tariff Reform and Imperfect Competition, *European Economic Review*, 31(1–2): 103–10.

Venables, Anthony (1996). Equilibrium Location with Vertically Linked Industries, *International Economic Review*, 37(2): 341–59.

Williamson, Jeffrey and Saif I. Shah Mohammed (2004). Freight Rates and Productivity Gains in British Tramp Shipping 1869–1950, *Explorations in Economic History*, 41(2): 172–203.

WTO (2011). The WTO and Reciprocal Preferential Trading Agreements, World Trade Report, Geneva.

Yamamoto, Kazuhiro (2003). Agglomeration and Growth with Innovation in the Intermediate Goods Sector, *Regional Science and Urban Economics*, 33(3): 335–60.

Yi, Kei-Mu (2003). Can Vertical Specialization Explain the Growth of World Trade? *Journal of Political Economy*, 111(1): 52–102.

2

Hollowing Out of the Japanese Economy: A Long-term Perspective

Michael J. Ryan and Farid Toubal

2.1 Introduction

The debate over the possible adverse effect of multinational firms has gained particular attention in developed countries. These firms are suspected to increase domestic labour inequality. By reallocating their production across borders, multinationals may substitute domestic unskilled labour intensive manufacturing activities with relatively more skilled labour-intensive activities related to the conception stage, the design of the goods, or the coordination of the production process. These firms might also add to the process of de-industrialization by shifting manufacturing jobs to locations with lower wages or lower labour standards. It remains unclear whether such offshored activities have an impact on aggregate employment as their activities abroad may or may not substitute for employment within the domestic parent and because they must be sufficiently large to influence the aggregates.

The idea that the impact of multinationals depends on the degree of substitution between the activities of parent and affiliate firms has been developed theoretically by Markusen (1989) and Markusen and Maskus (2001). Recent micro-level studies have shown that the impact of off-shoring on parent employment depends significantly on the location and type of the offshored activities. Harrison and McMillan (2011) show that offshoring by US multinationals to low-wage countries substitutes for US domestic employment. The effect is, however, positive when foreign and domestic employees perform complementary activities.[1]

[1] A large body of the literature has investigated the impact of foreign direct investment on domestic employment using different samples and different estimation methodologies.

Overall, the empirical literature finds little effect from the overseas activities of multinational firms.

In this chapter, we examine over a long period—from 1982 to 2002—whether Japanese firms have conducted similar strategies by exporting manufacturing jobs overseas. Examining Japan over these two decades is of particular interest as it has experienced a dramatic increase in foreign direct investment (FDI), especially in South and East Asia. FDI took off in the 1980s for administrative reasons. Prior to 1982, overseas investments were heavily regulated and not subject to market forces (Bayoumi and Lipworth 1997). In the 1980s, international competition led Japanese manufacturing firms to expand abroad to take advantage of the cheaper production costs in their neighbouring Asian countries. Japan's growth slowdown, associated with a sharp appreciation of the Yen after the 1985 Plaza Accord, intensified Japanese overseas' production. Interestingly, while almost all labour-intensive stages of production were offshored in Asia, overall Japanese manufacturing employment did not fall. The offshoring of some low-wage stages of production made Japanese firms sufficiently competitive in the EU and the US markets to maintain high-wage manufacturing jobs (Baldwin 2006).

After the bubble collapse in 1991, the Yen appreciated sharply again through mid-1995 and made it cheaper to acquire overseas firms and land. The so-called Lost Decade is characterized by a sharp slowdown in economic growth more or less associated with the foreign activities of Japanese manufacturers. This tendency, called the *hollowing out* of the Japanese economy, is a phenomenon whereby Japanese firms export manufacturing (labour-intensive) jobs abroad and then ship the final product to Western markets or back to Japan. Studies on the impact of Japanese FDI on domestic employment, however, find mixed evidence. Ando and Kimura (2011), Tanaka (2012), and Edamura et al. (2011) find a positive effect on employment. Earlier papers by Fukao (1995) and Fukao and Yuan (2001) find a negative effect of FDI in East Asia on the employment of Japanese parents. This effect is, however, dampened when the Japanese firms' aim to supply goods and services to local consumers (market-oriented FDI). In a recent study, Kiyota and Kambayashi (2014) show that domestic disemployment by Japanese multinationals during the 1995–2009 period was mainly driven by the

---

Interesting contributions include Blomström et al. (1997), Braconier and Ekholm (2000), Brainard and Riker (2001a, 2001b), Hanson et al., (2003) and recent contribution by Kleinert and Toubal (2007), Becker and Muendler (2010), Barba Navaretti et al. (2010), Hijzen et al. (2010), and Godart et al. (2013), who use European datasets.

substitution between capital and labour, rather than by the reallocation of activities from Japan to foreign countries.

To investigate the impact of Japanese overseas investment on domestic employment, our empirical work is based on a unique dataset that matched detailed information on the domestic activities of Japanese firms as well as overseas activities. We create this parent–affiliate dataset by manually matching Toyo Keizai Inc.'s data on the activities of its overseas affiliate with the Pacific-Basin Capital Markets Research Center (PACAP) data on the income statement of the parent companies. The PACAP database collects information on the income statements of over 2,000 Japanese listed firms providing us with information on Japanese parents' employment levels as well as their domestic sales and other firm-level controls such as the sector of activity. Toyo Keizai Inc. collects data on the activity of foreign affiliates of Japanese firms as well as their main business line. Our econometric analysis covers the period 1982–2002. We can therefore analyse whether the post-1991 period has led to a significant destruction of domestic jobs due to the foreign activities of Japanese manufacturers.

Our econometric methodology employs a labour demand function as in recent studies using micro-level data (Barba-Navaretti et al. 2010; Görg et al. 2009; Godart et al. 2013; Harrison and McMillan 2011). We apply two complementary empirical approaches to estimate the effect of overseas investment on the domestic employment of Japanese firms. First, we use the event study technique and compare average differences in domestic employment of firms that did not internationalize to the employment levels of Japanese multinational firms. We introduce a discontinuity in time in order to take into account the pre- and post-bubble periods. Second, we use a difference-in-difference estimator to compare average differences in employment before and after overseas investment. This technique requires more information on the status of the firm before it switches. However, the difference-in-difference analysis allows us to control for all non-random elements of the switching decision that are time invariant and persistent over time (Smith and Todd 2005). The remaining unobserved heterogeneity is averaged out by the large size of the sample. Using the difference-in-difference estimator, we also account for the post-1991 period by interacting a $Post_{1991}$ dummy variable with the firm status.

Our findings suggest that multinational firms have no significant effect on the hollowing out process during the sample period. However, our results confirm a negative impact within Japanese multinationals on their domestic employment in the post-1991 period, although this effect is small. Compared to non-multinationals, Japanese multinationals reduced their domestic employment by 0.17 per cent per year from 1992 to 2001. This effect is mostly due to the activities of vertical multinational firms.

The rest of this chapter is organized as follows. In Section 2.1.1, we present the Japanese data and provide some facts on the extent of Japanese FDI over the sample period. In section 2.2, we introduce the methodology and the empirical framework. In Section 2.3, we present the results. We conclude in Section 2.4.

2.1.1 The Japanese Data

In this section we use a different dataset to provide information on the process of internationalization of Japanese firms. In the following we have chosen to present some facts from the raw files, which covers subsequent periods. This choice is motivated by the willingness to provide accurate facts on the activity of multinational firms and their locations.

OVERSEAS AFFILIATES

This study is based on a unique set of survey data collected by Toyo Keizai Inc. (Tokyo, Japan) entitled *Japanese Overseas Investments: A complete list by firms and countries* (Japanese: *Kaigai Shinshutsu Kigyou Souran*). We use five editions of the survey (1984/85, 1986/87, 1992, 1995, 2001) for this study. For each edition of the survey, Toyo Keizai queries Japanese firms about their overseas affiliate holdings, and the survey provides numerous pieces of information on the investing parent as well as the overseas affiliate. Importantly for this chapter, we can determine not only the affiliate's geographic location and establishment date, but also the affiliate's level of employment (at year of survey) as well as a verbal description of its main line of business. Typically, this business line data will allow the affiliate industry classification to be determined to at least the two-digit US SIC, but usually to the three- or four-digit level. Note that we begin with the 1984/85 survey, which is prior to the explosion of Japanese outward FDI noted in the second half of that decade. In addition, Mason (1994) indicates that most Japanese firms were unable to invest abroad prior to 1970 due to government restrictions on their overseas activities. Thus, our dataset encompasses a majority of the Japanese FDI experience over the past three decades.

Given these datasets, we are able to determine a number of significant FDI-related pieces of information for each firm, including the number of foreign affiliates it operates, in how many different countries these affiliates operate (to establish a measure of the parent's foreign affiliate network), and how many of these affiliates are located in any particular country. We are also able to characterize, for each survey year, the number of Japanese listed firms that have operating foreign affiliates, the average and median number of operating affiliates per investing firm, as well as the average and median number of operating affiliates per investing firm by affiliate location. To make sense of the geographic dispersion of these affiliates, affiliate locations are grouped into eight categories: China, non-China Asia, Middle East, Europe, North America (USA and Canada), Latin America and the Caribbean, Africa, and Oceania.

We present summary statistics on this dataset in several ways. First, Table 2.1 reveals information on the number of investing firms and their average holdings.

There are numerous takeaways from even this simple set of aggregated descriptive statistics. Note that the number of investing firms jumps by 290 per cent between 1985 and 1992, and then continues to rise through 2001. This is the explosion of outward FDI that corresponds to the time that Japan started worrying about the hollowing out of its economy. This jump in investment results in a more than doubling of the number of affiliates (16,166 in 1992 compared to 6,664 in 1987). However, many of the newly investing firms during the late 1980s and early 1990s are smaller in size, and only have a few established affiliates (which may be, in part, because of our use of 1992 as a survey year due to data availability). This results in a significant drop in the average (10.6 to 5.3) and median (4 to 2) number of established affiliates per investing parent. We also note that the Japanese bubble economy appears to impact outward FDI, as the pace of foreign expansion slows (but, importantly, does not reverse). Between the 1992 and 1995 survey years, only 399 new investors are noted, and the number of affiliates increases only by about 20 per cent. The average and median number of affiliates does not change over this period as

Table 2.1 Summary statistics on Japanese outward FDI

	1982	1985	1987	1992	1995	2001
No. of investing firms	763	795	860	3092	3491	4201
No. of established affiliates	5718	6084	6664	16166	19608	22962
Avg. no. of affiliates per parent	7.49	7.65	10.61	5.27	5.62	5.47
Median no. of affiliates per parent	3	3	4	2	2	2
Avg. no. of unique countries	4.48	4.58	4.68	3.07	3.26	3.22
Median no. of unique countries	3	3	3	1	2	2

Source: author calculations from Toyo Keizai Data.

well. Finally, post-2000 investment data show increases in total affiliates operating abroad, as well as the average number of established affiliates per firm. However, given that the median number of per firm affiliates has not changed since 1992, it appears that much of the foreign affiliate establishment is being done by Japanese parents that have large foreign affiliate networks.

Table 2.1 addresses the expanse of foreign affiliate networks and reveals the average and median number of countries in which parent firms operate. Note the drop between 1987 and 1992, which corresponds to the significant foreign investment by firms new to outward FDI. In fact, the average and median number of countries in which a firm operates has yet to rise to its pre-bubble level. However, these aggregates do not tell us the extent to which firms are using FDI as part of the hollowing out of the Japanese economy. To do this, we disaggregate the affiliate geographic location to the aforementioned eight regions. Table 2.2 focuses on the statistically most important of these regions: China, non-Chinese Asia, North America, and Europe.

Several key characteristics of the Japanese affiliate network pattern can be noted here. In 1985 few, if any, Japanese parent firms had any foreign presence in China. However, by 1987, there was a ten-fold increase in the average number of investments per firm in China, from 1 in 200 investing firms having a presence in China in 1985 to approximately one in twenty in 1987; by 1992, another ten-fold increase could be noted as well, with one in every two foreign investors having a Chinese presence. For the rest of Asia, there was a drop in investment in these locations during the 1990s, but a rebound beginning in 2000. Note also the continued (relative) decline in North American and European investment. At the start of the sample, firms

Table 2.2 Japanese FDI by major geographic region

	1982	1985	1987	1992	1995	2001
China	0.004	0.005	0.048	0.455	0.418	0.834
	(0)	(0)	(0)	(0)	(0)	(0)
Non-China Asia	2.798	2.815	2.859	1.881	1.373	3.071
	(1)	(1)	(1)	(1)	(1)	(1)
North America	1.622	1.653	1.743	1.423	1.358	1.048
	(1)	(1)	(1)	(1)	(1)	(0)
Europe	1.219	1.225	1.328	1.032	1.090	0.849
	(0)	(0)	(0)	(0)	(0)	(0)

Source: author calculations from Toyo Keizai Data. Per firm average (median) data reported for Japanese MNEs only.

on average had three investments located in the combined North American–European continents. There is a steady decline in the average number of investments per firm in these locations, down to less than two by 2001. Combined, these results reveal a geographic change in the foreign affiliate networks of Japanese foreign investors over the past thirty years.

While the FDI dataset shows Japanese firms increasing their foreign presence through growing foreign affiliate networks, the FDI dataset alone cannot tell the entire hollowing out story. To do that, we look to additional data to support our claim that hollowing out was indeed happening. One place to look is METI, the Japanese Ministry of Economy, Trade, and Industry. Previously, METI published data on employment trends of Japanese-based parents and their overseas affiliates. Figure 2.1

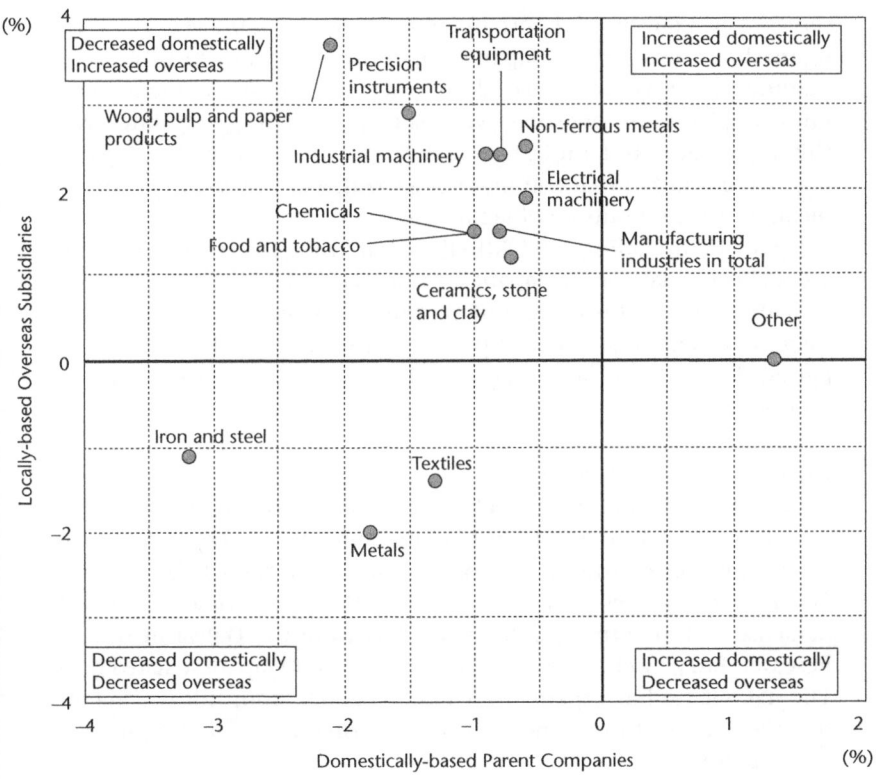

Figure 2.1 Growth rates in the numbers employed by domestically-based parent companies and overseas subsidiaries

Source: www.meti.go.jp/english/statistics/tyo/genntihou/h2c3720e/h2c3723e.html

Table 2.3 Japanese overseas production ratio

Year	%	Year	%
1982	3.2	1993	7.4
1984	4.3	1994	8.6
1985	3.0	1995	9.0
1986	3.2	1996	11.6
1987	4.0	1997	12.4
1988	4.9	1998	13.1
1989	5.7	1999	12.9
1990	6.4	2000	13.4
1991	6.0	2001	16.7
1992	6.2	2002	17.1

Note: no data reported for 1983.
Source: METI.

serves as an example of these employment trends for the year 1997. This figure shows a majority of Japanese manufacturing industries, as well as manufacturing as a whole, see decreased domestic employment growth rates coupled with increased overseas employment growth rates. Note this figure does not indicate negative growth rates for the Japanese parents, but rather that employment growth was slowing in Japan, and picking up steam outside of Japan.[2]

Up to and including 2002, METI's Research and Statistics Department also collected data on the Japanese Overseas Production Ratio. Table 2.3 provides data on this for manufacturing as a whole. Note the five-fold increase in Japanese overseas production during the 1982–2002 time period. These data clearly suggest an increasing percentage of Japanese production occurring outside of Japan.

PARENT FIRM DATA
As this study focuses on the behaviour of Japanese parents, we restrict our empirical estimation to only publicly held Japanese parent firms. Determination of this status comes from both Toyo Keizai's annual *Japan Company Handbook* as well as the PACAP database. The PACAP database collects firm-level financial data from the Daiwa Institute of Research Ltd as well as Toyo Keizai for over 2,000 Japanese listed firms. The dataset we have spans from 1982 to 2002. From this, we are able to collect a wealth of parent-specific information, including its main business line and employment levels.

[2] METI Census of Manufactures; www.meti.go.jp/english/statistics/tyo/genntihou/h2c3720e/h2c3723e.html

74

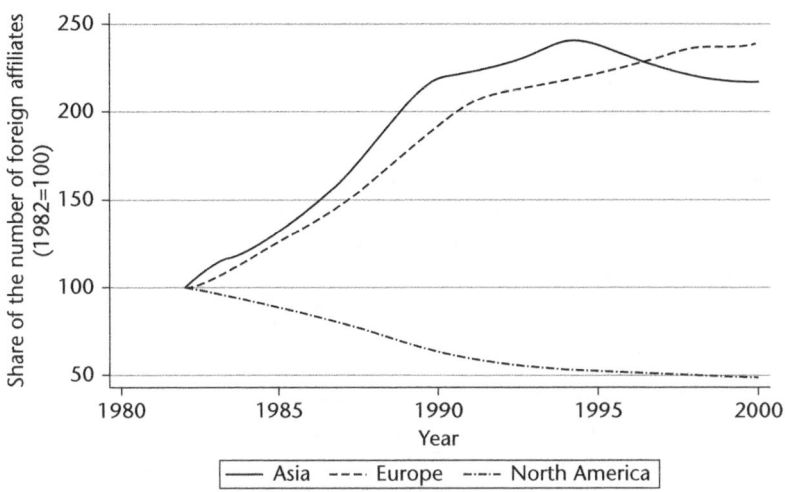

Figure 2.2 Share of overseas affiliates classified in a different business line than their Japanese parent
Source: author calculations from Toyo Keizai Data.

An interesting feature of the dataset is that it contains the parent firm's main business line. Combining the parent and affiliate main business line information, we can roughly appreciate the extent of vertical fragmentation operated by Japanese firms by creating variables focusing on vertical FDI both globally as well as for each geographic area.[3] In Figure 2.2, we concentrate on the main destination of Japanese FDI—Asia, Europe, and North America—and show the share of overseas affiliates classified in a different business line than their Japanese parent.[4] The figure shows that Japanese multinational firms have reallocated their vertical production network from North America to Asia and Europe. The share of overseas affiliates classified in a different business line than their Japanese parent has more than doubled in these two regions while it is halved in North America.

Importantly, we combine the parent information with information on affiliate employment. In Figure 2.3, we aggregate the employment figures at sector level and show the change in domestic and foreign employment for Japanese multinational firms between 1991–2011. The

---

[3] See the interesting contribution of Yamashita (2010) for a detailed analysis of the international fragmentation of the Japanese production process.

[4] We follow Buch et al. (2005) and assume that all affiliates classified in another business line than their parent belong to a vertical production network.

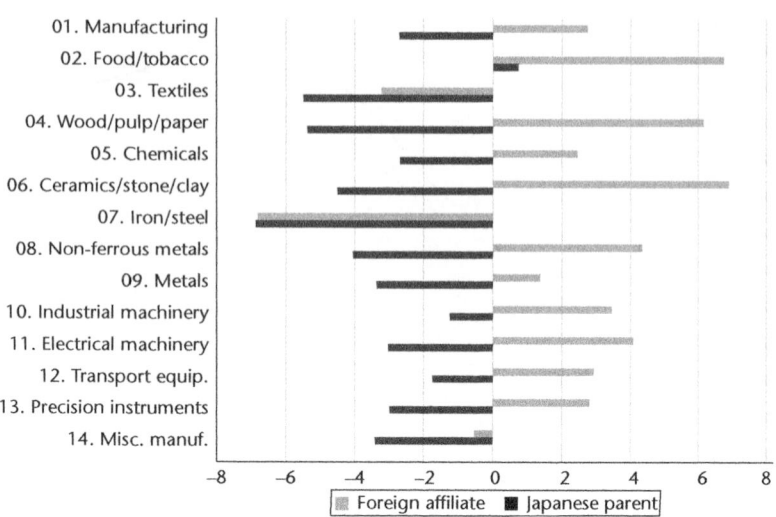

Figure 2.3 Average annual percentage change in parent and overseas affiliate employment (1991–2000)

Source: author calculations from Japanese Ministry of Economy, Trade, and Industry (METI) employment data.

evidence is striking. In the manufacturing sector, the Japanese parents have reduced their domestic employment by almost 3 per cent on average. This reduction has partly been absorbed by an increase in employment by foreign affiliates. The most important changes are reported in the textile and iron industries. In both industries, the reduction concerns the share of employment of parent and affiliates. In the other sectors, a reduction in the domestic employment of multinational firms is always (at least) partly compensated by an increase in the share of foreign affiliate employment.

We can classify the firms in the PACAP database into three categories. The first category concerns *domestic* firms that have never invested in a foreign country. The second category concerns *multinational* firms that have at least one overseas affiliate over the sample period. The third category concerns firms that have changed their status and become multinationals. We call these firms *switchers*. Figure 2.4 shows the density distribution of domestic employment of multinationals and switchers for the years 1983 and 2000. We show that multinational firms and switchers have reduced their domestic employment. This is, in fact, in line with the hypothesis that part of the *hollowing out* process is driven by firms that have affiliates in foreign countries. These firms substitute domestic jobs with foreign employment. However, Figure 2.4

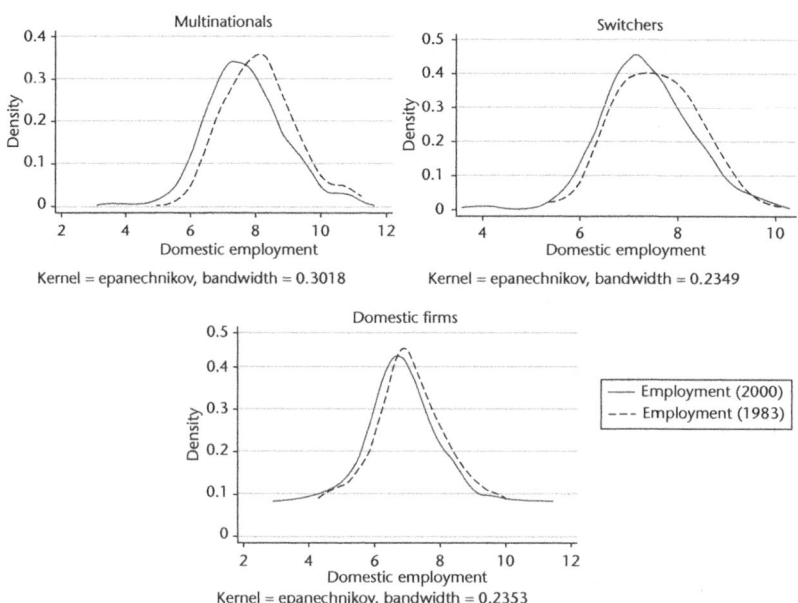

Figure 2.4 Domestic employment and firms' status, 1983 and 2000
Source: author calculations from Toyo Keizai Data.

shows that domestic firms have experienced a similar reduction in employment during the same sample period.

The main issue is therefore to characterize and identify the impact of Japanese multinationals on the reduction of manufacturing employment. In Section 2.2, we present our empirical methodology and identification strategy.

2.2 Methodology and Empirical Framework

To identify the effect of offshoring on domestic employment, we estimate an augmented labour demand function which is based on a generalized cost function as in Hamermesh (1993). This estimation procedure has been implemented in several recent papers investigating the impact of offshoring on domestic employment by parent firms including Barba-Navaretti et al. (2010), Görg et al. (2009), Godart et al. (2013), and Harrison and McMillan (2011). The standard labour demand can be written as follows:

$$ln(L_{it}) = \alpha ln(w_{it}) + \beta ln(Q_{it}) + \gamma ln(r_{it}) \qquad (2.1)$$

To estimate equation 2.1, we need information on Japanese employment, wages, outputs, and capital prices. We measure $ln(L_{it})$ as the natural logarithm of net domestic employment of the Japanese parent i in Japan at time t.

The PACAP dataset does not report information on the firm-level wage bill. We therefore approximate w_{it} by firm-level labour productivity defined as the ratio of value added over employment. We also proxy the firm-level output, Q_{it}, by the consolidated level of sales. The price of capital is approximated based on firm-specific capital stock. The firm-level controls are lagged one year and they are all taken in logarithms.

The labour demand equation is extended to include the multinational status of the Japanese firm. MNE_{it} is a dummy variable that takes the value of 1 if a Japanese firm has at least one affiliate abroad. In order to investigate whether Japanese multinationals significantly affected domestic employment during the *lost decade*, we add a $Post_{1991}$ dummy variable that we also integrate with the MNE dummy.

We can write the empirical labour demand as:

$$ln(L_{it}) = \zeta MNE_{it} + \delta(MNE_{it} \times Post_{1991}) \qquad (2.2)$$

$$+ \xi Post_{1991} + \alpha ln(w_{it-1}) + \beta ln(Q_{it-1}) + \gamma ln(r_{it-1}) + \epsilon_{it-1}$$

ϵ_{it} is the error term. The standard errors can be adjusted for clustering at the firm level to account for heteroscedasticity and non-independence across the repeated observations within firms.

In order to estimate (2.2), we develop two empirical methodologies. In the first set of estimations, we add two types of variables to the conditional labour demand equation. The first variables are sector × year specific dummy variables. They allow us to control for cyclical effects that are common to each sector. The second set of variables are *Japanese Prefecture* × year specific effect. They account for localized labour market changes, such as external shocks (localized earthquakes or exogenous shocks) or changes that are specific to each Prefecture. In the first methodology, we therefore compare the conditional labour demand of Japanese multinationals with non-multinational firms.[5]

In the second set of estimations, we use a fixed effect model. We include firm-specific effects and time dummies to control for year-specific shocks. In this methodology, we are examining the within estimates of labour demand. As we use the within variation, we compare the employment level of firms before and after becoming a

---

[5] Note that the $Post_{1991}$ dummy variable cannot be estimated in this first methodology as it is collinear with the Prefecture × year and sector × year specific dummy variables.

Table 2.4 Sample summary statistics (1983–2000, number of observations: 15,944)

Variables	Mean	Std. Dev
$\ln(L_{it})$	7.510	1.141
MNE_{it}	0.548	0.498
$\ln(w_{it})$	−3.575	1.493
$\ln(Q_{it})$	11.558	1.285
$\ln(r_{it-1})$	9.159	1/178
$\ln(fin_{it-1})$	−4.150	9.600

Note: Author calculations from Toyo Keizai Data.

multinational firm. As our methodology involves an interaction term between the MNE and the $Post_{1991}$ indicators, we analyse whether multinationals have reduced their domestic employment in the post-1991 period. Since employment is likely to be jointly determined by output and also by firm-level wages, we apply in a robustness check a first differenced two-step generalized methods of moments (GMM) estimator as developed by Arellano and Bond (1991). This estimator uses lagged levels of the endogenous variables as instruments in the first differenced equation. The results are reported in Table 2.A1 in the Appendix at the end of this chapter. The results are consistent with our previous findings.

In Table 2.4, we report the summary statistics of the variables used in the estimation. The average firm in the sample is about 1,800 employees. The firms are therefore large enough to affect the Japanese economy. Consistent with Figure 2.4, Japanese parents' employment fell by 31.5 per cent during the sample period.

2.3 Results

Table 2.5 reports the results of regressions without firm and year fixed effects to study the relationship between the level of employment and multinational status over time across firms. The log of Japanese employment is our dependent variable and we use the sector × year and Prefecture × year fixed effects in all specifications. Column 1 of Table 2.5 reports the estimated coefficient on the full sample. In column (2) we introduce the lagged MNE variable. The results indicate that domestic employment by Japanese firms is not affected by MNE status at least on average over the sample period.

Table 2.5 Between estimates of labour demand: Japanese parent

	Full sample			Vertical MNEs	Horizontal MNEs
MNE (1/0)	0.001		0.006	0.004	0.004
	(0.005)		(0.005)	(0.007)	(0.007)
MNE (1/0, lag)		0.000			
		(0.005)			
MNE × Post$_{1991}$			-0.016^b	-0.033^c	-0.033^c
			(0.007)	(0.019)	(0.019)
Output (lag)	0.528^a	0.529^a	0.528^a	0.533^a	0.533^a
	(0.005)	(0.005)	(0.005)	(0.007)	(0.007)
Capital (lag)	-0.007	-0.007	-0.007	-0.014^b	-0.014^b
	(0.005)	(0.005)	(0.005)	(0.007)	(0.007)
Wages (lag)	-0.460^a	-0.460^a	-0.460^a	-0.468^a	-0.468^a
	(0.008)	(0.008)	(0.008)	(0.007)	(0.007)
Sector × Year FE	Yes	Yes	Yes	Yes	Yes
Region × Year FE	Yes	Yes	Yes	Yes	Yes
Obs.	15,944	15,944	15,944	8,548	4,584
Adj. R^2	0.974	0.974	0.974	0.977	0.981
$\beta_{MNE} = \beta_{MNE*Post_{1991}}$			4.818^b	2.801^c	2.801^c

Robust standard errors in parentheses. Clustered at the firm level
$^a p<0.01$, $^b p<0.05$, $^c p<0.1$

In the third column, we introduce the interaction term between the
MNE and the $Post_{1991}$ dummy variables. We find a negative and significant effect of the cross term. The effect is estimated with a sufficient
degree of precision at the 5 per cent level of significance. Compared
to non-multinationals, Japanese multinationals have reduced their
domestic employment by 1.5 per cent during the post-1991 period.
There is no significant difference between Japanese multinationals and
domestic firms in the pre-bubble period, before 1991. In columns
(4) and (5), we investigate whether the impact is due to vertical or
horizontal activities. In our crude approximation of these types, we
use the nomenclature of activities of the parent and their affiliates in
order to classify firms. Vertical MNEs are firms that declare affiliates in
a sector other than their own. We find the effect to be twice as large as
the average effect for vertical multinational firms. As shown in column
(5), there is no differential impact for horizontal MNEs.

In Table 2.6, we use the difference in difference methodology by
introducing firm and year fixed effects. We investigate the impact of
overseas investments using the within variation in domestic employment over time and therefore analyse the impact on domestic employment of becoming a multinational firm. Note that we can now provide
an estimate for the $Post_{1991}$ dummy variable as it is no longer collinear
with the set of specific effects.

Table 2.6 Within estimates of labour demand: Japanese parent

	Full sample			Vertical MNEs	Horizontal MNEs
MNE (1/0)	0.001		0.005	0.017^c	0.023^c
	(0.007)		(0.007)	(0.009)	(0.012)
MNE (1/0, lag)		0.001			
		(0.007)			
MNE × Post$_{1991}$			-0.022^b	-0.049^b	-0.075
			(0.009)	(0.020)	(0.048)
Post$_{1991}$	-0.112^a	-0.112^a	-0.098^a	-0.060^a	-0.014
	(0.013)	(0.013)	(0.013)	(0.023)	(0.051)
Output (lag)	0.514^a	0.514^a	0.514^a	0.522^a	0.512^a
	(0.016)	(0.016)	(0.016)	(0.019)	(0.020)
Capital (lag)	0.011	0.011	0.012	0.001	0.029^b
	(0.009)	(0.009)	(0.009)	(0.012)	(0.012)
Wages (lag)	-0.260^a	-0.260^a	-0.260^a	-0.286^a	-0.258^a
	(0.033)	(0.033)	(0.033)	(0.028)	(0.042)
Firm FE	Yes	Yes	Yes	Yes	Yes
Year FE	Yes	Yes	Yes	Yes	Yes
Obs.	15,944	15,944	15,944	8,548	4,584
Adj. R^2	0.982	0.982	0.982	0.982	0.985
$\beta_{MNE} = \beta_{MNE*Post_{1991}}$			4.776^a	8.270^a	3.686^b

Robust standard errors in parentheses. Clustered at the firm level
$^a p<0.01$, $^b p<0.05$, $^c p<0.1$

In columns (1) and (2), we report the estimates using the MNE dummy variable and its lag. The within estimates are insignificant. Over the long sample period, there is no effect on domestic employment of switching from domestic to multinational status. However, the lost decade is a period of job destruction. We find a negative and significant effect in the $Post_{1991}$ statistics. Compared to the previous period, Japanese firms have reduced their employment levels by about 2.2 per cent.

In column (4), we introduce the interaction term between the MNE and the $Post_{1991}$ dummy variables. The interaction term is significant and negative. This implies that Japanese firms that have switched to multinational status have reduced their domestic employment level in the period post-1991. The reduction is about 2 per cent.

We find an amplification of this effect for vertical multinational firms. In column (4), we find a reduction of domestic employment by about 4 per cent during the lost decade for the Japanese firms that had started to fragment their production process. The negative effect is not significant for horizontal multinational firms.

Our results partially confirm the prediction of Baldwin (2006). Over the sample period, firms that had started to split up their production process exert a negative effect on their domestic employment (0.017 − 0.022 = −0.005). However, this effect is positive and significant in the pre-1991 period. Concerning the sample of horizontal multinational firms, we find a positive effect on domestic employment for firms that switched from domestic to multinational status in the pre-1991 period. The coefficients of the MNE dummy variable are, however, estimated with a low degree of precision.

2.4 Conclusion

This chapter investigates the impact of multinational overseas activities on domestic employment. For many years numerous empirical studies have examined the relationship between Japanese outward FDI in manufacturing and the *hollowing out*, or employment loss, in the Japanese domestic economy. Our contribution to this literature is unique in that we merge Japanese firm-level balance sheet and employment datasets with the firms' FDI activities during the 1982–2001 period. Our empirical approach focuses both on employment comparisons between firms with (MNEs) and without (domestic) foreign affiliates, as well as on how changes from domestic to MNE status affect firm-level domestic employment. In addition, we examine employment pre- and post-economic collapse to gain a better picture of how MNE employment activity changed in these two significantly different periods in the Japanese economy.

We find some limited evidence of the *hollowing out* of the Japanese economy by Japanese MNEs moving production out of Japan during the period after the 1991 economic collapse. While the aggregated data on overseas production ratios suggest a significant increase in the amount of Japanese production occurring outside of Japan, this outsourcing appears to have had only minor effects on Japanese domestic employment. Japanese vertically oriented MNEs did realize a drop in domestic employment, as they most likely outsourced some of their labour-intensive manufacturing activities, which is in contrast to horizontally oriented MNEs, who could not do this. But, combining the limited employment impact on individual MNEs with the relatively small number of vertically oriented MNEs when compared to the entirety of the Japanese economy, it is difficult to attribute hollowing out to FDI. Why domestic employment did not drop as many predicted is outside of the scope of this chapter, but the significant literature on Japanese employment rigidity points to several possibilities, including the well-known lifetime employment policies adopted by many Japanese firms.

Appendix

Table 2.A1 Dynamic panel analysis: Arellano Bond estimates

	Full sample		
Domestic employment (lag)	-5.054^a	-4.503^a	-5.281^a
	(1.068)	(1.130)	(1.476)
MNE (1/0), lag		0.286^c	0.440^b
		(0.171)	(0.193)
MNE $\times$ Post$_{1991}$			-1.856^c
			(1.016)
Post$_{1991}$	-0.062^a	-0.063^a	1.097^c
	(0.006)	(0.006)	(0.635)
Output (lag)	2.977^a	2.727^a	3.035^a
	(0.532)	(0.558)	(0.700)
Capital (lag)	-0.076^a	-0.128^a	-0.144^a
	(0.020)	(0.034)	(0.035)
Wage (lag)	-2.736^a	-2.483^a	-2.798^a
	(0.511)	(0.541)	(0.690)
Obs.	11,444	11,444	11,444
Number of firms	1,112	1,112	1,112
Sargan P-value	0.0177	0.0209	0.478

Robust standard errors in parentheses. Two-step GMM Arellano and Bond (1991) estimator.
$^a p<0.01$, $^b p<0.05$, $^c p<0.1$

Bibliography

Ando, M. and F. Kimura (2011). Globalizing Corporate Activities in East Asia and Impact on Domestic Operations: Further Evidence from Japanese Manufacturing Firms, RIETI Discussion Paper 11-E-034, Research Institute of Economy, Trade and Industry.

Arellano, M. and S. Bond (1991). Some Tests of Specification for Panel Data: Monte Carlo Evidence and an Application to Employment Equations, *Review of Economic Studies*, 58: 277–97.

Baldwin R. (2006). Globalisation: the great unbundling(s). Contribution to the project Globalisation Challenges for Europe and Finland organised by the Secretariat of the Economic Council.

Barba Navaretti, G., D. Castellani, and A.C. Disdier (2010). How Does Investing in Cheap Labour Countries Affect Performance at Home? Firm-Level Evidence from France and Italy, *Oxford Economic Papers*, 62(2): 234–60.

Bayoumi T. and L. Lipworth (1997). Japanese Foreign Direct Investment and Regional Trade, *Finance & Development*, September 1997.

Becker, S.O. and M.A. Muendler (2010). Margins of Multinational Labor Substitution, *American Economic Review*, 100(5): 1999–2030.

Blomström, M., G. Fors, and R.E. Lipsey (1997). Foreign Direct Investment and Employment: Home Country Experience in the United States, and Sweden, *Economic Journal*, 107(445): 787–1797.

Braconier, H. and K. Ekholm (2000). Swedish Multinationals and Competition from High and Low Wage Locations, *Review of International Economics*, 8(3): 448–61.

Brainard, L. and D. Riker (2001a). US Multinationals and Competition from Low Wage Countries, NBER Working Paper 5959.

Brainard, L. and D. Riker (2001b). Are US Multinationals Exporting US Jobs? In D. Greenaway and D. R. Nelson (eds), *Globalization and Labour Markets*, Northampton, MA: Edward Elgar Publishing, 410–26.

Buch, C., J. Kleinert, A. Lipponer, and F. Toubal (2005). Determinants and Effects of Foreign Direct Investment: Evidence from German Firm-Level Data, *Economic Policy*, 20(41): 52–110.

Desai, M., F. Foley and J. Hines (2005). Foreign Direct Investment and Domestic Economic Activity, NBER Working Paper 11717. Cambridge, MA, National Bureau of Economic Research.

Edamura, K., L. Hering, T. Inui, and S. Poncet (2011). The Overseas Subsidiary Activities and Their Impact on the Performance of Japanese Parent Firms, RIETI Discussion Paper 11-E-069, Research Institute of Economy, Trade and Industry.

Fukao, K. (1995). Outward Direct Investment and Jobs in Japan, *The Monthly Journal of the Japan Institute of Labour*, 37(7): 2–12 (in Japanese).

Fukao, K. and T. Amano (1998). Outward Foreign Direct Investment and Manufacturing Hollowing-out, *The Keizai Kenkyu*, 49(3): 256–76 (in Japanese).

Fukao, K. and T. Yuan (2001). Japanese Outward FDI and Hollowing Out, RIETI Discussion Paper Series 003, Tokyo, Research Institute of Economy, Trade and Industry.

Godart, O., Görg, H., and D. Greenaway (2013). Domestic Multinationals, Foreign Affiliates, and Labour Demand Elasticities, *Review of World Economics*, forthcoming.

Görg, H., M. Henry, E. Strobl, and F. Walsh (2009). Multinational Companies, Backward Linkages and Labour Demand Elasticities, *Canadian Journal of Economics*, 42(1): 332–48.

Hamermesh, Daniel S. (1993). *Labor Demand*. Princeton, NJ: Princeton University Press.

Harrison, A. and M. McMillan (2011). Offshoring Jobs? Multinationals and U.S. Manufacturing Employment, *The Review of Economics and Statistics*, 93(3): 857–75.

Hanson, G. H., J. Raymond J. Mataloni, and M. J. Slaughter (2003). Expansion abroad and the domestic operations of US multinational firms. In Susan Collins and Dani Rodrik (eds), *Brookings Trade Forum*, Washington, DC: Brookings Institution, 245–94.

Hijzen, A., S. Jean, and T. Mayer (2011). The Effects at Home of Initiating Production Abroad: Evidence from Matched French Firms, *Review of World Economics*, 147(3): 457–83.

Kleinert, J., and F. Toubal (2007). The Impact of Locating Production Abroad on Activities at Home, *Tübinger Diskussionsbeitrag*, No. 314.

Kiyota, K. and R. Kambayashi (2014). Disemployment Caused by Foreign Direct Investment? Multinationals and Japanese Employment, RIETI Discussion Paper Series 14-E-051.

Markusen, J. R. (1989). Trade in Producer Services and in Other Specialized Intermediate Inputs, *American Economic Review*, 79, 85–95.

Markusen, J.R., and K. Maskus (2001). General-Equilibrium Approaches to the Multinational Firm: A Review of Theory and Evidence, NBER working paper 8334.

Mason, M. (1994). Historical perspective on Japanese foreign direct investment in Europe. In Mark Mason and Dennis Encarnation (eds), *Does Ownership Matter? Japanese Multinationals in Europe*, Oxford: Clarendon, 411–34.

Muendler, M-A. and S.O. Becker (2010). Margins of Multinational Labor Substitution, *American Economic Review*, 100(5): 1999–2030.

Smith, Jeffrey A. and Petra E. Todd, 2005. Does Matching Overcome LaLonde's Critique of Nonexperimental Estimators? *Journal of Econometrics*, 125(1–2): 305–53.

Tanaka, A. (2012). The Effects of FDI on Domestic Employment and Workforce Composition, RIETI Discussion Paper Series 12-E-069, Research Institute of Economy, Trade and Industry.

Yamashita, N. (2010). *International Fragmentation of Production: The Impact of Outsourcing on the Japanese Economy*. Cheltenham: Edward Elgar.

Yamashita, N. and K. Fukao (2010). Expansion Abroad and Jobs at Home: Evidence from Japanese Multinational Enterprises, *Japan and the World Economy*, 22(2): 88–97.

3

Structural Change in the OECD: Some Facts

Jean Imbs

3.1 Introduction

Low frequency changes in the structure of production, and the associated allocation of factors across sectors, are issues of renewed importance with the emergence of large new players in world trade. The de-industrialization of rich economies appears to be accelerating, as labour moves from industrial sectors into services. This reallocation is taking centre stage in political circles, where calls for industrial policy, rising regulation, or protectionism are heard increasingly loudly. The conventional view of structural change describes patterns of production that go from agricultural goods to industries, and then from industries to services. Thus mature economies are by definition specialized in services.[1] In its own right, this fact does not sound necessarily problematic. Thus the question arises why such a venerable topic has regained prominent policy relevance.

There are two theoretical mechanisms that can explain structural change. First, technological progress is asymmetric across sectors. High productivity growth frees up labour, which tends to leave sectors with high productivity growth, towards sectors with low technology growth. This is the famous 'cost disease' first proposed by Baumol (1967). Thus wage earners are subjected to a double pain: first, they must reallocate across sectors, which can have substantial welfare consequences if skills are sector specific. Second, inasmuch as they reflect productivity,

---

[1] See for instance Chenery, Robinson, and Syrquin (1986). This chapter uses indifferently the terms 'manufactures' and 'industries'.

wages tend to grow at lower rates in the sectors that create jobs. It is understandable that such a mechanism would be of direct concern to policy makers. Two key parameters govern its magnitude: the substitutability between capital and labour in production, depending on which labour does not have to suffer the brunt of cross-sectoral reallocation. And the substitutability between goods that belong to different sectors: under strong complementarities, demand survives even in sectors with rising relative prices (i.e. those with low productivity growth), which exacerbates the reallocation of labour towards low productivity sectors.[2]

The second mechanism is demand-driven: under non-homothetic preferences, increases in income have asymmetric consequences on demand, across sectors. With an income elasticity above unity for services, and below unity for manufactures, the economy undergoes conventional structural change as it grows rich. Interestingly, the mechanism is purely demand driven, without any immediate prediction on the patterns of wages across sectors. In particular, there is no implication that labour reallocation is accompanied by a systematic fall in wage growth. With non-homothetic preferences, demand policies can hope to have permanent effects on structural change, for instance via subsidies towards sectors with high income elasticities. It is therefore not surprising that such preferences have been the object of a large literature.[3]

This chapter documents the salient features of structural change in fourteen OECD countries since 1970. The dynamics of employment and output shares are described at a variety of different aggregation levels. The purpose is to illustrate the correlations between the growth rates of employment, of labour productivity, and of wage growth at the sector level across the developed world. It is done by estimating the trend growth rates in the sector shares of employment versus real value added in the cross-section of OECD countries, and by comparing their magnitudes for each sector. The supply-side view of structural change implies that sectors with negative employment trends should display larger output growth than employment growth. Whenever this does not happen, other forces are at play than the pure 'cost disease' mechanism. The cross-country dimension makes it possible to differentiate sectors that verify this pattern from others that do not.

---

[2] See Ngai and Pissarides (2007) or Acemoglu and Guerrieri (2008).
[3] Kongsamut, Rebelo, and Xie (2001), Foellmi and Zweimuller (2008), or Gollin, Parente, and Rogerson (2002) have proposed models with non-homothetic preferences of the Stone–Geary type.

Table 3.1 Employment growth (yearly average, %)

	Manufacturing	Services	Total
Austria	−1.21	2.17	0.59
Belgium	−1.44	1.13	0.05
Czech Republic	−1.65	1.09	−0.17
Germany	−2.90	1.70	−0.49
Denmark	−1.11	1.45	−0.06
Finland	−1.02	2.09	0.37
France	−1.62	1.60	−0.33
Hungary	−1.79	2.83	0.76
Italy	−0.61	1.60	0.39
The Netherlands	−0.92	1.86	0.47
Norway	0.01	2.40	0.95
Slovenia	−2.81	2.23	−0.06
Sweden	−0.46	1.68	0.30
USA	−1.64	1.09	−0.63
TOTAL	−1.26	1.82	0.21

Structural change has been at play in the sample considered in this chapter. Table 3.1 documents that employment shares have decreased in manufacturing for all but one of the countries considered.[4] They unanimously increased in services. On average employment in manufacturing sectors shrank by 1.26 per cent per year since 1970, whereas employment in services increased by 1.82 per cent per year. The starting point of this chapter is to recognize that the same has not been true of value added: the share of manufacturing in value added has essentially remained unchanged over the period in the OECD, while the share of services has increased. In other words, labour productivity rose drastically faster in manufactures than in services. This suggests that on average, Baumol's view of structural change constitutes an accurate representation of structural change in the rich world: sectors with relatively high productivity growth tend to lose employment.

The share of the manufacturing sector in value added did not fall between 1970 and 2011, whereas the share of services increased. This is quite different from the conventional view going back to Chenery, Robinson, and Syrquin (1986), where in developed countries the reallocation goes from manufactures to services. I show that the resilience of value added in manufacturing comes from heavy industries, whose relative share in GDP actually rose over the period, and where therefore productivity growth was highest. Light industries, in contrast saw

[4] The exception is Norway, where manufacturing increased by an average of 0.01 per cent per year, presumably because of the oil sector.

their share of GDP fall, albeit at a lower rate than employment, so that productivity was still growing there.[5] The resilience of heavy manufactures was in fact prevalent well into the 1990s, as their share of GDP continued to increase until 2000, stabilized, and has only started falling since 2007. But then, since the share of services in GDP increased, what sectors saw their share fall, if not manufactures? I find that it is the share of construction in value added that fell between 1970 and 2011 in the OECD. Given the absence of any significant trend in the share of employment in construction, this suggests that productivity in construction was actually falling over the period, but at a slower rate than in services. In other words, the 'cost disease' appears to have been instrumental in allocating labour from manufactures to services, where the differential in productivity growth rates was largest. Parallel to this, wage growth was highest in manufacturing, second highest in construction, and lowest in services. Structural change meant job destruction in high wage growth activities, and job creation in low wage growth sectors.

There are two prominent exceptions to this pattern. I find that relative productivity growth was highest in ICT sectors, and second highest in the financial industry. Yet, employment growth was positive, especially in the ICT sector until the 2000s. The pattern is less significant in financial services, yet it is apparent that the growth in value-added share has tended to exceed that in employment share, while the sector was hiring. These are therefore highly productive sectors that hired, at least until the 2000s. They constitute an exception to the cost disease explanation of structural change. For all other services, the opposite pattern obtains: employment growth was positive, but it was also larger than value-added growth. This is especially true of administrative and non-business services—whose share in value added fell in the 1980s and 1990s, even though they were hiring.

There are two potential explanations. First, ICT and financial services are highly substitutable with other sectors: then employment can freely move into these high productivity sectors as there is no need to continue producing other, less productive, goods. Elasticities of substitution are typically estimated to be low in the aggregate, and high at a more microeconomic level (see for instance Herrendorf, Rogerson, and Valentinyi 2013; Samaniego and Sun 2014; or Imbs and Méjean 2015). But the evidence at the disaggregated level mostly builds from goods that are traded internationally: there is little evidence about elasticities

---

[5] Heavy industries include metals, metal products, machinery, equipment, and transport equipment. Light industries include food products, textiles, leather, wood, paper, printing, rubber, plastics, pharmaceutical, and furniture.

of substitution as regards services, and even less for specific services such as ICT or financial services. Given the time pattern apparent from the data, that hiring in ICT and financial services had stopped by the 2000s, it is difficult to think of an explanation based on these services being highly substitutable with the rest of the economy: they would presumably have to be substitutable throughout the period.

An alternative explanation rests on the existence of non-homotheticities in preferences. If the demand for ICT and financial services increases with income, then it follows directly that both sectors would be hiring even during periods of high productivity growth. In fact, they would represent an illustration of what McMillan and Rodrik (2011) document across a broad sample of countries: a reallocation of factors from low to high productivity sectors. In fact, this chapter documents a systematic positive correlation between the growth rate of employment share in ICT and the overall growth of GDP. In other words, these exceptions to Baumol's cost disease appear to have sizeable consequences for the aggregate performance of the countries where employment is reallocated. This suggests an interesting interpretation of the facts documented by McMillan and Rodrik (2011): there are non-homotheticities in preferences, and the reallocation of labour towards sectors with high income elasticities tends to be associated with high GDP growth.

This chapter is far from the first to take an interest in the mechanics that underpin structural change. Two recent contributions have attempted to distinguish the contributions of heterogeneous sector-level total factor productivity (TFP) growth versus non-homothetic preferences. Boppart (2014) constructs a model with non-Gorman preferences, where non-homotheticities can be combined with heterogeneous TFP without loss of tractability. He is able to document that, for US data, roughly half of structural change comes from each mechanism. Buera and Kaboski (2009) construct a model that also has both ingredients, and identify the shortcomings of its predictions, as well as some avenues to correct them. Rather than a model-based decomposition, this chapter proposes a purely empirical approach, whose purpose is not to establish that non-homotheticities exist (after all, we do know the poor consume more subsistence goods than the rich). Rather, the purpose here is to document the sectors in which non-homotheticities are most likely to prevail. Using coarse data limited to OECD countries, the analysis shows they seem to have prevailed in a specific type of services, with important aggregate consequences.

One of the key advantages of sector-level data is the availability of value-added information, which aggregates directly into GDP. Thus it is possible to relate structural change with aggregate performance. In that sense, this chapter is closest to Chapter 10 in this volume, although with less of a focus on international trade and the role of developing economics. The approach stands in contrast with firm-level data, where it is typically only information on sales that is available. Of course, the question of structural change can readily be analysed from firm-level data. For instance, the classification of firms into different sectors is affected by the emergence of vertical trade at a global level, and by the possibility of international trade in tasks rather than in goods only. And so, as argued in Chapters 4 and 5 of this volume, the very characterization of structural change can be altered depending on the sectors to which firms are allocated. But the bridge between firm-level activity and aggregate income remains virtually impossible to cross, because of the difficulties involved in isolating value added in firm-level data.[6] This chapter focuses firmly on the correlation between structural change and aggregate performance, taking as given the allocation of economic activity to different sectors.

The rest of the chapter is structured as follows. Section 3.2 describes the data, and introduces the empirical methodology. Section 3.3 presents the results. Section 3.4 concludes.

3.2 Data and Methodology

Data on employment and real value added were collected from the June 2013 release of the OECD Structural Analysis (STAN) database. Employment is measured by the total number of persons at work, and value added is expressed in real 2005 prices using sector-specific deflators, in local currency. Data are available from 1970 to 2011, for fourteen OECD countries, with varying year coverage.[7]

The data are reported at the two-digit level, with up to ninety-nine categories for all sectors in the economy. A few sectors are divided up to the three-digit level, but these are ignored in this chapter. Most countries do not report information on all ninety-nine two-digit sectors, and instead regroup several two-digit sectors into ad hoc categories. For instance, the USA does not report separate information on Agriculture,

---

[6] Chapter 9 in this volume constitutes an exception, being based on unique data available for France.

[7] The fourteen countries along with their respective time coverage are: Austria 1976–2011, Belgium 1995–2011, Czech Republic 1995–2011, Germany 1991–2008, Denmark 1970–2010, Finland 1975–2011, France 1978–2010, Hungary 1995–2009, Italy 1992–2010, the Netherlands 1988–2011, Norway 1970–2011, Slovenia 1995–2010, and Sweden 1994–2010, and USA 1987–2010. Korea has no employment data, and so is omitted.

Forestry, Hunting, and Fishing: instead the four sectors are regrouped into an intermediate category, effectively between one- and two-digit classifications. These regroupings are different across countries, so that a panel of sector data at two-digit aggregation level is by construction unbalanced, and contains many missing observations.

But all countries classify the two-digit categories into two main manufacturing sectors (heavy and light manufactures), and six main service sectors (trade, information and communication, financial industry, real estate, administrative services, and non-business services). I used the observed cross-section of two-digit sectors to identify trends in each of these eight main categories in the OECD. This presents the key advantage that trends can be estimated for each of the eight categories, using both the cross-country and the cross-sector dimension of the data.

I estimated average yearly growth rates in sector shares. The main estimation is given by

$$\ln S_{ict} = \alpha_{ic} + \beta_i t + \varepsilon_{ict} \tag{3.1}$$

where i indexes observed two-digit sectors, c are countries, and t denotes time. S_{ict} denotes the time t share of sector i in country c's GDP or in aggregate employment; α_{ic} is an intercept that is specific to each sector in each country. To account for the possibility that structural change happens because of aggregate, or sector-specific shocks, the residuals ε_{ict} are clustered at country and sector levels. The coefficient of interest is β_i, which captures the average yearly growth rate in the shares of sector i, where the share can be that of employment or of value added.

Equation (3.1) is estimated on a variety of sub-samples: for manufacturing, construction, and service sectors, for their sub-components (i.e. the eight categories just mentioned), and decade by decade. The chapter's main contribution is a description of estimates of β_i across sectors and across sub-samples. No causal inferences are made.

For each sample, the estimation was performed for $S_{ict} = \frac{N_{ict}}{\sum_i N_{ict}} = \frac{N_{ict}}{N_{ct}}$ and $S_{ict} = \frac{Y_{ict}}{\sum_i Y_{ict}} = \frac{Y_{ict}}{Y_{ct}}$, where N_{ict} is labour and Y_{ict} is real value added. Denote with β_i^N the estimated trend in the share of employment in sector i, and with β_i^Y the estimated trend in the share of value added. It is immediately apparent that

$$\beta_i^Y - \beta_i^N = \left(\frac{\dot{Y}_{ict}}{Y_{ict}} - \frac{\dot{N}_{ict}}{N_{ict}} \right) - \left(\frac{\dot{Y}_{ct}}{Y_{ct}} - \frac{\dot{N}_{ct}}{N_{ct}} \right)$$

The difference between coefficient estimates captures the productivity growth rate in sector i relative to the country's aggregate: $\beta_i^N < \beta_i^Y$ means sector i has relatively high productivity growth in country c. The cost disease mechanism implies that $\beta_i^N < 0$ whenever $\beta_i^N < \beta_i^Y$, and that $\beta_i^N > 0$ whenever $\beta_i^N > \beta_i^Y$. In other words, sectors that hire are those where labour productivity falls. The point of this chapter is to document the cross-sector patterns in such estimates for the OECD.

In order to document the consequences of structural change for wages, I also estimated a version of equation (3.1) on wages w_{ict}:

$$\ln w_{ict} = \alpha_{ic} + \beta_i^w t + \varepsilon_{ict} \tag{3.2}$$

Estimates of β_i^w represent the time pattern of wage growth in sector i.

3.3 Results

The chapter's results are presented in three steps. First, the evidence on structural change is discussed, using estimates of equation (3.1) for manufacturing, construction, and services, and then for their eight components. Second, the estimates are split over time, into the four decades since 1970, and for the crisis years. Third, evidence is presented on the correlation between structural change and aggregate economic performance.

3.3.1 Structural Change in the OECD

Table 3.2 reports the estimates of β in equation (3.1), estimated on the sub-samples of all manufacturing sectors, construction, and all service sectors. The table confirms the de-industrialization of the OECD between 1970 and 2011. The average growth rate in the share of manufacturing in employment is negative: the share contracted by 1.7 per cent per year on average. At the other end of the spectrum, the share of services in employment rose, at an average annual rate of 1.3 per cent. Employment in construction displays no significant trend. Such reallocation is the epitome of de-industrialization: labour shifted from manufactures to services. The lower panel of Table 3.2 shows that wage growth was slightly faster in manufacturing than in services, which emphasizes the potential welfare costs of structural change motivated by different rates of productivity growth.

Estimates of β_i^Y complete the picture. They confirm the rise of services in the average OECD economy: for services, β_i^Y is positive on

Table 3.2 Structural change in the OECD

	β_i^N	β_i^Y	β_i^N	β_i^Y	β_i^N	β_i^Y	Wage growth
Manufacturing	-1.679** (-9.13)	-0.249 (-0.83)					0.0499** (44.45)
Construction			-0.357 (-2.00)	-1.297** (-5.81)			0.0477** (10.64)
Services					1.338** (8.75)	0.827** (4.06)	0.0447** (41.36)
Obs	7,938	9,005	356	397	11,008	11,828	7,432 / 344 / 10,295

Notes: The table reports average yearly percentage change over 1970–2011. Employment, wage, and value-added shares are in logs, measured at two-digit aggregation level. All regressions include intercepts specific to each industry at the two-digit level, in each country. Standard errors are clustered by country-industry. Numbers in parentheses are t-values. ** (*) denotes significance at 1% (5%) level.

average. In contrast, β_i^Y is essentially zero for manufacturing sectors. This is interesting for two reasons. First, in manufactures, $\beta_i^Y > \beta_i^N$ while in services $\beta_i^Y < \beta_i^N$. This means that labour productivity growth was relatively higher in manufactures than in services between 1970 and 2011. Since labour was reallocated from manufactures to services over the same period, this is a clear illustration of the cost disease. De-industrialization happens as labour goes from high to low productivity activities.

Second, the share of manufactures in GDP has in fact been constant since 1970 even though employment has shrunk. This is surprising, because it suggests quite some resilience in industrial production. In fact, de-industrialization would not be apparent on output data alone. Since $\sum_i S_{ict} = 1$ we also ask where value added is shrinking, to compensate that it is increasing in services. Table 3.2 shows that it is the relative value added in construction sectors that has shrunk since 1970—not that in manufactures per se. In fact, comparing estimates of β_i^Y and β_i^N across all three sectors, it is apparent that labour productivity fell drastically in the construction sector. While growth in value added fell in construction, growth in employment increased in services. In both cases labour productivity fell, but for very different reasons. Even so, the difference in labour productivity growth is largest between manufactures and services—hence the reallocation of labour between these two.

Table 3.3 decomposes the panel of S_{ict} into subsets of the manufacturing categories. In particular, I distinguish between heavy and light manufactures. Heavy manufactures include metals, metal products,

Table 3.3 Detailed trends in manufactures

	β_i^N	β_i^Y	Wage growth	β_i^N	β_i^Y	Wage growth
Manufacturing						
Heavy	−1.385**	1.140*	0.0514**			
	(−7.19)	(2.70)	(30.95)			
Light				−1.838**	−0.969**	0.0491**
				(−6.97)	(−2.85)	(33.48)
Obs	2,773	3,101	2,597	5,165	5,904	4,835

Notes: The table reports average yearly percentage change over 1970–2011. Employment and value-added shares are in logs, measured at two-digit aggregation level. All regressions include intercepts specific to each industry at the two-digit level, in each country. Standard errors are clustered by country-industry. Numbers in parentheses are t-values. ** (*) denotes significance at 1% (5%) level. Heavy industries include: Metals, Metal Products, Machinery, Equipment, and Transport Equipment (incl. Repairs).

machinery, equipment, and transport. Light industries include food products, textiles, leather, wood, paper, printing, rubber, plastics, pharmaceuticals, and furniture. Table 3.3 estimates equation (3.1) for each subset of the manufacturing sector. The results are striking: the value added share of heavy manufactures did in fact increase between 1970 and 2011. Since their employment shares fell by 1.38 per cent per year over the same period, productivity gains were sizeable: more than 2.5 per cent per year faster than the aggregate. Additionally, there were productivity gains in light industries, since $\beta_i^Y > \beta_i^N$ there as well. Jobs were destroyed faster than in heavy industries (-1.84 percent per year versus -1.38), while value added actually contracted at 0.97 per cent per year, that is, light industries saw their share in GDP actually fall. Consistent with these differential rates of productivity growth, heavy manufactures experienced a slightly higher wage growth rate than light manufactures. The resilience of output in heavy manufactures (and fall in light industries) is an interesting and novel fact.

Table 3.4 turns to services, with estimates of β_i^Y and β_i^N for each of the six categories of services: trade, ICT, financial services (FI), real estate, administrative services, and non-business services. Administrative services include legal and accounting activities, architects, engineers, scientific R&D, advertising, rental and leasing, travel agencies, security, and services to buildings. Non-business services include public administration, defence, education, health, social work, arts, entertainment, and other personal services.

Several results are worth mentioning. First, not all service sectors were net recipients of labour flows: there are two exceptions—trade and financial services—that do not display any significant trends in $\frac{N_{ict}}{N_{ct}}$. At the other extreme, administrative services were the number one recipient of employment, with a labour share rising by almost 3 per cent per year since 1970. Relative gains in output are, in turn, centred on ICT, with an annual growth rate in value added almost equal to 4 per cent. The financial industry comes second, with relative value added growing at 1.74 per cent. In contrast, output in non-business services actually contracted, denoting negative growth in labour productivity.

In fact, most services mirror the cost disease: real estate, administrative services, and non-business services all display positive employment trends that exceed output trends. In other words, most services verify $\beta_i^Y < \beta_i^N$ and $\beta_i^N > 0$: the relative growth of employment is high in sectors that display relatively low productivity growth. The reallocation of labour is especially detrimental for non-business

Table 3.4 Detailed trends in services

	β_i^N	$\beta_i^{Y_i}$	β_i^N	β_i^Y	β_i^N	β_i^Y	β_i^N	β_i^Y	β_i^N	β_i^Y	β_i^N	β_i^Y	Wage growth					
Services																		
Trade	0.009	0.209											0.0439**					
	(0.49)	(0.63)											(24.51)					
ICT			1.607**	3.822**										0.0466**				
			(2.74)	(5.47)										(11.67)				
FI					1.047	1.742**									0.0498**			
					(1.49)	(3.39)									(15.22)			
RE							2.034*	−0.224								0.0474**		
							(2.80)	(−0.99)								(7.49)		
Admin									2.972**	1.385**							0.0436**	
									(11.80)	(3.41)							(18.85)	
Non-business											0.926**	−0.550*						0.0438**
											(4.16)	(−2.00)						(21.81)
Obs	2,704	2,827	1,325	1,489	913	954	356	397	2,567	2,731	3,143	3,430	2,538	1,228	847	334	2,377	2,971

Notes: The table reports average yearly percentage change over 1970–2011. Value added shares are in logs, measured at the two-digit level, in each country. All regressions include intercepts specific to each industry at the two-digit aggregation level. Standard errors are clustered by country-industry. Numbers in parentheses are *t*-values. ** (*) denotes significance at 1% (5%) level. ICT denotes the information and communication sector, FI regroups finance and insurance, RE is real estate, Admin includes professional, scientific, technical, administrative, and support service activities. Non-business are community, social, and personal services.

services, where value added actually grows slowly relative to the aggregate.

What is interesting in these data are the exceptional results for ICT services, where the opposite situation from the cost disease seems to prevail. In this sector, we have $\beta_i^N > 0$, and yet $\beta_i^Y > \beta_i^N$. In other words, this is a recruiting sector (at a rate of 1.6 per cent per year) whose labour productivity is growing faster than the aggregate (by approximately 2 per cent per year). According to the OECD, ICT services include publishing, audiovisual and broadcasting activities, telecommunications, and information technology, and other information services. These constitute a striking exception to the explanation of structural change based on the cost disease. Here, labour is reallocated from low to high productivity sectors. The same can be said, albeit to a lesser extent, of financial services, where both output and (weakly) employment display a positive trend, and $\beta_i^Y > \beta_i^N$.

The lower panel in Table 3.4 reports the estimated trends for wage growth across service sectors. The three sectors with the fastest wage growth rates are financial services, real estate, and ICT services. The two slowest are administrative and non-business services. The ranking of wage growth is therefore largely in line with that of productivity growth. The reallocation of labour from manufactures towards administrative and non-business services meant that wage earners saw the growth rate of their earnings decrease with structural change. This is less so for the two exceptional services in Table 3.4, ICT and financial services.

3.3.2 Structural Change over Time

The measurement of production and productivity gains in service activities is notoriously problematic. See, among many others, Baily and Zitzewitz (2001) or Gordon (1995). Thus, Table 3.4 is liable to under-estimate productivity gains, which could explain non-positive estimates of β_i^Y for instance in non-business services, or real estate. It is, however, harder to think of measurement difficulties changing over time: Table 3.5 estimates equations (3.1) and (w) (equation 3.2) for the three broad sectors over each of the four decades in the sample, and over the crisis years since 2007. Three results are worth mentioning.

First, de-industrialization did not start in earnest until the 1980s. In the 1970s, the share of manufacturing labour did not fall, and the share of manufacturing output actually rose very significantly, at 3.6

Table 3.5 Structural change over time

	70s β_i^N	70s β_i^Y	80s β_i^N	80s β_i^Y	90s β_i^N	90s β_i^Y	00s β_i^N	00s β_i^Y	Crisis β_i^N	Crisis β_i^Y	Wage 70s	Wage 80s	Wage 90s	Wage 00s	Wage crises
MFG	−0.751	3.581**	−1.444**	1.863	−1.814**	−0.476	−2.070**	−0.837**	−2.616**	−2.393**	0.1128**	0.0709**	0.0381**	0.0387**	0.0227**
	(−1.06)	(3.69)	(−5.67)	(0.43)	(−9.69)	(−1.45)	(−11.49)	(−2.82)	(−10.93)	(−6.03)	(52.59)	(39.86)	(40.04)	(31.02)	(17.71)
Obs	671	932	1,202	1,462	2,536	2,796	3,132	3,392	1,318	1,422	521	1,102	2,361	3,092	1,258
CONS	−1.695*	−0.722	−0.596	−0.473	−0.268	−1.729**	1.082*	−0.992	−0.597	−2.842**	0.1038**	0.0742**	0.0293**	0.0347**	0.0188**
	(−3.14)	(−0.32)	(−1.00)	(−0.84)	(−0.54)	(−3.33)	(2.49)	(−2.12)	(−0.92)	(−3.31)	(15.81)	(8.56)	(7.26)	(7.35)	(4.51)
Obs	31	41	55	41	113	123	139	149	59	63	31	52	105	139	58
SERV	1.803**	0.854	1.985**	1.218**	1.356**	1.099**	0.770**	0.237	0.586**	−0.012	0.1029**	0.0695**	0.0308**	0.0367**	0.0241**
	(4.64)	(1.78)	(7.57)	(3.67)	(8.04)	(4.86)	(5.11)	(1.29)	(3.73)	(−0.05)	(56.79)	(37.47)	(27.87)	(32.87)	(20.85)
Obs	911	1,111	1,603	1,803	3,510	3,710	4,412	4,612	1,871	1,951	581	1,392	3,374	4,412	1,835

Notes: The table reports average yearly percentage change over four decades. Each point estimate corresponds to a separate regression. Crisis years are defined as 2007–2011, when available. Employment, wage, and value-added shares are in logs, measured at two-digit aggregation level. All regressions include intercepts specific to each industry at the two-digit level, in each country. Standard errors are clustered by country-industry. Numbers in parentheses are t-values. ** (*) denotes significance at 1% (5%) level.

per cent per year. This represented large relative productivity gains, not accompanied by a fall in the employment share of manufactures, and in fact also not accompanied by structural change. The reallocation of labour away from manufactures started in the 1980s, and in fact accelerated until the crisis years, when the share of employment in manufactures shrank by 2.6 per cent annually. The resilience of value added in manufacturing is confirmed, with non-negative estimates of β_i^Y until the 2000s. The two decades from 1980 to 2000 were characterized by clear job destruction in manufacturing, associated with non-falling GDP shares, that is, structural change motivated by the cost disease. From 2000 onwards, value added in manufacturing stopped growing relative to the economy, and in fact β_i^Y and β_i^N were almost equal to each other during the crisis years: both contracted at around 2.5 per cent per year. In other words, relative productivity growth in manufacturing has fallen since 2000. The exact same patterns can be seen in wage growth, in the lower panel of Table 3.5. The growth rate of wages in manufacturing fell from 11.3 per cent in the 1970s to barely 2.3 per cent since 2007.

Second, the share of construction in value added contracted some-what in the 1990s, but most noticeably in the crisis years since 2007. This is unsurprising given the devastation of the housing sector during the great recession, which can be seen in the last cell for Table 3.5, where the share of construction in value added collapses (−2.8 per cent). In other words, the fall in the construction share of value added that prevailed in Table 3.4 appears to be mostly coming from the recent crisis. This explains why construction does not seem to have contributed to structural change in the previous tables: relative productivity growth in construction did not display much of a trend over the four decades that preceded the crisis, and so did not drive much of a reallocation of labour.

Third, while β_i^N has been consistently positive in services since 1970, estimates of β_i^Y decreased significantly over the period. The share of services in GDP rose significantly in the 1980s and 1990s, but the trends essentially became zero from 2000 onwards. This illustrates the degradation of the cost disease: labour shifted to services throughout the period, but the share of services in GDP was actually falling. Not only did labour reallocate to sectors with relatively low productivity growth, but the level of that productivity growth fell throughout the period. And wage growth behaved accordingly: the lower panel of Table 3.5 confirms that, until 2007 and the Great Recession, wages grew consistently faster in manufacturing than in services.

It is hard to explain away these changes in sign estimates of β_i^Y with the argument that value added cannot be measured precisely in services. Presumably, the difficulty in measuring value added in services is constant over time.

Table 3.6 and Table 3.7 combine sector- and time-decompositions of equations (3.1) and (3.2). Table 3.6 focuses on manufactures, with the purpose of timing the collapse in light industry output, and the resilience of heavy manufactures. The table confirms once again the timing of de-industrialization in the OECD. Job destruction only began in both sectors in the 1980s. While it was accompanied by rising estimates of β_i^Y in heavy manufactures, the share of light industries in value added started falling as early as the 1990s. In other words, both sectors displayed productivity gains from the beginning of the period, and both shed labour. But productivity gains were substantially larger in heavy industries, with rising shares of GDP, than in light industries, with a falling share of aggregate value added. This asymmetry continues into the 2000s, and it was only with the crisis that the value added share of heavy industries actually started falling.

In fact, the crisis years constitute a striking exception to Baumol's disease: while relatively high productivity growth is associated with falling labour shares throughout the period since 1980, from 2007 relative productivity growth rates in OECD manufacturing actually turned negative, as $\beta_i^Y < \beta_i^N$. The last six years were in fact the only period during which both labour and output shares collapsed simultaneously in heavy manufactures. The violence of this reversal constitutes a plausible reason why structural change is back with a vengeance in policy conversations: even in the sector where labour productivity grew over the past decades (and where employment shrank as a result), the crisis resulted in a fall in value added that exceeded the fall in employment.

Table 3.7 helps to illustrate the time pattern of structural change within the six main categories of services. Several results are worth mentioning. First, ICT constitutes a striking and long lasting exception to Baumol's disease: the sector was a net recipient of labour from 1970 until 2000, *and* it was also the sector with the highest relative productivity growth. Across all three decades, the estimates of equation (3.1) for ICT imply that $\beta_i^N < \beta_i^Y$ by margins that reached a peak in the 1990s and 2000s. At the same time, both β_i^N and β_i^Y are significantly positive. In other words, labour shifted towards sectors with high relative productivity growth. By the time of the crisis the engine stopped: both labour and output shares stabilized.

Table 3.6 Decomposition of manufactures over time

	70s β_i^N	70s β_i^Y	80s β_i^N	80s β_i^Y	90s β_i^N	90s β_i^Y	00s β_i^N	00s β_i^Y	Crisis β_i^N	Crisis β_i^Y	Wage 70s	Wage 80s	Wage 90s	Wage 00s	Wage crises
Heavy	-1.340**	4.977*	-1.713**	1.333	-1.077**	1.499**	-1.271**	0.655	-2.973**	-3.288**	0.1098**	0.0741**	0.0414**	0.0393**	0.0218**
	(-3.58)	(2.56)	(-5.28)	(1.68)	(-3.62)	(2.64)	(-4.92)	(1.14)	(-7.30)	(-4.27)	(45.53)	(30.34)	(28.97)	(23.15)	(11.41)
Obs	236	316	420	500	884	964	1,094	1,172	463	495	166	386	820	1,090	455
Light	-0.542	2.838**	-1.242**	-0.400	-2.226**	-1.517**	-2.497**	-1.627**	-2.427**	-1.911**	0.1139**	0.0691**	0.0364**	0.0382**	0.0233**
	(-0.50)	(2.68)	(-3.55)	(-0.79)	(-9.55)	(-3.94)	(-10.63)	(-4.96)	(-8.21)	(-4.27)	(40.62)	(29.41)	(29.94)	(22.60)	(13.69)
Obs	443	616	792	962	1,655	1,832	2,041	2,220	856	927	363	726	1,544	2,001	804

Notes: The table reports average yearly percentage change over four decades. Each point estimate corresponds to a separate regression. Crisis years are defined as 2007–2011, when available. Employment, wage, and value added shares are in logs, measured at two-digit aggregation level. All regressions include intercepts specific to each industry at the two-digit level, in each country. Standard errors are clustered by country-industry. Numbers in parentheses are t-values. ** (*) denotes significance at 1% (5%) level. Heavy industries include: Metals, Metal Products, Machinery, Equipment, and Transport Equipment (incl. Repairs).

Table 3.7 Decomposition of services over time

	70s β_i^N	70s β_i^Y	80s β_i^N	80s β_i^Y	90s β_i^N	90s β_i^Y	00s β_i^N	00s β_i^Y	Crisis β_i^N	Crisis β_i^Y	Wage 70s	Wage 80s	Wage 90s	Wage 00s	Wage crises
Trade	−0.204 (−058)	−0.383 (−0.62)	0.418 (1.31)	0.897 (1.44)	0.007 (0.03)	0.874* (2.08)	−0.098 (−0.36)	−0.144 (−0.41)	−0.566 (−1.85)	−2.289** (−3.38)	0.1075** (24.77)	0.0686** (23.46)	0.0313** (17.28)	0.0384** (16.21)	0.0246** (10.67)
Obs	211	241	382	419	873	903	1,091	1,121	461	473	131	368	817	1,091	452
ICT	3.142* (2.76)	4.136** (3.00)	2.309** (3.13)	3.004** (3.13)	1.963** (3.09)	4.362** (6.67)	−0.210 (−0.49)	2.392** (5.11)	−0.372 (−0.89)	1.162 (1.67)	0.1032** (27.96)	0.0711** (10.84)	0.0335** (10.90)	0.0350** (12.56)	0.0232** (10.02)
Obs	112	152	197	237	422	462	526	566	223	239	72	168	398	526	219
FI	2.059** (3.27)	0.188 (0.09)	3.917* (2.34)	3.376 (1.69)	−1.421 (−0.23)	1.207 (1.27)	0.421 (0.87)	1.301 (1.44)	1.083 (1.52)	1.241 (1.60)	0.0961** (14.81)	0.0756** (13.49)	0.0429** (7.93)	0.0407** (9.29)	0.0133** (3.21)
Obs	64	74	125	135	299	309	377	387	159	163	34	116	275	377	156
RE	3.875** (5.00)	0.330 (0.25)	2.717** (−3.72)	−0.651 (−1.41)	1.844 (1.91)	0.084 (0.15)	1.747** (3.82)	−0.350 (1.50)	0.977 (1.85)	1.412** (3.98)	0.0992** (14.54)	0.0628** (4.45)	0.0346** (5.35)	0.0381** (7.97)	0.0193** (3.52)
Obs	31	41	55	65	113	123	139	149	59	63	21	52	105	139	58
Admin	2.157** (3.56)	2.802* (2.60)	3.997** (8.30)	2.148** (3.09)	3.321** (9.61)	1.680** (3.01)	2.388** (6.78)	0.586 (1.40)	0.914** (2.91)	−0.120 (−0.24)	0.1001** (17.9)	0.0664** (14.72)	0.0303** (13.77)	0.0369** (15.97)	0.0237** (8.87)
Obs	219	259	371	411	813	853	1,031	1,069	438	454	129	288	805	1,031	429
Non-bus	2.130* (2.25)	−1.041 (−1.46)	0.934* (2.42)	−0.316 (−0.69)	1.092** (5.37)	−0.537* (−2.15)	0.609** (2.49)	−0.890** (−3.35)	1.514** (5.83)	0.978** (3.05)	0.1028** (43.72)	0.0709** (21.11)	0.0263** (12.54)	0.0342** (16.60)	0.0279** (12.90)
Obs	274	344	466	536	990	1,060	1,250	1,320	531	559	194	400	974	1,250	521

Notes: Each point estimate corresponds to a separate regression. Crisis years are defined as 2007–2011, when available. Employment, wage, and value-added shares are in logs, measured at two-digit aggregation level. All regressions include intercepts specific to each industry at the two-digit level, in each country. Standard errors are clustered by country-industry. Numbers in parentheses are t-values. ** (*) denotes significance at 1% (5%) level. ICT denotes the information and communication sector, FI regroups finance and insurance, RE is real estate, Admin includes professional, scientific, technical, administrative, and support service activities. Non-business are community, social, and personal services.

A similar exception is present in financial services, but it is weaker statistically: the point estimates of β_i^N and β_i^Y suggest the sector displays relatively high productivity growth from 1990, with positive inflows of labour. But the estimates are weakly significant at best decade by decade, perhaps because of the difficulty inherent in measuring value added in financial services.

A third exception concerns administrative services. They have been a net recipient of labour since 1970, and well into the Great Recession. In the 1970s (and only in the 1970s), they also displayed the fastest rate of productivity growth, with $\beta_i^N \ll \beta_i^Y$. However, from the 1980s relative productivity growth became negative, with increases in employment that were consistently significantly larger than growth in value added. In fact, relative productivity growth in administrative services collapsed over the period, with fast growing employment in the 2000s (2.4 per cent) and even during the crisis (0.91 per cent), but no trend in output. In other words, employment was reallocated towards services with low *and* falling relative productivity growth. The exact same pattern can be observed for non-business services, also a net recipient of employment throughout the period, but with a shrinking contribution to GDP.

Tables 3.6 and 3.7 paint a dismal picture of the de-industrialization of OECD economies since 1970. The reallocation of labour from manufactures to services accelerated from 1980. In the 1980s and 1990s, this reallocation happened towards sectors with relatively high productivity growth and relatively high wage growth, ICT, or financial services. But from the 2000s, labour was reallocated increasingly towards sectors with low and falling productivity growth, especially administrative and non-business services. Since then, the cost disease has been the first reason for structural change, with labour moving from relatively high to relatively low productivity sectors. The Great Recession exacerbated this pattern. This must have had aggregate consequences, which are examined in Section 3.3.3.

3.3.3 *Aggregate Implications and Policy*

Since 1970, most sectors in OECD countries display either job destruction and relatively fast growing labour productivity, or job creation but relatively slow growing labour productivity. ICT services in the 1980s and 1990s constitute a striking exception to this pattern of structural change: in this sector, labour productivity grows relatively fast, *but* employment also grows. To a lesser extent, the same can be said of financial services, perhaps in the 2000s. On the other side of the spectrum, heavy manufactures are the epitome of the cost disease, since they display job destruction and an exceptionally high rate of productivity growth. Until the 1990s, labour productivity in heavy manufactures grew both because labour was shed and value added grew; but from the 2000s, productivity gains occurred only via job destruction. In this section, I investigate the aggregate consequences of this pattern of structural change.

The approach takes inspiration from McMillan and Rodrik (2011). I check for any aggregate consequences of the three exceptions just listed. I construct a panel of country growth indicators, measured decade by decade, and investigate whether economic growth displays any exceptional behaviour during the periods when ICT (or FI) created jobs, or when heavy manufactures destroyed jobs. I also consider the role of administrative and non-business services, that tend to create jobs at low productivity growth (i.e. the mirror image of manufacturing). As dependent variables, I consider real GDP growth, real capital accumulation, TFP growth, and real per capita GDP growth. All data come from version 8.0 of the Penn World Tables.

The exercise is based on binary variables that capture the exceptional (or non-exceptional) features of five sectors: ICT, FI, heavy manufactures, administrative, and non-business sectors. For the first two sectors, I construct a dummy variable taking value one in decades (and countries) when ICT (or FI) created jobs while displaying relatively high labour productivity growth. For heavy manufactures, I construct a dummy variable taking value one in decades (and countries) when jobs were destroyed but labour productivity growth remained relatively high. And for administrative and non-business services, the dummy variables take value one for decades and countries when employment grew and labour productivity was relatively slow. The specification can be rewritten:

$$g_{c,T} = \alpha_c + \beta \; SECTOR_{c,T} + \varepsilon_{c,T} \tag{3.3}$$

where $g_{c,T}$ denotes the growth performance of country c in decade T, measured as GDP growth, capital growth, TFP growth, or per capita GDP growth, and $SECTOR_{c,T}$ captures the countries and decades when the relevant combinations of growth rates in employment and labour productivity occurred. We have $SECTOR_{c,T} = \{ICT, FI, HEAVY, ADM, NONBUS\}$, with obvious notation. All regressions include country specific intercepts.

For all intents and purposes, this is a growth regression. As such, it falls victim to the gigantic literature that seeks to determine the 'correct' specification, that includes all significant and relevant co-variates. Equation (3.3) is no exception, and thus omitted variables can be a concern. Different from the bulk of the empirical growth literature, however, the relevant regressor is measured at sector level and it is not a measure of the aggregate specialization of the economy. Of course, it is only inasmuch as they correlate with $SECTOR_{c,T}$ that omitted variables have damaging consequences on estimates of β. It is not clear that they do.

Table 3.8 presents estimates of β, for successive combinations of sector-level data. The first set of specifications in the table's first row confirms that countries and decades when ICT created employment are ones when GDP growth was relatively higher. It was higher because of fast TFP growth, with sizeable consequences on per capita GDP growth. Thus, the reallocation of factors from low to high productivity, which did happen in the case of ICT, has large and significant growth consequences: an additional 1.26 per cent in per capital growth rate. This is consistent with McMillan and Rodrik (2011): structural change boosts growth.

Interestingly, the allocation of employment to financial services seems to have detrimental consequences on GDP growth, and that happens because of lower capital accumulation. It is worth noting that the FI sector barely created any jobs in the sample, with the dummy variable FI taking value one in barely one-fifth of the cases. The results on the effects of FI may be driven by a few extreme observations.

The second set of specifications in Table 3.8 focus on heavy manufactures. The sector displayed exceptionally fast productivity growth over most of the period considered, and destroyed jobs. Consistent with this, the estimates of β point to growth enhancing consequences of de-industrialization, with positive consequences on GDP growth. Interestingly, virtually all of the increase in GDP growth works via accelerated capital accumulation: the sector grows as it substitutes capital for labour. This appears insufficient for it to have any significant effect on per capital GDP growth.

The third row of Table 3.8 shows that the reallocation of labour into administrative services had a mild positive effect on TFP growth, which translated into accelerating per capita GDP growth. Non-business services have no aggregate consequences, perhaps because the reallocation of employment towards these sectors has only started in earnest relatively recently. The final row of Table 3.8 combines all regressors, to confirm the positive roles of ICT and heavy manufacturing, via TFP growth and capital accumulation, respectively, and the negative role of financial services, albeit weakly. None of the services that have recently become home to most job creation seem to have any growth effects.

Table 3.8 Growth consequences of structural change

	GDP growth	Capital accumulation	TFP growth	Growth in GDP per capita
ICT	0.0234**	0.0130	0.0097**	0.0126**
	(0.0103)	(0.0105)	(0.0031)	(0.0048)
FI	−0.0255**	−0.0254**	−0.0035	−0.0117**
	(−0.0122)	(−0.0123)	(−0.0037)	(−0.0057)
Obs	54	54	54	54
HEAVY	0.0305*	0.0307**	0.0010	0.0071
	(0.0151)	(0.0146)	(0.0048)	(0.0075)
Obs	54	54	54	54
ADM	0.0161	0.0096	0.0088*	0.0163**
	(0.0156)	(0.0153)	(0.0047)	(0.0071)
NONBUS	0.0199	0.0197	0.0051	0.0089
	(0.0159)	(0.0156)	(0.0047)	(0.0072)
Obs	54	54	54	54
ICT	0.0196*	0.0092	0.0088**	0.0104**
	(0.0107)	(0.0108)	(0.0033)	(0.0050)
FI	−0.0237*	−0.0242*	−0.0021	−0.0091
	(−0.0126)	(−0.0127)	(−0.0039)	(−0.0059)
HEAVY	0.0266*	0.0277*	−0.0006	0.0056
	(0.0150)	(0.0152)	(−0.0047)	(0.0071)
ADM	0.0072	0.0031	0.0059	0.0117
	(0.0151)	(0.0152)	(0.0046)	(0.0071)
NONBUS	0.0026	0.0049	0.0023	0.0027
	(0.0155)	(0.0157)	(0.0048)	(0.0073)
Obs	54	54	54	54

Notes: The dependent variables are given by each column heading, where growth rates are computed decade by decade. The table reports the coefficient estimate on a binary variable that reflects the dynamics of employment and labour productivity in four relevant sectors. ICT (respectively FI) reports the coefficient estimate on a binary variable that takes value 1 in country-decades where employment growth in ICT (resp. FI) is positive, and labour productivity growth relatively high. HEAVY reports the coefficient estimate on a binary variable that takes value 1 in country-decades where employment growth in heavy industries is negative, and labour productivity growth relatively high. ADM and NONBUS report the coefficient estimates on a binary variable that takes value 1 in country-decades where employment growth in administrative and non-business services is positive, and labour productivity growth relatively low. Finally, ICT FI HEAVY ADM NONBUS reports the coefficient estimates when all binary variables are combined. All regressions include intercepts specific to each country. Numbers in parentheses are t-values. ** (*) denotes significance at 1% (5%) level. ICT denotes the information and communication sector, FI regroups finance and insurance, HEAVY includes Metals, Metal Products, Machinery, Equipment, and Transport Equipment (incl. Repairs); ADMIN includes professional, scientific, technical, administrative, and support service activities. NONBUS are community, social, and personal services.

What are the implications of these findings for policy? First, the last four decades have witnessed enormous movement of employment across sectors. A few have had positive growth effects: the emergence of ICT services in the 1980s and 1990s has boosted TFP growth, and thus growth in per capita income. The substitution of capital for labour in heavy manufactures has also boosted growth in income, though little seems to have trickled down to the individual level. These two sectors constitute exceptions: the bulk of structural change, especially in recent decades, has meant employment reallocation towards services with low—and diminishing—labour productivity growth, such as administrative and non-business services. These reallocations do not seem to have translated in aggregate growth, which does not bode well looking forward.

What can the ICT exception teach us? There are three reasons why a sector with a relatively high rate of productivity growth should hire. First, the good or service produced in the sector is highly substitutable with the rest of the economy: then employment growth may be needed to meet the fast increasing demand. Second, there are non-homotheticities in preferences. Then demand shifts towards the services with high income elasticities, which motivates further hiring. Third, international trade enables the economy to specialize, which can happen in those sectors with fast growing productivity, provided that happens to be the country's comparative advantage. It is not entirely clear why the substitutability between ICT services and the rest of the economy should have been especially high during the 1980s and 1990s, only to fall subsequently in the 2000s, when the sector stopped hiring. The possibility that the income elasticity of demand for ICT services should be above unity may be more compelling. If that is what happens, the exceptions documented in this chapter suggest that a very specific kind of industrial policy can actually manage to affect aggregate outcome: it is one that subsidizes the sectors with income elasticity higher than one, thus making it possible to transform a temporary demand shock into a permanent feature of the pattern of production. Of course, the issue then becomes the identification of income elasticities, which is in and of itself the object of a large literature.

Finally, the rest of this volume takes seriously the possibility that international trade should accelerate structural change, possibly with desirable growth consequences. To my knowledge, however, there is no theory available to helps us think through the potentially growth enhancing consequences of structural change in an open economy environment. This would seem to be a promising area of research.

3.4 Conclusion

This chapter documents the pattern of structural change in fourteen OECD economies since 1970. The data confirm, on average, Baumol's conjecture that labour shifted from high productivity growth manufactures to low productivity growth services. But the data also point to two prominent exceptions. The first is heavy manufacturing early in the period, which destroyed jobs but experienced an exceptionally high rate of productivity growth, with a positive effect on GDP growth. The second are ICT services, that were net recipients of labour until the 2000s, *and* displayed fast productivity growth until the 2000s. ICT services constitute an interesting illustration of structural change from low to high productivity growth, with positive consequences for GDP growth. I conjecture the exception may have come from non-homotheticities in preferences, which can motivate sector specific subsidies.

Since the Great Recession, things have observably taken a turn for the worse: manufacturing and construction continue to shed labour, but productivity growth has collapsed. And services have returned to the normalcy of Baumol's cost disease, as ICT lost their productivity advantage. Employment now shifts towards administrative or non-business services, that display falling relative productivity growth.

Bibliography

Acemoglu, D. and V. Guerrieri (2008). Capital Deepening and Nonbalanced Economic Growth, *Journal of Political Economy*, 116(3): 467–97.

Baily, M. and E. Zitzewitz (2001). Service Sector Productivity Comparisons: Lessons for Measurement. In Charles R. Hulten, Edwin R. Dean, and Michael J. Harper (eds), *New Developments in Productivity Analysis*, Chicago: University of Chicago Press.

Baumol, W. (1967). Macroeconomics of Unbalanced Growth: The Anatomy of Urban Crisis, *American Economic Review*, 57(3): 415–26.

Boppart, T. (2014). Structural Change and the Kaldor Facts in a Growth Model with Relative Price Effects and Non-Gorman Preferences, *Econometrica*, 82(6): 2167–96.

Buera, F. and J. Kaboski (2009). Can Traditional Theories of Structural Change Fit the Data? *Journal of the European Economic Association* 7(2-3): 469–77.

Chenery, H., S. Robinson, and M. Syrquin (1986). *Industrialization and Growth: A Comparative Study*. Oxford: Oxford University Press.

Foellmi, R. and J. Zweimuller (2008). Structural Change, Engel's Consumption Cycles and Kaldor's Facts of Economic Growth, *Journal of Monetary Economics*, 55(7): 1317–28.

Gollin, D., S. Parente, and R. Rogerson (2002). The Role of Agriculture in Development, *American Economic Review*, 92(2): 160–4.

Gordon, R. (1995). Problems in the Measurement and Performance of Service-Sector Productivity in the United States. In Palle Andersen, Jacqueline Dwyer, and David Gruen (eds), *RBA Annual Conference Volume*, Sydney: Reserve Bank of Australia.

Herrendorf, B., R. Rogerson, and A. Valentinyi (2013). Two Perspectives on Preferences and Structural Transformation, *American Economic Review*, 103(7): 2752–89.

Imbs, J. and Isabelle Méjean (2015). Elasticity Optimism, *American Economic Journal: Macroeconomics*, 7(3): 43–83.

Imbs, J., and R. Wacziarg (2003). Stages of Diversification, *American Economic Review*, 93(1): 63–86.

Kongsamut, P., S. Rebelo, and D. Xie (2001). Beyond Balanced Growth, *Review of Economic Studies*, 68(237): 869–82.

McMillan, M. and R. Rodrik (2011). Globalization, Structural Change, and Economic Growth, NBER WP 17143.

Ngai, R. and C. Pissarides (2007). Structural Change in a Multi-Sector Model of Growth, *American Economic Review*, 97(1): 429–43.

Samaniego, R. and J. Sun (2014). Productivity Growth and Structural Transformation, *mimeo* George Washington University.

4

The Servitization of French Manufacturing Firms

Matthieu Crozet and Emmanuel Milet

4.1 Introduction

In the early 2010s, manufacturing accounted for 15 per cent of GDP and 10 per cent of total employment in OECD countries, making them undoubtedly 'service economies' according to Fuchs (1965).[1] This is the result of a slow and regular shift of developed economies toward services, thoroughly described in this volume by Jean Imbs and Fiorini et al.[2]

A vast literature suggests that the shift toward services is a natural consequence of economic development. It is, for instance, the main prediction of Baumol's models of unbalanced growth, which emphasize the fundamental difference in long-term productivity growth between the manufacturing and the service sectors (Baumol and Bowen 1966; Baumol 1967). This argument has been recently revived by Acemoglu and Guerrieri (2008) and Ngai and Pissarides (2007), and is corroborated by the evidence shown in this volume by Jean Imbs. An alternative explanation stems from the difference in the income elasticity of demand between services and goods (Kuznets 1957, 1973; Chenery 1960).

---

[1] Fuchs noted that by 1960 in the United States, more than half of the workforce was employed in service sectors. 'We are now a "service economy"—that is, we are the first nation in the history of the world in which more than half of the employed population is not involved in the production of food, clothing, houses, automobiles, and other tangible goods.'

[2] These two chapters focus on the recent decades. However, the shift toward services started centuries ago: using historical data from the Maddison Project, Pilat et al. (2006) find that the manufacturing sector in total employment has been decreasing for more than 300 years in the main OECD countries.

Finally, the outsourcing strategy of firms can also help explain the decline of the manufacturing sector (see in this volume Chapter 2 by Ryan and Toubal, and Chapter 6 by Fontagné and d'Isanto).[3] Nevertheless, de-industrialization remains a major concern for policy makers. It is essentially because it generates potentially large labour market adjustment costs (see Chapter 8 by Ebenstein, Harrison, and McMillan and Chapter 9 by Francis Kramarz in this volume), and also because the relative importance of manufacturing is now so small in some countries that further shifting toward services creates uncertainty about the nature and the strength of possible engines of long-term growth (Jean Imbs, Chapter 3).

The debate on the extent, the causes, and the consequences of the shift toward services is implicitly based on a representation of the economy as a collection of distinct sectors. It largely ignores the complex interdependencies between sectors and the real nature of manufacturing production. Although official statistics draw arbitrary lines between the two types of activities, a vast literature in management and marketing stresses that the frontier between manufacturing and services is quite blurry. This fact has been stated by Levitt (1972) in the following provocative words: 'There are no such things as service industries. There are only industries whose service components are greater or less than those of other industries. Everybody is in service.' Acknowledging that the manufacturing sector is not only about the production of goods, this literature delivers another way of looking at the de-industrialization process. Repeated evidence suggests that more and more manufacturing firms in developed economies engage in the provision of services. For instance, Neely et al. (2011) show that, within a sample of more than 10,000 large manufacturing companies from various countries, the proportion of firms selling services rose from 29.5 per cent in 2007 to 30.1 per cent in 2011. Dachs et al. (2012) exploit input–output matrices to show that the share of services in total output of manufacturing industries increased steadily from 1995 to 2005 in most EU countries. Lodefalk (2013, 2015) presents firm-level evidence based on Swedish data, and Kelle (2013) exploits German trade data. In Chapter 5 of this volume, Bernard and Fort look at the extreme case of US firms registered as non-manufacturers but heavily involved in the pre- and post-production of manufacturing goods.

---

[3] Firms can outsource part of their production locally, or rely on foreign suppliers. In both cases, this implies a relocation of labour toward other firms, and perhaps other sectors. Some firms may outsource most (if not all) of the production process to focus only on service activities. Apple, with its 'Designed by Apple in California, assembled in China' label is a famous example of such an organization choice.

The shift towards services within the manufacturing sector is known as the 'servitization' of the manufacturing sector.[4] In addition to the structural adjustments that occur between sectors, the servitization of manufacturing is clearly an additional margin through which the global shift towards services takes place. The existing literature identifies three main reasons why manufacturing firms engage in service activities (Gebauer et al. 2005). First, by producing both goods and services, firms can expect marketing advantages. The provision of services may increase the consumer's loyalty and provide a faster and more appropriate response to the consumer's needs. The service provision can also improve the firm's corporate image. Second, the production of services may offer a strategic benefit since the firm is making a product–service bundle which is harder to imitate, and perceived as less substitutable by consumers. Third, firms may expect financial benefits because services make up an additional source of revenue, and may generate higher profit margins. In some cases, services also provide more stable revenues over time. While the sale of a product can be a one-time operation for a firm, the sales of related services can be spread over time. Rolls-Royce is an example of such a successful strategy of mixing the supply of goods and services, as mentioned in *The Economist* (8 January 2009): 'Rolls-Royce earns its keep not just by making world-class engines, but by selling "power by the hour"— a complex of services and manufacturing that keeps its customers' engines burning. If it did not sell services, Rolls-Royce could not earn enough money from selling engines'. Similarly, Apple's iPod/iTunes combines a physical product with online services where the customer can purchase and download music and movies. Between 2002 and 2010, Apple sold over 206 million iPods, and over a billion songs from the iTunes music store (Benedettini et al. 2010).[5]

In this chapter, we document the importance of the servitization of French manufacturing firms over the period 1997–2007, by looking at their supply of services. We define servitization as the increase in

[4] The term 'servitization' was first defined by Vandermerwe and Rada (1988). See Baines et al. (2009) for a review of this literature and a detailed definition.

[5] However, the provision of services can be a risky business, and the expected benefits listed here may not come to fruition. The fact that the firm's performance may be lower after engaging in servitization is known as the 'service paradox' (Gebauer et al. 2005): 'most product manufacturers were confronted with the following phenomenon: extended service business leads to increased service offerings and higher costs, but not to the corresponding higher returns'. When selling services, firms may dilute their resources so that neither business reaches the critical size required to become successful. More details and examples on the benefits and costs of servitization can be found in Bharadwaj et al. (1993); Oliva and Kallenberg (2003); Gebauer et al. (2005); Malleret (2006); Windahl and Lakemond (2006, 2010); Nelly (2007); Fang et al. (2008); Gebauer (2008); Brax and Jonsson (2009).

the share of services in the firms' production sales. Let us clarify one important point. We *do not* aim to assess the importance of service tasks in the production process of manufactured products, but to highlight the importance of the production and the *sales* of services to third parties by firms registered in the manufacturing sector. We exploit a quasi-exhaustive database providing detailed information on about 635,000 French manufacturing firms. We take advantage of a very nice feature of the data, which for each firm reports the value of the production of goods and the production of services sold during the year. We exploit this information to assess the extent and the evolution of the servitization of French manufacturing over a decade. Compared to subsequent studies, which often rely either on aggregated data or on a limited sample of firms (i.e. very large companies or exporting firms), we exploit firm-level data covering a large and representative sample of firms. This allows us to conduct a very detailed study of the servitization of the French manufacturing sector.

A rapid overview of the data shows that the production of services by manufacturing firms is not an anecdotal phenomenon. Simple counting for the year 2007 tells us that, in our sample of French manufacturing firms, services accounted for 11.4 per cent of aggregate sales. About 83 per cent of French manufacturing firms sold some services, 40 per cent sold more services than goods, and 26 per cent did not even produce goods. In 2007, the average firm-level share of services in total sales was close to 35 per cent of the total production sold. Compared to pure manufactures, firms simultaneously producing goods and services are, on average, larger, more productive, and pay higher wages.

Regarding the change in the service intensity (i.e. the share of services in the production sales) of manufacturing firms, we find evidence of a moderate but significant and steady trend of servitization over the period. Service intensity increased steadily between 1997 and 2007, in each industry. Even if recently established manufacturing firms are, on average, more engaged in the production of services than exiting ones, the aggregate trend in the level of servitization is mainly driven by changes that occur within firms. We find that taking firms' servitization into account provides a harsher diagnosis about the de-industrialization of the French economy. We estimate that the decline in the proportion of workers involved in the production of goods has been up to 8 per cent higher than the usual measures of de-industrialization based on the proportion of workers employed in manufacturing firms.

The aim of this chapter is to document the shift towards services within the French manufacturing sector. Whether this trend represents good news and whether it should be encouraged or not is beyond the scope of our study. It is noteworthy, however, that the servitization of manufacturing firms is not directly comparable to the inter-sectoral shift toward services described elsewhere in this volume. Inter-sectoral adjustments involve a combination of job losses in manufacturing and job creation in service sectors and, consequently, potentially large social costs and changes in the structure of productivity gains. The servitization of manufacturing firms themselves probably has very different consequences. As highlighted by the example of Rolls-Royce, the services provided by manufacturing firms are typically strongly linked to the product they sell. This strong complementarity is likely to support the sales of manufacturing products and to defend manufacturing employment and enhance productivity. Another important message we want to stress is the increasing difficulty of clearly identifying manufacturing firms, and by extension giving an accurate definition of the manufacturing sector. This fuzziness has important consequences for the way industrial policies are designed, as they should not focus solely on the production of manufacturing goods but should include services as well. For instance, changes in the regulation of services markets are very likely to impact also manufacturing production, export, and employment; not only because services are essential inputs of the manufacturing value added chain, but also because manufacturing firms are often direct producers of services.

The rest of the chapter is organized as follows. Section 4.2 presents and describes the data. In Section 4.3, we take a first look at the extent of the service intensity of French manufacturing firms. In Section 4.4, we look at the servitization of French firms between 1997 and 2007. We propose another view of the de-industrialization process in Section 4.5. Section 4.6 concludes and proposes questions for future research.

4.2 Data

We use firm-level information from the BRN (Bénéfice Réels Normaux) dataset. It is collected by the French fiscal authority (Direction Générale des Impôts) and provides exhaustive information on the balance sheets of French firms. It includes about 635,000 firms from the private non-financial, non-agricultural sectors. We have information on a firm's main activity (identified by a four-digit level NACE code), employment, value added, purchase of intermediate inputs, total cost, exports of goods, production, and total sales. Of particular interest to us is the distinction between the sales of services and the sales of goods produced by the firm.[6] This distinction allows us to compute the share of services in the total production sold by each firm. We call this ratio the service intensity of the firm. Note, once again, that we do not look at the importance of service activities in the production process of the firm. We are interested in the services that the firm is producing and *selling* to a third party. The services that a firm produces for its own consumption are therefore not considered in our analysis. We call servitized firms those firms with strictly positive sales of services. Because of changes in the industry classification and incomplete data for the year 2002, we split our sample into two periods: 1997–2001 and 2003–2007.

Figure 4.1 presents a visual description of the importance of the service intensity in different industries in both periods. It reports the average share of services in the total production sold by each two-digit industry. Unsurprisingly, services account for most of the sales in the service sectors, as well as in the wholesale and retail industries.[7] In the manufacturing industries, the share of services in the total production sold is much smaller, of course, but it is clearly far from zero. The service intensity ranges from 5 per cent in food production or in the manufacturing of basic metals, to over 20 per cent in industries such as the manufacturing of fabricated metal products, the manufacturing of computer, electronic, and optical products, or the repair and installation of machinery and equipment. Figure 4.1 also suggests that the

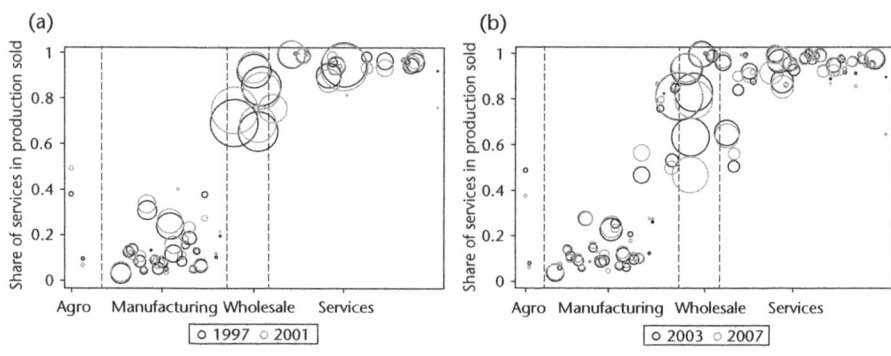

Figure 4.1 Service intensity: share of services in production sold. (a) 1997–2001 and (b) 2003–2007

[6] Total sales also include the sales of merchandise, i.e. products that have been bought and sold without transformation. We discard this information as we focus on the production of the firm only.

[7] Note that we do not consider the total sales in each industry, but only the production sales. In the wholesale-retail sector, most of the revenues stem from the sales of merchandise.

Table 4.1 Number of firms, employment, and value added in manufacturing

	1997	2001	Δ	2003	2007	Δ
Number of firms	68,634 (0.21)	65,078 (0.19)	−1.3%	55,847 (0.16)	50,721 (0.14)	−2.4%
Employment (thousands)	3,136 (0.34)	3,120 (0.30)	−0.1%	2,738 (0.28)	2,438 (0.23)	−2.9%
Value added (thousands)	198,650 (0.39)	212,379 (0.35)	+1.7%	194,455 (0.32)	194,730 (0.27)	0%

Δ = Annualized growth rate. Share of manufacturing in our total sample of firms in parenthesis.
Sources: BRN database, authors' calculations.

manufacturing industries are selling relatively more services over time. We formally investigate this question in Section 4.4.

In the rest of the chapter, we focus on manufacturing firms only, that is, the ones reporting a manufacturing NACE code as their main activity. Table 4.1 gives detailed information on the change in the number of firms, employment, and value added in the manufacturing sector during the two periods. Our sample consists of 68,634 manufacturing firms in 1997, which represent 21 per cent of the firms in the full sample. Table 4.1 also shows the extent of the de-industrialization of the French economy. Between 1997 and 2001, the number of manufacturing firms decreased by 1.3 per cent on average each year. In 2001, the manufacturing sector accounted for 19 per cent of the firm population. This decline was more pronounced between 2003 and 2007, when the number of manufacturing firms decreased on average by 2.4 per cent per year. The figures for employment also reveal the shrinking importance of the manufacturing sector in terms of jobs. During the first period, the number of jobs in manufacturing remained quite stable despite a 1.3 per cent yearly decrease in the number of firms. In the second period, however, employment declined by almost 3 per cent per year. By 2007, the workers employed in the manufacturing sector accounted for 23 per cent of the workforce in the whole BRN database. Figures for employment and the firm population suggest that the manufacturing sector declined in both absolute and relative terms. Nevertheless, the manufacturing sector benefited from positive growth in terms of value added. In the first period, value added grew by 1.7 per cent on average, while growth was much more limited—although still positive—in the second period. In relative terms, however, the contribution of the manufacturing sector to total value added declined by about 5 percentage points in both periods. In 2007, the manufacturing sector accounted for 27 per cent of the total value added reported in the BRN database.

4.3 Service Intensity of French Manufacturing Firms

Figure 4.2 presents the distribution of service intensity across manufacturing firms in 2007. Panel (a) shows the distribution for all manufacturing firms, and panel (b) presents the distribution for a subset of industries. The distribution of service intensity across firms is clearly bimodal, with peaks at both ends of the distribution. The left peak is quite as expected and can be easily explained. It reflects the fact that most manufacturing firms sell few or no services at all. About two-thirds of manufacturing firms have less than 20 per cent of their production sales in services. The distribution then approaches zero as the service intensity increases. This monotonic trend breaks at about 90 per cent, where we encounter the second peak. Thirty per cent of French manufacturing firms are gathered in this second part of the distribution. This bimodal shape is found in each manufacturing industry. The intermediate section of the distribution, where firms have a service intensity between 20 and 90 per cent is very small, although it is not empty. A mere 7 per cent of the firms are to be found there.[8] Panel (b) of Figure 4.2 shows the distribution of service intensity in four different manufacturing industries: Textiles, Metal

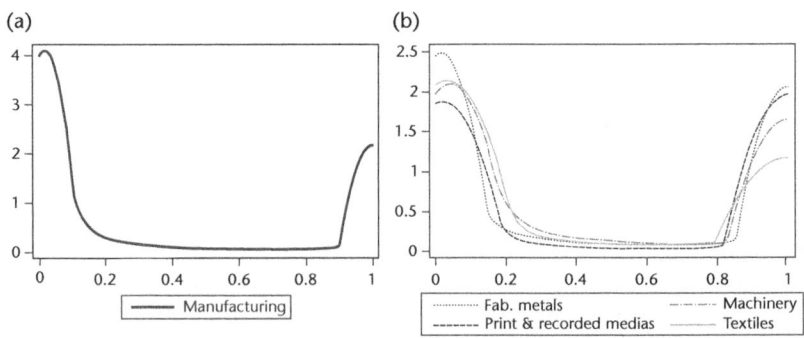

Figure 4.2 Distribution of the share of services in production. (a) manufacturing and (b) selected industries

[8] The share of firms with an intermediate level of service intensity ranges from 2 per cent in the food or tobacco industries to 13 per cent in the manufacture of computer, electronic, and optical products.

Products, Machinery, and Printing and Recorded Media. All of these industries exhibit a very similar distribution.[9] Firms with a very high service intensity are probably firms that have outsourced most of the production of goods to focus on the provision of services. They may also have progressively increased the sales of services that are linked to the goods they produce, but they have remained registered in the manufacturing sector. It is important to notice that, in France, firms are not systematically reclassified when their main activity changes over time. This is partly due to the fact that collective labour agreements are defined at the sectoral level, which can make the reclassification very costly and cumbersome for both employers and employees.

Table 4.2 provides additional information on the firms that form the second peak of the distribution. For each two-digit manufacturing industry, it describes the share of firms with at least 50 per cent of

Table 4.2 Share of firms with at least 50 per cent of services production sales, 2007

Industry	Nb firms	Nb firms (%)	L (%)	VA (%)
Other transport equipment	269	51.34	9.05	5.63
Recorded media	2,012	49.81	31.37	30.79
Fabricated metal products	4,910	43.92	27.23	25.24
Machinery	1,703	41.46	14.48	11.90
Computer, electronic products	673	39.82	14.68	12.88
Motor vehicles	408	37.81	7.63	6.70
Other manufacturing	860	36.75	15.63	13.14
Furniture	703	35.85	11.41	11.54
Wearing apparel	510	34.91	23.49	24.79
Textiles	550	34.9	22.87	18.26
Coke, petroleum	19	33.93	25.22	4.29
Electrical equipment	412	32.16	5.42	4.03
Leather	155	31.63	22.73	14.31
Other non-metallic mineral products	646	27.42	10.97	7.65
Wood products	546	22.11	12.61	11.37
Pharmaceutical products	63	21.72	18.64	19.98
Beverages	152	20.13	5.20	3.55
Tobacco	1	20.00	3.97	0.16
Paper products	204	19.63	6.92	7.28
Chemical products	266	18.95	13.95	30.77
Plastic products	477	16.33	6.15	6.04
Basic metals	95	14.91	4.15	4.29
Food products	1,036	14.67	9.31	7.48
Total	16,670	32.86	14.01	12.64

[9] Figure 4.2 uses the two-digit industry classification. The bimodal shape remains intact whether we look at three-digit or four-digit industries.

their production sales in services. Their corresponding share in industry employment and value added is shown in the last two columns of the table. Across the different industries, the share of firms with a high service intensity ranges from 50 per cent (Other transport equipment) to less than 15 per cent (Food production). However, these firms represent a much smaller share of employment and value added in their industry. Taken altogether, they make up as much as a third of the firms in the manufacturing sector, but only 14 per cent of the employment and 12 per cent of the value added. This pattern is quite stable over time.

As mentioned in the introduction, selling a product–service bundle instead of just a product is a way for manufacturing firms to differentiate themselves from their competitors. We can expect firms producing more differentiated products to sell relatively more services. We do not have direct information on the nature of the goods produced and sold by the manufacturing firms in our sample. However, an indirect way of knowing whether firms produce differentiated products is to use Rauch's classification of international traded goods. Rauch (1999) classifies goods into three categories: goods with a reference price (either in an organized market or with a price listed in trade publications), and goods without a reference price. The former are referred to as homogenous products, and the latter constitute the group of differentiated products. Using data from the French Customs, we compute for each industry the share of differentiated products in the industry's exports. The greater the share, the more differentiated the exports of the industry are. We use this as a measure of product differentiation in each industry and link this to the service intensity of each industry. We cross-reference these two pieces of information in Figure 4.3, using data for the year 2005. Perhaps unsurprisingly, we observe a positive correlation between the share of differentiated products in an industry's exports and the service intensity of that industry. Some cross-industry differences are worth noticing. Industries in the bottom left corner of the figure export mainly homogenous products and have a low service intensity. These industries include the manufacture of food products, beverages, or tobacco (NACE 10, 11, and 12 resp.) and the manufacture of basic metals, paper products, and refined petroleum products (NACE 24, 17, and 19 resp.). On the top right corner of the figure, we find industries with a high service intensity which export mainly differentiated products. These are the manufacture of fabricated metal products (NACE 25), the manufacture of computer, electronics, and optical products (NACE 26), and the manufacture of other transport equipment such as ships, railways, motorcycles, etc. (NACE 30). The industry of printing and reproduction of recorded media also shows

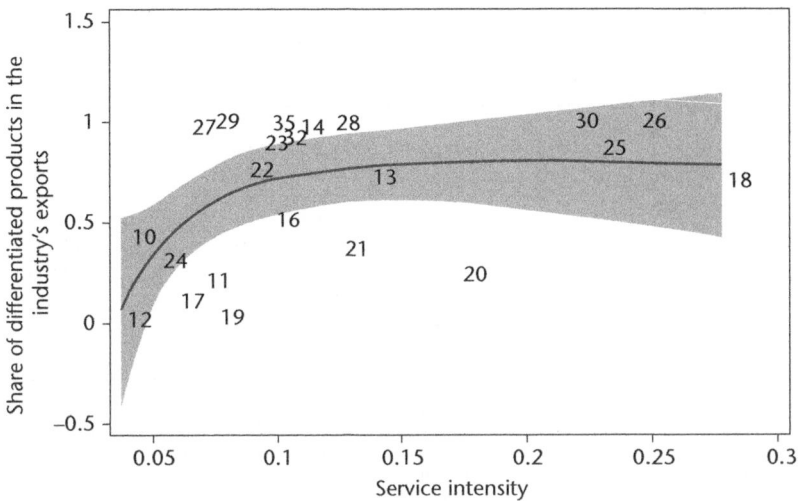

Figure 4.3 Exports of differentiated products and service intensity

a high service intensity with exports mostly of differentiated products (NACE 18). Figure 4.3 also suggests that there is some heterogeneity in the service intensity of industries that mainly export differentiated products. Considering industries where at least 80 per cent of exports consist of differentiated products, the service intensity ranges from 6 per cent (manufacture of electrical equipment—NACE 27) to 24 per cent (manufacture of computer, electronics, and optical products—NACE 26) or to 28 per cent (printing and recorded media—NACE 18).

We now turn our attention to the individual characteristics of servitized firms. We first calculate various premia for servitized firms by estimating the following equation:

$$Performance_{i,t} = \alpha \mathbb{1}(servitized_{i,t}) + \delta_{j,t} + \epsilon_{i,t}, \tag{4.1}$$

where $Performance_{i,t}$ is a variable characterizing the performance of firm i in year t, $\delta_{j,t}$ is a 2-digit industry×year fixed effect, $\epsilon_{i,t}$ is the error term. $\mathbb{1}(servitized_{i,t})$ is a dummy variable which takes the value 1 if the firm i is selling services at time t, and α is then the premium associated with being a servitized firm. $Performance_{i,t}$ is alternatively the firm's (log of) employment, (log of) labour productivity, (log of) capital–labour ratio, and the log of its average wage. Results are presented in Table 4.3. We first estimate equation (4.1) on the full sample of firms (Panels A and B), and then restrict the sample to firms that are mainly

Table 4.3 Servitization premia

	Ln emp. (1)	Ln lab. prod. (2)	Ln capital/Labour (3)	Ln avg. wage (4)
		Panel A		
$\mathbb{1}(servitized_{i,t})$	0.431^a	0.056^a	0.093^a	0.042^a
	(0.038)	(0.012)	(0.034)	(0.010)
		Panel B		
$\mathbb{1}(servitized_{i,t})$		0.039^a	0.012	0.032^a
		(0.010)	(0.027)	(0.009)
		Panel C		
$\mathbb{1}(servitized_{i,t})$		0.057^a	0.159^a	0.034^a
		(0.010)	(0.026)	(0.009)

Significance level: ^{a}: $p<0.01$. Robust standard errors in parentheses clustered at the NACE2 × year level. All samples include manufacturing firms only. Panels A and B use the full sample of firms (601,129 observations and 99,611 firms), while Panel C uses the sample of firms with a service intensity lower than 50% (357,942 observations and 55,383 firms). All regressions include industry × year fixed effects. In Panels A and B we control for the firm-level log of employment.

producing goods (i.e. firms selling more goods than services) in Panel C. In addition, we control for firm-level employment in Panels B and C. We only report α, the coefficient on $\mathbb{1}(servitized_{i,t})$. Results are to be read and interpreted as simple correlations. The estimated coefficients reported in Panel A suggest that, compared to firms that do not sell services, servitized firms employ on average 43 per cent more workers, have a higher productivity (+5.6%), are more capital intensive (+9.3%), and pay higher wages (+4.2%). In Panel B, we control for the log of employment. Premia become smaller (or non-significant for the capital–labour ratio) once we add this control, suggesting a positive correlation between size and labour productivity, capital–labour ratio, and average wage. Results obtained with Panel C (i.e. with firms for which service sales account for less than half of their production sales) are roughly similar to the one obtained in Panel A.

We now examine the characteristics of manufacturing firms with different service intensities. We classify firms into three categories: firms that do not sell services, firms with a low service intensity (less than 20% of services in total production sold), firms with a high service intensity (larger than 20%). Firms that are fully specialized in services, but still registered as manufacturing firms are not included in this picture. Figure 4.4 shows the distribution of employment and labour productivity for these three categories of firms. Panel (a) confirms that non-servitized firms are on average smaller than servitized firms. However, among this latter group, firms with a service intensity greater than 20 per cent are slightly smaller than firms with a low service

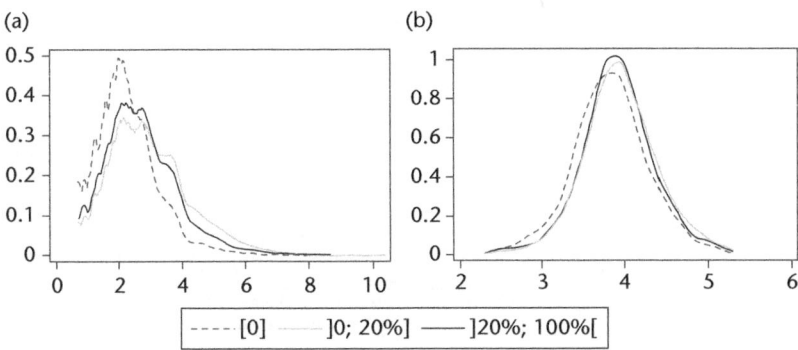

Figure 4.4 Firm characteristic and production mix in 2007. (a) employment (log) and (b) labour productivity (log)

intensity. The same pattern is observed in panel (b) for labour productivity. Servitized firms exhibit a greater labour productivity than non-servitized firms. The difference in labour productivity is much smaller between firms with a low service intensity and firms with a high service intensity.

4.4 The Servitization of French Manufacturing: 1997–2007

In this section, we look at the servitization of French manufacturing firms, that is, at how the service intensity of manufacturing firms has changed over time. In Figure 4.5, we look at change in aggregate servitization between 1997 and 2001, and between 2003 and 2007. The aggregate servitization is computed as the aggregate sales of services divided by the total production sales (goods and services) in our sample. The years 1997 and 2003 are taken as reference years in panels (a) and (b) respectively. The plain line denotes the manufacturing sector as a whole, and the dashed lines represent selected industries. Between 1997 and 2001, the aggregate service intensity of manufacturing firms increased by more than 10 per cent, going up from 10.8 per cent in 1997 to 12 per cent four years later. This is equivalent to a 2.8 per cent average yearly growth rate over the period.[10] This average change hides large sectoral differences. The manufacture of fabricated machinery increased its service intensity by more than 30 per cent over the period, while the

---

[10] The simple (unweighted) average of the share of services in production sold across all firms in the manufacturing sector produces much higher shares. The unweighted share was 36.5 per cent in 1997, and 38 per cent in 2001. This means that small firms increased their service intensity more than larger ones.

(a)   (b)

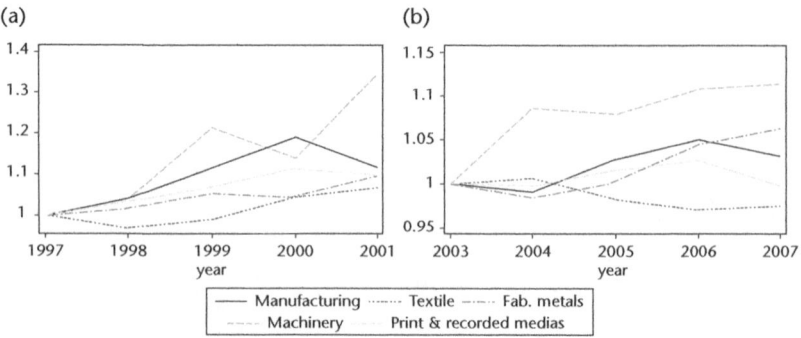

Figure 4.5 The servitization of manufacturing: aggregate trends

average service intensity did not change much in the textile industry (+6%). The trends are qualitatively similar for the period 2003–2007, but smaller in magnitude.

Three margins of adjustment can explain the change in the aggregate service intensity in each manufacturing industry. The first margin is due to entries and exits of firms with different service intensities. Then, considering a constant sample of firms, aggregate changes can be decomposed into a 'between-firms' margin and a 'within-firms' margin. The 'between-firms' margin refers to the shift of market shares between firms with different service intensities. The 'within-firms' margin refers to the average change in the share of services in firms' total output. In order to assess the importance of firm-level servitization, for each industry we decompose the changes in aggregate service intensity into the between and the within margin for the 1997–2001 and 2003–2007 periods respectively. Here, we consider a constant sample of firms for each period, thus ignoring the first margin due to entries and exits. A standard way of decomposing an aggregate change into terms reflecting the reallocation between and within firms is as follows:

$$\Delta S_j = \sum_i \Delta Y_{i,j} \bar{S}_{i,j} + \sum_i \Delta S_{i,j} \bar{Y}_{i,j}, \qquad (4.2)$$

ΔS_j denotes the aggregate change in service intensity in the constant sample of firms in industry j. $\bar{Y}_{i,j}$ is the average share of firm i in the production of industry j, $\Delta Y_{i,j}$ is its change. $\bar{S}_{i,j}$ is the average service intensity of firm i in industry j, $\Delta S_{i,j}$ is its change (i.e. the servitization whenever this is positive). The first term on the right-hand side of equation (4.2) captures the aggregate change in service intensity due to shifts in market shares between firms with different service intensities (the between margin). The second term captures the within margin, that is, the aggregate evolution of service intensity attributable to changes in individual firms' shares of services in total production sold (the within margin). The results for the 1997–2001 and 2003–2007 periods are displayed in Tables 4.4 and 4.5 respectively.[11] Taking the manufacturing sector as a whole, the share of services in production sales increased by almost 1 percentage point between 1997 and 2001, and by 0.65 percentage point between 2003 and 2007 (these results differ from those in Figure 4.5 as we focus here on a constant sample of firms). In both periods, the between-firms component contributed negatively to the shift toward services. This indicates that firms with low service intensity grew faster than firms with high service intensity, thus pulling the overall change down. But these between-firms effects are more than compensated for by the within-firm changes. The increase in the average firm-level service intensity accounts for 170 per cent of the aggregate servitization in the first period, and for 272 per cent in the second period. Looking at the details industry by industry, we observe that the within-firm component contributes positively to the overall servitization and dominates the between effect in almost every industry. The exceptions are the leather and petroleum industries in the first period, and recorded media and other transport equipment in the second period. The findings presented in Tables 4.4 and 4.5 suggest that the main driver behind the servitization of the French manufacturing sector is not that highly servitized firms performed better than less servitized ones. It is that each manufacturing firm, on average, shifted away from the production of goods and toward the production of services. We now further describe this firm-level shift toward servitization.

Figure 4.2 has highlighted the bimodal shape of the distribution of firms' service intensity, and the decomposition exercise shown in Tables 4.4 and 4.5 suggests that, on average, firms have increased this intensity. We now want to look at how the distribution of service intensity has shifted over time. Do firms become fully specialized in the provision of services (moving to the right peak of the distribution), or do they only marginally change their service intensity? To answer this question, we consider a sample of firms continuously present over the period 1997–2007 (32,053 manufacturing firms). We divide firms into ten bins, according to their initial service intensity in 1997. Firms in the first bin (d1) have a service intensity below 10 per cent (and strictly

---

[11] Results remain very similar if we exclude firms that are fully specialized in the production of either goods or services over the period.

Table 4.4 Change in service intensity between 1997 and 2001 (percentage point change)

Industry	Total change	Within	Between
All manufacturing	0.95	1.62	−0.67
Office machinery	17.52	19.07	−1.55
Machinery, n.e.c.	4.03	2.67	1.36
Radio, TV	4.01	5.19	−1.18
Medical, optical instruments	3.61	3.31	0.30
Electrical machinery	3.25	2.07	1.18
Publishing	2.32	2.56	−0.24
Plastic products	2.3	2.29	0.01
Wood products	1.19	0.28	0.92
Non-metallic products	1.11	0.69	0.41
Fabricated metals	1.03	1.10	−0.08
Textiles	0.99	1.65	−0.66
Motor vehicles	0.93	1.66	−0.74
Manufacturing, n.e.c.	0.91	0.83	0.08
Tobacco	0.89	0.90	−0.02
Food products	0.81	0.74	0.07
Paper products	0.31	0.80	−0.50
Other transport equipment	0.09	0.90	−0.81
Basic metals	−0.03	0.18	−0.21
Chemical products	−0.24	2.71	−2.94
Leather	−0.40	−0.70	0.30
Wearing apparel	−0.51	2.18	−2.68
Petroleum	−5.13	−2.01	−3.12

positive). Firms in the second bin (b2) have a service intensity between 10 and 20 per cent, and so on. Additionally, we consider firms that do not sell services (0%), and firms that only sell services (100%). We then look at the position of these firms in the classification ten years later. Each cell of the transition matrix in Table 4.6 indicates the share of firms that moved from one bin to another during the period.

Several key features of the matrix have to be emphasized. First, most of the firms are on the diagonal of this matrix. Between 1997 and 2007, two-thirds of the firms did not greatly change their service intensity. Second, most of the changes happen in the top left corner and in the bottom right corner. The four cells in the top left corner account for 58 per cent of firms, while the four cells in the bottom right corner account for 21 per cent of firms. Looking at the top left corner, we see that 4.98 per cent of the firms that had a service intensity in the first bin (i.e. below 10%) in 1997 stopped their production of services ten years later. Conversely, 6.67 per cent of the firms that did not sell services in 1997 sold some services in 2007 (they accounted for less than 10% of their production sold). Regarding the bottom right corner,

Table 4.5 Change in service intensity between 2003 and 2007 (percentage point change)

Industry	Total change	Within	Between
All manufacturing	0.65	1.77	−1.12
Tobacco	9.19	9.33	−0.13
Pharmaceutical products	5.22	9.22	−4.00
Other non-metallic mineral products	2.68	3.53	−0.85
Chemical products	1.82	5.48	−3.66
Motor vehicles	1.51	1.66	−0.15
Recorded media	1.43	−0.10	1.53
Beverages	1.35	0.93	0.42
Electrical equipment	1.35	2.21	−0.86
Fabricated metal products	1.32	1.16	0.16
Furniture	1.18	0.60	0.58
Machinery	0.96	2.19	−1.23
Computer, electronic products	0.72	2.95	−2.24
Other manufacturing	0.57	2.26	−1.69
Food products	0.51	0.51	0.00
Wearing apparel	0.41	4.64	−4.23
Plastic products	0.39	0.56	−0.17
Wood products	0.18	0.26	−0.08
Paper products	0.17	0.24	−0.07
Textiles	−0.29	1.05	−1.34
Basic metals	−0.39	0.55	−0.94
Leather	−0.51	0.53	−1.04
Coke, petroleum	−0.79	0.08	−0.87
Other transport equipment	−2.98	−3.43	0.44

the same kind of pattern emerges. If firms were to increase their service intensity substantially (enough to move to another bin over time), then we should see higher figures above the diagonal rather than below it. We find that 21 per cent of firms are strictly above the diagonal, and 13 per cent below. On average, more firms have increased their service intensity than decreased it. We also observe a substantial share of firms in the top right and bottom left corners of the matrix. These are firms that switch from one peak of the distribution to another. In the top right corner, we find firms that produced few or no services in 1997 and that were almost entirely servitized ten years later. The four cells in the top right corner of Table 4.6 account for 3.4 per cent of firms, and for 16 per cent of the firms above the diagonal. Conversely, the four cells in the bottom left corner account for 2.4 per cent of firms (or 18% of the firms below the diagonal). These firms were highly servitized in 1997 and almost stopped selling services in 2007. Table 4.6 suggest that there is no radical change in service intensity. Instead, we find a slow and steady trend toward a greater share of services in production for a

Table 4.6 Transition matrix between 1997 and 2007, 32,053 firms

from\to	0%	d1	d2	d3	d4	d5	d6	d7	d8	d9	d10	100%
0%	**10.00**	6.67	0.35	0.15	0.07	0.05	0.04	0.05	0.04	0.03	**0.20**	1.00
d1	4.98	**36.07**	2.56	0.68	0.34	0.15	0.11	0.09	0.05	0.08	**0.41**	1.75
d2	0.17	1.55	**1.02**	0.41	0.16	0.08	0.04	0.04	0.01	0.03	0.04	0.18
d3	0.06	0.51	0.39	**0.34**	0.19	0.11	0.04	0.02	0.03	0.03	0.04	0.12
d4	0.04	0.22	0.12	0.16	**0.14**	0.08	0.09	0.05	0.01	0.01	0.03	0.11
d5	0.03	0.12	0.07	0.08	0.10	**0.13**	0.04	0.05	0.04	0.01	0.04	0.07
d6	0.01	0.10	0.04	0.04	0.04	0.06	**0.08**	0.06	0.03	0.02	0.03	0.08
d7	0.01	0.05	0.03	0.04	0.04	0.04	0.05	**0.07**	0.04	0.07	0.04	0.07
d8	0.02	0.07	0.01	0.02	0.02	0.02	0.03	0.04	**0.07**	0.07	0.09	0.10
d9	0.02	0.06	0.01	0.01	0.01	0.02	0.02	0.02	0.05	**0.12**	0.17	0.18
d10	**0.07**	**0.28**	0.04	0.02	0.02	0.02	0.02	0.04	**0.05**	0.11	1.76	1.39
100%	**0.69**	**1.34**	0.21	0.15	0.08	0.07	0.07	0.11	0.09	0.14	1.14	16.25

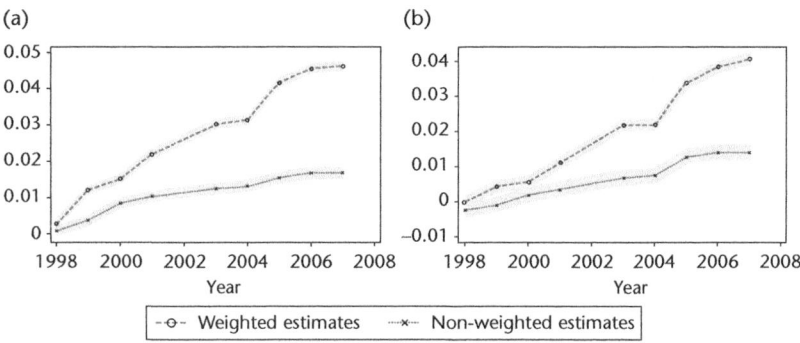

(a)   (b)

-○- Weighted estimates   ···×··· Non-weighted estimates

Figure 4.6 Firm-level trend in service intensity. (a) with entries and exits and (b) constant sample

substantial number of firms. To evaluate the statistical significance of this trend, we estimate the following equation:

$$ServiceIntensity_{it} = \theta_i + \gamma_t + \epsilon_{it}, \tag{4.3}$$

where $ServiceIntensity_{it}$ is the service intensity of firm i at date t, θ_i is a firm fixed effect, γ_t is a set of year dummies, and ϵ_{it} is the error term. The firm fixed effect controls for all observable or unobservable factors which are firm-specific and constant over time. This means that the time dummies, γ_t, measure the average yearly change in service intensity within firms. Figure 4.6 displays these time dummies graphically, along with a 95 per cent confidence interval. The year 1997 is taken as reference. A positive coefficient means that, on average, each firm has increased its service intensity with respect to its initial level in 1997. In panel (a), we use the full sample of firms, allowing for the entry and exit of firms. Instead, panel (b) shows the estimates obtained with a sample of firms that were continuously active between 1997 and 2007. In each panel, the dashed line shows unweighted estimates, while the dotted line shows estimates obtained from regressions weighted by the firm size (i.e. average firms' employment over the period).

The results confirm that on average, after controlling for firm-specific factors, each firm increased its service intensity between 1997 and 2007. The unweighed regression indicates that the service intensity of each firm increased by 1.7 percentage point on average in panel (a), and 1.4 percentage points on average in panel (b). Comparing panels (a) and (b), we see that service intensity increased at a slower pace when considering a constant sample of firms. This means that firms entering during the period increased their service intensity faster than incumbent firms, and exiting firms increased their service intensity less than incumbent firms.

4.5 Hidden De-industrialization

The usual assessments of de-industrialization such as the one shown in Table 4.1 are based on simply counting the relative importance of the manufacturing sector in the economy. However, the evidence presented in the previous sections suggests that the boundary between manufacturing and service activities is very blurry and that de-industrialization may also take a more insidious form. If, as shown already, a large proportion of manufacturing firms also supply services, then de-industrialization is not only a shift of production and employment away from the manufacturing sector, it is also a shift within the manufacturing sector (and within manufacturing firms), towards the production of services. The within-manufacturing shift towards services is invisible to the analyses based on industry classifications. In this section, we try to quantify the importance of this 'hidden' de-industrialization process.[12]

For each firm, we approximate the number of workers employed in the production of goods by multiplying the total employment of the

---

[12] It is worth mentioning that other points of view can be expressed. While we are using the lens of de-industrialization, one could see the servitization of the manufacturing industry as a manifestation of the change in the essence of the manufacturing industry itself. With increased competition, both domestically and internationally, manufacturing firms need to attract and keep customers. Proposing services along with the product, firms hope to make their product *perceived* as more differentiated by the consumer. For instance, one could say that Nespresso is selling more than just coffee, it is selling 'the perfect coffee experience'. In this regard, the 'hidden' de-industrialization can be seen as a mutation of the industry, rather than simply as a loss of industrial jobs.

firms by the share of goods in production sold (i.e. one minus our measure of service intensity). Summing over all firms gives us a rough but simple approximation of the number of workers actually employed in the production of manufactured products. The evolution over time of this aggregate employment is a measure of the de-industrialization that accounts for the shift toward services both between firms and sectors (i.e. the net entry rates of firms and their relative growth) as well as within firms. The same method is applied to firms' value added to obtain a measure of manufacturing value added net of the servitization of manufacturing firms.

The results are presented in Figure 4.7. It compares the evolution of the different measures of employment and value added for the two periods (1997–2001 and 2003–2007). For each period, figures are taken

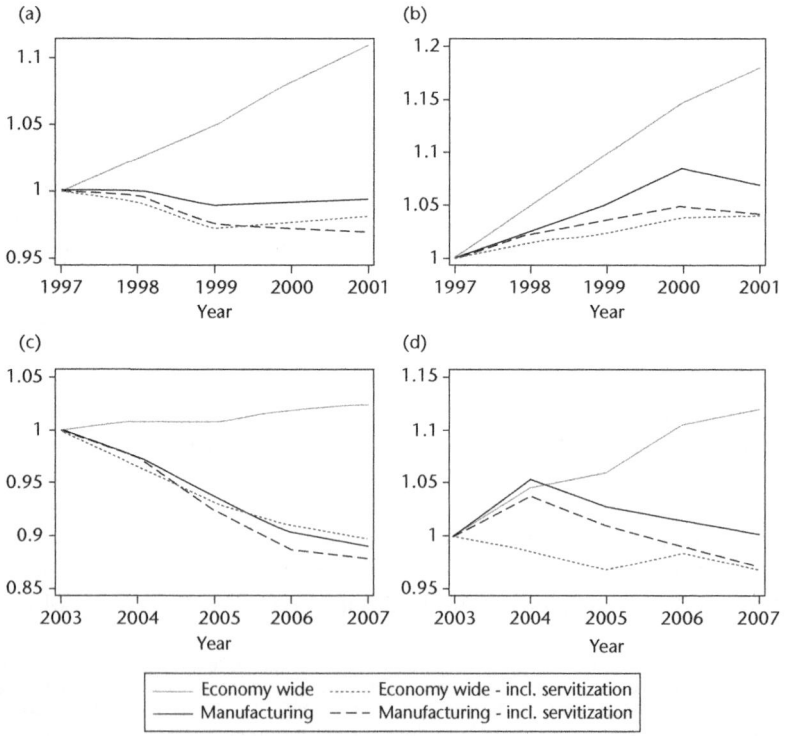

Figure 4.7 Evolutions of employment and value added using the share of services in production sold as weights. (a) employment: 1997–2001, (b) value added: 1997–2001, (c) employment: 2003–2007 and (d) value added: 2003–2007

in reference to the initial year of the period. Panels (a) and (b) present the evolution of employment and value added in the first period, respectively. Let us start with the description of Panel (a). The top solid line represents the change over time in the total number of workers in our sample of firms, with no distinction between sectors. Between 1997 and 2001, the total employment recorded in our database increased steadily by about 2.5 per cent per year. The bottom solid line shows the evolution of the number of workers in manufacturing firms (classified according to their main activity). Unsurprisingly, this line is declining, supporting the abundant evidence for the de-industrialization of the French economy. The decline is moderate, but considering that total employment grew over the period, this trend denotes a sharp decrease in the share of workers employed by manufacturing firms, by about 12 per cent between 1997 and 2001. The dotted line incorporates the within-firm shift toward services obtained by using the information on the service intensity of manufacturing firms. It represents the change over time of the estimated number of workers in manufacturing firms employed in the production of goods. The previous sections have shown that service intensity increased over the period. It is not a surprise then to observe that taking this dimension into account provides a harsher diagnosis of the de-industrialization of the French economy. The share of workers employed in the production of goods in manufacturing firms decreased by 3 per cent between 1997 and 2001. This figure is to be added to the 12 per cent decrease obtained when the firms' servitization is not considered. However, to have a comprehensive assessment of the evolution of the share of workers involved in the production of manufacturing goods, the production of goods in firms registered in the service sector must be taken into account. This is what the dashed line shows. Here, we ignore the information on firms' main activity. For each firm in our sample, we simply compute the total number of workers presumably involved in the production of goods, and sum these numbers over all the firms in our sample. The results suggest that firms in the service sector decreased their own service intensity, producing relatively more goods over time. All in all, the estimated share of workers employed in the production of goods decreased by 13 per cent between 1997 and 2001. This number is higher than the 12 per cent decrease provided by the usual measures of de-industrialization based on the observation of total employment by firms registered in the manufacturing sector. This simple counting exercise suggests that there is indeed 'hidden' de-industrialization which occurs within firms, and that the usual assessment of the de-industrialization process, which is simply based on sectoral classification, underestimates the shift of employment toward services by more than 8 per cent (=13/12).

Panel (b) confirms this conclusion by showing similar evidence based on value added rather than employment. Accounting based on sectoral classifications (represented by the spread between the two solid lines) reveals that the share of manufacturing firms' value added in total value added declined by 10 per cent between 1997 and 2001. But our measure of de-industrialization based on firms' actual production of goods suggests that the share of manufacturing value added declined by almost 12 per cent during this period, that is, 20 per cent more than the usual measure.

Panels (c) and (d) of Figure 4.7 replicate the same counting exercise for the 2003–2007 period. During these five years, the total employment registered in the BRN database remained roughly unchanged. However, the employment in manufacturing firms decreased by 10 per cent (the bottom solid line in Panel c). Using our measure of the total number of workers employed in manufacturing firms for the production of goods, we find a decline of 12 per cent, due to the growing servitization of manufacturing firms. However, this effect is almost entirely compensated for by the increase in the production of goods in service firms (or by the fact that service firms which also produce goods grew faster than others). In terms of value added, however, the growth of the production of goods in service firms has almost no impact on our measure of de-industrialization. In our sample, there was virtually no change in the share of manufacturing firms in total value added between 2003 and 2007. However, when we take into account the servitization of these firms, we obtain a 3 per cent decrease in manufacturing value added over the period.

4.6 Concluding Remarks

During the last decades, the importance of the manufacturing sector has been declining steadily in most developed economies. These profound changes in the economic structure of developed countries, in a context of relatively slow growth and/or persistent unemployment, is a very serious concern for policy makers.

A vast literature has discussed the possible causes for the shift of employment and value added away from manufacturing and towards services. Factors such as differences in productivity growth between the manufacturing and the service sector, changes in consumer preferences, international competition, or outsourcing strategies have been put forward to explain the decline of the manufacturing sector. However, the vast majority of the existing studies do not consider the possibility for manufacturing firms to produce both goods and services. Our investigation of the production of services by manufacturing firms, based on a very large sample of more than 635,000 French manufacturing firms, suggests that a shift towards services is occurring within the manufacturing sectors. More and more manufacturing firms are selling services, and the relative importance of these sales (compared to the sales of goods) is slowly but steadily increasing over time. French manufacturing produces many services and tends to produce more and more. On average over the 1997–2007 period, services accounted for more than 11 per cent of the total production sold by manufacturing firms. This proportion increased steadily over the period, by more than 10 per cent between 1997 and 2001 and by almost 3 per cent between 2003 and 2007. The main driver behind this servitization of the French manufacturing sector is a dynamic that occurred within firms. Even if the proportion of firms which radically changed their production mix toward services is small, the average change in the individual share of services in total production is non-negligible. During the 1997–2007 decade, the share of services in the total sales of each firm increased by 1.7 percentage points on average. It is important to note that firms in the service sector are also producing and selling more goods over time. This parallel trend offsets to some extent to servitization of the manufacturing sector.

An important message of this study is the need for a reconsideration of the industry classifications. The sector-by-sector approach of the economy is becoming less and less relevant. Firms registered in the manufacturing sector or in the service sector produce both goods and services. The industry classification only gives imperfect information regarding the actual activity of the firm. This calls for caution in the design of economic policies that use such classification to target the right firm. What this study highlights is that a study designed on these grounds is likely to miss potential candidates. Further research is needed to go beyond the simple empirical evidence presented in this study. It would be necessary to explore the causes and consequences of the servitization of manufacturing firms in terms of firm performance and economic growth.

Bibliography

Acemoglu, D. and V. Guerrieri (2008). Capital Deepening and Nonbalanced Economic Growth, *Journal of Political Economy*, 116(3): 467–98.

Baines, T., H. Lightfoot, O. Benedettini, and J. Kay (2009). The Servitization of Manufacturing: A Review of Literature and Reflection on Future Challenges, *Journal of Manufacturing Technology Management*, 20(5): 547–67.

Baumol, W. J. (1967). Macroeconomics of Unbalanced Growth: The Anatomy of Urban Crisis, *American Economic Review*, 57(3): 415–26.

Baumol, W. J. and W. Bowen (1966). *Peforming Arts The Economic Dilemma: A Study of Problems Common to Theatre, Opera, Music and Dance*. New York: Twentieth Century Fund.

Benedettini, O., B. Clegg, M. Kafouros, and A. Neely (2010). The Ten Myths of Manufacturing. What Does the Future Hold for UK Manufacturing? Report prepared for the Engineering and Physical Science Research Council.

Bharadwaj, S. G., P. R. Varadarajan, and J. Fahy (1993). Sustainable Competitive Advantage in Service Industries: A Conceptual Model and Research Propositions, *Journal of Marketing*, 57(4): 83–99.

Brax, X. and K. Jonsson (2009). Developing Integrated Solution Offerings for Remote Diagnostics. A Comparative Case Study of two Manufacturers, *Journal of Operations and Production Management*, 29(5), 539–60.

Chenery, H. B. (1960). Patterns of Industrial Growth, *The American Economic Review*, 50(4): 624–54.

Dachs, B., S. Biege, M. Borowiecki, G. Lay, A. Jager, and D. Schartinger (2012). The Servitization of European Manufacturing Industries, MPRA paper 38873, University Library of Munich, Germany.

Fang, E., W. R. Palmatier, and J.-B. E. Steenkamp (2008). Effect of Service Transition Strategy on Firm Value, *Journal of Marketing*, 72(5): 1–14.

Fuchs, V. R. (1965). Introduction Chapter. In *The Growing Importance of the Service Industries*, NBER Chapters, pp. 1–4. National Bureau of Economic Research, Inc.

Gebauer, H. (2008). Identifying Service Strategies in Product Manufacturing Companies by Exploring Environment–Strategy Configurations, *Industrial Marketing Management*, 37(3): 278–91.

Gebauer, H., E. Fleisch, and T. Friedli (2005). Overcoming the Service Paradox in Manufacturing Companies, *European Management Journal*, 23(1): 14–26.

Kelle, M. (2013). Crossing Industrial Borders: German Manufacturers as Services Exporters, *The World Economy*, 36(12): 1494–515.

Kuznets, S. (1957). Quantitative Aspects of the Economic Growth of Nations: II. Industrial Distribution of National Product and Labor Force, *Economic Development and Cultural Change*, 5(4): 3–111.

Kuznets, S. (1973). Modern Economic Growth: Findings and Reflections, *American Economic Review*, 63(3): 247–58.

Levitt, T. (1972). Product-Line Approach to Service, *Harvard Business Review*, 50(5), 20–31.

Lodefalk, M. (2013). Servicification of Manufacturing—Evidence from Sweden, *International Journal of Economics and Business Research*, 6(1): 87–113.

Lodefalk, M. (2015). Servicification of Manufacturing Firms Makes Divides in Trade Policy-Making Antiquated, Orebro University, working paper 2015:1.

Malleret, V. (2006). Value Creation through Service Offers, *European Management Journal*, 24(1): 106–16.

Neely, A., O. Benedittini, and I. Visnjic (2011). The Servitization of Manufacturing: Further Evidence. Euoma conference, Cambridge.

Nelly, A. (2007). The Servitization of Manufacturing: an Analysis of Global Trends. Paper presented at the 14th European Operations Management Association Conference, Ankara.

Ngai, L. R. and C. A. Pissarides (2007). Structural Change in a Multisector Model of Growth, *American Economic Review*, 97(1): 429–43.

Oliva, R. and R. Kallenberg (2003). Managing the Transition from Products to Services, *International Journal of Service Industry Management*, 14(2): 160–72.

Pilat, D., A. Cimper, K. Olsen, and C. Webb (2006). The Changing Nature of Manufacturing in OECD Economies, STI working paper 9.

Rauch, J. E. (1999). Networks Versus Markets in International Trade, *Journal of International Economics*, 48(1): 7–35.

Vandermerwe, S. and J. Rada (1988). Servitization of Business: Adding Value by Adding Services, *European Management Journal*, 6(4): 314–24.

Windahl, C. and N. Lakemond (2006). Developing Integrated Solutions: The Importance of Relationships within the Network, *Industrial Marketing Management*, 35, 806–17.

Windahl, C. and N. Lakemond (2010). Integrated Solutions from a Service-Centered Perspective: Applicability and Limitations in the Capital Goods Industry, *Industrial Marketing Management*, 39(8): 1278–90.

5

Factoryless Goods Producers in the USA

Andrew B. Bernard and Teresa C. Fort

5.1 Introduction

The global economy has undergone a series of rapid, connected transformations in recent years that are changing the way we think about
firms and sectors and that have potentially large consequences for
future policy, productivity, and prosperity. International trade in goods
has surged with the ratio of trade to GDP increasing for almost all
exporter–importer country pairs. This substantial increase in trade
has been accompanied by the rise of the importance of global value
networks and the fragmentation of production activities across national
borders even within narrowly-defined goods categories. At the same
time, there has been renewed interest in the fragmentation of production activities across the boundaries of the firm and its links to the
increases in trade and offshoring of production. The different activities
of the value chain for a product can be performed by one or more
establishments of a single firm, or can involve many different firms. In
both cases, the activities can be performed in different locations within
and across country borders. However, to date, almost all analyses of
these trends and their consequences for output, employment, or productivity, either aggregate or firm-level, have focused on establishments
and firms in the manufacturing sector and their decisions to outsource
or offshore.

In this chapter we consider an extreme form of the fragmentation of
production activities where the establishment is outside the manufacturing sector according to official government statistics but nonetheless
is heavily involved in activities related to the production of manufactured goods. These establishments are found in the wholesale sector and

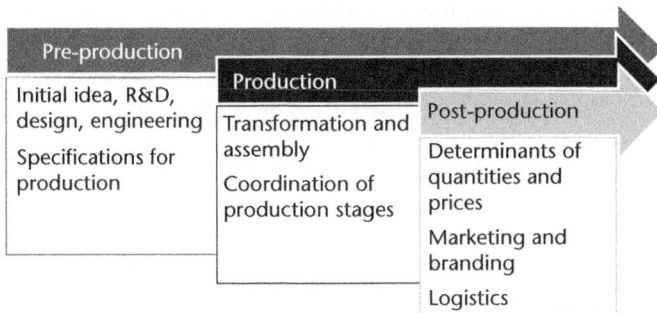

Figure 5.1 From idea to customer

are formally known as 'factoryless goods producers' (FGPs). Traditional wholesalers are primarily, or exclusively, involved in intermediating goods between producers and retailers/consumers. Factoryless goods producers, in contrast, design the goods they sell and coordinate the production activities, either at the establishment itself or through the purchase of contract manufacturing services. In other words, FGPs are manufacturing-like in that they perform many of the tasks and activities found in manufacturing establishments themselves.

There are many ways to classify the activities or tasks needed to take a product from an initial concept through production until its delivery to the final customer. Pre-production activities can include development of the initial idea or conceptualization, R&D, product design and engineering, as well as development of specifications for production. Production itself involves the transformation and assembly of inputs and coordination of the various production stages. Post-production tasks might cover the determination of prices and quantities, marketing and branding, logistics and the ultimate sale of the good to final customers.[1]

Traditionally, these activities were undertaken by the same firm in one location. Today, firms may perform different parts of each production stage, as well as the stages themselves, in different domestic and foreign locations. When the activities are separated in space, firms can also decide whether they should outsource them to others. We define a factoryless goods producer as an establishment that is outside of the manufacturing sector but performs pre-production activities

---

[1] Our focus is on tasks related to production of the goods themselves. We do not address the issue of services provided to the customer by the firm. This growing activity is discussed in Chapter 4.

such as design and engineering itself and is involved in production activities either by doing (some of) them at the establishment or through the purchase of contract manufacturing services (CMS).[2] CMS purchases entail an arrangement in which the FGP provides design and production criteria to a manufacturer who performs the physical transformation activities, generally on materials or inputs specified by the FGP.

FGPs are not hard to find. Perhaps the best-known example of a factoryless goods producer is Apple Inc. Apple designs, engineers, develops, and sells consumer electronics, software, and computers. However, since 2004, Apple has not owned any production lines in the USA and the actual production is conducted by other firms, such as Foxconn, in China and elsewhere. While Apple is known for its goods and services and closely controls all aspects of a product, from the idea until the product lands in the hands of the consumer, none of Apple's US establishments would be in the manufacturing sector.[3]

The semiconductor industry is well-known to have factoryless goods producers in the form of 'fabless' firms.[4] Mindspeed Technologies, a fabless semiconductor manufacturer in Newport Beach, CA with 500+ employees, 'designs, develops and sells semiconductor solutions for communications applications in wireline and wireless network infrastructure equipment'.[5] Mindspeed outsources all semiconductor manufacturing to other merchant foundries, such as TSMC, Samsung, and others. As with Apple, Mindspeed's establishments would not be in the manufacturing sector.

Perhaps the canonical example of a factoryless goods producer is the British appliance firm Dyson, best known for its innovative vacuum cleaners. The firm initially designed, engineered, and produced household appliances in Wiltshire, England but subsequently chose to offshore and outsource all its production to Malaysia while leaving several hundred research and other employees in the UK.[6]

All three of these FGPs started with production facilities inside the firm in the home country and subsequently shed their production lines and outsourced and offshored production. In addition, these

[2] Our definition differs from that currently under consideration by statistical agencies in the USA, see Appendix 5.B.

[3] As of June 2013, Apple has announced but not yet implemented an investment in new manufacturing facilities in the USA. For a description of the distribution of value in several of Apple's products, see Kraemer, Linden, and Dedrick (2011).

[4] Bayard, Byrne, and Smith (2015) document the extent and characteristics of FGPs in the US semiconductor industry.

[5] See the company profile at www.mindspeed.com.

[6] See *Financial Times* 23 August 2011.

firms retained or expanded other activities including research and development, design, engineering, marketing, and distribution.

Anecdotes aside, however, there is very little systematic evidence on the extent of these types of firms and establishments. In this chapter, we use data from the US Census of Wholesale Trade in 2002 and 2007 to systematically document the extent of FGP activities in the wholesale sector in the USA and to examine the characteristics of plants and firms that are factoryless goods producers. Statistical agencies in the USA and elsewhere are grappling with the problem of how to collect information about the evolving variety of manufacturing-related companies in the economy (OMB 2010). The US Census Bureau has historically classified many FGP plants in the wholesale trade sector, but beginning in 2017, will move these FGP establishments into manufacturing.[7] In addition there may be substantial numbers of non-wholesale FGPs in other sectors such as business services.[8]

There are several reasons why distinguishing FGPs from traditional wholesale establishments may be important for economic welfare or policy. First, the mere existence of the FGPs highlights a new type of production function in the global economy involving extreme fragmentation of tasks. Second, the types of workers, and as a result jobs and wages, employed by FGPs may differ significantly from those at integrated manufacturing plants or traditional wholesalers. Third, the relative importance of R&D and innovation is likely to be more important at FGPs. These potential differences between FGPs and traditional manufacturers and wholesalers introduce the possibility of very different wage, employment, and productivity dynamics if factoryless goods production grows in aggregate activity. We do not address these issues directly, but as a final exercise we attempt to calculate how much employment and output would be shifted from the wholesale sector to the manufacturing sector if FGPs are reclassified. Moving FGP establishments to the manufacturing sector would have shifted at least 595,000 to as many as 1,311,000 workers from wholesale to manufacturing sectors in 2002 and at least 431,000 to as many as 1,934,000 workers in 2007.

Our research is related to a broader set of questions that asks how production, innovation, knowledge, and productivity are related. One perspective is that, without production activities located nearby, in the long run a firm cannot continue to generate new ideas, improve

---

[7] Doherty (2015) discusses the expected impact of reclassifying FGPs on US economic statistics including the value of imports and exports and sectoral employment and wages.

[8] Our data do not cover sectors beyond wholesale trade and manufacturing so we are unable to document how many FGPs might exist in other sectors.

product quality, innovate its designs, and raise productive efficiency. The counterpoint suggests that the advent of dramatic improvements in telecommunication technology, the rise of the internet, and the reduction of transportation and trade costs have combined to allow firms to separate their activities geographically and potentially locate them outside the firm. This perspective suggests firms will thrive if they can take advantage of comparative advantage and relative cost differences in the performance of the tasks involved in the creation, production, distribution, and marketing of a product. Co-location of these tasks may not be necessary and might be more costly.

We provide a first step in developing an understanding of these complex processes by documenting the extent to which plants are engaged in different activities in the production value chain. Our focus is on establishments that are currently characterized by statistical authorities as performing wholesale trade, that is, those that are thought to be outside manufacturing. We are motivated by the idea that the rapid decline in manufacturing employment in the USA in recent years has been accompanied at least in part by a rise in employment in manufacturing-related activities in other sectors.[9]

5.1.1 *Relation to Existing Work*

This chapter contributes to a growing empirical literature about the importance of international fragmentation of production (i.e. offshoring). A number of papers use industry-level input–output (IO) tables to show the importance of offshoring across countries and over time (e.g. Hummels, Ishii, and Yi 2001; Johnson and Noguera 2012). While these papers provide strong evidence that international fragmentation of production is an important and growing phenomenon, their analyses focus on the manufacturing sector. In this chapter, we show that when establishments relocate the entire physical production process to another location, they become FGPs and so are no longer included in official manufacturing statistics. As a result, current work that relies on IO tables, or manufacturing more generally, will miss this potentially important type of production fragmentation.[10]

There is also research into the determinants of firms' vertical production networks. One strand of this literature focuses on multinational production to assess production sharing across countries (e.g. Yeaple

---

[9] See Pierce and Schott (2016) for a description and trade-related explanation of the decline in US manufacturing sector employment.

[10] While the IO tables do include information for the wholesale sector, it is at such a high level of aggregation that it does not allow for a comparable analysis.

2003; Hanson, Mataloni, and Slaughter 2005). These papers find an important role for wages, distance, taxes, and human capital in firms' sourcing decisions. In more recent work, Fort (2016) uses the 2007 Census of Manufactures (CM) to asses the role of labour costs, distance to suppliers, and communication technology in US firms' domestic and foreign fragmentation decisions. While the findings in that paper show that firm use of communication technology significantly increases the likelihood of domestic fragmentation, it does not necessarily lead firms to offshore. Most of the firms considered in Fort's paper offshore to low wage countries, but the use of communication technology only increases the likelihood of sourcing from high-technology countries. An open question is whether these results also apply to offshoring by FGPs that have relocated the entire physical production process overseas.

The vast majority of the existing evidence on international fragmentation is based on manufacturers' decisions to offshore production. In this chapter, we show that focusing exclusively on manufacturing misses an important element of production fragmentation. Existing evidence on fragmentation by non-manufactures is much more limited. Bernard, Jensen, and Schott (2009) and Bernard, Jensen, Redding, and Schott (2010) show that firms with wholesale establishments account for more than 40 per cent of US imports. However, these papers are silent on the relationship between wholesalers and production fragmentation, either domestic or foreign.[11]

The chapter also relates to the theoretical literature on offshoring by providing evidence on the types of producers who fragment, the extent to which they do so, and their import activity. Grossman and Rossi-Hansberg (2008) conceptualize the production process in terms of tasks that are costly to separate from the headquarter location. The FGPs documented here provide some of the first direct evidence on establishments that have completely outsourced their production activities. Baldwin and Venables (2010) take the physical production process seriously to distinguish between 'snakes', in which production is sequential, and 'spiders' in which multiple parts can be made at the same time. This paper highlights the importance of extending the concept of production to include product design and engineering. In this sense, the theoretical framework in Antràs and Helpman (2004) is closely related to the producers we describe here. In that paper,

---

[11] The new empirical literature on intermediaries in exports implicitly or explicitly assumes that wholesale firms are merely reselling goods from other producers, i.e. acting as traditional wholesale resellers, see Akerman (2010), Blum, Claro, and Horstmann (2010), and Bernard, Grazzi, and Tomasi (2015).

producers combine headquarter services with intermediate good production that can occur within or outside the boundaries of a producer's firm and country. The FGPs we identify provide the precise type of headquarter services modelled in Antràs and Helpman (2004) and source their intermediate inputs both domestically and offshore.

Although Antràs and Helpman (2004) is one of the few theoretical papers to consider both domestic and foreign fragmentation within the same framework, a burgeoning empirical literature explores the domestic fragmentation option. Fort (2016) shows that US manufacturers that fragment production domestically are far more prevalent than those that offshore. Using IO tables for the USA, Fally (2012) assesses the number of production stages within industries and over time. While that paper documents a decrease in production fragmentation over time, we note that the emergence of FGPs introduces error into the IO tables since they do not capture outsourcing by wholesalers. Akerman and Py (2011) employ firm-level data on Swedish manufacturers to show that firms in large cities contain fewer occupations, consistent with the premise that these firms are specialized in a smaller range of tasks. The FGPs documented in this paper have undertaken an extreme form of fragmentation in which all the physical production processes have been relocated to another location. To the extent that domestic fragmentation allows for gains to specialization, it represents a dimension of firms' organizational choices with potentially large aggregate productivity effects.

This chapter is most closely related to several working papers on measuring the extent of FGP activity in the US economy. Doherty (2015) looks at the response of international and US statistical organizations to the phenomena of rapid improvements in ICT and transportation and the resulting increase in offshore outsourcing. Kamal, Moulton, and Ribarsky (2015) analyse data on CMS from US firm surveys focusing on the 2011 Company Organization Survey. They find that 5 per cent of US firms purchase CMS and 4 per cent supply CMS, with 1 per cent both supplying and purchasing. Bayard, Byrne, and Smith (2015) present a case study of FGP semiconductor production identifying domestic establishments of FGP firms with a unique dataset combining outside company directories of FGP semiconductor firms with Economic Census data for 2002 and 2007. Within wholesale trade, they find that FGP establishments are larger in terms of both employment and sales, their employees have higher average earnings, and they are more geographically concentrated than establishments of other firms. This chapter revisits the definition of an FGP and expands the analysis to cover the entire wholesale sector.

5.2 Data

The data employed in this chapter are from the 2002 and 2007 US Census Bureau Census of Wholesale Trade (CW). The CW is conducted in years that end in 2 and 7 and covers the universe of establishments classified in the wholesale trade sector. The data analysed here are from a new set of 'Establishment Activities' (EA) questions that were asked in the 2002 and 2007 censuses. In 2002, the CW asked each establishment whether (i) product design/engineering and (ii) materials fabrication/processing/assembly/blending were (a) performed by the establishment; (b) performed for the establishment by another company; or (c) not provided by the establishment. In 2007, the CW asked each establishment whether (i) it designed, engineered, or formulated the manufactured product it sold, produced, or shipped; (ii) its primary activity was to provide contract manufacturing services for other establishments, manufacture its own goods, resell goods produced by others, or other; and (iii) it purchased contract manufacturing services from another establishment (within or outside the firm) to process its inputs. Copies of the exact questions as they appeared in the censuses are in the appendix at the end of the chapter.

The EA data are not available for every wholesale plant. In 2002, all establishments in every wholesale industry were asked the EA questions. In 2007, only establishments in forty-nine of the seventy-one NAICS industries were sent a form with the EA questions. [12] All establishments that receive a census form in the mail are legally required to return the completed form. Despite the legal requirement, a number of establishments in both years did not respond to the question. The appendix provides a list of the excluded wholesale industries in 2007 and discusses sample selection issues.

Establishments are given a single industry (sector) classification based on their production process, that is, they can either be classified as manufacturing or wholesale trade but not both. However, a given establishment may perform activities in both sectors and have employment in both sectors. The practical implication of the assignment process is that plants in the wholesale trade sector may, and many do, perform some physical transformation activities. [13] These wholesale establishments' manufacturing activities are not captured by aggregate statistics

---

[12] In practice, there are answers to the EA questions in every industry since information was collected from establishments that switched from one of the included forty-nine industries in 2002 into an excluded industry in 2007.

[13] See Appendix 5B for more detail.

since all employment and sales are designated to an establishment's uniquely assigned industry and sector.

The EA data are also available for manufacturing establishments in 2007. The CM included the same set of EA questions asked on the 2007 CW. For manufacturers, all large plants and all plants that belong to multi-unit firms, as well as a random sample of small and medium-sized plants within industries, were asked the EA questions. The smallest manufacturing plants, generally those with fewer than five employees, are never surveyed.[14] The EA data on manufacturers allow us to compare FGPs in the wholesale sector to manufacturing establishments that are similar along several key dimensions.

We supplement the EA data with additional establishment and firm-level variables. Sales, employees, and wages are available in the censuses. We link the census data to the Longitudinal Business Database (LBD) to determine establishment and firm age, as well as the firm's employment in all other sectors. We also link the census data to Customs Trade Transactions data to obtain measures of each firm's imports. The Customs data provide value, transaction type (whether the imports are intra-firm), country, and product information at the firm level.

We construct a value-added labour productivity measure for establishment i as $vap_i = va_i/te_i$, where va denotes value added and te denotes total employment. For manufacturing establishments, value added is provided in the census. For wholesalers, we calculate a proxy measure for value added as $va_i = sales_i - merch_i - invb_i + inve_i$, where $merch_i$ denotes the establishment's purchases of merchandise for resales and $invb_i$ and $inve_i$ denote inventory at the beginning and end of the year respectively. It may therefore be more appropriate to think of wholesaler productivity as a gross-margin, but this provides the most comparable productivity measure available for wholesale establishments given the existing data. Establishment sales, employment, wages, and productivity all vary significantly across industries. To make meaningful comparisons of these variables across establishments in different industries, we provide information on a relative measure for each characteristic, $x_{ij}/\bar{x}_j$, where $\bar{x}_j$ is the mean of variable x in industry j.

At first glance, manufacturing production by wholesalers appears paradoxical. Traditional wholesalers simply distribute goods and have no involvement in the manufacturing process. While the majority

---

[14] Manufacturing has short and long forms, and only the long forms asked the EA purchase questions. While all large and multi-unit firm establishments receive the long form, only a random sample of small, single-unit firms received the long form. Data for the smallest establishments is imputed from Federal tax returns and industry averages.

of wholesalers still function as distributors, the sector has evolved to include establishments that design, market, and sell their own goods. Because these establishments perform few or no physical transformation activities, they are classified as wholesalers. From an economic theory perspective, however, plants that design goods and coordinate their production are closer to manufacturers than distributors. As such, the wholesale sector contains plants whose behaviour sheds light on manufacturing activity in the US economy.[15]

5.3 Design and Manufacturing at Wholesale Establishments

Since individual establishments (plants) are assigned a single primary industry code, each plant is covered by only one sector of the quinquennial Economic Census.[16] As discussed in section 5.2, in 2002, every establishment in the Census of Wholesale Trade was asked questions about its activities in product design and manufacturing. We focus on these questions to explore the manufacturing-related activities of wholesale establishments and ultimately to create a formal definition of an FGP plant.

5.3.1 *2002*

In Table 5.1, we tabulate the counts of plants in the wholesale sector that responded to both the design and manufacturing questions in the 2002 Census.[17] In each case, a plant could either perform the activity at the plant, have it provided by another company, or not provide the activity. Of the 207,494 responding establishments, 63.2 per cent participated in neither design nor manufacturing activities,

[15] The Census Bureau has recognized this issue and attempted to address it in the 2017 Economic Census by identifying every manufacturing or wholesale establishment that does not perform its own manufacturing activities, but 'undertakes all of the entrepreneurial steps and arranges for all required capital, labor, and material inputs required to make a good' (OMB 2010, pp. 3–4). In 2017, these establishments will be classified in the manufacturing industry that corresponds to the good they sell, with an additional flag identifying them as FGPs. The flag will distinguish FGPs from the traditional 'integrated manufactures' (IMs) that perform their own transformation activities, and establishments whose main activity is to provide contract manufacturing services for others (referred to as manufacturing service providers or MSPs).

[16] For example, a plant is either in the Economic Census in the manufacturing sector or in the wholesale sector but not both. This is true even if the plant performs both activities.

[17] The exact questions from the 2002 CW can be found in Appendix 5A in Figure 5.A1. Many more plants responded to one of the two questions. The distribution of responses was similar for plants answering one or two questions.

Table 5.1 Design and manufacturing activities at wholesale plants, 2002

		Manufacturing			
		At plant	Outside	No	Total
Design	At plant	18,539	9,792	6,450	34,781
	Outsourced	2,137	17,193	2,039	21,369
	Not provided	13,130	6,983	131,231	151,344
	Total	33,806	33,968	139,720	207,494

Note: Each cell gives a count of the number of establishments. Establishments had to answer both the design and manufacturing questions to be included. *Design* refers to design or engineering activity in product development. *Manufacturing* refers to materials fabrication, processing, assembly, or blending. *At plant*—activity was performed by this plant; *Outsourced/Outside*—activity was performed for this plant by another company; *No*—activity not provided by this plant. All plants were covered by the Census of Wholesale Trade.

either inside the plant or purchased from another firm, see Figure 5.2. These plants match the typical perception of a wholesaler that is not involved in the creation of the product but rather is active in delivery, warehousing, order fulfilment, logistics, or other services that intermediate between a producer and a customer.

However, more than 36 per cent of wholesale establishments are involved in either design or manufacturing activities or both. Almost a third of the responding wholesale plants are involved in manufacturing, evenly split between plants that are doing manufacturing themselves or those purchasing contract manufacturing services. Similarly more than a quarter of wholesale plants are involved in design and engineering activities; 16.8 per cent design at the establishment while 10.0 per cent outsource design activities to others. These results challenge the stereotype of a wholesale establishment that simply intermediates between producer and consumers. The wholesale sector is a heterogeneous mix of traditional resellers and plants that are actively involved in production activities.

There is also new evidence in the other direction, that is, that manufacturing firms are increasingly producing services. Crozet and Milet (Chapter 4) document the shift away from goods towards services in French manufacturing firms. They find that one-third of French manufacturing firms have more than half of their revenue from services.

Plants that perform design activities themselves are most likely to conduct manufacturing activities as well, or to have manufacturing provided by an outside company. More than one in twelve wholesale

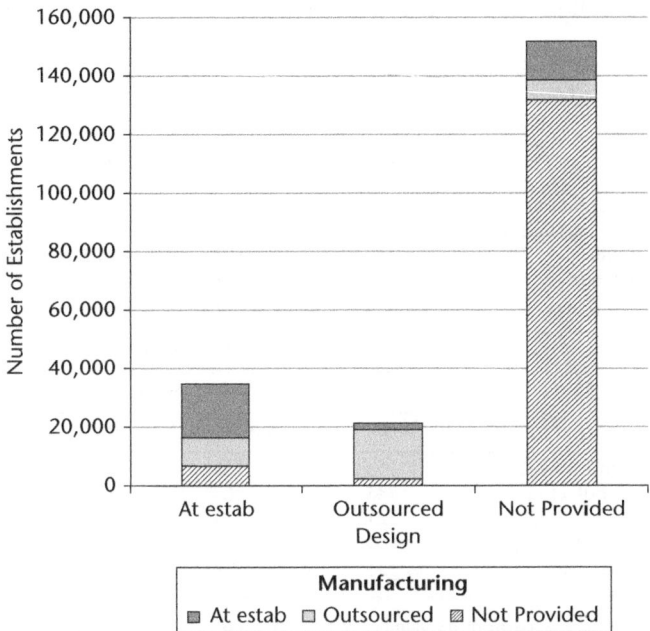

Figure 5.2 Design and manufacturing activities at wholesale establishments, 2002

plants both design and manufacture at the establishment itself. For those plants that outsource design activities, a large majority (more than 80 per cent) also contract for manufacturing services.

5.3.2 *2007*

As discussed in Section 5.2, the coverage and format of the questions changed between the 2002 and 2007 Economic Censuses. In Table 5.2 we report three dimensions of the underlying sample of plants for 2007: those that did or did not perform design activities at the plant, the primary activity of the plant, and whether or not the plant contracted for manufacturing services, either inside or outside the US. To be included in the table, an establishment had to provide a response to all three of the questions.[18]

[18] The exact questions from the 2007 CW form can be found in Appendix 5A in Figure 5.A2. This requirement that a plant provides an answer to all three questions results in the smaller sample size in Table 5.2 than in Table 5.1. One- and two-way tabulations that are not limited to the subset of plants that responded to all three questions result in comparable percentages of plants across the categories.

Table 5.2 Design, contract manufacturing, and primary activity at wholesale plants, 2007

		Did design at plant			
		Contract manufacturing			
		In US	Outside US	No	Total
Primary	Contracting	632	207	932	1,771
	Manufacturing	2,507	495	3,827	6,829
	Other	480	545	1,256	2,281
	Resales	3,294	1,548	5,707	10,549
	Total - Yes	6,913	2,795	11,722	21,430
		Did **not** design at plant			
		Contract manufacturing			
		In US	Outside US	No	Total
	Contracting	596	139	1,657	2,392
	Manufacturing	745	84	2,457	3,286
	Other	821	301	17,141	18,263
	Resales	7,085	1,945	86,345	95,375
	Total - No	9,247	2,469	107,600	119,316

Note: Each cell gives a count of the number of establishments. Only establishments that answered the design, contract manufacturing, and primary activity questions are included. *Design*: did this plant design, engineer, or formulate the manufactured products that it sold, produced, or shipped (yes/no)? *Primary* refers to the establishment's primary activity: *Contracting*—providing contract manufacturing services to others; *Manufacturing*—transforming raw materials or components into new products that this plant owns or controls; *Other*—other (sector-specific); *Resales*—reselling goods manufactured by others (with or without minor final assembly). The *contract manufacturing* question is 'Did this establishment purchase contract manufacturing services from other companies or other establishments of your company to process materials or components that this establishment owns or controls?' *In US*—primarily with plants within the 50 States and DC; *Outside US*—primarily with establishments outside the 50 States and DC; *No*—no. All plants were covered by the Census of Wholesale Trade.

Of the 140,726 responding establishments, 15.2 per cent indicated that they perform design activities at the plant, down slightly from 2002. More than a fifth of wholesale plants (21.5%) are involved in activities related to manufacturing either through the purchase or sale of contract manufacturing services or because they report their primary activity to be manufacturing. There is substantial variation in manufacturing activities depending on whether or not the plant does design in-house. A total of 67.5 per cent of designing establishments buy or sell CMS or have their primary activity as manufacturing. Only 13.3 per cent of non-designing plants are similarly involved in manufacturing activities.

For those plants with no design activities, 95.2 per cent report their primary activity to be in 'resales' or 'other'. These establishments conform to the traditional view of a wholesalers. The remaining 5,678 establishments with no design activity at the plant describe their primary activity as manufacturing or contract manufacturing for others. Among the 21,430 establishments that do report design activities, 6,829 (31.9%) report their primary activity as manufacturing and another 8.3 per cent are primarily contract manufacturers for other companies, see Figure 5.3. Although categorized as wholesalers, these plants are performing a substantial range of manufacturing-related activities. Even among establishments that describe themselves as resellers (or other), almost 46 per cent are purchasing contract manufacturing services from domestic or foreign locations in addition to their own design activity.

The 2007 questions also shed light on the role these non-traditional wholesale establishments play in global production chains. Two per

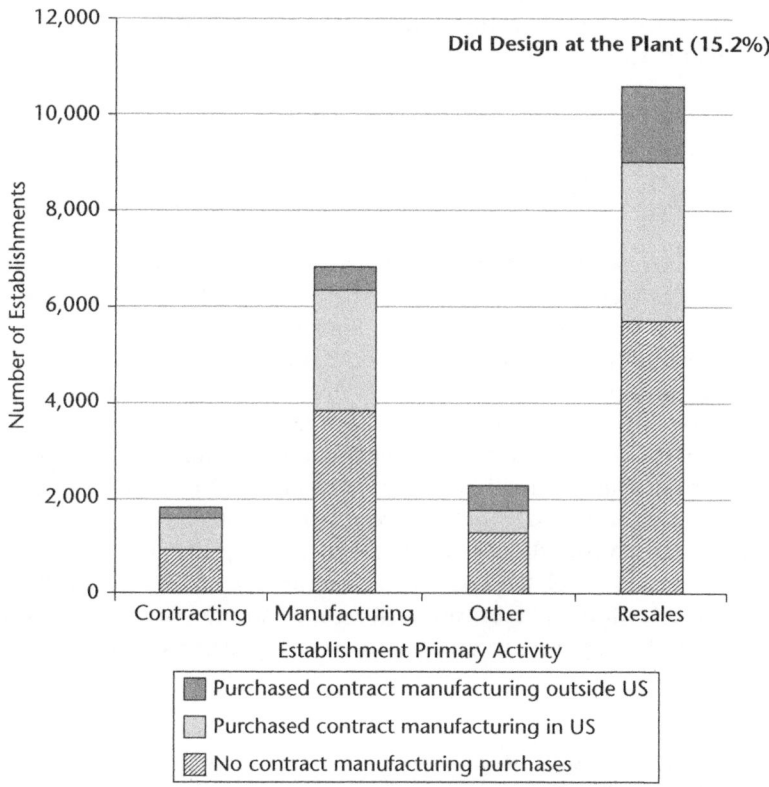

Figure 5.3 Design and manufacturing activities at wholesale plants, 2007

cent of establishments that do not design their products purchase CMS offshore. In contrast, 13 per cent of wholesale plants that design their own goods also offshore customized production (i.e. purchase CMS abroad). Fort (2016) examines offshore CMS purchases in the manufacturing sector and finds that the share of offshoring establishments is close to 2 per cent. The share of designing wholesale establishments that offshore is therefore more than six times the share of manufacturing establishments that offshore. We do note that, as in the results for manufacturing reported in Fort (2016), establishments with domestic CMS purchases are still more prevalent than establishments with offshore purchases.[19]

In both 2002 and 2007, a sizeable fraction of wholesale plants are conducting a range of manufacturing-related activities from design to the purchase of contract manufacturing services to manufacturing itself. Establishments that perform design are much more likely to have manufacturing activity at the plant or purchase contract manufacturing than plants that report no design activities.

5.4 FGPs

The results in Section 5.3 suggest that there are multiple types of wholesale plants engaged in a range of activities related to the production and distribution of manufactured goods. Both national statistical agencies and researchers are faced with the difficult question of how to conceptually and practically define an establishment that performs a sufficient range of manufacturing-related activities to be categorized as an FGP. Whether or not FGPs should be moved from non-manufacturing sectors to manufacturing is a separate question.[20] Not every wholesale plant that does design, purchases contract manufacturing services, or manufactures onsite should qualify for this change in status. The range of manufacturing-related activity must be sufficient to cover both the conceptualization and fabrication of a good. Additional complications arise from the variation in underlying survey questions over time.

---

[19] Fontagné and d'Isanto (Chapter 6) find that 4.2 per cent of French non-financial firms source activities from abroad.

[20] One practical reason to classify FGPs in the manufacturing sector is to ensure adequate data collection. The CM collects much more detailed information on the inputs and outputs of the physical production process.

5.4.1 *Definition of an FGP*

Our definition is based on a combination of activities at the plant: the wholesale establishment must perform design (pre-production) *and* be involved in manufacturing in some capacity (physical transformation activities). Wholesale establishments by definition are also involved in post-production activities.

> **Definition 5.1** A *Factoryless Good Producer (FGP)* is a wholesale establishment that performs design/engineering/R&D activity at the establishment and either conducts manufacturing operations at the establishment itself or purchases manufacturing services from a domestic or foreign company.

By this definition the wholesale plant has manufacturing-related activity both before (design) and during the production of the good. Wholesale establishments that are not FGPs (non-FGPs) include those that contract for design services, those that report no purchases of contract or onsite manufacturing even if design itself is occurring at the establishment, and those that are not involved in product design at all.[21] In theory the definition covers all wholesale establishments and divides them into FGPs and non-FGPs. In practice, wholesale establishments might not be able to be categorized if they did not answer the relevant questions about design and manufacturing and thus will be classified as missing.[22] The implementation of our definition varies between 2002 and 2007. We caution that comparisons across the years are difficult both due to changes in the underlying sample of responding establishments as well as to changes in the nature of the questions in the Economic Censuses.

5.4.2 *FGPs in 2002*

For 2002, using our definition, an FGP is an establishment in the wholesale sector that reports design activity in-house and either conducts

---

[21] International and US definitions of FGPs differ according to the ownership of inputs but both use a definition that ignores manufacturing activity at the establishment. Using the same CW data, Bayard, Byrne, and Smith (2015) adopt a version of this narrower definition of an FGP as a wholesale establishment that performs design and purchases contract manufacturing services. Wholesale establishments that both design and manufacture onsite are excluded from these definitions but are included in ours.

[22] In practice it is sometimes possible to classify a plant based as non-FGP based on their answer to a single question. For example, if they indicated they did no design but did not answer the other questions or if they indicated they were not involved in manufacturing at the plant or through the purchase of contract manufacturing services but gave no information about their design activity.

Table 5.3 Plants, sales, and employment by FGP status and census, 2002

	Plants	Sales	Employment
		FGP Status	
	Plants	Sales	Employment
No	181,671	2,750	2,897
Yes	28,331	253	595
Total	210,002	3,003	3,492
		Census	
	Plants	Sales	Employment
Wholesale	431,013	4,570	5,830
Manufacturing	348,813	3,900	14,600
Total	779,826	8,470	20,430

Note: FGP Status: Yes indicates the establishment performed design or engineering activity in product development and did manufacturing at the plant or purchased contract manufacturing services; No indicates the plant did no design or engineering activity in product development and/or was not involved in manufacturing either at the plant or through the purchase of contract manufacturing services. In 2002, only plants in the Census of Wholesale Trade were asked the design question. Census: Manufacturing indicates the plant was covered by the Census of Manufactures; Wholesale indicates the plant was covered by the Census of Wholesale Trade. The numbers in the cells represent the sums within the category. Employment is in thousands of workers, Sales are in billions of 2002 dollars.

manufacturing activity itself or purchases manufacturing services from outside the company.[23] These criteria mean that, for the 2002 CW, the establishment must have provided an answer to both the design and manufacturing questions to be classified as an FGP.[24]

The upper panel of Table 5.3 reports the counts of FGP and non-FGP plants in the wholesale sector along with their total sales and employment, while the bottom panel of the table provides similar totals for the population of wholesale and manufacturing establishments. We are able to classify almost half of the wholesale establishments in 2002 according to their FGP status. Of the plants with non-missing FGP status, 13.5 per cent are FGPs doing both design and manufacturing

[23] In 2002, the Economic Census does not distinguish between domestic and foreign contract manufacturing purchases.

[24] However, we are able to categorize some plants as non-FGP even if they answered only one of the questions on design or manufacturing. All plants with no design and all plants that report no manufacturing are classified as non-FGP (regardless of their answer to the other question) and as a result the total number of plants in Table 5.3 is greater than the totals in Table 5.1.

activities.[25] The FGP plants have $253 billion in sales and employ 595,000 workers. Compared to the population of wholesale establishments, FGP establishments represent 6.5 per cent of total establishments and account for 10.2 per cent of employment and 5.2 per cent of output.[26]

5.4.3 FGPs in 2007

As mentioned in Section 5.2, the questions about manufacturing-related activities at the establishment changed between the 2002 and 2007 Censuses. In addition, in 2007 not every wholesale industry was asked the questions. To qualify under our definition of FGP in 2007, a plant had to either (a) do design and have its primary activity as manufacturing, contracting, or other or (b) do design with the primary activity of resales and purchase contract manufacturing services. A plant was non-FGP if it either (a) did not perform design or (b) did design with the primary activity of resales but did not purchase contract manufacturing services.

Table 5.4 gives plant, sales, and employment totals for FGP and non-FGP plants in 2007 in the upper panel. The numbers of plants that are classified as FGP or non-FGP drops between 2002 and 2007 even as the population of wholesale establishments grows slightly.[27] This is likely due to the difference in the questions asked in the 2007 Census, the need for responses to three questions instead of two, and the fact that not all industries in the wholesale trade sector were asked the EA questions. Of the wholesale plants with non-missing status in 2007, 10.5 per cent are classified as FGP with $279 billion in sales employing 431,000 workers.

Interestingly, in the 2007 Economic Census, a subset of manufacturing establishments was asked the same questions about design, primary activity, and CMS purchases and thus we are able to classify

[25] These 28,331 FGP establishments represent the sum of the 18,539 plants that did design and manufacturing at the plant (Table 5.1 row 1 column 1) and the 9,792 plants that did design at the plant and purchased CMS (Table 5.1 row 1 column 1).

[26] We caution that these shares represent the activity at plants we can identify as FGP, i.e. a lower bound, as the FGP status of more than half of plants in the wholesale sector is missing.

[27] The 16,752 FGP establishments in 2007 represent the sum of the 10,881 plants that did design at the plant and had contracting, manufacturing, or other as their primary activity (Table 5.2 rows 1–3 column 4) and the 4,842 plants that did design at the plant, purchased CMS, and had resales as their primary activity (Table 5.2 row 4 columns 1–2). Note that these numbers sum to only 15,723 since Table 5.2 is limited to establishments that answered the design question, the primary activity question and the CMS question. In contrast, FGP status is defined for all plants that answered the design question and at least one of the primary activity and CMS questions.

Table 5.4 Plants, sales, and employment by FGP status and census, 2007

		FGP status		
		Plants	Sales	Employment
Wholesale	No	142,961	2,600	2,487
	Yes	16,752	279	431
Manufacturing	No	43,676	1,360	3,024
	Yes	61,427	2,520	6,031
	Total	264,816	6,750	11,973

	Census		
	Plants	Sales	Employment
Wholesale	434,984	6,520	6,230
Manufacturing	332,536	5,320	13,400
Total	767,520	11,840	19,630

Note: *FGP status*: *Yes* indicates that the plant did design and the primary activity was manufacturing, contracting, or other, or that the plant did design and the primary activity was resales and the plant purchased contract manufacturing services; *No* indicates that the plant did not design or that the plant did design and the primary activity was resales and the plant did not purchase contract manufacturing services. Plants in both the Census of Manufactures and the Census of Wholesale Trade were asked the design, primary activity, and contract manufacturing questions—for the exact coverage see the Data Appendix. *Census*: *Manufacturing* indicates the plant was covered by the Census of Manufactures; *Wholesale* indicates the plant was covered by the Census of Wholesale Trade. The numbers in the cells represent the sums within the category. Employment is in thousands of workers, Sales are in billions of 2007 dollars.

manufacturing firms according to the same criteria. The majority of manufacturing establishments with non-missing data satisfy the FGP criteria (58.4 per cent) and they account for just under half of total manufacturing sales and employment.

5.5 Characteristics of FGP Establishments

In this section we compare FGP establishments, non-FGP establishments, all wholesalers, and manufacturing establishments in terms of employment, wages, sales, labour productivity, and age. As there is no formal theoretical guidance from the literature on how these characteristics should vary across plant types, we describe two possible wholesale establishments. The FGP plant creates, designs, and engineers the product itself and coordinates the production, possibly through the purchase of CMS. Wholesale status means it is likely that the establishment is involved in post-production logistics and distribution. The traditional wholesale establishment (non-FGP) is not involved with pre-production activities, purchases the finished good directly from the producer, and is primarily involved in post-production activities.

The addition of the design activities would tend to raise employment and measured value added at the FGP plant, especially when adjusting for total sales. If pre-production workers are relatively skill intensive, average wages would also be higher at the FGP facility. Sales volume itself might be higher at the non-FGP plant, especially sales per employee, in part because the traditional wholesaler is likely to handle a wider variety of goods in any given market.

5.5.1 *2002*

Table 5.5 reports unweighted means for each characteristic by plant FGP status in the top panel for 2002. Since differences in the means

Table 5.5 Plant characteristics by FGP status and census, 2002

	Sales	Employment	Log VA/worker	Age	Wage
	FGP status				
No	15,136	16.0	4.81	12.2	39.9
Yes	8,918	21.0	4.47	11.6	39.9
Total	14,297	16.6	4.77	12.1	39.9
	Relative to NAICS 6-digit industry means				
	Sales	Employment	Log VA/worker	Age	Wage
No	1.29	1.15	0.155	1.11	1.06
Yes	1.23	1.67	0.010	1.11	1.07
Total	1.28	1.22	0.136	1.11	1.06
	Census				
	Sales	Employment	Log VA/worker	Age	Wage
Wholesale	10,600	13.5	4.55	10.8	37.1
Manufacturing	11,173	41.9	4.16	13.0	29.7
Total	10,856	26.2	4.37	11.8	33.6

Note: FGP status: Yes indicates the establishment performed design or engineering activity in product development (row 1 of Table 5.1) and did manufacturing at the plant or purchased contract manufacturing services (columns 2 or 3 of Table 5.1); *No* indicates the plant did no design or engineering activity in product development and/or was not involved in manufacturing either at the plant or through the purchase of contract manufacturing services. Plants in both the 2007 Census of Manufactures and the 2007 Census of Wholesale Trade were asked the design, primary activity, and contract manufacturing questions—for the exact coverage see the Data Appendix. *Census: Manufacturing* indicates the plant was covered by the Census of Manufactures; *Wholesale* indicates the plant was covered by the Census of Wholesale Trade. The numbers in the cells represent the sums within the category. Sales and Wage are in thousands of 2002 dollars.

can come from a combination of within industry differences at FGP and non-FGP plants and the mix of industries in the sample of plants with non-missing FGP status (and the industry mix difference between FGP and non-FGP), we report the average unweighted ratio (or log difference) relative to the mean in the industry of the establishment in the middle panel. The bottom panel in the table gives unweighted means across all establishments in the wholesale and manufacturing sectors for comparison.

Within the sample of establishments where we can identify FGP status, we find that FGP plants have much lower sales and log value added per worker than traditional wholesale plants (non-FGP), while employment is substantially larger and the average wage is comparable. They are also slightly younger.

The middle panel shows the extent to which the differences between FGPs and non-FGPs depend upon the industry composition of each group. In this panel, a value of one indicates that a plant is exactly at its industry mean (zero for log VA/worker). First, it is clear that, on average, plants in the FGP sample are larger and more productive than establishments with a missing status. Both FGPs and non-FGPs have values greater than one. Second, the relative means reveal important within-industry differences from the raw averages presented in the top panel. Although non-FGPs still have more sales than FGPs, their relative mean is only 4.7 per cent larger than the FGP mean, whereas the raw numbers suggested a 41 per cent difference in size. In contrast, the relative means reveal even bigger differences in employment at FGPs versus non-FGPs. FGPs employ 1.67 times more workers than their industry average, compared to just 1.15 times for non-FGPs.

5.5.2 2007

We repeat the exercise for 2007 in Table 5.6. Within the sample of wholesale establishments where we can identify FGP status, we find that FGP plants have somewhat lower sales and substantially higher employment than traditional wholesale establishments as in 2002. However, in this sample, FGP plants on average have higher wages and comparable, rather than lower, productivity. FGP plants are also younger than non-FGPs.

Looking at the middle panel, we find that relative to their industry averages, FGP establishments have substantially higher sales, wages, productivity, and especially employment. On average, FGP plants are also larger, more productive, and pay higher wages than non-FGP plants in the same industry.

Table 5.6 Plant characteristics by FGP status and census, 2007

		FGP status				
		Sales	Employment	Log VA/worker	Age	Wage
Wholesale	No	18,189	17.4	4.79	14.0	44.6
	Yes	16,667	25.7	4.78	12.9	49.4
Manufacturing	No	40,959	98.2	4.59	19.1	41.9
	Yes	31,111	69.2	4.52	17.9	39.0
	Total	25,506	45.2	4.70	15.8	43.3
		Relative to NAICS 6-digit industry means				
		Sales	Employment	Log VA/worker	Age	Wage
Wholesale	No	1.11	1.06	0.126	1.12	1.05
	Yes	1.31	1.65	0.154	1.10	1.13
Manufacturing	No	2.26	2.15	0.016	1.25	1.12
	Yes	1.78	1.72	-0.004	1.17	1.09
	Total	1.50	1.46	0.081	1.16	1.08
		Census				
		Sales	Employment	Log VA/worker	Age	Wage
Wholesale		14,979	14.3	4.79	12.1	43.4
Manufacturing		15,997	40.3	4.48	14.7	34.9
Total		15,420	25.6	4.66	13.2	39.6

Note: *FGP status*: *Yes* indicates that the plant did design and the primary activity was manufacturing, contracting, or other, or that the plant did design and the primary activity was resales and the plant purchased contract manufacturing services; *No* indicates that the plant did not design or that the plant did design and the primary activity was resales and the plant did not purchase contract manufacturing services. *Census*: *Manufacturing* indicates the plant was covered by the Census of Manufactures; *Wholesale* indicates the plant was covered by the Census of Wholesale Trade. Sales and Wage are in thousands of 2007 dollars.

5.6 FGP Firms

Having established a number of plant-level facts, we turn our focus to the firm. While the Economic Censuses collect information at the unit of the establishment, economic decision-making in many cases takes place at the firm level. Most firms in both manufacturing and wholesale trade are single-plant (SP) organizations but the smaller number of multi-plant (MP) firms are disproportionately important in aggregate output, and employment and are more likely to produce multiple products (see Dunne, Roberts, and Samuelson 1988 and Bernard, Redding, and Schott 2010). For SP firms, FGP status is a straightforward application of Definition 5.1; however, for MP firms we need a new definition.

Definition 5.2 A *Factoryless Goods Producing Firm (FGPF or FGP firm)* is a firm with at least one FGP wholesale establishment.

The practical implementation of Definition 5.2 is complicated by the fact that each wholesale plant can be in one of three categories: FGP, non-FGP, or missing. As a result, firms can also be in one of three categories: *FGPF*—at least one wholesale plant is an FGP; *non-FGPF*—where none of the wholesale plants at the firm is identified as an FGP and at least one plant is identified as not being an FGP; and *missing*—where every wholesale plant in the firm has missing for its FGP status.[28]

MP firms can be comprised of only wholesale establishments, a mix of manufacturing and wholesale establishments, and only manufacturing establishments. FGP firms come from the first two firm types, any firm that has no wholesale (only manufacturing) establishments is not an FGPF.[29]

Table 5.7 reports the number of firms by FGP status and firm type in 2002 (upper panel) and 2007 (lower panel). In 2002, 16.5 per cent of the firms with non-missing status are FGPFs and only a small fraction

Table 5.7 Firm counts by FGPF status, 2002 and 2007

		Firm type, 2002			
		Manufacturing	Mixed	Wholesale	Total
FGPF status	Missing	298,025	1,894	185,484	485,403
	No	–	2,612	125,732	128,344
	Yes	–	961	24,388	25,349
	Total	298,025	5,467	335,604	639,096
		Firm type, 2007			
		Manufacturing	Mixed	Wholesale	Total
	Missing	282,020	2,654	213,871	498,545
	No	–	2,152	100,883	103,035
	Yes	–	757	13,505	14,262
	Total	282,020	5,563	328,259	615,842

Note: *Firm type*: *Manufacturing* indicates firms with no wholesale plants; *Mixed* indicates firms with both manufacturing and wholesale plants; *Wholesale* indicates firms with only wholesale plants. *FGPF status*: *Missing* indicates firms with no FGP wholesale plants and at least one wholesale plant with missing FGP status; *No* indicates firms with no FGP wholesale plants and no wholesale plants with missing FGP status; *Yes* indicates firms with at least one FGP wholesale plant.

[28] We note that this is a conservative definition of an FGP firm since a plant with missing status at a non-FGP firm may be an FGP. An alternative definition would have classified all firms with one or more plants with a missing status as missing. However, this classification scheme would likely have resulted in a much bigger allocation of the larger, MP firms to the missing category.

[29] We note that all firms may have employment in other sectors, such as retail trade or business services, but we do not measure those activities here.

of FGPFs are mixed firms. However, FGPFs are almost twice as likely to be a mixed firm (3.8%) than are non-FGPFs (2.0%) or missing firms. For 2007, as with the plant-level data, fewer firms have non-missing FGPF status and among those a smaller fraction are FGPF. Again the share of mixed firms among FGPFs is much higher (5.3%) than for non-FGPFs (2.0%).

Table 5.8 reports on firm characteristics by FGPF status and firm type (upper panel) as well as by Census (lower panel) for 2002.[30] The comparable firm characteristics for 2007 are given in Table 5.9. Sales, employment, and imports are much larger at FGPFs than at other type of firms (non-FGPF or missing) in both years. FGPFs also have more manufacturing plants on average (almost four times as many in 2002 and five times as many in 2007) than non-FGPFs. A portion of these differences is driven by the increased presence of mixed firms in the FGPF category. Within each group, mixed firms are dramatically larger, more productive, and more involved in imports. Despite this compositional component, the mixed FGPFs are still different from the mixed non-FGPs. They are more productive and have more sales, employment, and imports than the non-FGPFs. In addition, the mixed FGPFs have twice as many manufacturing and wholesale establishments on average than non-FGPFs in both 2002 and 2007.

Tables 5.8 and 5.9 also show the average share of intra-firm (related party) imports by FGP status and firm type. The share of intra-firm imports for mixed firms is between 0.25 and 0.27 for both FGPFs and non-FGPFs in 2002 and 2007. In contrast, FGPF wholesale-only firms have a noticeably lower share of intra-firm imports compared to non-FGPFs. In 2002, the average share of intra-firm imports for FGPFs was only 0.09 compared to 0.13 for non-FGPFs. A similar pattern is evident in 2007. Wholesale-only FGPFs had an average share of intra-firm imports of 0.08 compared to 0.13 for non-FGPs.

5.7 Aggregate Implications

In this section we consider how employment and output aggregates for manufacturing would have been different if FGP establishments had been included in the manufacturing sector in 2002 and 2007 instead of in the wholesale sector. In 2017, the US Census Bureau is scheduled to do exactly this by recording FGPs in the manufacturing sector.

---

[30] We do not report normalization within industries due to the multi-industry nature of many firms.

Table 5.8 Firm characteristics by FGPF status, firm type, and census, 2002

FGPF status

	Sales	Employment	Log VA/worker	Age	Imports	Intra-firm	M-plants	W-plants	Wage
Missing	5,703	22.8	3.83	11.9	514	0.092	0.67	0.43	30.6
Manufacturing	4,691	27.1	4.07	12.8	291	0.096	1.07	–	30.3
Mixed	344,818	787	4.59	22.6	42,405	0.228	3.55	4.49	36.1
Wholesale	3,866	8.25	3.44	10.2	446	0.082	–	1.07	31.1
No	30,320	46.4	4.64	12.8	2,873	0.135	0.11	1.40	37.8
Mixed	960,767	1,497	4.57	23.6	100,990	0.269	5.34	8.97	38.8
Wholesale	10,991	16.2	4.65	12.6	835	0.125	–	1.24	37.8
Yes	71,258	134	4.38	12.3	9,334	0.105	0.39	1.78	38.5
Mixed	1,651,635	2,983	4.59	22.9	203,373	0.271	10.3	16.9	37.5
Wholesale	8,984	21.9	4.37	11.9	1,688	0.089	–	1.19	38.5
Total	13,247	32.0	4.01	12.1	1,338	0.105	0.55	0.674	32.4

Census

	Sales	Employment	log VA/worker	Age	Imports	Intra-firm	M-plants	W-plants	Wage
Manufacturing	4,691	27.1	4.07	12.8	291	0.096	1.07	–	30.3
Mixed	868,818	1,512	4.58	23.2	98,691	0.256	5.59	8.81	37.6
Wholesale	6,907	12.2	3.96	11.3	682	0.099	–	1.14	34.5
Total	13,247	32	4.01	12.1	1,338	0.105	0.55	0.674	32.4

Note: Firm type: Manufacturing indicates firms with only manufacturing plants; Mixed indicates firms with both manufacturing and wholesale plants; Wholesale indicates firms with only wholesale plants. FGPF status: Missing indicates firms with no FGP wholesale plants and at least one wholesale plant with missing FGP status; No indicates firms with no FGP wholesale plants and no manufacturing plants with missing FGP status; Yes indicates firms with at least one FGP wholesale plant. Sales, Imports, and Wage are in thousands of 2002 dollars. Intra-firm is the share of firm imports from related parties abroad. M-plants (W-plants) is the number of manufacturing (wholesale) establishments in the firm.

Table 5.9 Firm characteristics by FGPF status, firm type, and census, 2007

FGPF status

		Sales	Employment	log VA/worker	Age	Imports	Intra-firm	M-plants	W-plants	Wage
Missing		11,146	24.0	4.00	13.5	1,436	0.075	0.63	0.50	35.7
	Manufacturing	6,279	26.9	3.80	14.7	516	0.070	1.07	—	33.3
	Mixed	765,646	836	4.87	26.2	139,905	0.215	4.18	5.32	52.0
	Wholesale	8,202	10.1	4.24	11.7	931	0.075	—	1.10	39.0
No	Manufacturing	41,747	51.5	4.52	15.3	5,859	0.095	0.12	1.49	41.6
	Mixed	960,767	1,497	4.57	23.6	100,990	0.269	5.34	8.97	38.8
	Wholesale	10,991	16.2	4.65	12.6	835	0.125	—	1.24	37.8
Yes	Manufacturing	138,619	166	4.50	14.5	17,561	0.092	0.62	2.18	45.7
	Mixed	2288467	2,692	4.92	27.3	286,731	0.247	11.7	19.8	53.0
	Wholesale	18,113	24.9	4.48	13.7	2,473	0.076	—	1.19	45.3
Total		19,218	31.9	4.10	13.8	2,549	0.080	0.54	0.71	36.9

Census

	Sales	Employment	log VA/worker	Age	Imports	Intra-firm	M-plants	W-plants	Wage
Manufacturing	6,279	26.9	3.80	14.7	516	0.070	1.07	—	33.3
Mixed	1194406	1,370	4.85	26.8	181,869	0.224	5.71	9.18	51.5
Wholesale	10,419	13.5	4.33	12.8	1,257	0.080	—	1.17	40.0
Total	19,218	31.9	4.10	13.8	2,549	0.080	0.54	0.71	36.9

Note: Firm Type: Manufacturing indicates firms with no wholesale plants; Mixed indicates firms with both manufacturing and wholesale plants; Wholesale indicates firms with only wholesale plants. FGPF status: Missing indicates firms with no FGP wholesale plants and at least one wholesale plant with missing FGP status; No indicates firms with no FGP wholesale plants and no wholesale plants with missing FGP status; Yes indicates firms with at least one FGP wholesale plant. Sales, Imports, and Wage are in '000s of 2007 dollars. M-plants (W-plants) is the number of manufacturing (wholesale) establishments in the firm. Intra-firm is the share of firm imports from related parties abroad.

We emphasize that the results in this section depend on our definition of FGP in each year. The difference in the survey questions and coverage over time makes even the comparison of the 2002 and 2007 numbers problematic.

A major concern for policy makers in advanced, industrialized economies has been the rapid and systematic decline in the manufacturing sector in recent decades. The focus of this chapter is on the presence of FGPs that reside outside the manufacturing sector but conduct manufacturing-like or manufacturing-related activities. Broadly construed FGPs employ workers and produce output that is similar in many dimensions to traditional manufacturing operations but their employment and output do not count towards manufacturing aggregates.

Here we report the results of two exercises that shift FGPs to the manufacturing sector with adjustments to the aggregate manufacturing employment and output statistics.[31] In the first adjustment, we add employment (output) by establishments that we have identified as FGPs in 2002 and 2007 to existing manufacturing aggregates. In the second adjustment, we assume that the prevalence of FGPs in our samples of responding establishments holds for the entire population of wholesale plants and that employment and output at all those plants differs from their industry means to the same extent as found in the samples of responding establishments. The two methods provide rough lower and upper bounds on the extent of manufacturing-like activity due to the presence of FGPs in the wholesale trade sector. To the extent that FGPs are present in other sectors, such as business services, both of our estimates may understate the presence of FGPs and their employment and output.

The first method is quite straightforward and merely involves adding the employment and output aggregates at establishments identified as FGP in Section 5.4 to the reported manufacturing totals for each year. Reclassifying FGP establishments to the manufacturing sector would have increased reported manufacturing jobs by 595,000 in 2002 and by 431,000 in 2007, corresponding to a 4.0 per cent increase in manufacturing employment in 2002 and 3.2 per cent increase in 2007.

---

[31] Using a narrower definition of FGPs and focusing on the semiconductor industry, Bayard, Byrne, and Smith (2015) estimate that US manufacturing output would have been 7–30 per cent higher in 2002 and 2007 if FGPs has been included. We consider FGPs more broadly and include a focus on employment which is typically the focus of policy debates on the manufacturing sector. They find a larger share of output in FGPs in the semiconductor sector than we do for manufacturing overall. This difference might exist in part because the semiconductor industry has undergone more production fragmention than the average manufacturing sector.

The same method of adjustment would have resulted in increased reported manufacturing output by \$253 billion (6.5%) in 2002 and by \$279 billion (5.2%) in 2007.

The second method involves two strong additional assumptions. First, we assume that the fraction of FGPs in the overall wholesale sector is the same as that among those plants answering both the design and manufacturing questions in 2002, and those answering the design, primary activity, and outsourcing questions in 2007. Second, we assume that all these FGPs are proportionally different from (larger than) the average in their industry in terms of employment and output to the same degree as the observed FGP plants (see Tables 5.5 and 5.6).

Applying the first assumption results in 58,147 FGPs in 2002 and 45,624 FGPS in 2007. Average employment at wholesale plants was 13.5 workers in 2002 and 14.3 workers in 2007 and the within-industry FPG-adjustment factors were 1.67 and 1.65 respectively, yielding an average of 22.5 workers per FGP in 2002 and 23.6 workers per FGP in 2007.

This more liberal set of assumptions results in 1,311,000 more manufacturing jobs in 2002 and 1,934,000 in 2007, 9 per cent and 14.4 per cent respectively. The same method of adjustment would have resulted in increased reported manufacturing output by \$758 billion (19.4 per cent) in 2002 and by \$895 billion (16.8 per cent) in 2007.

5.8 Conclusions

Large numbers of workers in the wholesale sector are employed at plants that engage in manufacturing-related activities. Unlike traditional wholesalers, these establishments are not primarily engaged in intermediation but instead undertake design and engineering of products themselves and exert control over the production process. To date, many of these FGPs have been hidden in the wholesale sector. Our findings open a window into the extent and characteristics of FGPs in the US wholesale sector. The potential for increasing fragmentation of production across firms and borders means that FGPs are likely to play an even larger role in industrialized economies in years to come.

The findings in this chapter raise issues for academic researchers and statistical agencies. There is the relatively straightforward question of how to assign FGPs to broad sectors such as manufacturing or wholesale trade. Our results suggest that merely asking plants about their outsourcing activities might miss an important segment of FGPs, those that design their goods and still do some manufacturing but not enough to be reclassified as traditional manufacturers. Our findings suggest that moving FGPs to manufacturing will substantially raise measured manufacturing employment. These results also raise questions about the production process itself and how it is fragmented across locations and firms. Measurement of outputs and inputs may be fundamentally different at FGPs than at integrated manufacturing firms or at more traditional wholesalers with obvious consequences for measuring value added and productivity. The presence of FGPs in an industry also complicates the already-difficult job of measuring productivity, both within FGPs over time and between FGPs and other plants. We lack evidence on their production function, or on how their existence may bias existing estimates of productivity.

Our results suggest a fruitful area of research related to theoretical models of tasks, outsourcing, and offshoring. The largely neglected wholesale trade sector contains a sizeable number of establishments that are at the forefront of this type of production fragmentation. The FGPs we document in this chapter suggest that, at least for some producers, it is optimal to fragment the majority of the physical transformation activities to another location. We also find that these plants are systematically different from integrated manufacturers or traditional wholesale intermediaries. Rodríguez-Clare (2010) develops a dynamic model of offshoring in which the reallocation of factors of production away from manufacturing and towards design activities can result in long-term productivity gains for the offshoring country. The FGPs we document in this chapter provide evidence of a production process that is consistent with this mechanism. However, our results only provide a snapshot of FGPs at two points in time. We know nothing about how they are created, for example whether they are new establishments or transformations of existing ones, or how they perform over time in terms of output, employment growth, and survival.

Appendix

A. Data

The industry classifications for all establishments covered by the Economic Census and surveys are based on the North American Industry Classification System (NAICS). The method of assigning industry classifications and the level of detail at which establishments were classified depends on whether a report form is obtained for the establishment. Establishments that returned a report form are classified on the basis of their self-designation; product line sales, products produced, or services rendered; and responses to other industry-specific inquiries. Establishments that do not return a report form and those that were not sent a report form were classified using the following

Form WH-42101   Page 12

㉗ Not Applicable.

㉘ ESTABLISHMENT ACTIVITIES

A. Indicate activities that were performed by this establishment or were performed for this establishment by another company during 2002.
(Mark "X" ALL that apply.)

1. Product Development	This activity was performed by this establishment	This activity was performed for this establishment by another company	This activity was not provided by this establishment
a. Product design/engineering	0921 ☐	0941 ☐	0961 ☐
b. Materials fabrication/processing/assembly/blending	0922 ☐	0942 ☐	0962 ☐

Figure 5.A1 Census design and manufacturing questions, 2002

Form WH-42301 (12/04/2006)   Page 12

㉖ SPECIAL INQUIRIES - Continued

C. OTHER ESTABLISHMENT ACTIVITIES

1. Did this establishment design, engineer, or formulate the manufactured products that it sold, produced, or shipped?

0318 ☐   Yes

0319 ☐   No

2. Which of the following best describes this establishment's primary activity? *(Mark "X" only ONE box.)*

0362 ☐   Providing contract manufacturing services for others

0363 ☐   Transforming raw materials or components into new products that this establishment owns or controls

0364 ☐   Reselling goods manufactured by others (with or without minor final assembly)

0365 ☐   Other - *Specify*

0366 _____

3. Did this establishment purchase contract manufacturing services from other companies or other establishments of your company to process materials or components that this establishment owns or controls?

0496 ☐   Yes, primarily with establishments WITHIN the 50 States and the District of Columbia

0497 ☐   Yes, primarily with establishments OUTSIDE of the 50 States and the District of Columbia

0498 ☐   No

Figure 5.A2 Census design, primary activity, and outsourcing questions, 2007

methods: (a) the most current industry classification available from the applicable Census Bureau current surveys or the previous Economic Census, (b) the classification from administrative records of other federal agencies, (c) a brief inquiry requesting information necessary to assign a kind-of-business code, and/or (d) research done by Census Bureau analysts. Figures 5.A1, 5.A2, and 5.A3 illustrate the report forms.

B. Definitions of FGPs

The Economic Classification Policy Committee (OMB 2010) gives the following definition of an FGP:

NAICS Code	NAICS Description
423210	Furniture Merchant Wholesalers
423220	Home Furnishing Merchant Wholesalers
423410	Photographic Equipment and Supplies Merchant Wholesalers
423420	Office Equipment Merchant Wholesalers
423440	Other Commercial Equipment Merchant Wholesalers
423450	Medical, Dental, and Hospital Equipment And Supplies Merchant Wholesalers
423460	Ophthalmic Goods Merchant Wholesalers
423490	Other Professional Equipments and Supplies Merchant Wholesalers
423710	Hardware Merchant Wholesalers
423720	Plumbing and Heating Equipment and Supplies (Hydronics) Merchant Wholesalers
423730	Warm Air Heating and Air-Conditioning Equipment and Supplies Merchant Wholesalers
423740	Refrigeration Equipment and Supplies Merchant Wholesalers
423840	Industrial Supplies Wholesalers Merchant
423990	Other Miscellaneous Durable Goods Merchant Wholesalers
424610	Plastics Materials and Basic Forms and Shapes Merchant Wholesalers
424690	Other Chemical and Allied Products Merchant Wholesalers
424710	Petroleum Bulk Stations and Terminals
424720	Petroleum and Petroleum Products Merchant Wholesalers (except Bulk Stations and Terminals)
424910	Farm supplies Merchant Wholesalers
424990	Other Miscellaneous Nondurable Goods Merchant Wholesalers
425110	Business to Business Electronic Markets
425120	Wholesale Trade Agents and Brokers

Figure 5.A3 Industries not asked the establishment activity questions, 2007

The factoryless goods producer (FGP) outsources all of the transformation steps that traditionally have been considered manufacturing, but undertakes all of the entrepreneurial steps and arranges for all required capital, labor, and material inputs required to make a good. Characteristics of FGPs include:

Owns rights to the intellectual property or design (whether independently developed or otherwise acquired) of the final manufactured product;

- May or may not own the input materials;
- Does not own production facilities;
- Does not perform transformation activities;
- Owns the final product produced by manufacturing service provider partners; and
- Sells the final product.

The FGP can provide information on the purchase of the manufacturing service, that is, the cost of the contract, but would not necessarily have production worker payroll or capital expenditures on plant and equipment. However, it can provide data on the number of units that were produced and the market value of the final product.

Bibliography

Akerman, A. (2010). A Theory on the Role of Wholesalers in International Trade Based on Economies of Scope. Research papers in economics, Stockholm University, Department of Economics.

Akerman, A. and L. Py (2011). Outsourcing and the Division of Labor between Firms: Evidence from Swedish Cities, *mimeo*, Stockholm University.

Antràs, P. and E. Helpman (2004). Global Sourcing, *Journal of Political Economy*, 112(31): 552–80.

Baldwin, R. and A. Venables (2010). Relocating the Value Chain: Offshoring and Agglomeration in the Global Economy, NBER working paper 16611.

Bayard, K., D. Byrne, and D. Smith (2015). The scope of U.S. factoryless manufacturing. In Susan Houseman and Michael Mandel (eds), *Measuring Globalization: Better Trade Statistics for Better Policy*, Vol. 2, ch. 4, Kalamazoo, Michigan: W.E. Upjohn Institute.

Bernard, A. B., J. B. Jensen, and P. K. Schott (2009). Importers, exporters, and multinationals: a portrait of firms in the U.S. that trade goods. In T. Dunne, J. Jensen, and M. Roberts (eds), *Producer Dynamics: New Evidence from Micro Data*, Chicago: University of Chicago Press.

Bernard, A. B., S. J. Redding, and P. K. Schott (2010). Multiple-Product Firms and Product Switching, *American Economic Review*, 100(1): 70–97.

Bernard, A. B., J. B. Jensen, S. J. Redding, and P. K. Schott (2010). Wholesalers and Retailers in US Trade, *American Economic Review*, 100(2): 408–13.

Bernard, A. B., M. Grazzi, and C. Tomasi (2015). Intermediaries in International Trade: Products and Destinations, *Review of Economics and Statistics*, 97(4): 916–20.

Blum, B. S., S. Claro, and I. Horstmann (2010). Facts and Figures on Intermediated Trade, *American Economic Review*, 100(2): 419–23.

Doherty, Maureen (2015). Measuring 'factoryless' manufacturing: evidence from U.S. surveys. In Susan Houseman and Michael Mandel (eds), *Measuring Globalization: Better Trade Statistics for Better Policy*, Vol. 2, ch. 1, Kalamazoo, Michigan: W.E. Upjohn Institute.

Dunne, T., M. J. Roberts, and L. Samuelson (1988). Patterns of Firm Entry and Exit in U.S. Manufacturing Industries, *Rand Journal of Economics*, 19: 495–515.

Fally, T. (2012). Production Staging: Measurement and Facts, working paper, University of Colorado-Boulder.

Fort, Teresa C. (2016). Technology and Production Fragmentation: Domestic versus Foreign Sourcing, NBER working paper 22550.

Grossman, G. M. and E. Rossi-Hansberg (2008). Trading Tasks: A Simple Theory of Offshoring, *The American Economic Review*, 98(5): 1978–97.

Hanson, G. H., R. J. Mataloni, and M. J. Slaughter (2005). Vertical Production Networks in Multinational Firms, *Review of Economics and Statistics*, 87(4).

Hummels, D., J. Ishii, and K.-M. Yi (2001). The Nature and Growth of Vertical Specialization in World Trade, *Journal of International Economics*, 54(1): 75–96.

Johnson, R. and G. Noguera (2012). Fragmentation and Trade in Value Added Over Four Decades, working paper 18186, NBER.

Kamal, Fariha, Brent. R. Moulton, and Jennifer Ribarsky (2015). Measuring 'factoryless' manufacturing: evidence from U.S. surveys. In Susan Houseman and Michael Mandel (eds), *Measuring Globalization: Better Trade Statistics for Better Policy*, Vol. 2, ch. 3, Kalamazoo, Michigan: W.E. Upjohn Institute.

Kraemer, K. L., G. Linden, and J. Dedrick (2011). Capturing Value in Global Networks: Apple's iPad and iPhone, working paper, Personal Computing Industry Center, UC Irvine.

OMB (2010). Economic Classification Policy Committee Recommendation Recommendation for Classification of Outsourcing in North American Industry Classification System (NAICS) Revisions for 2012. Federal register, Office of Management and Budget.

Pierce, Justin and Peter Schott (2016). The Surprisingly Swift Decline of U.S. Manufacturing Employment, *American Economic Review*, 106(7): 1632–62.

Rodríguez-Clare, A. (2010). Offshoring in a Ricardian World, *American Economic Journal: Macroeconomics*, 2(2).

Yeaple, S. R. (2003). The Role of Skill Endowments in the Structure of U.S. Outward Foreign Direct Investment, *The Review of Economics and Statistics*, 85(3): 726–34.

6

Fragmentation: Survey-based Evidence for France

Lionel Fontagné and Aurélien D'Isanto

6.1 Introduction

Since the mid-1990s, the global business environment has changed profoundly.[1] There has been a drop in both import tariffs and transaction and data processing costs, which has been accompanied by the emergence of low-wage new industrialized countries. In contrast to the traditional vertical integration model centred on the home country, goods, and in many cases services, have become internationalized. Value chains have become fragmented globally leading to trade in tasks rather than in intermediate goods and services (Hummels, Ishii, and Yi 2001; Grossman and Rossi-Hansberg 2008; Miroudot, Lanz, and Ragoussis 2009). The 'great unbundling' (Baldwin 2012 and this book) has led firms to adopt a global perspective on their organization and to reconsider the location of their activities. Outsourcing of certain services is a longstanding practice in industry, but the norm was using nearby service providers. The reduction in communication and information processing costs has made it more likely for both industry activities and services to be outsourced internationally. Offshoring—defined here as international sourcing—has become common for many tasks. For French firms, the European Union (EU) enlargement in 2004 to Central and Eastern European countries was a first step to more global fragmentation of production processes. This fragmentation of value chains has raised several issues.

---

[1] The views expressed in this chapter are those of the authors and not necessarily INSEE.

First, the traditional way of measuring international trade as gross amounts leads to possible multiple counting of the same flow if intermediate goods and services are traded. The response has been to compute the value-added content of trade, combining input–output and detailed trade data to construct world input–output tables (Johnson and Noguera 2012; Stehrer 2012; Koopman, Wang, and Zei 2014).

A second issue is related to the international organization and boundaries of multinational firms (Antras and Rossi-Hansberg 2009). For each value chain segment, firms now have to choose the global location of activities. Depending on the technological intensity of the activity, the intrinsic difficulty to contract, transaction costs in general, and the business environment in the alternative locations, the perimeter of the firm in the origin country is optimally adjusted. How the international organization of the firm is shaped by the interaction of these constraints has been well documented. Insourcing (defined here as internalization via subsidiaries, joint-ventures, and parent or sister firms) versus outsourcing (defined here as externalization to firms which are neither subsidiaries, joint-ventures, nor parent or sister firms) mirrors firms' 'make or buy' decisions. At the international level, the choice of internalizing or externalizing the sourcing will be driven by firm, country, and also industry characteristics (Antras 2003; Yeaple 2006).

Third, since firms optimally adjust their internal organization, there is an impact on the location of jobs. The international location of activities is shaped by international differences in factor costs (Dixit and Grossman 2002), differences in the probability of making mistakes (Costinot, Vogel, and Wang 2013), and differences in the quality of the contractual environment (Nunn 2007). Low-wage countries tend to specialize in labour intensive tasks, while countries with higher technology skills specialize in the final segments of sequential value chains where errors are more costly. Finally, countries with more favourable contracting environments will have advantages in activities where relationship-specific investments are important. The ultimate impact of such international allocation of activities by multinational firms on domestic employment, skill composition, and jobs in the parent country is a key concern for economic policy. A wide range of methods and data is used in the literature—sectoral evidence (Feenstra and Hanson 1999), firm-level data (Harrison and McMillan 2011), individual-level worker data (Ebenstein, Harrison, and McMillan, Chapter 8 in this book)—but is limited to actual cost savings in the context of survey-based evidence (Bryan 2013).

Complementing previous research, mostly based on aggregated data or microeconomic evidence relying on administrative sources, this chapter exploits the result of the 2012 survey of global value chains in fifteen European countries, including France. The *International Sourcing and Global Value Chains* (IS-GVC) survey—in French the *Chaînes d'activité mondiales* (CAM) survey, focuses on the 28,000 firms located in France, with more than fifty employees at the end of 2008, belonging to the industry, trade, and non-financial services sectors.

This chapter provides an in-depth treatment of this survey with a focus on detailed results for France, the largest European country involved in the survey. Our conclusions are very much in line with the predictions of recent theories of global organization of multinational firms. We identify reasons why leading firms do not offshore certain activities, and we characterize what might be the direct consequences for employment of French firms' offshoring strategies.

We found that offshoring decisions were made by only 4.2 per cent of French industry, trade, and non-financial services sector firms with more than fifty employees at the end of 2008, over a three-year period (2009–2010–2011). These firms accounted for almost 500,000 employees in 2011, representing 6.5 per cent of employees in the 28,000 firms covered by the survey. We found also that 3.1 per cent of these firms contemplated offshoring, but eventually decided not to. Among the determinants of the offshoring decision, distance, as expected, is an important barrier: more than half of the firms that do offshore choose a European country including the twelve new Member States of the 2004–2007 enlargement. More strategic segments of the value chain are generally offshored within the firm's foreign boundaries (foreign subsidiary, joint-venture, or foreign sister or parent firm), pointing to the potential for problems related to incomplete contracts. Lastly, we estimate that 20,000 jobs (or 0.3% of employment in the surveyed firms in 2011) were offshored between 2009 and 2011, based on decisions identified in the survey. This figure, though it downplays the threats related to a massive relocation of activities, takes no account of general equilibrium effects and is not based on a proper counterfactual. The definition of offshoring used in the survey is restrictive as well, as it excludes situations where relocations of activity abroad go hand-in-hand with an expansion of the activity at home. Thus, 20,000 jobs offshored over a three-year period must be considered as indicative.

The rest of the chapter is organized as follows. In Section 6.2 we present the survey methodology. The potential impact on employment of offshoring is discussed in Section 6.3. Section 6.4 describes the firms that decide to offshore and Section 6.5 analyses the decision not to offshore. In Section 6.6 we show that the fragmentation of value chains is mostly regional and is mostly within the boundaries of the group. We demonstrate in Section 6.7 that reducing costs is the main determinant of offshoring, although lower wages is only one facet of this strategy. The last section concludes.

6.2 An Original Survey of Global Value Chains

The IS-GVC survey of global value chains is a European initiative, implemented in France as the *Enquête Chaînes d'Activités Mondiales (CAM)*. The survey approach has few precedents in France. The *Globalization* survey (*'enquête mondialisation'*) launched in 1999 by the French Ministry of Industry aimed at measuring the importance of within group inter-firm trade in industry.[2] The *survey of inter-firm relations* (*'enquête sur les relations inter entreprises'*) carried out in 2003 by SESSI, was wider in scope (industry, services, trade, construction). It provided a panorama of the inter-firm relations that required minimum cooperation (essentially subcontracting, but not buying or selling directly from a catalogue).[3] A joint survey (*'Enquête sur les Changements organisationels et technologies de l'information et de la communication'*—*'Enquête COI-TIC 2006'*) by the French national institute of statistics (INSEE), the statistical service of the French ministry of labour (DARES), and the French centre for employment studies (CEE), conducted in 2006, focused on international expansion and sourcing by manufacturing firms.[4] Finally, the survey of the competitiveness of French enterprises (*'enquête sur la compétitivité de "l'entreprise France" et des entreprises françaises'*), administered jointly by INSEE and the French committee of foreign trade advisers (CNCCEF) in 2008, was aimed at gathering business leaders' views on globalization and French firms' competitiveness. It focused on the manufacturing sector.[5]

In comparison, the survey described in this chapter is innovative in many aspects. The questionnaire was designed at European level (IS-GVC survey), although its French implementation (CAM survey) included additional questions. It was administered by INSEE and was compulsory for the sampled firms; the number of non-responses was

---

[2] 'L'industrie en France et la mondialisation', SESSI (*Service des études et des statistiques industrielles*), Collection Analyse et chiffres clés, (257), 2005.

[3] La sous-traitance internationale: l'Europe, partenaire privilégié, SESSI, Collection Le 4 pages des statistiques industrielles, (205), 2005.

[4] 'Les implantations à l'étranger des entreprises industrielles françaises: entre délocalisations et conquête de nouveaux marchés', SESSI, Collection Le 4 pages des statistiques industrielles, (246), 2008.

[5] Bardaji J. and Scherrer P., Mondialisation et compétitivité des entreprise françaises: l'opinion des chefs d'entreprise de l'industrie, Insee Première, (1188), 2008.

small. It was aimed at uncovering the strategic choices made by firms regarding the 'make or buy' choice: either performing the activities themselves inside the firm, or sourcing in France or abroad. The survey questions were careful and precise and the definition of terms was clearly explained and exemplified to the surveyed firms.

The survey defines the 'sourcing of an activity in France' as total or partial transfer of this activity to another firm located in France (which may or may not be within the boundaries of the original firm's group). 'Offshoring of an activity' or 'international sourcing of an activity' was defined as total or partial transfer of this activity to another firm located abroad (which may or may not be part of the original firm's group).

'Firm subsidiaries' are defined as all firms directly or indirectly controlled (more than half of the shareholder voting power or more than 50% of the shares) by the firm. A 'group' is defined in the survey as the set of firms, located in France or abroad, controlled directly or indirectly by a common parent firm, or 'group head'. Prior to being sourced internationally, the activity could have been carried out within the firm or have been sourced to another firm located in France.[6]

Importantly, for the purposes of this survey, offshoring of the activity must have resulted in a *reduction* in the same activity in France. For example, setting up a new production line abroad not accompanied by a corresponding reduction in production in France is not considered offshoring. This definition could indeed be questioned on analytical grounds. Although defining international sourcing as a substitute to domestic production is restrictive enough to avoid misinterpretation of the questions by respondents, it neglects more complex strategies where outsourcing and domestic activity are complements. One mechanism consistent with such complementarity is the productivity gain described in Grossman and Rossi-Hansberg (2008).

The survey was carried out by INSEE between June and October 2012 within the framework of a European project to improve knowledge of firms' internationalization strategies. It covers the period from January 2009 to December 2011 and looks at non-financial firms with fifty or more employees at the end of 2008, whose sector of activity corresponds to sections B to N (excluding section K) of the NACE Rev. 2 classification. The surveyed entity is the statistical unit as per the legal definition of a firm ('legal unit' identified by its administrative identifier, the 'SIREN' number), and not the statistical unit used in the French Law on the Modernization of the Economy. To take into

---

[6] Thus, it is a fairly broad definition: if a firm is the ordering party and hands over to a subcontractor abroad an activity that until then had been carried out by a subcontractor located in France, the survey considers this activity to be offshored.

account that some issues about global value chains pertain more to groups than legal units, the questionnaire includes several questions linked to the group organization of the surveyed entity. Similarly, using US firm-level data, Harrison and McMillan (2011) oppose offshoring to low-wage countries, which substitutes for domestic employment, to more complex strategies with tasks differing at home and abroad. In the latter case, foreign and domestic employment are complements, not substitutes. The restrictive definition used in the survey must accordingly be kept in mind when interpreting our quantification exercise: the measure of job losses that we provide must be considered as indicative, as it excludes by assumption all offshoring activity that could be complementary with domestic activity.

The survey is subdivided by activity. Central to this study is the distinction between core business activity and support business activities. Core business activity represents the production of goods or services destined for markets or third parties, carried out by the firm and generating a turnover. This is usually the firm's main activity. It may also include secondary activities if the firm considers that they constitute part of its essential functions. Support business activities are those activities carried out by the firm to allow or facilitate the production of goods or services for the market or for third parties. The output of support activities is not destined directly for the market or for third parties.

The survey considers a value chain split into support functions in six segments beyond the core business of the surveyed firm:

- Distribution and logistics consists of transportation activities, warehousing, and order processing functions.
- Marketing, sales, and after sales services including help desks and call centres. This consists of market research, advertising, direct marketing services (telemarketing), exhibitions, fairs, and other marketing or sales services including call-centre services and after sales services such as help desks and other customer support services.
- ICT services include IT services and telecommunication. IT services consist of hardware and software consultancy, customized software data processing and database services, maintenance and repair, web-hosting, other computer related and information services, but exclude packaged software and hardware.
- Administrative and management functions include legal services, accounting, book-keeping and auditing, business management and

consultancy, human resources management (e.g. training and education, staff recruitment, provision of temporary personnel, payroll management, health and medical services), corporate financial and insurance services, and also procurement functions.

- Research and development, engineering, and related technical services include R&D, intramural research and experimental development, engineering, and related technical consultancy, technical testing, analysis, certification, and also design services.
- Other support functions are all other functions including manufacturing as a secondary activity for services enterprises.

The survey also defines a world economy split into twelve regions:

- France;
- EU15 but excluding France: Belgium, Denmark, Germany, Greece, Spain, Ireland, Italy, Luxembourg, Netherlands, Austria, Portugal, Finland, Sweden, and the United Kingdom;
- EU12: the Czech Republic, Estonia, Cyprus, Latvia, Lithuania, Hungary, Malta, Poland, Slovenia, Slovak Republic, Bulgaria and Romania;
- Russia;
- other European countries: Switzerland, Norway, Turkey, Belarus, Ukraine, and the Balkan states;
- China;
- India;
- Oceania and other Asian countries: Japan, Korea, Near-, Middle- and Far-East, and Oceania (including Australia and New Zealand);
- USA and Canada;
- Brazil;
- other American countries;
- Africa.

The universe of legal units comprising the survey population is created with 'SIRENE', the French business register. The legal units considered:

- are located in France (mainland and French overseas departments);
- have a number of employees (at the end of the year 2008) greater than or equal to fifty;
- have a main activity from section B to section N (excluding section K) in NACE Rev. 2.

After out-scope correction, the survey population includes 28,370 legal units.

This population was stratified combining two criteria:

- the activity at a detailed level (seventy-one headings). These categories are defined to maximize the estimated accuracy of results, particularly for the six analytical breakdowns requested by Eurostat;
- the number of employees at the end of the year 2008 (three categories: 50–99 employees, 100–249 employees, 250 employees and more).

This stratification created 213 strata.

All legal units with 250 or more employees were surveyed (seventy-one strata and about 5,000 units). In the remaining 142 strata and 23,000 units, the number of legal units included in the sample is proportional to the total number of employees in each stratum. The results of the algorithm were slightly modified based on expert judgement:

- if a stratum sample size is less than six, the number is increased to six in order to have a minimum quality of results even in small strata;
- the sampling rate was slightly decreased in the trade sector.

Sample selection in these 142 strata was achieved by applying the algorithm of 'systematic selection' while taking care to respect the proportion of the following categories of legal units in each stratum:

- legal unit not in group;
- affiliate of an entirely French group (French parent with no foreign affiliate);
- parent of an entirely French group (French parent with no foreign affiliate);
- parent of an international group;
- legal unit with foreign affiliates in a French group;
- legal unit with foreign affiliates in a group with foreign parent;
- legal unit without foreign affiliates in a French group;
- legal unit without foreign affiliates in a group with a foreign parent.

The final sample size is 8,093 legal units. The survey was compulsory (validated as part of the public statistics) and had 6,428 respondents.

For convenience, we use 'firm' instead of 'legal unit' in the rest of the chapter.

6.3 How Many Jobs?

This new survey helps to shed light on the overall impact of offshoring strategies in terms of jobs displacement. Recall, however, the restrictive nature of the definition used for offshoring—substitution between domestic and offshored activities.

The econometric literature addressing the impact of offshoring on employment uses aggregate branch or sector level data. The share of the manufacturing sector in total employment is regressed on a series of controls and on the intensity of trade (imports over GDP) with low wage countries hosting offshoring. This method was proposed by Rowthorn and Ramaswamy (1998) and has been applied to France for different periods (Boulhol and Fontagné 2006; Demmou 2010). A second approach is an accounting method that uses input–output tables to compute the labour content of the changes in net trade. Barlet, Blanchet, and Crusson (2009) and Demmou (2010) implement it for France and for different periods. Finally, individual firm data can be used. Aubert and Sillard (2005) match customs data with social and taxation declarations. They define offshoring accurately as two simultaneous events in a group: a significant drop in the workforce in one establishment of the group, and a surge of importations of products corresponding to the main output of this establishment. Hijzen, Jean, and Mayer (2011) use matching techniques to assess the impact of a first investment abroad. They distinguish between horizontal and vertical investments by firms belonging to advantaged or disadvantaged sectors. While obtaining quite contrasting results in terms of impact on the labour market, most of these studies point to limited losses related to offshoring. These approaches have several shortcomings. It is difficult to disentangle pure offshoring from imports generally when applying an econometric or accounting approach. Neither of these methods accounts for general equilibrium effects. The method for defining a proper counterfactual is subject to the quality of firm matching and relies on a simple split between horizontal and vertical investment strategies.

The advantage of our approach based on a survey is to define offshoring precisely (although restrictively) and to observe directly what are the firm's *perceived* motivations for and obstacles to this activity. Also, collecting information on firms that decided not to offshore provides an interesting counterfactual.

Table 6.1 provides preliminary evidence, comparing changes in employment, in France, in firms that offshored or not. Employment in firms that considered, but did not offshore—a category that is

Table 6.1 Evolution of firm employment, according to the offshoring status, as a percentage of number of employees in firms

	Firms reporting			
	Increase	Stability	Decrease	Total
All firms	42	25	33	100
Of which:				
Firms having offshored	*32*	*9*	*59*	*100*
Firms having considered offshoring but eventually did not	*75*	*9*	*16*	*100*
Firms having not offshored and not considerer offshoring	*40*	*27*	*33*	*100*

Note: the scope is non-financial firms with fifty or more employees (at end 2008) located in France, whose sector falls within sections B to N (excluding section K) of the NACE Rev. 2.

Source: INSEE Survey, Chaînes d'Activité Mondiales.

difficult to identify in econometric exercises based on administrative data—increased the most. This contrasts with employment in the French branch of firms that offshored, which often show decreased employment. The conclusion, though rather qualitative, is that offshoring of tasks is not only about the nature of jobs maintained in the origin country, but also about the number of jobs. Firms that find alternative reorganizations to offshoring tend to show (or to claim) better employment performance. These two results should be examined in future research.

We can tentatively measure the magnitude of job displacement induced by the decision to offshore, assuming that the overall employment performance of offshoring firms is reduced by this decision. Note that we do not know the exact counterfactual, although we got information on firms deciding not to offshore: what would have been the evolution of employment in France in those firms offshoring, if they had decided against it. Comparing offshoring and not offshoring firms is not a good way to properly answer this question.

With this caveat in mind, we turn to the survey. The *CAM survey* includes two questions whose responses provide a rough estimate of jobs directly lost in France due to the offshoring decision. Based on these responses, we estimate that about 20,000 jobs were shed in France between 2009 and 2011 as a direct result of offshoring by non-financial firms in the industry, trade, and services sector with fifty or more employees, or about 6,600 jobs per year over the three years. These 20,000 jobs lost represent 0.3 per cent of salaried employment in 2011 in all the firms within the scope of the survey and 4 per cent of jobs in firms that sourced internationally. Two-thirds of the jobs shed concerned core business functions in the offshoring firms. In the manufacturing industry, 11,500 jobs appear to have been shed as a result of offshoring between 2009 and 2011, or 0.6 per cent of salaried employment in all firms in the manufacturing industry included in the survey.

These figures, which reflect the microeconomic impact of offshoring in terms of employment, should however be interpreted with much care for the following reasons. (i) In the survey, job losses are counted only for firms that transferred at least part of one activity from France to abroad: we already stressed the drawbacks of such a restrictive definition assuming substitutability between activities abroad and at home, in contrast with more nuanced findings of the economic literature on global value chains. (ii) Job losses are declarative figures and only take account of direct shedding of jobs without considering those lost in the firm's subcontractors or, conversely, jobs that might be created in France as a result of the same type of movement from abroad. (iii) Situations where a firm offshores an activity, but develops another activity in parallel in France are considered only in terms of the negative side of jobs displaced abroad. (iv) Finally, we need also to consider how the job situation would have changed had the offshoring not taken place.

Although the order of magnitude obtained is in line with previous studies addressing the impact of offshoring on employment in the French case (Aubert and Sillard 2005; Boulhol and Fontagné 2006; Demmou 2010; Hijzen, Jean, and Mayer 2011), the most comparable study, which is based on microeconomic evidence, is Aubert and Sillard (2005). Considering the group level and focusing on the manufacturing industry, they define offshoring as two simultaneous events in a group: a significant drop in the workforce in one establishment of the group and a surge of importations of products corresponding to the main output of this establishment from a foreign subsidiary of the group. In Aubert and Sillard's (2005) paper as well, offshoring is considered as a substitution of activity. They estimate job losses in the manufacturing industry due to offshoring at between 9,000 and 20,000 per year (versus almost 4,000 per year according to the CAM survey), but this might include a large proportion of jobs shed by subcontractors (that are part of the group). Also, Aubert and Sillard's study covers the period 1995–2001, which corresponds to a period of massive expansion in China and the emerging countries in central and eastern Europe, whereas 2009–2011 was a period of crisis during which firms expanded abroad much less.

Notwithstanding the intrinsic limitations of this rough quantification exercise, the advantage is to provide an indication on the magnitude of the phenomenon at stake which can be compared with alternative methods. Let us now characterize offshoring firms and related strategies.

6.4 Large and More Productive Firms Offshore More

In 2012 there were 28,370 non-financial firms with at least fifty employees at the end of 2008, located in France.

According to the CAM survey, 4.2 per cent of these firms offshored some or all of their activities in the course of the three years from 2009 to 2011 (Table 6.2). Almost as many (3.1%) considered offshoring, although did not actually do it. Finally 7.3 per cent of firms sourced part of their activities to another firm located in France.

Sourcing in general and offshoring in particular, are strategies pursued by larger firms. Table 6.3 considers employment as a proxy for size, it shows the impact of sourcing: 13.6 per cent of employment is in firms that sourced at least one activity in France in the period 2009–2011, and 6.4 per cent is in firms that sourced internationally.

Fourteen smaller European countries administered the survey in 2012. European scope is limited to non-financial sector firms with 100 or more employees (at end 2008), as opposed to fifty or more employees for France. After adjusting for this different threshold, Table 6.4 shows that 5.9 per cent of non-financial firms located in France with 100 or more employees, sourced at least one activity internationally (totally

Table 6.2 Firms with fifty or more employees that sourced in France or off-shored activities, over the period 2009–2011, as a percentage of the number of firms

Business function	Offshoring	Sourcing in France
At least 1 activity	**4.2**	**7.3**
Core business	2.7	3.0
At least 1 support, of which:	2.1	5.7
Administrative and management functions	*0.9*	*1.8*
ICT services	*0.7*	*2.8*
Marketing, sales services and after sales services, incl. help desks and call centres	*0.5*	*1.2*
Distribution and logistics	*0.4*	*2.9*
R&D, engineering, and related technical services	*0.4*	*1.0*
Other support functions	*0.4*	*1.4*

Note: the scope is non-financial firms with fifty or more employees (at end 2008) located in France, whose sector falls within sections B to N (excluding section K) of the NACE Rev. 2.

Source: INSEE Survey, Chaînes d'Activité Mondiales.

Table 6.3 Firms with fifty or more employees that sourced in France or off-shored activities over the period 2009–2011, as a percentage of the number of employees in firms

Business function	Sourcing in France	Offshoring
At least 1 activity	**13.6**	**6.4**
Core business	3.8	4.1
At least 1 support activity, of which:	12.2	3.8
Administrative and management functions	*5.8*	*2.1*
ICT services	*7.3*	*1.9*
Marketing, sales services and after sales services, incl. help desks and call centres	*4.8*	*1.0*
Distribution and logistics	*6.9*	*0.5*
R&D, engineering, and related technical services	*1.2*	*0.5*
Other support functions	*3.1*	*0.7*

Note: the scope is non-financial firms with fifty or more employees (at end 2008) located in France, whose sector falls within sections B to N (excluding section K) of the NACE Rev. 2.

Source: INSEE Survey, Chaînes d'Activité Mondiales.

Table 6.4 European countries (that carried out the survey) firms with 100 or more employees that offshored activities between 2009 and 2011, as a percentage of the number of firms

	Non-financial sector	Industry
Denmark	25.2	33.6
Finland	20.6	28.7
Belgium	15.9	23.5
Portugal	15.3	18.2
Sweden	13.2	17.4
Norway	12.0	18.0
Ireland	11.8	15.8
Slovakia	11.0	10.1
Netherlands	9.8	15.8
Estonia	8.7	14.7
Latvia	6.8	8.2
France	5.9	10.5
Romania	3.3	3.4
Bulgaria	1.1	1.4
Lithuania	0.7	0.0

Note: the European scope is non-financial firms with 100 or more employees (at end 2008), whose sector falls within sections B to N (excluding section K) of the NACE Rev. 2. Industry refers to Sections B to E of NACE Rev. 2.

Source: Eurostat, Statistics explained 'International sourcing of business functions', summer 2013, http://ec.europa.eu/eurostat/statistics-explained/ index.php/International_ sourcing_of_business_functions

or partially), and for the industry sector this figure is 10.5 per cent. The large proportions of firms that offshore observed for some countries (notably Denmark and Belgium) can be explained in part by country size. Indeed, for firms located in smaller European countries, geography and the limited variety of potential domestic contractors are strong determinants of offshoring.

We are also interested in characterizing the sectors of firms located in France that offshored some activities at least partially over the period 2009–2011 (Table 6.5).

The manufacturing industry and information and communication services are the two broad sectors where offshoring is most frequent—8.8 per cent of firms in each category. This is explained by the tradability of many of the tasks in these sectors. Between 2009 and 2011, employment in firms offshoring new activities represented 13.6 per cent and 19.2 per cent respectively of all employees in manufacturing and information communication services firms with fifty or more employees.

Within manufacturing, production of electrical equipment (25% of firms declared offshoring of new activities) and computers, electronic, and optical products (respectively 22% of firms) were the most important. In the information and communication services sector, services linked to computer activities mainly offshored (11%) compared to the

Table 6.5 Share of firms that offshored activities during the period 2009–2011, according to different criteria (%)

Multinational status	
Companies belonging to a group and controlling subsidiaries abroad in 2009	12.7
Companies belonging to a group and controlling no subsidiary abroad in 2009	4.3
Exporter status	
Exporting companies in 2009	7.7
Non-exporting companies in 2009	0.7
Firm size	
Workforce of 250 or more at end 2008	7.6
Workforce of 100–249 at end 2008	4.9
Workforce of 50–99 at end 2008	2.7
Sector	
Manufacturing industry	8.8
Information and communication services	8.8
Specialized scientific and technical activities	5.5
Other non-financial market sectors	1.5

Note: the scope is non-financial firms with fifty or more employees (at end 2008) located in France, whose sector falls within sections B to N (excluding section K) of the NACE Rev. 2.
Source: INSEE Survey, Chaînes d'Activité Mondiales.

construction, transport, hotel, catering, and real estate sectors which offshored very little between 2009 and 2011 (less than 1% of the firms).

Offshoring firms are different; more productive firms not only export and invest abroad, but also optimize their value chain on a global basis. Between 2009 and 2011, the larger a firm's employment, the more likely it was to offshore parts of its activity: 5.9 per cent of firms with 100 or more employees (at end 2008) compared with 2.7 per cent of firms with 50–99 employees. For firms with 250 or more employees, the percentage was 7.6 per cent, and 10 per cent for firms with over 5,000 employees. Similarly, many more exporting (7.7%) than domestic-only firms (0.7%) offshored. Also, the proportion of firms that offshore is increasing with the share of exports in their turnover. Finally, for a given sector, size, and firm type (type meaning whether or not the firm is part of a group, is French or foreign, and controls or does not control subsidiaries abroad), exporting firms offshored on average four times more often than non-exporting firms. These results are in line with what is expected among heterogeneous firms where only the most efficient are able to cope with the fixed and variable costs of exporting (Melitz 2003), and where only the most efficient overcome the higher costs of investing abroad (Helpman, Melitz, and Yeaple 2004).

Not all firms are independent. Ownership is used to trace the boundaries of groups of French firms controlled by a common parent (French or not). Firms belonging to a group in 2009 offshored more than independent firms (5.2% against 1.6%). Among international groups, the strategy increases: 12.7 per cent of firms already present abroad in 2009 through subsidiaries, offshored between 2009 and 2011. This share is 20.8 per cent for firms already present abroad in 2009 through subsidiaries and having a foreign parent. Table 6.6 presents the intensity of offshoring as a function of firm size. Size classes are defined as class 1 50–99 employees, class 2 100–249, and class 3 over 250 employees. We observe that 6 per cent of firms in the lowest size class in manufacturing offshored at least one activity compared to 13.5 per cent in highest size class. For business support functions, this positive relation between size and offshoring intensity is particularly evident for IT services and administration and management. Manufacturing industries are the most heavily engaged in offshoring.

From this we can conclude that firms that offshore are not only bigger and more productive, they are also members of international groups. Large multinational corporations optimize their value chains at the global level, and what we observe in a national level survey is part of an ongoing global reorganization.

Table 6.6 Share of firms that offshored activities during the period 2009–2011, by activity sourced, sector, and size (%)

	All sectors			Manuf. industry			Other non fin. sectors		
Size class	1	2	3	1	2	3	1	2	3
Offshoring at least 1 activity	**2.7**	**4.9**	**7.6**	**6**	**9.7**	**13.5**	**1.6**	**2.9**	**4.7**
Offshoring core business activity	1.6	3.4	4.6	5.3	8.6	9.6	0.4	1.2	2.1
Offshoring at least 1 support activity, of which:	1.3	2.2	4.5	1.1	2.4	6.6	1.3	2.2	3.4
Computer services and telecommunications	*0.3*	*0.7*	*1.9*	*n.s.*	*n.s.*	*2.1*	*n.s.*	*0.8*	*1.7*
Administration and management	*0.4*	*1.1*	*2.4*	*n.s.*	*1.1*	*3.4*	*0.4*	*1.1*	*1.8*
Design, R&D, engineering, and technical services	*0.2*	*0.5*	*1*	*n.s.*	*n.s.*	*1.6*	*n.s.*	*0.5*	*0.6*

Note: the scope of the survey is non-financial firms with fifty or more employees (at end 2008) located in France, whose sector falls within sections B to N (excluding section K) of the NACE Rev. 2. Size classes are defined as [50–99], [100–249], and 250+ employees for class 1, 2, and 3 respectively. n.s: not significant due to limited number of units in the considered cell.

Source: INSEE Survey, Chaînes d'Activité Mondiales.

6.5 Firms May Decide *Not* to Offshore

The majority of offshoring is within the EU, reflecting the costs related to distance even for service activities (Head, Mayer, and Ries 2009; Fort 2013). Splitting the results by firm size shows that larger firms source to more remote places, where the enforcement of contracts can be more difficult. While 42 per cent of offshoring firms with more than 100 employees have offshored to at least two regions, only 23 per cent of firms with 50–99 employees have done so. In the presence of incomplete contracts, only the largest and most efficient firms will benefit from offshoring (Antras and Helpman 2004). Defever and Toubal (2013) using the *Enquête Mondialisation* referred to in Section 6.2, provide similar evidence.

Some firms contemplated offshoring, but eventually decided against it. An important value added of the CAM survey is that it allows us to identify these cases and the related perceived obstacles. The 3.1 per cent of firms that considered offshoring, but did not do so, represent 6 per cent of employment in the survey. The majority of these firms cited uncertainty about the quality of goods and services produced in the offshore location as the main obstacle, and also the need for close

Table 6.7 Barriers indicated as important or very important by firms that considered offshoring during the period 2009–2011, but decided against it, as a percentage of the number of firms that considered offshoring but decided not to offshore

Uncertainty of the quality to be supplied abroad	57
Proximity to existing clients needed	55
Legal or administrative barriers	48
Concerns of the employees and the trade unions	48
Lack of management resources and know-how	40
Tariffs and other trade barriers	39
Taxation issues	37
Difficulties in identifying potential/suitable providers	34
Linguistic or cultural barriers	31
Chance of patent violation or non-respect of IP	27
Access to finance or other financial constraints	25
Political or economic instability	22

Note: the table is based on non-financial firms with fifty or more employees (at end 2008) located in France, that considered offshoring but eventually decided against it, and whose sectors fall within sections B to N (excluding section K) of the NACE Rev. 2.

Source: INSEE Survey, Chaînes d'Activité Mondiales.

interaction with clients (Table 6.7). Legal and administrative barriers in the host country and union problems in the home country were also reasons for not offshoring. Interestingly, political and economic instability were the least mentioned barrier. For instance, 57 per cent of the firms that considered offshoring during the period 2009–2011, but eventually decided not to do so, referred to uncertainty about the quality of the products/services to be supplied abroad as a determinant of their decision. Proximity to existing clients and legal and administrative barriers were mentioned by 55 per cent and 48 per cent of firms respectively. When firms are making decisions about organizing their activities on an international basis, they are sensitive about just-in-time issues, possible interruptions to value chains due to deficient suppliers, and the quality of the contractual relations.

Interestingly, the obstacles faced by firms deciding to offshore differ across destination regions. We report these obstacles in Table 6.8, in which only firms who offshored in one region are counted. Uncertainty about the quality to be supplied abroad is the prominent concern for firms that offshored in China: 78 per cent of the firms that offshored in China mentioned this problem. In contrast only 15 per cent of the firms that offshored in the EU15 were concerned by potential quality issues. The next big problem faced in China is the difficulty in identifying potential or suitable providers of services. This is reported as a concern by 64 per cent of the firms offshoring in this country. The third main concern in China is about tariffs and non-tariff measures (resp. 52%).

Table 6.8 Barriers indicated as important or very important by offshoring firms
that offshored to only one region during the period 2009–2011 (for each region,
as a percentage of firms having offshored only in this region)

	EU15	new Member States	Africa	China	India
Uncertainty of the quality to be supplied abroad	15	46	58	78	68
Proximity to existing clients needed	27	29	48	44	36
Legal or administrative barriers	26	33	52	31	34
Concerns of the employees and the trade unions	55	41	44	47	27
Lack of management resources and know-how	13	21	52	40	37
Tariffs and other trade barriers	11	38	30	52	n.s.
Taxation issues	20	32	28	23	n.s.
Difficulties in identifying potential/suitable providers	11	25	24	64	n.s.
Linguistic or cultural barriers	30	35	38	47	43
Chance of patent violation or non respect of IP	12	16	n.s.	35	n.s.
Access to finance or other financial constraints	9	36	20	20	n.s.
Political or economic instability	n.s.	18	50	15	n.s.

Note 1: the table is based on non-financial firms with fifty or more employees (at end 2008) located in
France, that offshored at least one activity, and whose sectors fall within sections B to N (excluding section
K) of the NACE Rev. 2.
Note 2: n.s.: not significant.
Source: INSEE Survey, Chaînes d'Activité Mondiales.

Finally, linguistic or cultural barriers, concerns of the employees and
of trade unions in the home country, as well as a need for proximity
to existing clients were faced by more than 44 per cent of the firms
offshoring in China. This contrasts with the obstacles reported by
firms offshoring in India: although uncertainty about the quality to
be supplied is mentioned by more than two out of three firms, other
obstacles are less binding. The limited number of cases of offshoring
in India and the sectoral concentration unfortunately lead to several
non-significant figures. In Africa, legal and administrative barriers,
combined with a lack of management resources or uncertainty about
quality are considered to be a big obstacle by firms offshoring on this
continent. This is also the only region in the world where political
or economic instability is considered to be an important risk factor
(mentioned by half of the firms offshoring in Africa). Obstacles faced by
firms offshoring in new EU Member States are primarily the uncertainty

about the quality to be supplied locally, as well as the concerns of the labour trade unions in the home country. Finally, concerns of the labour unions play the biggest role when offshoring in the other fifteen countries. The latter concern of French firms points to the limited social acceptability of activity restructuring among rather similar countries.

6.6 Offshoring Strategies are Mostly Regional

European enlargement has provided French firms with a range of possible offshoring locations that are relatively nearby, offer stable legal environments, have no tariff barriers and, in certain cases, have attractive taxation schemes. This has led to the recent preference among offshoring firms located in France for new Member States.

A first glance at offshoring strategies is provided in Table 6.9. Percentages relate to the number of firms offshoring. The table presents the main host areas (in relation to potentially affected employment in the

Table 6.9 Main host areas for offshored activities during the period 2009–2011, as a percentage of the number of offshoring firms

	Firms offshoring	As a % of the number of firms offshoring					
		EU27	of which EU15	12 new MS	Africa	China	India
At least 1 activity	4.2	55	38	22	24	18	18
Core business	2.7	44	28	19	27	26	12
At least 1 support	2.1	65	48	24	16	9	26
activity, of which:							
Logistics and transport	0.4	69	53	17	2	21	15
Marketing, after sales, and call centres	0.5	52	42	16	44	6	13
Computer services and telecommunications	0.7	66	49	21	6	3	24
Administration and management	0.9	80	47	34	8	3	20
Design, R&D, engineering, and technical services	0.4	67	53	14	6	5	30

Note 1: for each activity, the percentages sum to more than 100 per cent because the firm may have offshored several activities to different geographical areas over this period.
Note 2: the scope is non-financial firms with fifty or more employees (at end 2008) located in France, whose sector falls within sections B to N (excluding section K) of the NACE Rev. 2.
Source: INSEE Survey, Chaînes d'Activité Mondiales.

originating country—France) for offshored activities during the period 2009–2011, for firms who offshored, at least partially, one function. We observe that 4.2 per cent of non-financial companies with fifty or more employees sourced internationally (totally or partially) at least one activity, and that 55 per cent of these companies sourced internationally at least in other countries of the EU. Within the EU, EU15 destinations are chosen for all offshored activities, although predominantly for logistics and transport and design and R&D. New Member States host predominantly offshored administrative and management activities. Africa specializes in marketing services and call centres. Interestingly, the percentages observed for R&D in India and core business activities in China, show that firms are prepared to offshore strategic activities even in countries where obstacles to offshoring are present, as referred to in Section 6.5.

Since large firms offshore more often and to more 'difficult' destinations, we now focus on the *share of employment* of firms that decided to offshore in the period 2009–2011 (instead of the share of firms). This approach in terms of employment is indeed a better metric, as it takes account of the larger size of offshoring firms. Table 6.10 presents information on firms' location decisions. Percentages are number of employees in offshoring firms. The Table presents again the main host areas for offshored activities during the period 2009–2011, for firms which offshored, at least partially, one function. For instance, firms that offshored at least part of their core business function to Africa between 2009 and 2011 represent 39 per cent of employment among firms that offshored at least part of their core business function. Firms that offshored at least part of a function to Europe between 2009 and 2011 represent 60 per cent of employment of firms that offshored at least part of one function: 38 per cent to the EU15 Member States and 31 per cent to the new Member States, with some firms sourcing certain activities to several countries. Africa is a favoured host country (31%), due to its geographic (and for certain countries linguistic) proximity to France, especially North Africa. The distant location of China (18%) and India (38%) and less favourable business environments are offset by the variety of local suppliers, low labour costs, and host market size. While the EU is the preferred destination for French firms' offshoring of support activities, 45 per cent of employment of firms that offshored at least one support activity is in firms that moved this activity to India (especially computer or telecommunications services). Offshoring of support activities to Africa is mainly related to call centres used for marketing and after sales service. Language is an important asset for these locations.

Table 6.10 Main host areas for offshored activities during the period 2009–2011, as a percentage of the number of employees in offshoring firms

	Firms offshoring (†)	As a % of the number of employees in firms offshoring						
		EU27 of which:	EU15	12 new MS	RoW of which:	Africa	China	India
At least 1 activity	6.4	60	38	31	75	31	18	38
Core business	4.1	49	26	29	77	39	21	32
At least 1 support activity, of which:	3.8	71	44	36	69	25	12	45
Logistics and transport	0.5	71	54	22	49	13	23	16
marketing, after sales, and call centres	1.0	52	27	31	84	45	11	29
Computer services and telecommunications	1.9	56	32	30	64	24	8	50
Administration and management	2.1	81	36	47	62	3	5	44
Design, R&D, engineering, and techn. serv.	0.5	68	54	14	67	12	8	35

(†) Offshoring firms, as a percentage number of employees of firms in the scope

Note 1: for each activity, the percentages sum to more than 100% because the firm may have offshored several activities to different geographical areas over this period.

Note 2: the scope is non-financial firms with fifty or more employees (at end 2008) located in France, whose sector falls within sections B to N (excluding section K) of the NACE Rev. 2.

Source: INSEE Survey, Chaînes d'Activité Mondiales.

Table 6.10 finally compares EU27 and other offshoring destinations. We observe that firms that offshored logistics to EU27 destinations between 2009 and 2011 represent 71 per cent of the employment of offshoring firms, and this contrasts with firms that offshore logistics to non-EU countries (only 49%). Thus, the EU is a favoured destination for logistics and administration activity, while non-EU destinations prevail for marketing services and computer services.

Table 6.11 presents the distribution of the main host areas of off-shored activities for the manufacturing sector only. This restriction explains that 6.4 per cent of employment is in firms offshoring one activity, as opposed to 13.6 per cent in the manufacturing sector. We list the main host areas for the offshored activities during the period 2009–2011 and gauge the importance of alternative destinations in terms of employment in offshoring firms, focusing on the manufacturing industry. For instance, firms in the manufacturing sector that offshored at least part of their administrative and management support functions

Table 6.11 Manufacturing sector: main host areas of offshored activities during the period 2009–2011, as a percentage of the number of employees in offshoring firms

	Firms offshoring (†)	As a % of the number of employees in firms offshoring						
		EU27 of which: *EU15*	*12 new MS*	RoW of which:	*Africa*	*China*	*India*
At least 1 activity	**13.6**	**64**	**40**	**33**	**72**	**23**	**25**	**29**
Core business	9.6	55	28	33	73	31	28	19
At least 1 support activity, of which:	6.9	77	47	39	61	5	13	38
Logistics and transport	*0.9*	*80*	*67*	*23*	*51*	*n.s.*	*38*	*n.s.*
marketing, after sales, and call centres	*1.1*	*92*	*39*	*53*	*69*	*n.s.*	*n.s.*	*n.s.*
Computer services and telecommunications	*2.7*	*69*	*39*	*36*	*47*	*n.s.*	*n.s.*	*40*
Administration and and management	*3.9*	*84*	*35*	*49*	*55*	*3*	*3*	*39*
Design, R&D, engineering, and techn. serv.	*1.1*	*60*	*37*	*24*	*65*	*14*	*7*	*36*

(†) Offshoring firms, as a percentage number of employees of firms in the scope
Note 1: for each activity, the percentages sum to more than 100% because the firm may have offshored several activities to different geographical areas over this period.
Note 2: the scope is restricted to manufacturing firms with fifty or more employees (at end 2008) located in France.
Source: INSEE Survey, Chaînes d'Activité Mondiales.

to the EU15 Member States between 2009 and 2011, represent 84 per cent of employment in those firms that offshored administrative and management support functions. Most of the offshored activities are related to the firms' core business functions, that is, the production of goods, and the main destination for offshoring these functions is the EU (mostly new Member States). Africa is an important destination for offshoring of core business activities from manufacturing firms, achieving similar levels to China. This shows that French-located firms consider Africa a feasible destination for production activities, which is in line with the regionalization of global value chains.

The treatment of the European surveys by Eurostat (in terms of number of firms rather of number of employees), albeit for very different origin countries of offshoring firms, confirms the importance of Europe-wide value chains, but does not support the French finding regarding Africa since it does not make this distinction (Table 6.12).

Table 6.12 Number of offshoring firms (100 employees or more) located in one of the fifteen countries which carried out the survey, by main offshoring destination

Offshoring region	EU surveys (1)	French survey (2)
EU15	1,590	357
New Member States	1,010	190
India	570	172
China	420	136
Other European countries †	410	97
Oceania and other Asian countries	310	115
USA and Canada	240	57

(1) Number of offshoring firms in the fifteen countries which carried out the survey
(2) Number of offshoring firms located in France
Note: the scope is non-financial firms with 100 or more employees (at end 2008) located in one of the fifteen countries who carried out the survey, whose sector falls within sections B to N (excluding section K) of the NACE Rev. 2.
†: European countries except EU27 and Russia.
Source: EUROSTAT Survey, IS-GVC and INSEE Survey, Chaînes d'Activité Mondiales

6.7 Firms Offshore within the Group

Another important issue is the organizational form of offshoring. Is it within or outside the foreign boundaries of the firm group? Table 6.13 shows the organizational mode for newly offshored activities between 2009 and 2011, by firms that belong to a group (in terms of numbers of firm employees). Column 1 shows the share of employment in firms that offshore: 7 per cent of total employment in these firms that belong to a group is in firms that offshored over the period under consideration. Among this 7 per cent, 82 per cent of employment in firms that decided to offshore (or 5.7% of total employment of firms belonging to a group that offshored or not: $100 \times 0.070 \times 0.82$) is in firms that decided to offshore within the group.

Thus, the fact that firms prefer offshoring within the group suggests there are risks associated with contractual relationships. Firms choose to relocate activity within their group in the vast majority of cases. Firms that offshore core business usually offshore within the group (91% of employment in firms that offshored core business) rather than outside (27%). The percentages sum to over 100 since the firm can make the decision to displace jobs within and beyond the boundaries of the group at the same time. For support functions, the gap is narrower (72% compared to 46%). However, for support activities related to design, R&D, engineering, and technical services, the group is the preferred target for offshoring (94% compared to 15%), which is in line with the literature.

Table 6.13 Organizational mode for newly offshored activities between 2009 and 2011, by firms belonging to a group, as a percentage of the number of employees in the offshoring firms

	Firms belonging to a group offshoring %	For each activity, as a % of the number of employees in firms offshoring					
		Within group of which:	Existing affiliate	M & A	Greenfield	Affiliate of the group	Arm's length
At least 1 activity	7	82	34	3	7	44	38
Core business	4.1	91	40	3	9	47	27
At least 1 support activity, of which:	4.4	72	25	2	4	43	46
Logistics and transport	0.5	68	14	n.s.	n.s.	44	52
Marketing, after sales, and call centres	1.1	72	24	n.s.	n.s.	45	47
Computer services and telecommunications	2.1	63	18	n.s.	n.s.	46	44
Administration and management	2.4	73	20	n.s.	3	50	44
Design, R&D, engineering, and techn. serv.	0.6	94	43	5	n.s.	53	15

Note 1: for each activity, the percentages sum to more than 100% because the firm may have offshored several activities to different geographical areas over this period.

Note 2: the scope is non-financial firms with fifty or more employees (at end 2008) located in France, whose sector falls within sections B to N (excluding section K) of the NACE Rev. 2.

Note 3: n.s.: not significant.

Source: INSEE Survey, Chaînes d'Activité Mondiales.

6.8 Killer Costs, beyond Wages

Having identified the destinations and organizational modalities of offshoring, we next examine its determinants. Table 6.14 presents the reasons for offshoring to the five most favoured host regions. To minimize bias due to possible multi-destination offshoring by firms, we focus on firms that offshored to only one of the eleven (now excluding France) foreign geographical regions defined in the survey. Note that these are the determinants reported by the offshoring firms in the survey. For instance, 98 per cent of firms that offshored only to Africa consider lower labour costs as important or very important in their decision to offshore. However, it is interesting that in Table 6.14 offshoring is driven primarily by cost savings, and is not just related to lower wages. Offshoring to emerging countries such as India and China is often motivated by access to low costs, which may include low wages, and to promising markets. In the case of the new EU Member States, low wage costs can be attractive, but access to these markets is not an important motivation because access is guaranteed by their membership of the EU. In offshoring to the EU15, firms are primarily looking to reduce production costs rather than wages, and their reasons for offshoring are more diverse. Finally, offshoring to Africa is driven mainly by the search for close locations offering low wages for labour-intensive activities. Note that for firms that belong to a group, the decision to offshore often stems from strategies imposed by the parent, irrespective of the area to which the offshoring is directed. This shows the value of distinguishing between legal unit and group or even firm from an economic perspective.

6.9 Conclusion

We have proposed a preliminary treatment of the *International Sourcing and Global Value Chains* (IS-GVC) survey, for France. The *Chaînes d'activité mondiales* survey (CAM) was carried out by INSEE in June to October 2012 within the framework of a European project to improve knowledge of firm internationalization strategies. It covers the period from the beginning of 2009 to the end of 2011 and looks at industry, trade, and non-financial services firms.

We observed that offshoring decisions have been limited with only 4.2 per cent of firms with more than fifty employees in the man-ufacturing and non-financial services sector making the decision to offshore over a three-year period. Interestingly, 3.1 per cent of firms

Table 6.14 Motivations indicated as important or very important by offshoring firms that offshored to only one region during the period 2009–2011 (for each region, as a percentage of firms having offshored only in this region)

	International sourcing to				
	EU15	12 new MS	Africa	China	India
Reduction of labour costs	37	82	98	68	82
Reduction of costs other than labour costs	62	69	50	54	49
Access to new markets	17	31	29	54	46
Lack of qualified labour	n.s.	17	36	n.s.	10
Improved quality or introduction of new products	8	15	n.s.	n.s.	n.s.
Focus on core business	26	25	18	19	35
Access to specialized knowledge/technologies	22	21	n.s.	n.s.	12
Reduced delivery times	19	22	15	24	n.s.
Less regulation affecting the enterprise	16	15	13	n.s.	n.s.
Risk exchange exposure reduction	8	n.s.	n.s.	34	n.s.
Relocation of an ordering party abroad	8	17	17	n.s.	14
Strategic decisions taken by the group head	69	32	42	59	44

Note 1: the scope is non-financial firms with fifty or more employees (at end 2008) located in France, whose sector falls within sections B to N (excluding section K) of the NACE Rev. 2.
Note 2: n.s.: not significant.
Source: INSEE Survey, Chaînes d'Activité Mondiales.

contemplated offshoring but decided against it. Distance remains a major obstacle and more than half of the moves reported were to other European countries, including the twelve Member States added by the most recent EU enlargement. More strategic segments of the value chain are generally offshored within the boundaries of the firm or firm group (foreign affiliates of the firm, joint ventures, or other foreign affiliates of the parent of the firm considered), pointing to potential issues raised by incomplete contracts.

Bibliography

Antras, Pol (2003). Firms, Contracts and Trade Structure, *Quarterly Journal of Economics*, 118(4): 1375–418.

Antras, Pol and Elhanan Helpman (2004). Global Sourcing, *Journal of Political Economy*, 112(3): 552–80.

Antras, Pol and Esteban Rossi-Hansberg (2009). Organizations and Trade, *Annual Review of Economics*, 1: 43–64.

Aubert, Patrick and Patrick Sillard (2005). Délocalisations et réductions d'effectifs dans l'industrie française, in Insee, *L'économie française: comptes et dossiers*, Insee - Référence, Edition 2005–2006: 57–89.

Baldwin, Richard (2012). Global Supply Chains: Why They Emerged, Why They Matter, and Where They are Going, CEPR discussion papers 9103.

Barlet, Muriel, Didier Blanchet and Laure Crusson (2009). Globalisation et flux d'emplois que peut-on dire d'une approche comptable? *Économie et Statistique*, (427–428): 3–20.

Boulhol, Hervé and Lionel Fontagné (2006). Deindustrialisation and the Fear of Relocations in the Industry, CEPII working paper, 2006-07.

Bryan, Jon L. (2013). Offshore Outsourcing: Will the Robust Growth Continue? *mimeo*, Bridgewater State University.

Costinot, Arnaud, Jonathan Vogel and Su Wang (2013). An Elementary Theory of Global Supply Chains, *Review of Economic Studies*, (80): 109–44.

Defever, Patrice and Farid Toubal (2013). Productivity, Relationship-Specific Inputs and the Sourcing Modes of Multinationals, *Journal of Economic Behavior & Organization*, 94(C): 345–57.

Demmou, Lilas (2010). Le recul de l'emploi industriel en France entre 1980 et 2007. Ampleur et principaux déterminants: un état des lieux, *Économie et Statistique*, (438–40): 273–96.

Dixit, Avinash K. and Gene M. Grossman (1982). Trade and Protection with Multistage Production, *Review of Economic Studies*, 49: 583–94.

Feenstra, Robert C. and Gordon Hanson (1999). The Impact of Outsourcing and High-Technology Capital on Wages: Estimates for the United-States, 1979–1990, *The Quarterly Journal of Economics*, 114(3): 907–40.

Fort, Teresa C. (2013). Breaking up is Hard to Do: Why Firms Fragment Production across Locations, working paper, Tuck School of Business, 1, 3.

Grossman, Gene M. and Esteban Rossi-Hansberg (2008). Trading Tasks: A Simple Theory of Offshoring, *American Economic Review*, 98(5): 1978–97.

Harrison, Ann and Margaret McMillan (2011). Offshoring Jobs? Multinational and U.S. Manufacturing Employment, *Review of Economics and Statistics*, 93(3): 857–75.

Head, Keith, Thierry Mayer, and John Ries (2009). How Remote is the Offshoring Threat? *European Economic Review*, 53(4): 429–44.

Helpman, Elhanan, Marc J. Melitz, and Stephen R. Yeaple (2004). Export Versus FDI with Heterogeneous Firms, *American Economic Review*, 94(1): 300–16.

Hijzen, Alexander, Sébastien Jean, and Thierry Mayer (2011). The Effects at Home of Initiating Production Abroad: Evidence from Matched French Firms, *Review of World Economics*, 147(3): 457–83.

Hummels, David, Jun Ishii, and Kei-Mu Yi (2001). The Nature and Growth of Vertical Specialization in World Trade, *Journal of International Economics*, 54(1): 75–96.

Johnson, Robert C. and Guillermo Noguera (2012). Accounting for intermediates: Production Sharing and Trade in Value Added, *Journal of International Economics*, 86(2): 224–36.

Koopman, Robert, Zhi Wang, and Shang-Jin Wei (2014). Tracing Value Added and Double Counting in Gross Exports, *American Economic Review*, 104(2): 459–94.

Melitz, Marc J. (2003). The Impact of Trade on Intra-Industry Reallocations and Aggregate Industry Productivity, *Econometrica*, 71(6): 1695–725.

Miroudot, Sébastien, Rainer Lanz, and Alexandros Ragoussis (2009). Trade in intermediate goods and services. OECD, TAD/TC/WP(2009)1/Final.

Nunn, Nathan (2007). Relationship-specificity, Incomplete Contracts and the Pattern of Trade, *Quarterly Journal of Economics*, 122: 569–600.

Rowthorn, Robert and Ramana Ramaswamy (1998). Growth, Trade and Deindustrialization, IMF working paper, WP/98/60.

Stehrer, Robert (2012). Trade in Value Added and Value Added in Trade, WIIW working papers, 81, The Vienna Institute for International Economics.

Yeaple, Stephen R. (2006). Offshoring, Foreign Direct Investment and the Structure of US Trade, *Journal of the European Economic Association*, 4(2–3): 602–11.

7

The Skill Bias of the US Trade Deficit

Rosario Crinò and Paolo Epifani

7.1 Introduction

In the past three decades, the US economy and a number of other developed and developing countries have experienced a dramatic rise in wage inequality. This fact has stimulated a vast theoretical and empirical literature pointing at skilled biased technical change (SBTC) and globalization as the basic forces behind the observed trends. Building on this literature, in this chapter we illustrate a new mechanism whereby international trade may raise the relative demand for skills, provided that it is accompanied by global imbalances of the type recently experienced by the world economy.

To motivate our analysis, Figure 7.1 plots the US manufacturing trade balance as a share of GDP (dashed line) and the wage bill share of nonproduction workers in manufacturing (solid line) between 1977 and 2005. The latter is a standard proxy for the relative demand for skills. The two variables are strongly negatively correlated, perhaps suggesting that the massive trade deficit accumulated by the US economy over the past thirty years may have led to skill upgrading in the manufacturing sector.[1]

In Section 7.2, building on Feenstra and Hanson (1996, henceforth FH) and Crinò and Epifani (2014, henceforth CE) we formulate a simple general equilibrium theory that can naturally explain a positive association between manufacturing trade deficits and skill upgrading in a skill-rich country such as the USA. In particular, we use a Heckscher-Ohlin model with a continuum of goods, as in Dornbusch, Fischer,

---

[1] Following a terminology widely used in the empirical trade literature, in this chapter we refer to skill upgrading as a within-industry increase in the relative demand for skills.

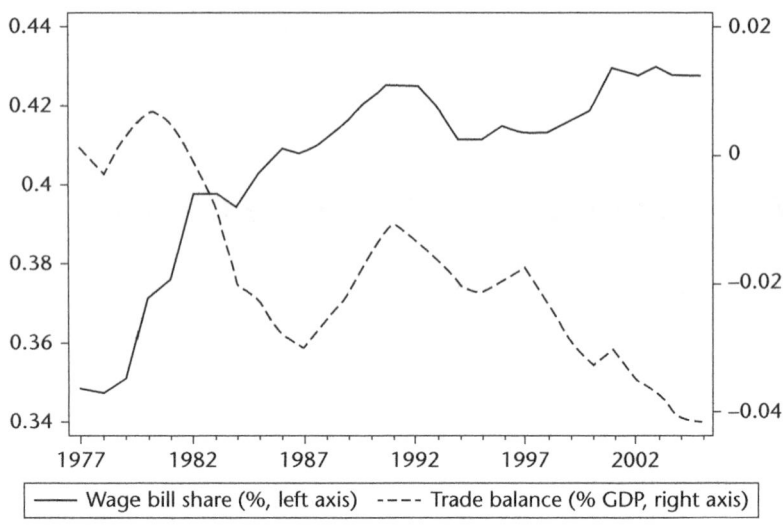

Figure 7.1 Trade imbalances and relative demand for skills in US manufacturing

and Samuelson (1980, henceforth DFS80), in which we allow for trade imbalances, modelled as transfers as in Dornbusch, Fischer, and Samuelson (1977) and more recently in Dekle, Eaton, and Kortum (2007, 2008). In our model, the skill-rich North and the South produce a final non-traded good by assembling physical capital and a range of traded intermediate inputs. The latter are produced using physical capital and different combinations of high-skill and low-skill workers. The model implies that a Southern (Northern) trade surplus (deficit) leads to skill upgrading and a rise of the skill premium in both countries. The intuition behind this result is the same as for why North–South capital flows are skill biased in FH: a Southern trade surplus leads the South to expand (at the expense of a de-industrializing North) into a range of traded activities which are more skill intensive than the Southern average but less skill intensive than the Northern average, thereby inducing skill upgrading in both regions.

The mechanics behind our result are the following. A Southern transfer to the North reduces final expenditure in the South and raises it in the North. Given that physical capital is used to produce (also) the final (non-traded) good, and its rental price is therefore increasing in the domestic expenditure for the final good, it follows that a Southern trade surplus reduces the rental price of capital in the South relative to the North. Notice that these mechanics are essentially the same as in

FH, where outsourcing reduces the Southern rental rate and increases Southern competitiveness relative to the North.

The empirical (and policy) implications of our analysis are, however, different. In Section 7.3, we therefore test our theory and compare it to competing explanations proposed in the empirical trade literature. Following most of this literature, we focus on the US economy, for which higher-quality and more detailed industry-level data are available. Using aggregate data for the overall manufacturing sector, drawn from the *NBER Productivity Database*, we start by showing that, consistent with our model and the evidence reported in Figure 7.1, our data feature a positive correlation between skill upgrading and the trade deficit, which holds strong even after controlling for standard proxies for offshoring, trade openness, and technical change.

Next, following the methodology proposed by Feenstra and Hanson (1996, 1999), we use a panel of 380 (six-digit NAICS) US manufacturing industries observed between 1977 and 2005 to test whether sectoral trade deficits are associated with a systematic within-industry increase in the relative demand for skills. Consistent with the aggregate results, but now taking full advantage of the high level of industry detail in our data, we find a strong impact of sectorial trade deficits on skill upgrading within US industries. Moreover, in our data the estimated impact of trade imbalances on within-industry reallocations is larger and more robust than that of offshoring, trade liberalization, and SBTC. Our results therefore suggest that the effect of trade imbalances may be no less relevant than that of competing explanations investigated in the empirical literature.

Our chapter is related to a vast literature that documents the recent increase in the US skill premium and tries to pin down its main determinants (see Acemoglu and Autor 2011, for a recent survey). Within this literature, we are not the first to point at the possible role played by the US trade deficit. Indeed, initial studies for the 1980s found the US trade deficit to have a strong impact on the relative demand for skills, thereby concluding that international trade was an important force of change. In particular, Murphy and Welch (1992) found that an increase in the US durable goods deficit equal to 1 per cent of GNP reduces wages for young and less educated workers by roughly 3 per cent while increasing the wages of older and more educated workers by 1–2 per cent. Similarly, Borjas, Freeman, and Katz (1991) argued that up to 25 per cent of the observed increase in the college premium between 1980 and 1985 is due to the concomitant increase in the US trade deficit. Importantly, however, lacking a theoretical foundation for a link between trade deficits and the relative demand for skills, the early literature interpreted the above findings through the lens of the standard neoclassical trade model. This soon led to discrediting the trade explanation in favour of SBTC (e.g. Bound and Johnson 1992; Berman, Bound, and Griliches 1994), in particular because the Stolper–Samuelson theorem was seemingly inconsistent with the observation of skill upgrading in the USA and rising skill premia in most trade liberalizing developing countries (Goldberg and Pavcnik 2007). Our main aim is therefore to contribute to a recent rehabilitation of the trade explanation (initiated by FH and Bernard and Jensen 1995, 1997) by illustrating a new mechanism, consistent with the early evidence, whereby trade *cum* imbalances can increase the relative demand for skills.[2]

As mentioned earlier, this chapter is more closely related to Feenstra and Hanson (1996) and Crinò and Epifani (2014). FH were the first to notice that North–South capital flows may increase skill premia worldwide in a Heckscher–Ohlin model with a continuum of goods. CE were instead the first to notice that the same logic applies to North–South trade imbalances. Specifically, CE use a model similar to the model in this chapter (with a continuum of *final* instead of intermediate traded goods, as in Chun Zhu and Trefler 2005, and without physical capital) to show that a Southern (Northern) trade surplus leads both countries to reallocate resources towards more (less) skill-intensive industries. This prediction is tested using a panel of more than 100 countries observed over three decades. Consistently, CE find strong evidence that a trade surplus leads to between-industry reallocations towards more or less skill-intensive industries depending on whether the country is skill poor or skill rich relative to the world economy. Importantly, CE also find no evidence of a significant impact of FDI and trade in intermediate goods on between-industry reallocations after controlling for trade imbalances. Their analysis is, however, silent on the impact of international trade on within-industry reallocations, which instead are the main focus of the empirical trade literature

---

[2] Using firm-level data, Bernard and Jensen (1995, 1997) have documented the relevance of trade-induced between-firm reallocations. This has led to a rethinking of the early evidence in support of SBTC (based on highly aggregated industry-level data), according to which trade-induced reallocations were small. Moreover, Bernard and Jensen's findings have led to the new heterogeneous-firm paradigm, which provides new mechanisms whereby trade liberalization, even between identical countries, can increase the relative demand for skills (e.g. Yeaple 2005; Verhoogen 2008; Helpman, Itskhoki, and Redding 2010; Bustos 2011). See also, *inter alia*, Epifani and Gancia (2006, 2008) for an analysis of the distributional implications of intra-industry trade, and Crinò (2009, 2010), Fontagné and d'Isanto (Chapter 6, this volume), Ebenstein, Harrison, and McMillan (Chapter 8, this volume), and Ebenstein et al. (2014) for evidence on the distributional effects of offshoring. In particular, the latter two papers find trade to have a stronger impact on US wages than offshoring.

studying the determinants of the recent increase in the relative demand for skills. In this chapter we therefore complement our previous work by studying, theoretically and empirically, how trade imbalances may affect within-industry reallocations.

7.2 Theory

7.2.1 Overview

In order to make our point that trade imbalances may lead to skill upgrading, in this section we illustrate a simple Heckscher–Ohlin setup *à la* DFS80 and FH featuring factor price differences (FPD) in the free-trade equilibrium. The model consists of two countries (a skill-poor South and the North, indexed by $c = s, n$) and three primary factors (high-skill labour H, low-skill labour L, and physical capital K). A nontraded final output Y is produced using a continuum of traded intermediate inputs (indexed by $z \in [0, 1]$) and physical capital. Intermediate inputs are instead produced using different combinations of the three primary factors. Finally, we allow for trade imbalances, modelled as a transfer T from the South to the North.

7.2.2 Technology

All goods are produced under perfect competition and constant returns to scale. Specifically, final output Y_c is produced by assembling physical capital K_c and a continuum of traded intermediate inputs with the following Cobb–Douglas production function (expressed in logs):

$$\ln Y_c = \theta \int_0^1 \ln d_c(z)dz + (1 - \theta) \ln K_{Y,c}, \qquad (7.1)$$

where $d_c(z)$ and $K_{Y,c}$ are the units the of intermediate input z and physical capital used to produce final output, and $(1 - \theta)$ is the output elasticity of capital.

Intermediate input z is produced with the following Cobb–Douglas production function:

$$q_c(z) = \left(\frac{H_c(z)}{\theta z} \right)^{\theta z} \left(\frac{L_c(z)}{\theta (1 - z)} \right)^{\theta(1-z)} \left(\frac{K_c(z)}{1 - \theta} \right)^{1-\theta}, \qquad (7.2)$$

where $q_c(z)$ is the output, and $H_c(z)$, $L_c(z)$ and $K_c(z)$ are, respectively, the units of high-skill labour, low-skill labour, and physical capital used to produce input z.

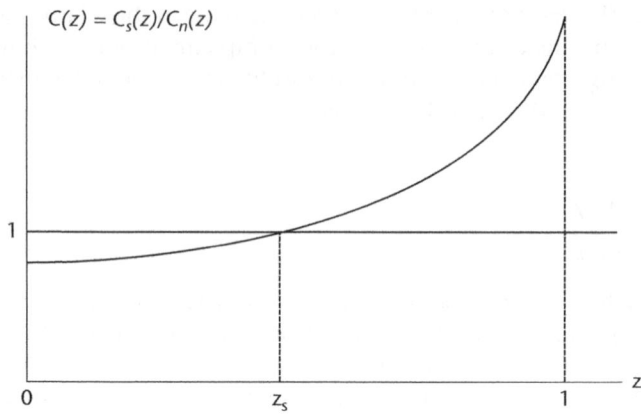

Figure 7.2 The borderline commodity

The unit cost function associated with (7.2) is

$$C_c(z) = w_{H,c}^{\theta z} w_{L,c}^{\theta(1-z)} r_c^{1-\theta} = \left(w_{L,c} s_c^z\right)^\theta r_c^{1-\theta},$$

where $w_{H,c}$ is the wage rate of high-skill workers, $w_{L,c}$ is the wage of low-skill workers, r_c is the rental price of capital, and $s_c = w_{H,c}/w_{L,c}$ is the skill premium. The unit cost of input z in the South relative to the North is thus

$$C(z) = \frac{C_s(z)}{C_n(z)} = w^\theta s^{\theta z} r^{1-\theta}, \tag{7.3}$$

where $w = w_{L,s}/w_{L,n}$ is the wage of Southern low-skill workers relative to Northern workers, $s = s_s/s_n$ is the Southern relative skill premium, and $r = r_s/r_n$ is the Southern relative rental price of capital. We assume that $s > 1$ in the free-trade equilibrium, which implies that $C(z)$ is upward sloping for given factor prices (see Figure 7.2).

7.2.3 Trade Pattern

The trade pattern is pinned down by the borderline input z_s, defined by the condition

$$C(z_s) = w^\theta s^{\theta z_s} r^{1-\theta} = 1. \tag{7.4}$$

It follows that country c produces and exports all intermediate inputs $z \in I_c(z_s)$, where

$$I_c(z_S) = \begin{cases} [0, z_S), & c = s \\ (z_S, 1], & c = n \end{cases}.$$

7.2.4 Factor Market Clearing

Consider labour markets first. Equation (7.2) and perfect competition imply industry z's cost (and revenue) shares of factors H, L, and K to equal θz, $\theta(1-z)$ and $(1-\theta)$, respectively. Moreover, equation (7.1) and goods market equilibrium imply industry z's revenue to equal a constant share θ of world expenditure $E_W = E_S + E_n$. Thus, market clearing conditions for factors H_c and L_c can be written in value terms as

$$w_{H,c}H_c = \theta^2 E_W \int_{z \in I_c(z_S)} z\,dz = \theta^2 E_W z_c \omega_c, \tag{7.5}$$

$$w_{L,c}L_c = \theta^2 E_W \int_{z \in I_c(z_S)} (1-z)\,dz = \theta^2 E_W z_c (1 - \omega_c), \tag{7.6}$$

where

$$z_c = \begin{cases} z_S, & c = s \\ 1 - z_S, & c = n \end{cases},$$

and

$$\omega_c = \frac{1}{z_c} \int_{z \in I_c(z_S)} z\,dz = \begin{cases} \frac{1}{2}z_S, & c = s \\ \frac{1}{2}(1 + z_S), & c = n \end{cases} \tag{7.7}$$

is the average wage bill share of high-skill workers in the traded sector. Equation (7.7) highlights a key property of the model. Specifically, although Cobb–Douglas production functions in (7.2) imply that in each traded industry the wage bill share of high-skill workers is constant and equal to $\theta z/(\theta z + \theta(1-z)) = z$, the average wage bill share of high-skill workers in the traded sector, ω_c, is endogenous as it depends on z_S. It follows that in this model, consistent with the seminal insight by FH, skill upgrading (a rise in ω_c) does not require an exogenous technical change that increases z, as it can also be induced by a change in the trade equilibrium that leads to a rise in z_S.

Consider now the capital market. Perfect competition and (7.1) imply that in the final good sector capital expenditure equals a share $(1-\theta)$ of domestic expenditure E_c. Moreover, capital is used to produce intermediate inputs and, by (7.2), its cost equals a share $(1-\theta)$ of world expenditure on country c's inputs. The latter is equal to $\theta E_w z_c$ by (7.5) and (7.6). Hence we can write:

$$r_c K_c = (1 - \theta)(E_c + \theta E_w z_c). \tag{7.8}$$

Finally, total income is given by

$$Y_c = w_{L,c} L_c + w_{H,c} H_c + r_c K_c = w_{L,c} L_c (1 + s_c h_c) + (1 - \theta)(E_c + \theta E_w z_c). \tag{7.9}$$

7.2.5 Trade Imbalances

We crucially assume that the South makes a transfer T to the North. A positive transfer ($T > 0$) is therefore equivalent to a trade surplus in the South, whereas a negative transfer ($T < 0$) corresponds to a trade surplus in the North. Trade imbalances also imply that expenditure does not equal income. In particular, we have that $E_s = Y_s - T$ and $E_n = Y_n + T$. Recalling that a share θ of total expenditure is on traded inputs, the trade (im)balance condition can be written as:

$$T = EXP_s - IMP_s = \theta \int_0^{z_s} E_n dz - \theta \int_{z_s}^1 E_s dz = z_s \theta (Y_n + T)$$
$$- (1 - z_s) \theta (Y_s - T),$$

where EXP_s (IMP_s) denotes Southern exports (imports). Thus, rearranging,

$$Y_s = \frac{z_s}{1 - z_s} Y_n - \frac{1 - \theta}{\theta} \frac{T}{1 - z_s}. \tag{7.10}$$

7.2.6 General Equilibrium

To characterize the general equilibrium properties of the model, we must express countries' incomes and relative factor prices as functions of z_s and model's parameters. To this purpose, note first that, taking the ratio of (7.5) to (7.6) and solving for the skill premium using (7.7) yields:

$$s_c = \frac{1}{h_c} \frac{\omega_c}{1 - \omega_c} = \begin{cases} \frac{1}{h_s} \frac{z_s}{2 - z_s}, & c = s \\ \\ \frac{1}{h_n} \frac{1 + z_s}{1 - z_s}, & c = n \end{cases}. \tag{7.11}$$

Thus,

$$s = \frac{s_S}{s_n} = \frac{z_S (1 - z_S)}{h (2 - z_S) (1 + z_S)}, \tag{7.12}$$

where $h = h_S/h_n$ is the Southern relative skill ratio.

Next, using (7.6) and (7.7) yields an expression for the relative wage of Southern low-skill workers:

$$w = \frac{w_{L,S}}{w_{L,n}} = \frac{z_S (1 - \omega_S)}{L (1 - z_S) (1 - \omega_n)} = \frac{z_S (2 - z_S)}{L (1 - z_S)^2}, \tag{7.13}$$

where $L = L_S/L_n$ is the Southern relative endowment of low-skill workers.

Moreover, using (7.8) and recalling that $E_s = Y_s - T$, $E_n = Y_n + T$ and $E_w = Y_s + Y_n$, we can express the relative rental rate as a function of the two countries' incomes:

$$r = \frac{r_S}{r_n} = \frac{1}{K} \frac{E_s + \theta E_w z_S}{E_n + \theta E_w (1 - z_S)} = \frac{1}{K} \frac{(1 + \theta z_S) Y_s + \theta z_S Y_n - T}{\left[1 + \theta (1 - z_S)\right] Y_n + \theta (1 - z_S) Y_s + T}, \tag{7.14}$$

where $K = K_S/K_n$ is the Southern relative capital stock.

To find the equilibrium value of Y_s and Y_n note first that, using (7.11) in (7.9), and setting $w_{L,n} = 1$ by choice of numeraire, we obtain:

$$Y_n = \frac{\frac{2L_n}{(1-z_S)\theta} + \left[(1 - \theta) /\theta\right] T + (1 - \theta) (1 - z_S) Y_s}{1 - (1 - \theta) (1 - z_S)}. \tag{7.15}$$

Solving (7.10) and (7.15) for Y_s and Y_n finally yields:

$$Y_n = \frac{2L_n}{(1 - z_S) \theta^2} + \frac{1 - \theta}{\theta} T, \quad Y_s = \frac{2L_n z_S}{(1 - z_S)^2 \theta^2} - \frac{1 - \theta}{\theta} T. \tag{7.16}$$

Thus, using (7.16) in (7.2.6), gives:

$$r = \frac{1}{K} \frac{z_S - \frac{(1-z_S)^2 \theta}{2(1+\theta)} \frac{T}{L_n}}{1 - z_S + \frac{(1-z_S)^2 \theta}{2(1+\theta)} \frac{T}{L_n}}. \tag{7.17}$$

Note that r is increasing in z_S. More importantly, r is decreasing in T and K for given z_S, thus implying that transfers and capital flows play a similar role in reducing Southern relative rental rate.

Rosario Crinò and Paolo Epifani

Finally, using (7.12), (7.13), and (7.17) in (7.4) to eliminate s, w, and r from $C(z_S)$, and simplifying, yields:

$$C(z_S) = \frac{F(z_S)^\theta}{AL^\theta K^{1-\theta} h^{\theta z_S}} \left(\frac{z_S - \frac{(1-z_S)^2\theta}{2(1+\theta)} \frac{T}{L_n}}{1 - z_S + \frac{(1-z_S)^2\theta}{2(1+\theta)} \frac{T}{L_n}} \right)^{1-\theta}, \qquad (7.18)$$

where

$$F(z_S) = \frac{z_S^{1+z_S} (2 - z_S)^{1-z_S}}{(1 - z_S)^{2-z_S} (1 + z_S)^{z_S}}$$

is a monotonically increasing function. Note that $h^{-\theta z_S}$ and r are also increasing in z_S (recall that $h < 1$ and that the expression in brackets in 7.18 equals rK); it follows that $C(z_S)$ is monotonically increasing in z_S, and thus the equilibrium is unique.

7.2.7 Trade Imbalances, Offshoring, and Skill Upgrading

Equation (7.18) allows us to immediately show our main results. First, as in FH, a reallocation of capital from a capital-abundant North to the South (an increase in K) shifts the curve $C(z_S)$ downwards, inducing an increase in the equilibrium value of z_S and thus leading, by (7.7) and (7.11), to skill upgrading (a higher ω_c) and a higher skill premium s_c in both regions. The reason is that North–South capital flows reduce the Southern relative rental rate r, thereby increasing the competitiveness of Southern industry and allowing the South to produce and export a broader range of inputs.

Second, and more importantly, (7.18) implies that a transfer from the South to the North ($T > 0$) also shifts the curve $C(z_S)$ downwards, thereby producing similar effects. The reason is that a transfer reduces Southern expenditure on domestic capital, thereby reducing the rental rate. Conversely, a transfer from the North to the South ($T < 0$) shifts the curve $C(z_S)$ upwards, thus reducing z_S. The model therefore suggests a close and so far neglected relationship between trade imbalances, skill upgrading, and skill premia.

7.3 Empirical Evidence

In this section, we look for a systematic relationship between trade imbalances and within-industry reallocations, as implied by our theory. To this purpose, we focus on a skill-rich country, the USA, and use data for a large panel of manufacturing industries observed over the last three decades (see Section 7.3.1). We start by showing that, in the overall manufacturing sector, larger trade deficits are associated with skill upgrading (Section 7.3.2). Then, we implement a well-established framework introduced by Feenstra and Hanson (1996, 1999), in order to fully exploit the industry detail of our data and provide more systematic evidence on the effects of trade imbalances on the relative demand for skills within industries (Section 7.3.3).

7.3.1 Data and Variables

In the spirit of FH, in our model there is one final-good sector, and all trade is in intermediate inputs produced with different skill intensities by countries endowed with different skill ratios. A rigorous test of the model would require highly disaggregated data on the traded activities, so as to proxy for the borderline input z_S. Unfortunately, as pointed out by Chun Zhu and Trefler (2005), at the level of detail at which trade data are usually reported, aggregation bias prevents us from observing the borderline activity z_S in practice. Importantly, however, a crucial feature of our model is that, by (7.7), the average wage bill share of high-skill workers in the traded intermediate activities, ω_C, only depends on the equilibrium value of the borderline input z_S, and is monotonically increasing. It follows that, even if we do not observe z_S, we can proxy for it using ω_C. This allows us to test our mechanism by studying how trade imbalances affect skill upgrading in a certain country.

To construct ω_C for the USA, we use data on employment and wages of low-skill (production) and high-skill (non-production) workers, sourced from the *NBER Productivity Database*. Overall, we have information for 380 (six-digit NAICS) manufacturing industries between 1977 and 2005. For a given industry i and year t, the wage bill share of high-skill workers is defined as $\omega_{i,t} = \left(\frac{w_H H}{w_H H + w_L L} \right)_{i,t}$, where H and L denote employment of non-production and production workers, respectively, while w_H and w_L indicate their wages. The same database provides us with a number of other variables used in our empirical analysis, namely real output, value added, capital stock, non-energy input purchases, and an index of Total Factor Productivity (TFP), which we use as a proxy for SBTC.

To measure trade imbalances, we merge these data with information on exports and imports at the industry level. In particular, we first retrieve trade data at the four-digit level of the SITC Rev. 2 classification, from Feenstra et al. (2005) for the period 1977–2000 and from *UN Comtrade* for more recent years. Then, we convert these data into the six-digit NAICS classification, using a correspondence table produced by Feenstra, Romalis, and Schott (2002). The conversion leaves us with 380 industries spanning the entire manufacturing sector of the USA.

Using these trade data, we compute the (normalized) trade deficit of each industry as the difference between imports and exports divided by value added, $T_{i,t} = \left(\frac{IMP-EXP}{VA} \right)_{i,t}$. In addition, we construct proxies for other factors that may lead to skill upgrading according to complementary theories. In particular, we proxy for trade liberalization using the openness ratio $OPEN_{i,t}$, defined as imports plus exports over industry value added. Moreover, following Feenstra and Hanson (1999), we proxy for offshoring using $MOS_{i,t}$, defined as the share of imported inputs in total non-energy input purchases.[3]

7.3.2 Results for the Aggregate Manufacturing Sector

We start by providing evidence of a strong positive association between trade deficits and skill upgrading using aggregate data for the overall manufacturing sector. In column (1) of Table 7.1, we regress the average wage bill share of non-production workers in manufacturing on the average normalized trade deficit, using twenty-nine yearly observations between 1977 and 2005. For comparability, we standardize the variables to have mean zero and standard deviation equal to 1. Consistent with our model, the coefficient on T_t is positive, precisely estimated and large, implying that a one standard deviation increase in the manufacturing trade deficit is associated with a rise of roughly 0.6 standard deviations in the average wage bill share of high-skill workers.

In columns (2)–(4) we replace T_t with MOS_t, TFP_t, and $OPEN_t$, respectively. The coefficients on these variables are positive and significant, suggesting that offshoring, SBTC, and trade liberalization may also be associated with skill upgrading in manufacturing. In column (5), we repeat instead our baseline specification after adding linear and quadratic time trends, in order to check that the correlation between T_t and ω_t is not driven by underlying trends in the data, and to account for possible skill upgrading due to within-industry specialization driven by comparative advantage. Reassuringly, the coefficient on the trade deficit remains positive and highly significant. Finally, in column (6) we include all variables jointly. Strikingly, the coefficient on T_t is still

---

[3] As standard in the empirical literature, we measure imported inputs as imports of products classified in Section 5 ('Chemicals and Related Products, NES'), Section 6 ('Manufactured Goods Classified Chiefly by Material'), or Section 7 ('Machinery and Transport Equipment') of the SITC Rev. 2 classification.

Table 7.1 Estimates for the aggregate manufacturing sector

Dependent variable: wage bill share of non-production workers, ω_t

	(1) Trade deficit	(2) Offshoring	(3) TFP	(4) Trade openness	(5) Trade deficit and time trends	(6) All variables
T_t	0.584*** (0.147)				0.333*** (0.075)	0.688*** (0.183)
MOS_t		0.809*** (0.128)				-1.763** (0.673)
TFP_t			0.630*** (0.139)			-0.154 (0.093)
$OPEN_t$				0.880*** (0.104)		-0.092 (0.443)
Observations	29	29	29	29	29	29
R-squared	0.34	0.65	0.40	0.77	0.92	0.95
Linear trend	no	no	no	no	yes	yes
Quadratic trend	no	no	no	no	yes	yes

Notes: all specifications are estimated on twenty-nine yearly observations for the aggregate manufacturing sector of the USA. The sample period is 1977–2005. T is trade deficit over value added. MOS is the share of imported inputs in total non-energy input purchases. TFP is the log TFP index, obtained as the weighted average of the industry-specific indexes, with weights given by the industries' shares in total manufacturing shipments. OPEN is log imports plus exports over value added. All coefficients are beta coefficients. Robust standard errors are reported in round brackets. ***, **, *: indicate significance at the 1, 5, and 10% levels, respectively.

positive and very precisely estimated, whereas the coefficients on the other variables become negative and, with the exception of MOS_t, statistically insignificant.

Overall these results suggest that, consistent with our theory, trade imbalances may be a crucial determinant of skill upgrading in the USA. In the next section, we provide more systematic evidence using a well-consolidated approach that takes full advantage of the high level of industry detail in our data.

7.3.3 Industry-level Analysis

As pointed out by Feenstra (2004, ch. 4), the approach used in the previous section raises a degrees-of-freedom issue, as only one observation on ω_C is available in each year. The empirical literature therefore suggests expanding on the degrees of freedom by using detailed industry-level data instead of aggregate data for the traded sector, an approach to which we now turn.

EMPIRICAL MODEL

As in Feenstra and Hanson (1996, 1999), we use our panel of six-digit manufacturing industries to estimate fixed-effects regressions of the following form:

$$\omega_{i,t} = \phi_i + \phi_t + \phi_s \ln \left(w_H/w_L \right)_{i,t} + \phi_Y \ln Y_{i,t} + \phi_K \ln (K/Y)_{i,t}$$
$$+\phi_T T_{i,t} + \varepsilon_{i,t}, \tag{7.19}$$

where ϕ_i and ϕ_t denote industry and time fixed effects, respectively, $\left(w_H/w_L \right)_{i,t}$ is the skill premium, $Y_{i,t}$ is real output, $(K/Y)_{i,t}$ is the capital/output ratio, and $\varepsilon_{i,t}$ is a random disturbance. As is well-known (see e.g. Feenstra 2004, ch. 4), (7.19) can be obtained by applying Shephard's lemma on a short-run translog cost function (a flexible functional form encompassing the Cobb–Douglas as a special case), where high-skill and low-skill labour are variable inputs, capital is a fixed production factor, and the trade deficit acts as a cost shifter.[4]

Before presenting our estimates, we note that this approach, while helping us to address a statistical problem, requires two important qualifications concerning the interpretation of the results. First, the general equilibrium mechanism whereby trade imbalances (or capital

---

[4] Following a large empirical literature (e.g. Berman, Bound, and Griliches 1994, and Feenstra and Hanson 1999), we will omit the skill premium $\left(w_H/w_L \right)_{i,t}$ from most of our specifications, in order to avoid introducing endogeneity. However, we will show that controlling for $\left(w_H/w_L \right)_{i,t}$ does not affect our main results.

mobility), by changing factor prices, affect skill upgrading in our model (and in models *à la* Feenstra and Hanson more generally) may not be identifiable at the industry level if labour is highly mobile across industries. Although this may be a concern in the long run, it is less so in the short run, as intersectorial labour mobility seems sluggish in the USA (Artuc et al. 2010).[5] It follows that sectorial imbalances are likely to induce temporary deviations of sectorial factor prices from the national norm that mimic on a smaller scale the aggregate long-run effects.

Second, our model implies that a trade deficit (surplus) induces skill upgrading in a skill-rich (skill-poor) country. When using disaggregated data to test this prediction for the USA, we will thus search for a positive association between industry-level trade deficits and skill upgrading (i.e. our prior is that $\phi_T > 0$). Note, however, that industry-level trade imbalances may also reflect comparative advantage, given that manufacturing industries feature different skill intensities. Specifically, trade liberalization and specialization according to comparative advantage imply larger trade deficits in comparative disadvantage industries and larger trade surpluses in comparative advantage industries, and therefore no systematic industry-level correlation between imbalances and skill upgrading. Conversely, our theory suggests a systematic positive correlation between trade deficits and skill upgrading in a skill-rich country like the USA.

BASELINE ESTIMATES

The baseline estimates are reported in Table 7.2, where all variables are standardized to have mean zero and standard deviation equal to 1. In column (1) we estimate (7.19) by including only $T_{i,t}$. Consistent with our model and the results for the overall manufacturing sector, the trade deficit enters with a positive and statistically significant coefficient at the 1 per cent level.

In columns (2)–(4) we include instead $MOS_{i,t}$, $TFP_{i,t}$, and $OPEN_{i,t}$, respectively. As expected, the coefficients on these variables are positive and significant. The results are broadly similar when including $T_{i,t}$ jointly with one of these variables (see columns (5)–(7)), but the coefficient on offshoring is now smaller and significant only at the 10 per cent level. In column (8), we include the four variables in the same specification. Except for the coefficient on offshoring, which is now insignificantly different from zero, the coefficients on the other variables are all significant at the 1 per cent level and roughly similar in magnitude. Finally, in column (9) we show that the results are

---

[5] See also the discussion in Autor, Dorn, and Hanson (2013) on this point.

Table 7.2 Industry-level regressions: baseline estimates

Dependent variable: wage-bill share of non-production workers, $\omega_{i,t}$

	(1) Trade deficit	(2) Offshoring	(3) TFP	(4) Trade openness	(5) Trade deficit and offshoring	(6) Trade deficit and TFP	(7) Trade deficit and trade openness	(8) All variables	(9) Controlling for the skill premium
$T_{i,t}$	0.080*** (0.012)				0.078*** (0.012)	0.071*** (0.012)	0.075*** (0.012)	0.067*** (0.011)	0.066*** (0.011)
$MOS_{i,t}$		0.040*** (0.015)			0.026* (0.015)			0.016 (0.015)	0.012 (0.013)
$TFP_{i,t}$			0.071*** (0.011)			0.060*** (0.011)		0.053*** (0.011)	0.063*** (0.010)
$OPEN_{i,t}$				0.083*** (0.019)			0.067*** (0.018)	0.056*** (0.017)	0.067*** (0.016)
$\ln(K/Y)_{i,t}$	0.137*** (0.018)	0.133*** (0.018)	0.247*** (0.025)	0.131*** (0.018)	0.138*** (0.018)	0.234*** (0.025)	0.137*** (0.018)	0.224*** (0.025)	0.241*** (0.023)
$\ln(Y)_{i,t}$	0.132*** (0.029)	0.098*** (0.030)	0.073** (0.029)	0.094*** (0.029)	0.134*** (0.029)	0.112*** (0.028)	0.133*** (0.029)	0.118*** (0.029)	0.137*** (0.027)
$\ln(\omega_H/\omega_L)_{i,t}$									0.200*** (0.011)
Observations	10,875	10,875	10,875	10,770	10,875	10,875	10,770	10,770	10,770
R-squared	0.95	0.95	0.95	0.95	0.95	0.95	0.95	0.95	0.95
Year FE	yes	yes	yes	yes	yes	yes	yes	yes	yes
Industry FE	yes	yes	yes	yes	yes	yes	yes	yes	yes

Notes: all specifications are estimated on a panel of 380 (6-digit NAICS) US manufacturing industries. The sample period is 1977–2005. T is trade deficit over value added. MOS is the share of imported inputs in total non-energy input purchases. TFP is the log TFP index. OPEN is log imports plus exports over value added. K/Y is the capital/output ratio. Y is real output. ω_H/ω_L is the relative wage of non-production workers. All coefficients are beta coefficients. All regressions are weighted by the industries' shares in total manufacturing wage-bill in the year 1977. Robust standard errors are reported in round brackets. ***, **, *: indicate significance at the 1, 5, and 10% levels, respectively.

unchanged when also including the skill premium $(w_H/w_L)_{i,t}$. Interestingly, across all specifications, the coefficient on $T_{i,t}$ is close in size to that on $OPEN_{i,t}$ and $TFP_{i,t}$ and much larger than that on $MOS_{i,t}$.

Overall, these results suggest that trade imbalances matter a great deal for skill upgrading, and that their impact is empirically no less relevant than that of trade liberalization, offshoring, or technical change. In the following, we submit these results to a number of robustness checks, using the regression in column (8) as our baseline specification.

ROBUSTNESS CHECKS
We start by addressing endogeneity concerns. In this respect, even if in our model trade imbalances are exogenous, in the real world they may either be jointly determined with the wage bill share of high-skill workers (simultaneity bias) or arise as a consequence of skill upgrading (reverse causality). In particular, simultaneity bias may occur if $T_{i,t}$ and $\omega_{i,t}$ are jointly driven by variables that are omitted from our baseline specifications. An important concern in this respect is that changes in trade imbalances and skill upgrading may reflect underlying trends in the data, such as ongoing specialization driven by comparative advantage in more finely disaggregated industries. We deal with this issue in Table 7.3. In columns (1)–(7), we control for possible heterogeneous trends based on pre-existing industry characteristics. To this purpose, following Goldberg et al. (2010), we add full sets of interaction terms between the time dummies and the initial value of the industry characteristics indicated in the columns' headings. The results are largely unchanged, except that $MOS_{i,t}$ enters with the wrong sign in one specification. In column (8) we follow instead a complementary approach by controlling for industry-specific linear trends. Note that the coefficients on $TFP_{i,t}$ and $OPEN_{i,t}$ are now imprecisely estimated, implying that both variables are dominated by a time trend. More importantly, the coefficient on $T_{i,t}$ remains positive and statistically significant at the 5 per cent level.

Reverse causality may instead arise if some unobserved shocks induce skill upgrading within industries, and this in turn leads to the emergence of trade deficits. To fully control for these shocks we would need to include a whole set of industry-year dummies, but this would clearly be unfeasible as these dummies would be collinear with $T_{i,t}$. However, assuming that unobserved shocks are correlated with observed changes in some industry characteristics, we can implement a simple empirical strategy to assess how these shocks may affect our main results. In particular, following CE, we can divide industries into ten bins of equal size, based on the average change during the sample period in a number

Table 7.3 Industry-level regressions: controls for underlying trends

Dependent variable: wage-bill share of non-production workers, $\omega_{i,t}$

	(1) Wage-bill share	(2) Trade deficit	(3) Capital–output ratio	(4) Real output	(5) Offshoring	(6) Trade openness	(7) TFP	(8) Industry-specific time trends
$T_{i,t}$	0.066***	0.073***	0.044***	0.055***	0.067***	0.052***	0.063***	0.031**
	(0.012)	(0.012)	(0.010)	(0.011)	(0.011)	(0.011)	(0.011)	(0.013)
$MOS_{i,t}$	0.013	0.027*	0.027*	0.013	0.016	−0.028*	0.015	−0.036**
	(0.015)	(0.014)	(0.015)	(0.015)	(0.016)	(0.016)	(0.015)	(0.015)
$TFP_{i,t}$	0.054***	0.056***	0.116***	0.038***	0.053***	0.050***	−0.016	−0.005
	(0.011)	(0.011)	(0.012)	(0.011)	(0.011)	(0.011)	(0.016)	(0.011)
$OPEN_{i,t}$	0.047***	0.053***	0.052***	0.029*	0.058***	0.151***	0.036**	0.016
	(0.015)	(0.017)	(0.016)	(0.016)	(0.017)	(0.017)	(0.017)	(0.013)
$\ln(K/Y)_{i,t}$	0.193***	0.227***	0.221***	0.183***	0.224***	0.224***	0.189***	0.124***
	(0.025)	(0.025)	(0.023)	(0.024)	(0.025)	(0.025)	(0.025)	(0.022)
$\ln(Y)_{i,t}$	0.048	0.115***	0.035	0.060*	0.118***	0.137***	0.089***	−0.034
	(0.031)	(0.029)	(0.027)	(0.028)	(0.029)	(0.030)	(0.030)	(0.040)
Observations	10,770	10,770	10,770	10,770	10,770	10,770	10,770	10,770
R-squared	0.95	0.95	0.95	0.95	0.95	0.95	0.95	0.98
Year FE	yes	yes	yes	yes	yes	yes	yes	yes

Notes: columns (1)–(7) include controls for heterogeneous trends based on pre-existing industry characteristics (coefficients unreported). These controls are obtained by interacting the time dummies with the initial value of the characteristics indicated in column headings. Column (8) includes instead a full set of industry-specific linear trends. All coefficients are beta coefficients. All regressions are weighted by the industries' shares in total manufacturing wage-bill in the year 1977. Robust standard errors are reported in round brackets. ***, **, *: indicate significance at the 1, 5, and 10% levels, respectively. See also notes to previous tables.

of observable characteristics. Then, we can create a dummy for each of these bins and interact it with the year dummies. By adding the full set of interactions to our specification, we thus control for shocks affecting in a similar way all industries that experienced similar developments in a given characteristic. Our coefficients of interest are identified only from the remaining variation within a given year across all industries that belong to the same bin. The results of these exercises are reported in columns (1)–(7) of Table 7.4. Each column's heading indicates the variable we use to construct the bins for that specification. Strikingly, our main results are confirmed across all these very demanding specifications. In column (8), we use instead a complementary approach by including a full set of two–digit industry-year dummies. Our main evidence is also preserved in this case.

US–CHINA IMBALANCES
A final concern is that our results may be entirely driven by the US trade deficit with China, which accounts for more than one-third of the total manufacturing trade deficit of the USA (see e.g. Dekle, Eaton, and Kortum 2007, 2008). To account for this, in Tables 7.5 and 7.6 we repeat our main specifications and robustness checks after dividing the normalized trade balance of each industry into the components accounted for by China ($TCH_{i,t}$) and the rest of the world ($TROW_{i,t}$). To construct $TCH_{i,t}$ and $TROW_{i,t}$, we rely on import and export data disaggregated by country of origin and destination, which are sourced from Schott (2008). These data are available for the period 1977–2005 at the four-digit level of the SIC classification. Accordingly, we match them with the SIC-based version of the *NBER Productivity Database*. After merging the two datasets we are left with information for 333 four-digit SIC industries. As shown in column (1) of Table 7.5, the results for the overall trade deficit $T_{i,t}$ obtained on this sample of industries are similar to those obtained on the sample of six-digit industries used in Tables 7.2–7.4. More importantly, across all specifications, the coefficients on $TCH_{i,t}$ and $TROW_{i,t}$ are positive, precisely estimated and similar in size. This implies that our findings are not driven by China, but hold true also for the US trade deficit with other countries.

7.4 Conclusion

It is well-known that, according to the standard trade theory, international trade cannot directly increase the relative demand for skills within the manufacturing industries of a skill-rich country.

Table 7.4 Industry-level regressions: controls for contemporaneous shocks

Dependent variable: wage-bill share of non-production workers, $\omega_{i,t}$

	(1) Wage-bill share	(2) Trade deficit	(3) Capital–output ratio	(4) Real output	(5) Offshoring	(6) Trade openness	(7) TFP	(8) Industry-time effects
$T_{i,t}$	0.013*	0.037***	0.050***	0.044***	0.059***	0.066***	0.060***	0.062***
	(0.007)	(0.011)	(0.011)	(0.011)	(0.011)	(0.011)	(0.011)	(0.011)
$MOS_{i,t}$	-0.020**	-0.038**	0.010	0.010	0.033*	0.013	0.014	0.006
	(0.008)	(0.015)	(0.015)	(0.014)	(0.018)	(0.013)	(0.015)	(0.015)
$TFP_{i,t}$	0.056***	0.053***	0.046***	0.029***	0.041***	0.051***	0.074***	0.059***
	(0.008)	(0.011)	(0.010)	(0.010)	(0.010)	(0.011)	(0.012)	(0.011)
$OPEN_{i,t}$	0.021**	0.045***	0.043***	0.049***	0.044***	0.068***	0.034**	0.027
	(0.009)	(0.015)	(0.015)	(0.014)	(0.016)	(0.021)	(0.015)	(0.017)
$\ln(K/Y)_{i,t}$	0.129***	0.245***	0.212***	0.148***	0.203***	0.204***	0.254***	0.251***
	(0.015)	(0.025)	(0.026)	(0.028)	(0.023)	(0.022)	(0.024)	(0.025)
$\ln(Y)_{i,t}$	0.003	0.146***	0.148***	-0.009	0.116***	0.095***	0.138***	0.140***
	(0.015)	(0.032)	(0.031)	(0.054)	(0.026)	(0.026)	(0.031)	(0.029)
Observations	10,770	10,770	10,770	10,770	10,770	10,770	10,770	10,770
R-squared	0.97	0.95	0.95	0.95	0.95	0.95	0.95	0.95
Year FE	yes	yes	yes	yes	yes	yes	yes	yes
Industry FE	yes	yes	yes	yes	yes	yes	yes	yes

Notes: columns (1)–(7) include controls for contemporaneous shocks (coefficients unreported). These controls are obtained by dividing industries into ten bins of equal size, based on the average change (over the estimation period) in the characteristics indicated in columns headings. A dummy for each bin is then interacted with a full set of year dummies. Column (8) includes instead a full set of 2-digit industry-time effects. All coefficients are beta coefficients. All regressions are weighted by the industries' shares in total manufacturing wage-bill in the year 1977. Robust standard errors are reported in round brackets. ***, **, *: indicate significance at the 1, 5, and 10% levels, respectively. See also notes to previous tables.

Table 7.3 Industry-level regressions: US trade balance with China and the rest of the world, baseline estimates

Dependent variable: wage-bill share of non-production workers, $\omega_{i,t}$

	(1) Trade deficit (overall)	(2) Trade deficit (China & RoW)	(3) Offsh.	(4) TFP	(5) Trade openness	(6) Trade deficit and offsh.	(7) Trade deficit and TFP	(8) Trade deficit trade openness	(9) All variables	(10) Controlling for the skill premium
$T_{i,t}$	0.128***									
	(0.017)									
$TCH_{i,t}$		0.097***				0.094***	0.092***	0.084***	0.090***	0.096***
		(0.017)				(0.015)	(0.017)	(0.019)	(0.019)	(0.018)
$TROW_{i,t}$		0.065***				0.056***	0.063***	0.050***	0.055***	0.060***
		(0.012)				(0.012)	(0.012)	(0.018)	(0.017)	(0.015)
$MOS_{i,t}$			0.087***			0.050***			0.045**	0.039**
			(0.018)			(0.017)			(0.019)	(0.017)
$TFP_{i,t}$				0.041***			0.027***		0.044***	0.060***
				(0.010)			(0.010)		(0.014)	(0.013)
$OPEN_{i,t}$					0.130***			0.031	-0.004	-0.010
					(0.016)			(0.025)	(0.026)	(0.023)
$\ln(K/Y)_{i,t}$	0.188***	0.189***	0.187***	0.238***	0.186***	0.193***	0.227***	0.189***	0.259***	0.266***
	(0.018)	(0.018)	(0.019)	(0.023)	(0.018)	(0.019)	(0.023)	(0.018)	(0.028)	(0.027)
$\ln(Y)_{i,t}$	0.249***	0.250***	0.251***	0.166***	0.246***	0.279***	0.214***	0.251***	0.255***	0.243***
	(0.030)	(0.030)	(0.039)	(0.034)	(0.030)	(0.037)	(0.033)	(0.030)	(0.036)	(0.035)
$\ln(w_H/w_L)_{i,t}$										0.188***
										(0.012)
Observations	7,425	7,425	7,213	7,425	7,425	7,213	7,425	7,425	7,213	7,213
R-squared	0.97	0.97	0.96	0.97	0.97	0.96	0.97	0.97	0.96	0.97
Year FE	yes	yes	yes	yes	yes	yes	yes	yes	yes	yes
Industry FE	yes	yes	yes	yes	yes	yes	yes	yes	yes	yes

Notes: all specifications are estimated on a panel of 333 (4-digit SIC) US manufacturing industries. The sample period is 1977–2005. TCH is the trade deficit with China over value added. TROW is the trade deficit with the rest of the world over value added. All coefficients are beta coefficients. All regressions are weighted by the industries' shares in total manufacturing wage-bill in the year 1977. Robust standard errors are reported in round brackets. ***, **, *: indicate significance at the 1, 5, and 10% levels, respectively. See also notes to previous tables.

Table 7.6 Industry-level regressions: US trade balance with China and the rest of the world, robustness checks

Dependent variable: wage-bill share of non-production workers, $\omega_{i,t}$

	(1) Real output	(2) Capital–output ratio	(3) Offsh.	(4) Trade openness	(5) TFP	(6) Industry-specific time trends	(7) Real output	(8) Capital–output ratio	(9) Offsh.	(10) Trade openness	(11) TFP	(12) Industry-time effects
$TCH_{i,t}$	0.075***	0.079***	0.085***	0.093***	0.099***	0.048*	0.086***	0.086***	0.080***	0.041***	0.089***	0.048***
	(0.019)	(0.019)	(0.020)	(0.020)	(0.019)	(0.027)	(0.018)	(0.020)	(0.019)	(0.015)	(0.019)	(0.016)
$TROW_{i,t}$	0.065***	0.044***	0.049***	0.046***	0.064***	0.046**	0.069***	0.061***	0.047***	0.036**	0.054***	0.034**
	(0.017)	(0.017)	(0.017)	(0.017)	(0.017)	(0.018)	(0.016)	(0.017)	(0.017)	(0.017)	(0.017)	(0.016)
$MOS_{i,t}$	0.036*	0.050***	0.065***	0.055***	0.057***	−0.010	0.045***	0.034*	0.036*	0.002	0.033*	0.049***
	(0.017)	(0.017)	(0.017)	(0.017)	(0.017)	(0.018)	(0.016)	(0.017)	(0.017)	(0.017)	(0.017)	(0.016)
$TFP_{i,t}$	0.010	0.062***	0.043***	0.037***	0.022	−0.020	0.015	0.035***	0.028**	0.017	0.054***	0.029**
	(0.013)	(0.014)	(0.014)	(0.013)	(0.018)	(0.018)	(0.017)	(0.019)	(0.021)	(0.016)	(0.018)	(0.017)
$OPEN_{i,t}$	−0.029	−0.002	0.007	0.011	−0.032	−0.070**	−0.046*	−0.010	0.013	−0.025	−0.001	−0.024
	(0.013)	(0.014)	(0.014)	(0.013)	(0.018)	(0.016)	(0.012)	(0.013)	(0.012)	(0.012)	(0.015)	(0.014)
$\ln(K/Y)_{i,t}$	0.170***	0.249***	0.258***	0.247***	0.233***	0.154***	0.165***	0.216***	0.200***	0.196***	0.229***	0.169***
	(0.025)	(0.027)	(0.027)	(0.027)	(0.027)	(0.032)	(0.025)	(0.026)	(0.025)	(0.026)	(0.026)	(0.025)
$\ln(Y)_{i,t}$	0.170***	0.249***	0.258***	0.247***	0.233***	0.154***	0.165***	0.216***	0.200***	0.196***	0.229***	0.169***
	(0.027)	(0.027)	(0.028)	(0.027)	(0.031)	(0.031)	(0.030)	(0.024)	(0.024)	(0.024)	(0.025)	(0.026)
	0.202***	0.203***	0.261***	0.264***	0.216***	0.079	0.113**	0.255***	0.226***	0.272***	0.193***	0.177***
	(0.035)	(0.037)	(0.036)	(0.036)	(0.038)	(0.058)	(0.055)	(0.033)	(0.031)	(0.033)	(0.035)	(0.034)
Observations	7,213	7,213	7,213	7,213	7,213	7,213	7,213	7,213	7,213	7,213	7,213	7,213
R-squared	0.96	0.96	0.96	0.96	0.96	0.98	0.97	0.97	0.97	0.97	0.97	0.97
Year FE	yes	yes	yes	yes	yes	yes	yes	yes	yes	yes	yes	yes
Industry FE	yes	yes	yes	yes	yes	yes	yes	yes	yes	yes	yes	yes

Notes: columns (1)–(5) include controls for heterogeneous trends based on pre-existing industry characteristics (coefficients unreported), which are constructed as explained in the footnote to Table 7.3. Column (6) includes a full set of industry-specific linear trends. Columns (7)–(11) include controls for contemporaneous shocks (coefficients unreported), which are constructed as explained in the footnote to Table 7.4. Column (12) includes a full set of 2-digit industry-time effects. All regressions are weighted by the industries' shares in total manufacturing wage-bill in the year 1977. Robust standard errors are reported in round brackets. ***, **, *: indicate significance at the 1, 5, and 10% levels, respectively. See also notes to previous tables.

Consequently, the vast literature documenting skill upgrading within US manufacturing industries pointed at skill-biased technical change as the main culprit. Yet, an early literature for the 1980s found trade deficits to strongly affect the relative demand for skills and the skill premium in the USA. Building on Feenstra and Hanson (1996) and our earlier work (Crinò and Epifani, 2014), we have provided a theoretical underpinning for such a link. Specifically, we have argued that, just as offshoring in Feenstra and Hanson's framework, a Southern trade surplus leads the South to acquire (and the North to dismiss) a range of activities that are more (less) skill intensive than the Southern (Northern) average, thereby acting as a sort of skill-biased technical change which induces skill upgrading in both regions. Using data for a panel of US industries, we have found robust support for our theory. Moreover, we have found that the impact of trade deficits on the relative demand for skills seems stronger than that of trade liberalization, offshoring, and TFP growth.

Bibliography

Acemoglu, D. and D. Autor (2011). Skills, tasks and technologies: implications for employment and earnings. In D. Card and O. Ashenfelter (eds), *Handbook of Labor Economics*, Amsterdam: Elsevier, 4B, 1043–171.

Artuc, E., S. Chaudhuri, and J. McLaren (2010). Trade Shocks and Labor Adjustment: A Structural Empirical Approach, *American Economic Review*, 100: 1008–45.

Autor, D., D. Dorn, and G. H. Hanson (2013). The China Syndrome: Local Labor Market Effects of Import Competition in the United States, *American Economic Review*, 103(6): 2121–68.

Berman E., J. Bound, and Z. Griliches (1994). Changes in the Demand for Skilled Labor within U.S. Manufacturing: Evidence from the Annual Survey of Manufactures, *Quarterly Journal of Economics*, 109: 367–97.

Bernard, A. and J. B. Jensen (1995). Exporters, Jobs, and Wages in US Manufacturing: 1976–87, *Brookings Papers on Economic Activity: Microeconomics*, 1995: 67–112.

Bernard, A. and J. B. Jensen (1997). Exporters, Skill Upgrading and the Wage Gap, *Journal of International Economics*, 42: 3–31.

Borjas, G., R. Freeman, and L. Katz (1991). On the Labor Market Effects of Immigration and Trade, NBER working paper 3671.

Bound, J. and G. Johnson (1992). Changes in the Structure of Wages in the 1980s: An Evaluation of Alternative Explanations, *American Economic Review*, 82: 371–92.

Bustos, P. (2011). The Impact of Trade Liberalization on Skill Upgrading. Evidence from Argentina, working paper, CREI.

Chun Zhu, S. and D. Trefler (2005). Trade and Inequality in Developing Countries: A General Equilibrium Analysis, *Journal of International Economics*, 65: 21–48.

Crinò, R. (2009). Offshoring, Multinationals and Labour Market: A Review of the Empirical Literature, *Journal of Economic Surveys*, 23: 197–249.

Crinò, R. (2010). Service Offshoring and White-collar Employment, *Review of Economic Studies*, 77: 595–632.

Crinò, R. and P. Epifani (2014). Trade Imbalances, Export Structure and Wage Inequality, *The Economic Journal*, 124(576): 507–39.

Dekle, R., J. Eaton, and S. Kortum (2007). Unbalanced Trade, *American Economic Review P&P*, 97: 351–5.

Dekle, R., J. Eaton, and S. Kortum (2008). Global Rebalancing with Gravity: Measuring the Burden of Adjustment, *IMF Staff Papers*, 55: 511–40.

Dornbusch, R., S. Fischer, and P. Samuelson (1977). Comparative Advantage, Trade and Payments in a Ricardian Model with a Continuum of Goods, *American Economic Review*, 67: 823–39.

Dornbusch, R., S. Fischer, and P. Samuelson (1980). Heckscher–Ohlin Trade Theory with a Continuum of Goods, *Quarterly Journal of Economics*, 95: 203–24.

Ebenstein, A., A. Harrison, M. McMillan, and S. Phillips (2014). Estimating the Impact of Trade and Offshoring on American Workers Using the Current Population Surveys, *Review of Economics and Statistics*, 96(3): 581–95.

Epifani, P. and G. Gancia (2006). Increasing Returns, Imperfect Competition and Factor Prices, *Review of Economics and Statistics*, 88: 583–98.

Epifani, P. and G. Gancia (2008). The skill Bias of World Trade, *Economic Journal*, 118: 927–60.

Feenstra, R. C. (2004). *Advanced International Trade: Theory and Evidence*. Princeton, NJ: Princeton University Press.

Feenstra, R. C. and G. H. Hanson (1996). Foreign investment, outsourcing and relative wages. In R. C. Feenstra *et al.* (eds), *The Political Economy of Trade Policy: Papers in Honor of Jagdish Bhagwati*, Cambridge, MA: MIT Press, 89–127.

Feenstra, R. C. and G. H. Hanson (1999). The Impact of Outsourcing and High-technology Capital on Wages: Estimates for the United States, 1979–1990, *Quarterly Journal of Economics*, 114: 907–40.

Feenstra, R. C., R. E. Lipsey, H. Deng, A. C. Ma, and H. Mo (2005). World Trade Flows: 1962–2000, NBER working paper 11040.

Feenstra, R. C., J. Romalis, and P. K. Schott (2002). U.S. Imports, Exports and Tariff Data, NBER working paper 9387.

Goldberg, P. K., A. K. Khandelwal, N. Pavcnik, and P. Topalova (2010). Imported Intermediate Inputs and Domestic Product Growth: Evidence from India, *Quarterly Journal of Economics*, 125: 1727–67.

Goldberg, P. K. and N. Pavcnick (2007). Distributional Effects of Globalization in Developing Countries, *Journal of Economic Literature*, 45: 39–82.

Helpman, E., O. Itskhoki and S. Redding (2010). Inequality and Unemployment in a Global Economy, *Econometrica*, 78: 1239–83.

Murphy, K. and F. Welch (1992). The Structure of Wages, *Quarterly Journal of Economics*, 107: 285–326.

Schott, P. K. (2008). The Relative Sophistication of Chinese Exports, *Economic Policy*, 23: 5–49.

Verhoogen, E. (2008). Trade, Quality Upgrading and Wage Inequality in the Mexican Manufacturing Sector, *Quarterly Journal of Economics*, 123: 489–530.

Yeaple, S. R. (2005). A Simple Model of Firm Heterogeneity, International Trade and Wages, *Journal of International Economics*, 65: 1–20.

8

Why are American Workers Getting Poorer? China, Trade, and Offshoring

Avraham Ebenstein, Ann Harrison, and Margaret McMillan

8.1 Introduction

Between 1983 and 2008, the US economy experienced a doubling of imports of manufactured goods, and US multinational corporations tripled their employment in low-income countries. Over this same period, domestic US manufacturing employment declined from 22 million to 16 million (Current Population Survey, CPS). Since the 'great recession' of 2008, US manufacturing has declined precipitously, with nearly 2 million additional jobs lost. Today, the US employment recovery remains anemic, and millions of Americans of working age are either unemployed or out of the labour force entirely. Many blame these trends on globalization, and in particular, on China.

Following China's accession to the World Trade Organization (WTO) in 2001, Chinese imports to the USA surged. Chinese imports currently represent over 8 per cent of total imports and nearly 600,000 Chinese workers were employed at US multinational affiliates by 2008. These parallel developments led some critics of globalization to conclude that 'good' manufacturing jobs have been shipped overseas, and the USA's pre-eminence in the world economy had been usurped by China. But defenders of globalization respond that the role of trade and offshoring in these trends is exaggerated. They argue that empirical support for a direct role of foreign competition in explaining the decline in US manufacturing is limited, in spite of popular opinion blaming globalization and China in particular.

One possible explanation for the lack of evidence regarding the impact of trade on US workers is that most research has focused on analysis of workers in affected industries. In the standard approach, the wage effects of import competition on wages are identified by exploiting variation in the prices (or quantities) of imported goods across different manufacturing industries and examining their impact within manufacturing. Examples include Feenstra and Hanson (1999), Bernard, Jensen, and Schott (2006), and Autor, Dorn, and Hanson (2013). However, these papers generally ignore a key marker for exposure to overseas competition, which is whether a worker's occupation can be performed more cheaply and reliably in China. Relying on analysis at the industry level may also fail to account for structural change that occurs in response to trade. Insofar as globalization affects the US labour market by pushing workers out of manufacturing and into services, a better measure of globalization's impact is found by focusing on occupational exposure to globalization. This is because workers can more easily switch industries than occupations (Kambourov and Manovskii 2009a, 2009b), and so the wage declines will be felt by workers who are forced to leave manufacturing or their occupation entirely.

In Ebenstein et al. (2014), we present evidence that an occupation-based analysis is more effective at uncovering the impact on worker wages of global competition. We find significant wage declines for American workers exposed to globalization, especially among workers performing tasks that are routine, and can presumably be performed offshore. In this chapter, we extend this work, and improve upon it in several ways. Due to data limitations, Ebenstein et al. (2014) focused on the period between 1983 and 2002.[1] In this chapter, we include the effects of trade observed up to 2008, which allows us to include a period characterized by rapid increases in offshoring, especially to China following its accession to the WTO at the end of 2001.

In this chapter, we also focus greater attention on the differences between offshoring and imports. Most recent papers analysing the impact of trade on labour outcomes (e.g. Autor, Dorn, and Hanson 2013 or Pierce and Schott 2012) focus on trade in goods. However, trade in tasks, or offshoring, has the ability to affect a much wider class of workers. As we will demonstrate, while imports are often found in low value added sectors (e.g. toys), offshore employment is most common in high value-added sectors, such as motor vehicles and electronics, where companies would not want to share their intellectual property with a foreign firm. These industries have historically had higher rates

---

[1] The updated analysis was made possible by recently-released trade and offshoring data, as well as IPUMS-Minnesota, which provided concordances necessary to generate industry and occupation codes consistent over time, including the switch between 2002 and 2003 from SIC to NAICS.

of unionization, and higher US wages. This new trend is potentially much more threatening to US workers by reducing their bargaining leverage. Insofar as the threat to move a factory overseas to China is credible, globalization can generate downward pressure on wages, and affect even those workers whose jobs are not sent overseas. If the wages prevailing in an occupation become sufficiently low relative to historical standards, many older workers may begin to exit the labour force entirely.

A second contribution of this chapter is to disaggregate the impact of geographically distinct sources of offshore employment changes on domestic US wages. In particular, we measure the impact of offshore employment by US multinationals in China, Mexico, India, and other low-income locations. We also compare their impact on domestic US wages with offshore employment growth in high-income locations. We concentrate our analysis on China, and compare the effects of import competition from China and offshore employment in China on US worker wages.

Consistent with our earlier results, we find that offshoring to low wage countries is associated with wage declines for US workers, and the workers most affected are those performing routine tasks. Our results indicate that a 10 percentage point increase in occupational exposure to import competition is associated with a 2.7 per cent decline in real wages for workers who perform routine tasks.[2] We also find substantial wage effects of offshoring to low wage countries: a 10 per cent increase in occupation-specific exposure to overseas employment in low wage countries is associated with a 0.27 per cent decline in real wages for workers performing routine tasks for our entire sample, and nearly a 1 per cent decline for 2000–2008. The wages of workers without higher education and older workers are disproportionaley affected by offshoring activities, as the point estimates are larger for these groups of workers. If instead we measure exposure to globalization at the industry level, we find no significant effects on US worker wages.

The downward pressure from trade and offshoring on US wages using occupational (but not industry-level) measures of globalization explains the puzzling results reported in Autor, Dorn, and Hanson (2013). They find a positive, but insignificant impact of import competition on local wages, leading them to conclude that 'manufacturing plants react to import competition by accelerating technological and

---

[2] This finding is consistent with recent work highlighting the differential impact of offshoring by worker skill type. Hummels et al. (2011) use matched worker and firm data from Denmark and find that offshoring raises skilled worker wages but lowers unskilled worker wages, while exporting raises the wages of all types of workers.

organizational innovations that increase productivity and may raise wages'. Our research suggests that occupational exposure to globalization puts significant downward pressure on wages because such a measure captures the movement of workers out of manufacturing and into lower wage services.

We explicitly test the importance of this mechanism to confirm the stark differences between occupational versus industry measures of globalization. Using a subset of the CPS data where we are able to follow the same worker over time, we measure what happens to worker wages when they switch industries or occupations. Since our original exercise was motivated by the possibility that globalization has affected US workers by forcing them out of manufacturing,[3] we directly examine the wage impact of switching within manufacturing, switching from manufacturing, and finally, both switching out of manufacturing and switching occupations. We find evidence that while the wage impacts of switches within manufacturing are mild, leaving manufacturing for services is associated with an appreciable loss in wages, and larger losses still for workers who are forced to switch occupation upon leaving manufacturing. This highlights the importance of examining the impact of globalization by looking beyond only workers employed directly in manufacturing.

We then turn to a more in-depth analysis of competition from China, the US's largest trading partner and second most popular destination for offshoring (after Mexico) in 2008. We present evidence that both imports from China and offshoring to China are associated with lower US worker wages. Increasing occupational import penetration from China by a 10 percentage point share of a market is associated with a 5.6 per cent wage decline, and increasing occupational offshore exposure to China is associated with a further 1.6 per cent decline in wages. The results suggest that focus on imports alone (as in Autor, Dorn, and Hanson 2013) may understate the role of globalization in contributing to falling US wages.

Lastly, we begin to examine the role played by trade and offshoring in explaining US labour force participation. In the wake of the global financial crisis and the slow recovery, the US has suffered persistently high rates of unemployment relative to historical averages, and generational lows in labour force participation rates. While some of this

---

[3] Our results corroborate results on employment declines within manufacturing by Harrison and McMillan (2011) who use firm-level data on multinational manufacturing firms, but stand in contrast to Desai, Foley, and Hines (2009). Desai, Foley, and Hines do not distinguish between high wage and low wage affiliate employment and find that offshoring is unambiguously positive for US employment.

is due to population ageing, the decline in labour force participation is thought to reflect the long-term weakness of the labour market. Many unemployed Americans have discontinued their job searches, but the extent to which this is related to globalization is unclear. We hypothesize that for workers who participated in the 'glory days' of American manufacturing, the offered wages available in the market where they could secure employment do not justify working or continuing a job search.

In our empirical analysis, we examine the relationship between trade, offshoring, and labour force participation. We find a robust negative correlation between offshore exposure to China and labour force participation, within age–year–occupation cells but interestingly, a positive relationship between labour force participation and import competition from China. The evidence suggests that factors associated with computer use and increasing capital intensity are much more significantly associated with declining employment. Consistent with Harrison and McMillan (2011), we find very small effects of globalization on labour force participation and large effects of computer use and the price of investment goods. Falling investment goods prices are associated with increasing use of capital. Greater use of computers and capital equipment is associated with lower employment, higher unemployment, and lower labour force participation. Taken together, our results indicate that while globalization as measured by trade and offshoring is associated with downward pressure on US wages, globalization is not strongly associated with the historically low rates of labour force participation. In fact, import competition appears to be associated with higher rates of labour force participation, higher employment, and lower unemployment.

The chapter is organized as follows. Section 8.2 describes our data, documents broad trends in trade and offshoring, and presents the empirical specification. Section 8.3 presents our main empirical findings regarding the impact of globalization on domestic wages at the occupation versus the industry level. Section 8.4 examines the role of imports from and offshoring to China and other destination countries in labour force participation in the USA. Section 8.5 concludes.

8.2 Data Description, Empirical Strategy, and Trends

8.2.1 *Data Description*

Our sample of US workers is taken from the Current Population Survey Merged Outgoing Rotation Groups for 1983–2008, which provides data for over 4.3 million workers who are assigned a consistent classification for their industry and occupation during the period.[4] Offshore activity in each industry is measured by the total employment of foreign affiliates by multinational US firms, separated into high- and low-income affiliate locations, as collected by the Bureau of Economic Analysis (BEA).[5] Our data on import penetration and export shares are taken from Bernard at al. (2006), which we recalculated and updated through 2007. We control for productivity changes that could also affect labour demand as well as wages using the NBER's calculations of total factor productivity provided by Wayne Gray, also updated through 2007. Additionally, the NBER data provides measures of the prices of investment goods, capital to labour ratios, and the real price of shipments by industry and year.[6] These are included in our main specifications to control for technological change that could also affect wage rates. We include an occupational exposure version of these variables, which are generated in a manner similar to the globalization variables. Lastly, we match our worker data with information on computer use rates by industry and occupation from CPS computer supplements conducted during our sample period (1984, 1989, 1993, 1997, 2000). Using the available surveys, we interpolate computer use rates for intervening years. Since the CPS changed the nature of the computer question following 2000, we freeze computer use rates by occupation at the rates in 2002.

We use Autor et al.'s (2003) distinction between routine and non-routine tasks to allow us to separately identify the impact of different measures of globalization across different types of workers.[7] To the

---

[4] We would like to express our gratitude to IPUMS-CPS, which generated a consistent coding scheme of industries and occupations for the period. We use occ1990 in our analysis for coding occupation. We use a tweaked version of ind1990 and create a concordance with the BEA industry scheme for coding industry. All programs and public data are available from the authors upon request.

[5] The BEA sample of multinational firms accounted for 80 per cent of total output in manufacturing in 1980, suggesting that the coverage is fairly extensive. However, using these data we are unable to distinguish between imports from affiliates (arms-length trade between firms) and imports from non-affiliates.

[6] These data were aggregated from the 4-digit to 3-digit SIC level using the employment distribution in 1979. The 3-digit SIC level was converted to our industry classification scheme using a concordance provided by David Autor that was a census-based scheme that consistently defined industries for our sample period. A similar method was used to match CPS workers to the trade data.

[7] These data were also provided by David Autor and are used in Autor et al. (1998). Autor et al. (2003) describe routine jobs as 'tasks that can be expressed using procedural or "rules-based" logic, that is, codified in a fully specified sequence of logical programming commands ("If-Then-Do" statements) that designate unambiguously what actions the machine will perform and in what sequence at each contingency to achieve the desired result.'

extent that routine tasks are more easily offshored or replaced with imports, we would expect globalization to have a larger impact on workers performing these types of tasks. While Autor et al. (2003) use routine-ness to designate which jobs can be easily performed by computers, we would argue that routine jobs are also more readily codified, communicated, and consequently transferred overseas. Examples of these jobs include attaching hands to faces of watches, sewing fasteners and decorative trimming to articles of clothing, and services tasks that we think of as offshorable, such as answering telephones. This is described in greater detail in Ebenstein et al. (2014).

8.2.2 Empirical Strategy

Our empirical strategy is to regress log wages of worker i in industry j in period t (W_{ijt}) on lagged measures of exposure to offshoring and international trade (G_{ijt-1}) using annual data from 1983 to 2008, first at the industry level and subsequently at the occupation level, which we define below.

We use lagged measures of exposure to offshoring and trade for two reasons. First, since offshoring requires time to implement, and wage adjustment is not instantaneous, it is unlikely that the causal effect of offshoring on wages will play out within a single calendar year. Second, within a given year, offshoring, trade exposure, and wages are likely to be affected by simultaneous shocks. In our basic specification in Tables 8.1 and 8.2, we use four measures of exposure to offshoring and international trade: offshoring to low-income affiliate locations, offshoring to high-income affiliate locations, export shares, and import penetration. Offshoring is measured as the log of summed employment in sector j and year t by US multinationals in low and high-income countries.

There are three additional challenges to identifying the causal effect of globalization on wages. First, the industries that are most likely to globalize may also be those with lower wages or greater volatility. We address this concern by including industry fixed effects (I_j) in our specification. Second, globalization and wages may be jointly affected by common time-varying shocks, such as the business cycle and exchange rate fluctuations. We control for these by including time-fixed effects (d_t). Third, we control for time-varying shocks at the industry level that could be confounded with changes in globalization by adding a number of additional controls. TFP_{jt-1} captures changes in productivity by industry and year that could affect demand for labour. We also control for productivity changes including two (arguably) exogenous measures, the price of investment goods and computer use rates. The price of investment goods $PINV_{jt-1}$ captures in part the role of falling computer prices and the potential impact of labour-saving technology on labour market outcomes. We also control for industry factor intensity (lagged capital to labour ratio $KLRATIO_{jt-1}$) and computer use rates by industry and year (COMPjt) to account for contemporaneous changes in an industry's wage rate based on the ability to substitute labour with computers.[8] Finally, we control for individual characteristics of the labour force by including age, sex, race, experience, education, and location (Z_{ijt}). The estimating equation at the industry level (for manufacturing only) is given by:

$$W_{ijt} = \beta_0 Z_{ijt} + \beta_1 G_{jt-1} + \beta_2 TFP_{jt-1} + \beta_3 PINV_{jt-1} + \beta_4 KLRATIO_{jt-1}$$
$$+ \beta_5 COMP_{jt} + \beta_6 d_t + \beta_7 I_j + \varepsilon_{ijt}. \tag{8.1}$$

To examine the relationship between wages and globalization at the occupation level, we retain the same setup as in 8.1 but expand the sample to include workers outside of manufacturing. We also modify the G vector to create a measure of occupational exposure to offshoring or trade. Each variable in the G vector was created from a merged dataset of BEA offshore employment data, trade data, and CPS monthly outgoing rotation group individual-level data, by industry and year. We calculate for each occupation its exposure to trade using as weights the distribution of workers employed in this occupation *across* industries in 1983. For each occupation k and industry j, we have: $\alpha_{kj83} = \frac{L_{kj83}}{L_{k83}}$ where L_{kj83} is the total number of workers in occupation k and industry j in 1983, and L_{k83} is the total number of workers across all industries in occupation k. We then calculate occupation-specific import penetration in year t for occupation k as:

$$\sum_{j=1}^{J} \alpha_{kj83} IMP_{jt}$$

where IMP_{jt} is the measure of import penetration for goods in industry j in year t. We continue to control for technological changes by industry, and set these technological changes equal to unity for workers outside of manufacturing.[9]

---

[8] Our results are similar if we control for computer use rates in the previous year.

[9] An alternative approach would be to create occupation-specific measures of each of our control variables. In the online appendix, we estimate models with occupational-specific measures of TFP, the price of investment goods, and the capital to labour ratio. The results are qualitatively similar to the results presented in the main text.

This leads to a specification of the form:

$$W_{ijkt} = \beta_0 Z_{ijkt} + \beta_1 G_{kt-1} + \beta_2 TFP_{jt-1} + \beta_3 PINV_{jt-1} + \beta_4 KLRATIO_{jt-1}$$
$$+ \beta_5 COMP_{kt} + \beta_6 d_t + \beta_7 I_j + \beta_8 Occupation_k + \varepsilon_{ijkt} \qquad (8.2)$$

where k indexes the worker's occupation, and workers within the same k occupation may be in different j industries.[10] For workers outside of manufacturing, the control variables for TFP, $PIINV$, and $REALSHIP$ are produced at an occupation level using the same method as with trade and offshoring, where movement is based on the weighted average of change across industries, where the weights are taken from the occupation's distribution across industries.

Our G vector and technology control variables are now an occupation-specific measure for each worker, and we have added occupation fixed effects to absorb variation specific to time invariant features of occupations. Note that we also control for variation in computer use rates by occupation and year, which is meant to account for wage changes driven by the ability of some occupations to benefit from computer technology (Autor et al. 1998). We will estimate this specification for routine and non-routine workers separately.[11]

8.2.3 Trends in Offshoring, Trade, Employment, and Wages

In this section we outline broad trends in the data for employment, wages, and the relationship between wages and measures of globalization. In Figure 8.1, we compare the trends in employment and wages in the manufacturing sector alongside the same trends in the service sector between 1979 and 2012. We present these trends separately for workers performing routine and non-routine tasks. Total manufacturing employment (using the CPS employment numbers) fell from 22 to below 16 million from 1979 to 2008, with rapid declines at the beginning of the early 1980s and in the late 1990s. Within manufacturing, the labour force has become increasingly high-skilled with a large decline of about 8 million in the number of workers in routine occupations. While there was a modest increase of 1.5 million

---

[10] For workers outside of manufacturing, the control variables for TFP, PIINV, and REALSHIP are not available and are therefore assumed constant in our main specifications.

[11] One important implicit assumption in our approach is that barriers to changing occupations are similar across routine and non-routine occupations. Kambourov and Manovskii (2008) show this to be the case. They also decompose occupation switching across routine and non-routine occupations and show that between 1968 and 1997 workers were not able to escape routine occupations by switching into non-routine ones.

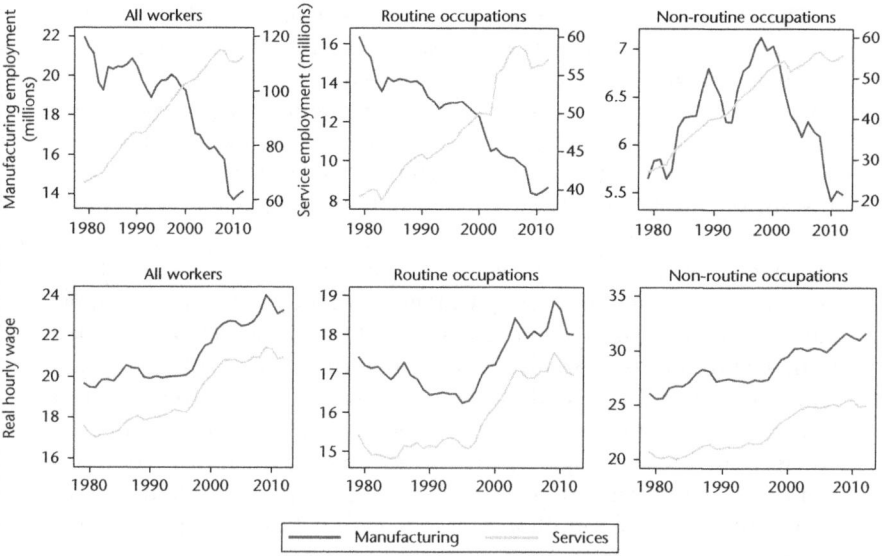

Figure 8.1 Trends in employment and wages in the manufacturing and service sectors

Notes: employment and wage calculations are based on the Current Population Survey Merged Outgoing Rotation Groups (MORG). Sample includes all part-time and full-time workers. Wages are in 2012 dollars. Definition of routine workers is based on occupational task content. Details are available in the data appendix.

between 1979 and 1999 in the number of workers performing non-routine occupations, this increase evaporated in the ten years that followed.

In contrast, demand for both types of workers continued to grow in the service sector, and many of the displaced routine manufacturing workers may have found employment in the service sector. These trends have important implications for the US wage distribution. As shown at the bottom of Figure 8.1, where we report the real hourly wage among CPS workers, manufacturing workers enjoyed a large wage premium during the entire period among both routine and non-routine workers. Insofar as manufacturing provided an opportunity to earn high relative wages—even for low-skilled workers—the fall in manufacturing employment might also have played a role in increasing US income inequality during the period.[12]

---

[12] See Autor et al. (2008) for a review of these trends. It is worth noting that while the trends in Figure 8.1 are informative, they do not control for other factors that affect

The three panels displaying wage trends exhibit significant differences during the sample period. Real wages grew in the 1980s, fell or stagnated in the 1990s, and then began to increase around 1995–1996. Over the entire period, the gap between manufacturing and service wages narrowed, particularly from the mid-1990s onwards. The persistently higher wage offered in manufacturing relative to services during the entire sample period, and present in both routine and non-routine occupations, is an important stylized fact that we emphasize in this chapter. As we will show in Section 8.3, much of the impact of globalization has operated by shifting workers from the higher paid manufacturing sectors to the lower paid service sectors in the US labour market.

In Figure 8.2, we turn to an examination of how offshoring and trade may be related to these employment and wage trends within manufacturing and in the overall economy. As shown in Figure 8.2, foreign affiliate employment in low-income countries by US multinationals nearly tripled from a base of less than a million workers to reaching almost 3 million workers, while affiliate employment in high-income countries remained roughly constant. The increase in developing country activity was accompanied by a reduction in the US workforce domestically from approximately 22 to 16 million from the beginning of the sample period to 2008 when our data on trade and offshoring end.

In Figure 8.3, we report changes in the distribution across destination regions for offshoring activity. The results show significant increases for Mexico, China, India, and other low-income destinations. In Section 8.3 we focus on these three countries, which have received significant attention and which represent important offshore destinations for US multinationals.

8.3 Offshoring, Trade, and the Impact on Domestic Workers

8.3.1 Wage Impacts of Offshoring and Trade at the Industry versus Occupation Level

In Table 8.1, we present our main results showing how the impact of offshoring and trade differ when using industry versus occupation

income, such as sex, age, and experience. We redid the trends in wages by educational attainment using wage residuals. These wage residuals were computed using Lemieux's (2006) approach for each educational category separately. We also added industry dummies to control for inter-industry wage differentials. The wage residuals show similar trends, with falling wage premia for less educated workers and rising wage premia for more educated workers. Similar results are observed for wage premia when workers are stratified by routineness of occupation. Results are available from the authors upon request.

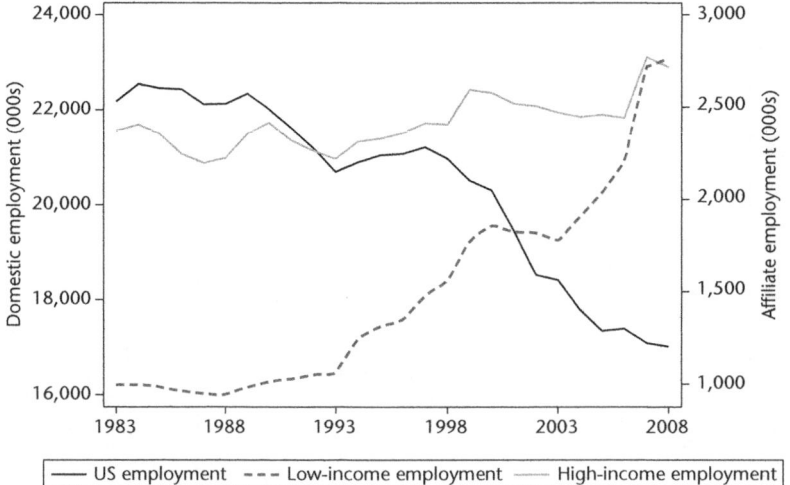

Figure 8.2 Trends in domestic and affiliate employment among multinational firms

Notes: Author's calculations based on the most comprehensive available data and based on firm-level surveys on US direct investment abroad, collected each year by the Bureau of Economic Analysis (BEA) of the US Department of Commerce. Using these data, we compute number of employees hired abroad by country and year, and then aggregate employment by Low (High) Income country according to World Bank income classifications.
Source: Bureau of Economic Analysis.

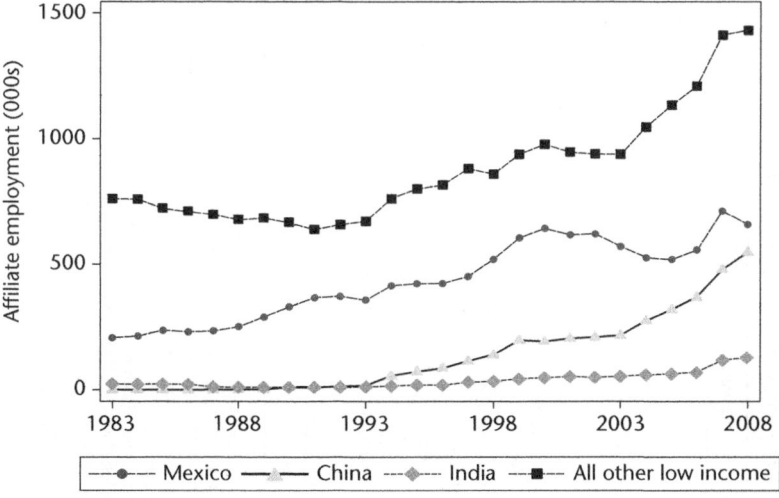

Figure 8.3 Trends in manufacturing affiliate employment in low-income countries

Notes: the 'alll others' category includes all employment in low-income countries other than Mexico, China, and India.
Source: Bureau of Economic Analysis.

Table 8.1 OLS estimates of wage determinants using industry and occupational exposure to offshoring and trade, 1983–2008

Dependent variable: log wage

Variable	Offshoring and trade measured by industry-specific exposure, manufacturing only				Offshoring and trade measured by occupation-specific exposure, all sectors			
	All occupations	Most routine	Intermediate routine	Least routine	All occupations	Most routine	Intermediate routine	Least routine
Lagged log of low-income affiliate employment	0.000 (0.001)	−0.001 (0.001)	−0.001 (0.002)	0.003 (0.003)	−0.0271*** (0.0090)	−0.0682*** (0.0130)	0.0256* (0.0150)	0.0510*** (0.0150)
Lagged log of high-income affiliate employment	0.001 (0.002)	−0.001 (0.002)	0.004 (0.003)	−0.003 (0.005)	0.0158** (0.0080)	0.0493*** (0.0100)	−0.013 (0.014)	−0.0178** (0.0070)
Lagged export share	0.0345* (0.020)	−0.001 (0.025)	0.0921** (0.038)	0.009 (0.050)	0.614*** (0.170)	0.750*** (0.231)	0.995*** (0.319)	−1.930** (0.967)
Lagged import penetration	−0.018 (0.011)	−0.010 (0.012)	−0.038 (0.027)	0.017 (0.031)	−0.277** (0.125)	−0.041 (0.100)	−1.548*** (0.340)	0.333 (0.877)
Number of observations	660,500	374,162	196,612	89,726	4,315,758	1,529,895	1,786,437	999,426
R-squared	0.49	0.39	0.43	0.31	0.51	0.42	0.53	0.38

* significant at 10%. ** significant at 5%. *** significant at 1%.

Note: robust standard errors are reported in parentheses below the coefficient estimates. The workers are taken from CPS samples from 1983–2008, with their lagged values of the independent variables taken from 1982–2007. The left side of the table is restricted to manufacturing workers and the right-hand side variables shown are based on the exposure to trade within a worker's industry. The right side of the table includes service workers as well, and all right-hand side variables shown are based on the exposure to trade within a worker's occupation. The standard errors are clustered by occupation and five-year period. The classification of occupations into routine categories is determined by the proportion of tasks which are routine in each occupation, with low being occupations with more than 2/3, intermediate being between 1/3 and 2/3, and high being occupations with less than 1/3 of tasks designated routine. We also control for the occupation-specific lagged log price of investment, lagged total factor productivity, lagged real price of shipments, and lagged capital to labour ratio. Wage specifications control for a worker's gender, age, race, experience, whether in a union, and include fixed effects for industry (3-digit), occupation (2-digit), year, education, and state. Controls for computer use rates are imputed by the worker's occupation using the CPS computer supplement and are included in all specifications.

Source: Current Population Surveys Merged Outgoing Rotation Groups (1983–2008). See Table 8.A1 for sources of the other variables.

measures of exposure. In the first four columns, we present our estimates for equation (8.1) which defines exposure to trade or offshoring at the industry level. In the last four columns, we redo the analysis using our occupation exposure measure, as outlined in equation (8.2). Note that the standard errors are clustered by industry and five-year period in columns (1) through (4) and by occupation and five-year period in the last four columns. Industry regressions include industry fixed effects and occupation regressions include occupation as well as industry fixed effects.

Columns (1) through (4) of Table 8.1 identify the impact on wages of workers in industries which were more exposed to international trade or offshoring during the 1984 through 2008 period.[13] In these four columns, only workers within the manufacturing sector are included in the estimation. The results suggest a very limited role for offshoring or trade in explaining log wages. There is no statistically significant relationship between low-income-affiliate employment, lagged export share, or lagged import penetration and industry-level wages; indeed, the point estimates are close to zero. We find a modest relationship between exports and wages, suggesting that workers with intermediate routine tasks gain the most from export demand. However, this evidence is from only a single significant coefficient, and in general, the table indicates that trade has had only a mild effect on workers within manufacturing. In these first four columns, which rely on differences in exposure to trade or offshoring across industries, the evidence indicates that trade has no substantial negative effect on worker wages for either routine or non-routine workers.

In columns (5) through (8) of Table 8.1, we present results from specification (1b) where we measure exposure to trade or offshoring at the occupation level. The effects of both offshoring and trade are larger in sign and generally significant at the 5 per cent level. In the first row of column (5), the coefficient on low-income affiliate employment indicates that a 10 per cent increase in employment offshored within an occupation is associated with a 0.27 per cent wage reduction for US workers. For workers in the most routine occupations, we find that a 10 per cent increase in low-income affiliate employment abroad is associated with a 0.68 per cent decline in domestic wages, whereas workers in less routine occupations were largely unaffected by offshoring. Although the magnitude of the effect is small, the results are consistent with the following interpretation: workers in low-income

---

[13] Note that we exclude 1983 for consistency with our occupation results, which can only be estimated from 1984–2002, since occupation was only coded consistently from 1983 onwards, and we are using lagged measures of our independent variables.

locations perform the same tasks that low-skilled workers perform in the USA and are therefore substitutes for workers in the USA.

We also find a positive effect of lagged high-income affiliate employment on wages, for all but the least routine workers. Workers in high-income locations appear to perform tasks that are complementary to workers in the USA and so expansion of employment in high-income countries can benefit domestic workers who engage in routine tasks. These results, which are consistent with Harrison and McMillan (2011), are robust to a range of specification choices, including whether we use prices of imported and exported goods instead of quantities, and our chosen set of control variables, such as controlling for the real price of shipments by sector to account for variation in product demand.[14] The results are qualitatively similar to the results presented here, and are available from the authors.

Our results indicate that a 10 percentage point increase in occupational exposure to import competition is associated with nearly a 3 per cent decline in real wages for workers. For intermediate routine workers, a 1 percentage point increase in import penetration translates into a 1.5 percentage point reduction in wages. While some occupations have experienced no increase in import competition (such as teachers), import competition in other occupations (such as shoe manufacturing) has increased by as much as 40 percentage points.[15] For occupations with significant export activity, wages are positively linked to export growth. For these workers, a 10 percentage point increase in export share at the occupation level is associated with a 6.1 per cent increase in wages over the sample period. The gains from growing exports are largest for routine workers and actually negative for less routine workers, which is a puzzle.

Krugman (2008) and Feenstra (2008) both hypothesize that the effects of international trade and offshoring may have increased recently relative to earlier decades. In Table 8.2, we split the sample into earlier and later time periods. In particular, we allow the impact of globalization to vary for 1983–1990, 1991–1999, and 2000–2008.

---

[14] The results indicate that workers with price decreases in their product market have suffered the largest wage declines, with this pattern most pronounced in routine occupations. Similar to our core results, however, this effect is only observed using occupational exposure measures of import price changes. Special thanks to Lawrence Edwards for generous use of his price series data on imports. Other specifications we have tested include removing measures of TFP and controlling for price changes in the service sector using a CPI/PPI index, both of which provide results similar to those presented in Table 8.2. Likewise, the results including the real price of shipments are similar to the results in Table 8.2.

[15] See the online appendix for further information on import exposure by occupation.

Table 8.2 OLS estimates of wage determinants using occupational exposure to offshoring and trade among subsamples of CPS workers, 1983–2008

Dependent variable: log wage

Specification	Lagged log of low-income affiliate emp	Lagged log of high-income affiliate emp	Lagged export share	Lagged import penetration	Observations	R-squared
1983–1990	-0.0140 (0.015)	0.0080 (0.011)	0.510 (0.324)	-0.151 (0.168)	1,385,716	0.55
1991–1999	-0.0150 (0.014)	0.0044 (0.012)	0.600*** (0.221)	0.016 (0.213)	1,434,790	0.51
2000–2008	-0.0395** (0.020)	0.0302* (0.017)	0.496* (0.270)	-0.170 (0.129)	1,495,252	0.47
Female	-0.0195** (0.009)	0.0097 (0.008)	1.015*** (0.237)	-0.228* (0.119)	2,101,141	0.49
Union	-0.0179* (0.010)	0.0070 (0.009)	-0.036 (0.189)	0.005 (0.130)	740,506	0.38
High school or less	-0.0466*** (0.010)	0.0366*** (0.009)	0.575*** (0.204)	-0.140 (0.121)	2,020,735	0.44
College or more	-0.0060 (0.011)	-0.0032 (0.009)	0.666*** (0.173)	-0.373** (0.146)	2,295,023	0.45
Under 35	-0.0280*** (0.009)	0.0155** (0.007)	0.958*** (0.181)	-0.422*** (0.142)	1,987,180	0.51
Over 40	-0.0337*** (0.010)	0.0209** (0.009)	0.283* (0.169)	-0.097 (0.120)	1,873,255	0.47
Over 50	-0.0387*** (0.010)	0.0249*** (0.009)	0.250 (0.172)	-0.079 (0.126)	851,052	0.47

* significant at 10% ** significant at 5%. *** significant at 1%.

Note: each row represents a separate regression. The independent variables are listed in the column headings, and the subsample of interest is listed in the row heading. Each regression is estimated in the same manner as those reported in Table 8.1.

Source: see Table 8.5.

We also explore whether the impact of globalization varied by gender, union status, education, and age.

The results in Table 8.2 suggest that there is no significant association between log wages and employment in offshore locations in the early years of our sample (1983–1990, 1991–1998). However, in the later periods (2000–2008) worker wages are negatively and significantly associated with increased offshore employment in low-income affiliate locations. In the years 2000–2008, the coefficient estimates in the third row of Table 8.2 indicate that a 10 per cent increase in low-income affiliate employment is associated with a 0.4 per cent decrease in domestic wages. These negative coefficients contrast with the positive coefficients on high-income affiliate employment, a 10 per cent increase in high-income affiliate employment is associated with a 0.3 per cent increase in domestic wages.

Table 8.2 also reports the coefficient on lagged imports and exports, measured at the occupation level. The point estimates for occupation-specific import penetration are statistically significant for some of the specifications. For example, among women, a 10 percentage point increase in import penetration is associated with a 2.28 per cent wage decline, significant at the 10 per cent level. The evidence also points to a positive and significant association between export share and domestic wages.

In Table 8.2, we also explore heterogeneity in our results across different demographic groups. Anecdotes in the popular press and elsewhere suggest that women, union workers, less educated workers, and older workers may have been disproportionately affected by international competition. If we restrict the sample to either women or union workers, there is no evidence that their wages were more negatively affected than the rest of the sample. In fact, the wages of unionized workers appear to have been relatively unaffected by either export activity or import competition. Women seem to have significantly benefited from export activity.

The wages of workers without higher education and older workers do appear to have been disproportionately affected by offshoring activities, as the point estimates are larger for these groups of workers. The estimates in Table 8.2 indicate that the largest negative and significant effects of offshore employment were concentrated among older or less educated workers. In contrast, the largest (negative) impacts of import competition and (positive) effects of export activity on wages are concentrated among individuals under 35 years of age and college educated workers.

8.3.2 Mechanisms for Differences between Occupation and Industry Results

In this section, we identify mechanisms for the differences between industry-level and occupation-level exposure to offshoring and trade. Our evidence and previous research suggest that switching occupations, but not sectors within manufacturing, significantly affects worker wages. In this section, we directly link changes in occupations for the same individual with changes in globalization and explore the impact on wages. We begin by examining the wage consequences of switching industries, sectors, and occupations using a panel of CPS workers who are followed for more than one period.

To explore the impact of switching sectors or occupations, we construct a sample of manufacturing workers observed in CPS samples in consecutive years between 1983 and 2008. We regress the change in log wages between period t and $t + 1$ for a given worker on an indicator for switching industries, sectors, or occupations. We also include a rich set of controls for the worker's age, sex, education, race, union status in the first period, and industry in the first period. If occupational exposure to globalization puts downward pressure on wages by inducing workers to exit high wage jobs in manufacturing, then we would expect to see this in the data. In particular, we would expect wages of manufacturing workers who retain their jobs to be relatively unaffected by globalization, whereas those who shift sectors or occupations would be negatively affected. In Table 8.3, we examine the impact on a worker's wages of shifting across manufacturing sectors, leaving manufacturing, and leaving an occupation within manufacturing. The first panel (Panel A) of Table 8.3 examines the impact on wages for workers who switch industries but remain within manufacturing during both periods. Consistent with the results in Table 8.1, we see that switching sectors (from textiles to steel, for example) but remaining in the same occupation within manufacturing is not associated with significant wage changes. For all types of occupations, including the most routine occupations, switching industries has no significant impact on worker wages. In Panel B of Table 8.3, we examine how the wages of an individual are affected when that worker leaves manufacturing. On average, a worker who leaves the manufacturing sector experiences a real wage decline of 3 per cent from one period to the next. The documented wage decline for an individual worker in the CPS who leaves manufacturing is consistent with Figure 8.1 showing a wage premium for workers in manufacturing. However, unlike Figure 8.1, the regression results in Table 8.3 control for a wide range of individual worker characteristics.

Table 8.3 Wage changes observed over two periods among manufacturing workers who switch industry, 1983–2008

Dependent variable: log wage change between periods

	All occupations	Most routine	Intermediate routine	Least routine
Panel A: Sample of Workers Who Stay in Manufacturing Both Periods				
Switched Industry Classification (1=yes)	−0.001	0.000	0.000	−0.0133**
	(0.003)	(0.003)	(0.005)	(0.006)
Observations	177,759	111,833	42,600	23,326
Panel B: Sample of Workers Who Switch Industry Classification between Periods				
Left Manufacturing (1=yes)	−0.0269***	−0.0267***	−0.0273***	−0.0220**
	(0.0040)	(0.0060)	(0.0050)	(0.0110)
Observations	208,979	130,105	50,364	28,510
Panel C: Sample of Workers Who Leave Manufacturing between Periods				
Switched Occupation (1=yes)	−0.0406***	−0.0276***	−0.0393***	−0.0852***
	(0.0100)	(0.0100)	(0.0110)	(0.0200)
Observations	32,212	18,696	7,947	5,569

* significant at 10% ** significant at 5%. *** significant at 1%.

Note: robust standard errors reported in parentheses below coefficient estimates. Standard errors are clustered by occupation. All models include year, state, and education level fixed effects. Other demographic controls are age, sex, non-white, and union status in the first period. Industries and occupations are defined by 3-digit census classifications. Classification of routine is based on first period occupation. The classification of occupations into routine categories is determined by the proportion of tasks which are routine in each occupation, with low being occupations with more than 2/3, intermediate being between 1/3 and 2/3, and high being occupations with less than 1/3 of tasks designated routine.

Source: sample is composed of CPS MORG workers observed in two consecutive samples and employed in manufacturing in the first period.

The last panel of Table 8.3 shows the highest real wage declines for workers who leave manufacturing *and* switch occupations. On average, workers who leave manufacturing and switch occupations experienced a real wage decline of 4 per cent, with a range of 2.7 to 8.5 per cent. To summarize, Table 8.3 shows that (1) remaining in the same occupation but switching industries within manufacturing does not significantly affect a worker's wages, (2) leaving manufacturing but remaining within the same occupation has a negative impact on an individual's real wage, and (3) leaving manufacturing is particularly costly for workers who also switch occupations.

The evidence presented in Table 8.3 is consistent with the results presented earlier in the chapter but does not establish a direct link with trade or offshoring. In Ebenstein, Harrison, McMillan, and Phillips (2014), direct linkages are explored between switching sectors or occupations and our different globalization measures. We decompose the results in the last four columns of Table 8.2 into manufacturing only and services only. The impact of offshoring and trade is significant using the occupational exposure measure for both manufacturing (only) and services (only).[16] What is particularly noteworthy is that the coefficients are the most negative for services. Paul Krugman (2008) has argued that globalization could not possibly affect wage outcomes in the USA because manufacturing is too small relative to the other sectors of the economy, so the 'tail can't wag the dog'. However, our results suggest that, in fact, the significant exposure at the occupational level to trade or offshoring does affect service sector wages. This is likely to operate both through the falling wages of workers who have moved from manufacturing to services (as documented in Figure 8.1 and Table 8.3) as well as by putting downward pressure on the wages of workers in services as labour supply in services shifts out to absorb workers formerly in manufacturing.

Our results are consistent with work by Kambourov and Manovskii (2008, 2009a, 2009b) who find large wage declines among workers who switch occupations; this evidence suggests an important role for occupation-specific human capital in a worker's wage profile. Kambourov and Manovskii (2008, 2009a, 2009b) also argue that occupation-switching may be an important cause of the increase in US wage inequality, as younger workers are missing out on the benefits that accrue to occupational tenure enjoyed by workers in previous decades. Insofar as this is partly driven by competition from overseas, this

---

[16] Those results are available in the Appendix to Ebenstein et al. (2014).

highlights another mechanism by which offshoring may be responsible for declining US wages and increasing wage inequality.

8.4 Offshoring to Low-income Countries and Labour Force Participation

8.4.1 Descriptive Statistics

Some theories of foreign investment emphasize the horizontal nature of FDI and the fact that it substitutes for international trade. Other theories emphasize the vertical nature of FDI and focus on offshoring as an outcome of strategic and profit-maximizing location decisions to increase the efficiency of global value chains. In this section, we begin our discussion of the impact of offshoring on US wages by summarizing the patterns in trade and offshoring in 2007, as reported in Table 8.4.

Table 8.4 reports the sectors with the greatest activity in imports, exports, and offshoring. Imports and exports are measured as a share of domestic production, while offshore activities are measured using total foreign affiliate employment. All the data are calculated for 2007, the latest year for which we have information on both trade and offshoring. Import penetration is highest in lower value added industries, and sectors which are traditionally thought to be labour-intensive. This includes toys, leather products, apparel and other textiles, and metal products.

In contrast, offshoring occurs primarily in high value added industries, such as motor vehicles and electronics. There are many possible reasons for this. Historically, the sectors where offshore employment for US multinationals has been highest in Mexico, China, and India and other emerging markets are those where domestic tariffs were the highest. This means that in order to access those markets, US companies needed to establish offshore operations there instead of exporting, which was more challenging given the size of local tariffs or other restrictions on entry. Foreign investment promotion efforts in many developing countries have also targeted these types of activities, as countries like India and China have sought to grow their own motor vehicle, electrical machinery, and other higher tech sectors. This evidence, while preliminary, may indicate that offshoring could expose a larger and different class of workers to international competition than trade alone.

8.4.2 Occupational Exposure by Country of Destination

Tables 8.5 and 8.6 redo our basic specification but replace the offshoring measure with location-specific measures of offshore activity. Table 8.5

Table 8.4 Summarizing patterns in trade and offshoring: five largest observations for each category

Panel A: patterns in exports and import penetration

Export share		Import penetration		Low wage country import penetration		China import penetration	
0.42	Toys, amusement, and sporting goods	0.93	Primary aluminum industries	0.47	Toys, amusement, and sporting goods	0.46	Toys, amusement, and sporting goods
0.39	Pottery and related products	0.88	Watches and clocks	0.40	Leather and leather products	0.37	Leather and leather products
0.32	Construction machines	0.68	Pottery and related products	0.37	Apparel and other textiles	0.33	Pottery and related products
0.32	Primary aluminum industries	0.63	Apparel and other textiles	0.36	Pottery and related products	0.22	Household appliances
0.25	Engines and turbines	0.59	Toys, amusement, and sporting goods	0.22	Household appliances	0.20	Apparel and other textiles

Panel B: patterns in offshore employment

Mexico		China		India		All other low-income countries	
193,498	Motor vehicles and equipment	106,971	Electrical machinery and equipment	19,760	Motor vehicles and equipment	228,401	Motor vehicles and equipment
100,674	Sugar and confectionery products	55,890	Motor vehicles and equipment	15,893	Sugar and confectionery products	139,338	Sugar and confectionery products
63,464	Electrical machinery and equipment	37,400	Drugs	14,411	Electrical machinery and equipment	119,144	Machinery and equipment (NEC)
36,412	Radio, TV, and related equipment	33,223	Other machinery (NEC)	12,178	Drugs	82,880	Apparel and textile products
33,701	Household appliances	32,460	Radio, TV, and related equipment	10,746	Other machinery (NEC)	78,860	Tobacco manufactures

Notes: NEC=Not Elsewhere Classified. Firms are reported as having offshore employment by the BEA when an overseas affiliate is at least 10% owned by a US-based parent corporation.

Source: export and import figures taken from Bernard, Jensen, and Schott (2006). Offshore employment figures are taken from the *Bureau of Economic Analysis* (2007).

Table 8.5 Occupational exposure to offshoring by destination

Dependent variable: log wage

	1983–1990 (1)	1991–1999 (2)	2000–2008 (3)
China	−0.028 (0.017)	0.0008 (0.003)	−0.0197** (0.009)
India	−0.0018 (0.009)	0.0020 (0.004)	−0.0198** (0.008)
Mexico	0.000 (0.008)	−0.0114 (0.008)	−0.0290*** (0.010)
Other low-income countries	−0.028 (0.018)	−0.020 (0.013)	−0.0486* (0.025)

* significant at 10% ** significant at 5%. *** significant at 1%.
Note: each cell represents the coefficient from a separate regression. The regressions are estimated in the manner described in Table 8.3, but the measure of offshore employment in low-income countries is replaced by employment in China, India, Mexico, and other low-income countries (not China, India, Mexico) in each row respectively, and estimated for the period listed in the column heading.
Source: see Table 8.5.

estimates by time period the impact of offshore employment in China, India, and Mexico. We replace the coefficients for offshoring to low-income countries with separate measures for each offshore destination. While in Table 8.5 the results are reported for each country in separate regressions, we also estimate the equation including all country destinations concurrently. While the point estimates remain the same, the significance falls due to multicollinearity. Consequently we only report the specifications in Table 8.5.

If we compare the coefficient estimates in Tables 8.1, 8.2, and 8.5, there is no evidence that offshoring to China, India, or Mexico is more likely to put downward pressure on domestic US wages than offshoring to other low-income country destinations. In fact, the evidence is consistent with offshoring to China being less costly or not significantly different than offshoring to other low-income country destinations. Similarly, offshoring activities in Mexico and India, the other top destinations for offshoring by US multinationals as measured by the number of employees at offshore affiliates, do not exert significantly larger downward pressure on US wages than offshoring to other low-income regions. The largest coefficient is for Mexico, which remained the location with the highest number of affiliate employees for US multinationals throughout the sample period (see Figure 8.3).

In Table 8.6 we compare the impact of import competition from China with offshoring to China by including both measures in the same regression. Other controls (see Tables 8.1 and 8.2), are also

Table 8.6 Comparing the wage impact of imports from China versus offshoring to China

Dependent variable: log wage			
	(1)	(2)	(3)
Panel A: 1983–1990			
Lagged import	−1.61		−1.26
penetration from China	(1.93)		(1.66)
Lagged log of Chinese		−0.0342***	−0.0194***
affiliate employment		(0.013)	(0.007)
Panel B: 1991–1999			
Lagged import	−0.318		−0.386
penetration from China	(0.388)		(0.417)
Lagged log of Chinese		0.002	0.003
affiliate employment		(0.002)	(0.003)
Panel C: 2000–2008			
Lagged import	−0.665***		−0.562**
penetration from China	(0.226)		(0.228)
Lagged log of Chinese		−0.0194***	−0.0158**
affiliate employment		(0.007)	(0.007)

* significant at 10% ** significant at 5%. *** significant at 1%.
Note: the columns report the results of regressing wages on occupational exposure to (1) import penetration from China, (2) offshoring to China, or (3) including both imports and offshoring simultaneously. The regressions are specified in the manner described in Table 8.2, except without including low-income offshoring or imports.
Source: see Table 8.A1.

included but not reported. The results show that the negative impact of import competition from China did not become significant until the last decade (2000–2008), when China joined the WTO and trade volumes significantly increased. The coefficient estimate, −0.562, is two to three times the magnitude of the import coefficients reported in Tables 8.1 and 8.2. The coefficient indicates that a 10 percentage point increase in import competition from China is associated with a 5.6 percentage point decline in the wages of workers in occupations affected by those imports.

In contrast, the impact of offshoring to China is small in magnitude. In comparison to offshoring activities in other low-income regions, the impact is also smaller, if we compare the point estimates in Table 8.6 with those in Tables 8.1 and 8.2. The coefficient, −0.0158, indicates that a 10 per cent increase in offshore employment in China would be associated with a small wage decline of 0.16 per cent. The evidence in Table 8.6 indicates that the impact through 2008 of Chinese competition on US wages was felt most significantly via imports and not through the offshoring activities of US companies to China. The point estimates on offshoring activities through 2008 were significantly below those for other offshore destinations, including Mexico and India.

8.4.3 Results for Labour Force Participation

Table 8.7 examines the determinants of labour force participation rates using the CPS data. Labour force participation is defined as the share of the labour force either employed or actively seeking employment. Labour force participation is calculated at the three digit occupation by year by five-year age group cell for ages 15 through 64. The measure is the labour force participation rate among workers in each of these cells weighted by their sample weight. We then regress labour force participation on all of the variables included in Table 8.1. We report results for all individuals as well as for individuals between the ages of 15 and 34, as there has been a significant decline in labour force participation for this age group.

The results, reported in the first two columns of Table 8.7, indicate that import competition is *positively* and significantly associated with labour force participation, as measured by import shares. The most significant determinant of labour force participation (apart from individual characteristics such as sex, age, and experience which are included as controls) is the use of computers in the occupation. Occupational exposure from offshore employment in China is also significantly and negatively associated with US labour force participation, but the point estimates indicate a very small effect.

The last four columns of Table 8.7 decompose labour force participation into its two components, individuals who are employed and those who are actively seeking employment (i.e. the unemployed). We felt that it would be useful to decompose labour force participation into these two components, since demand shocks are likely to have opposite effects on the percentage of individuals who are currently employed versus those who are seeking employment. The results in the last four columns of Table 8.7 show that the most important determinants of employment are computer use rates (negative) and investment goods prices (positive). These results are consistent with a viewpoint that technological change is leading to increasing use of computers or capital equipment to replace labour. Offshoring, on the other hand, is not an important determinant of employment or unemployment.

The results for trade, as measured by imports and exports, are quite different for labour force participation than they are for wages. While neither exports nor imports are significantly associated with labour force participation, they are significantly associated with employment

Table 8.7 Offshoring to China and labour force participation, 1983–2008

Dependent variable:	Participating (1=yes)		Employed (1=yes)		Unemployed (1=yes)	
	All	Ages 15–34	All	Ages 15–34	All	Ages 15–34
	(3)	(4)	(1)	(2)	(5)	(6)
Occupational exposure from employment in China	-0.00182*** (0.0007)	-0.00313*** (0.0010)	-0.00168* (0.00090)	-0.00356** (0.00140)	-0.0001 (0.0006)	0.0004 (0.0010)
Imports	0.057 (0.038)	0.082 (0.053)	0.173*** (0.049)	0.255*** (0.076)	-0.127*** (0.037)	-0.185 * ** (0.061)
Exports	0.019 (0.070)	-0.005 (0.099)	-0.168* (0.094)	-0.278* (0.142)	0.156** (0.070)	0.225** (0.111)
Computer use	-0.0411*** (0.0059)	-0.0338*** (0.0083)	-0.0615*** (0.0075)	-0.0549*** (0.0098)	0.0211*** (0.0042)	0.0223*** (0.0059)
Price of investment goods	0.0256* (0.016)	0.021 (0.024)	0.0837*** (0.020)	0.0956*** (0.029)	-0.0720*** (0.015)	-0.101*** (0.021)
Observations	89,749	34,696	89,749	34,696	89,749	34,696
R-squared	0.32	0.31	0.32	0.33	0.17	0.17

* significant at 10% ** significant at 5%. *** significant at 1%.

Note: each observation represents a 3-digit occupation × year × 5 year age group cell from ages 15–64. The dependent variable is the listed CPS category (participating in the labor force, employed, or unemployed but participating in the labour force) rate among workers in each cell (weighted by their sample weight), and the independent variable is the lagged log of occupational exposure to Chinese offshore employment. The other controls are as described in Table 8.2, except that the real value of shipments is used in place of the real price of shipments. The standard errors are clustered by 3-digit occupation and five-year period, and are robust.

Source: see Table 8.A1.

and unemployment rates. The evidence indicates that higher import penetration is associated with *higher* rates of employment, and lower rates of unemployment. These results are contrary to received wisdom. The evidence is equally surprising for exports: higher export shares in the previous period are associated with higher rates of unemployment, although the relationship with labour force participation in the first two columns and employment rates in the middle two columns is not statistically significant at conventional levels. We explored the robustness of the trade results in Table 8.7 by adding a number of controls, including controls for domestic production. The results remained unaffected.

We further explore the robustness of these results using the subset of the CPS that follows the same worker over time. In Tables 8.8 and 8.9, we are able to identify workers who worked in the previous time period but stopped working the current year. In particular, we would like to see whether employment for the same individual over time is affected by our measures of globalization. The results at the individual level are useful because they allow us to control for individual fixed effects which may not be captured in Table 8.7.

The results in Tables 8.8 and 8.9 are consistent with the earlier results presented in Table 8.6 on the determinants of employment. Individuals are more likely to stop working if they are in occupations that are more exposed to offshoring in low-income regions. Conversely, these individuals are less likely to stop working if they are in occupations where high-income affiliate employment is growing. Consistent with the results in Table 8.7, the evidence indicates that greater import shares are associated with a *lower* likelihood of leaving employment. When we split the sample into the degree of routineness of the occupation, we see that the results on import penetration are driven by the least routine workers. Increasing import penetration is associated with a higher likelihood of employment for non-routine workers, implying complementarity between non-routine activities and imports. The results are similar in Table 8.9, which replaces low-income offshore employment with offshore employment in China.

8.5 Conclusion

This chapter makes several contributions. First, it builds on the analysis in Ebenstein et al. (2014) by focusing on occupational exposure instead of industry-level exposure to identify the wage effects of competition from international trade and offshoring activities through 2008. We show that with China's entry into the WTO in late 2001, our results

Table 8.8 OLS estimates of employment determinants and occupational exposure to offshoring and trade among individuals observed over two periods, 1983–2008

Dependent variable: stopped working (1=yes)

Variable	All occupations	Offshoring and trade measured by occupation-specific exposure, all sectors		
		Most routine	Intermediate routine	Least routine
Lagged log of low-income affiliate employment	0.00643* (0.004)	0.0151*** (0.004)	-0.003 (0.005)	0.0100** (0.005)
Lagged log of high-income affiliate employment	-0.00566* (0.003)	-0.0123*** (0.004)	-0.011 (0.007)	-0.00890** (0.003)
Lagged export share	-0.137** (0.063)	-0.255*** (0.084)	0.103 (0.100)	1.164*** (0.366)
Lagged import penetration	-0.011 (0.033)	0.034 (0.037)	-0.120* (0.070)	-0.775*** (0.226)
Number of observations	1,377,706	472,215	565,291	340,200
R-squared	0.03	0.03	0.04	0.02

* significant at 10%. ** significant at 5%. *** significant at 1%.

Note: robust standard errors are reported in parentheses below the coefficient estimates. The workers are taken from CPS samples from 1983–2008, with their lagged values of the independent variables taken from 1982–2007. The sample is composed of individuals working in the first period and the dependent variable is whether they were working in the second period. The standard errors are clustered by occupation and five-year period. We also control for the occupation-specific lagged log price of investment, lagged total factor productivity, lagged real price of shipments, and lagged capital to labour ratio. Individual-specific controls include a worker's gender, age, race, experience, whether in a union, and fixed effects for industry (3-digit), occupation (2-digit), year, education, and state. Controls for computer use rates are imputed by the worker's occupation using the CPS computer supplement and are included in all specifications.

Source: see Table 8.A1.

Table 8.9 OLS estimates of employment determinants and occupational exposure to offshoring to China and trade among individuals observed over two periods, 1983–2008

Dependent variable: stopped working (1=yes)

Variable	Offshoring and trade measured by occupation-specific exposure, all sectors			
	All occupations	Most routine	Intermediate routine	Least routine
Lagged log of Chinese affiliate employment	0.00217*** (0.001)	0.00296*** (0.001)	0.002 (0.001)	0.001 (0.002)
Lagged log of high-income affiliate employment	−0.001 (0.001)	0.000 (0.001)	−0.0133** (0.005)	−0.001 (0.002)
Lagged export share	−0.161*** (0.061)	−0.295*** (0.086)	0.138 (0.094)	1.266*** (0.384)
Lagged import penetration	−0.016 (0.032)	0.042 (0.039)	−0.180*** (0.069)	−0.799*** (0.234)
Number of observations	1,377,706	472,215	565,291	340,200
R-squared	0.03	0.03	0.04	0.02

* significant at 10% ** significant at 5%. *** significant at 1%.
Note: robust standard errors are reported in parentheses below the coefficient estimates. The workers are taken from CPS samples from 1983–2008, with their lagged values of the independent variables taken from 1982–2007. The sample is composed of individuals working in the first period and the dependent variable is whether they were working in the second period. The standard errors are clustered by occupation and five-year period. We also control for the occupation-specific lagged log price of investment, lagged total factor productivity, lagged real price of shipments, and lagged capital to labour ratio. Individual-specific controls include a worker's gender, age, race, experience, whether in a union, and fixed effects for industry (3-digit), occupation (2-digit), year, education, and state. Controls for computer use rates are imputed by the worker's occupation using the CPS computer supplement and are included in all specifications.
Source: see Table 8.A1.

remain significant and robust. We also present results that indicate the mechanisms for differences in industry versus occupational exposure. We present evidence that globalization has led to the reallocation of workers away from high-wage manufacturing jobs into other sectors and other occupations, with large declines in wages among workers who switch, explaining the large differences between industry and occupational analyses.

Our data on offshoring from the BEA reveal differences in both the timing of offshoring and the industries that participate in offshoring, relative to conventional trade in goods. Offshoring is a more recent phenomenon and has grown significantly faster than trade in recent years, with implications for US wages and employment. Offshoring activities allow US multinational corporations to separate the production process for any given good into high-skill and low-skill tasks, and thereby take advantage of cheaper labour overseas, even for high value added goods.

This is particularly relevant for industries such as motor vehicles, which historically had powerful unions and were able to demand high wages for their workers.

The second contribution is that we are able to consider offshoring by destination country separately from imports. We find that the most significant low-income offshore destinations, measured in terms of total employment offshore by US parents, are not associated with larger downward pressure on US worker wages than offshoring to other low-income regions.

Third, we examine the role of China's entry into the global economy in much greater depth. Since China's accession to the WTO in 2001, scholarship has largely focused on China's growing role in international trade and its potential impact. In this chapter, we compare for the first time the impact of both import competition from China and offshore activities by US multinationals in China. Analysing wages of individuals who are actively in the labour force indicates that competition via international trade from China is economically much more important as measured by downward pressure on US wages than offshoring activities in China. The point estimates indicate that a 1 percentage point increase in import penetration from China during the 2000 through 2008 period would have been associated with a 0.6 percentage point decline in the wages of affected US workers. In contrast, a 1 per cent increase in offshore employment of US affiliates in China was associated with a 0.02 percentage point decline in wages.

Finally, we explore the impact of trade and offshoring on labour force participation. We demonstrate that neither offshoring nor international trade are associated with a significant reduction in labour force participation. Our results indicate that the most important factors associated with a reduction in US labour force participation during the sample period were computer use rates or increasing capital intensity, and that offshore activities to China or elsewhere played a very small role. Trade is positively associated with labour force participation between 1983 and 2008. Our preliminary results indicate that the 'discouraged worker effect' is unlikely to be linked to increasing import competition, from either China or elsewhere.

Appendix

Table 8.A1 Sample averages for Current Population Survey merged outgoing rotation group workers, 1983–2008

	Overall sample			1988			1993		
	All	Manufacturing	Services	All	Manufacturing	Services	All	Manufacturing	Services
Panel 1: Demographic and Wage Information									
Number of Observations	5,159,133	821,354	4,337,779	184,881	35,988	148,893	186,467	33,280	153,187
Age	37.7	39.3	37.4	36.2	37.9	35.8	37.2	38.8	36.9
Female	0.48	0.33	0.50	0.5	0.3	0.5	0.5	0.3	0.5
Years of Education	13.2	12.7	13.3	13.0	12.5	13.1	13.2	12.7	13.3
Real Hourly Wage ($2006)	16.9	18.3	16.6	15.6	17.2	15.2	15.8	17.0	15.6
Sample Weight	2,560	2,619	2,549	2341.8	2417.8	2323.4	2410.6	2449.7	2402.1
Routine	0.52	0.61	0.50	0.53	0.62	0.51	0.53	0.61	0.51
Panel 2: Offshoring and Trade Data									
Low-income Affiliate Emp	6,943.7	43,615.2	—	5,079.1	26,092.7	—	5,749.2	32,212.5	—
High-income Affiliate Emp	11,925.8	74,909.3	—	12,973.2	66,647.1	—	12,181.8	68,254.1	—
Low-income Affiliate Emp, Occupation	7,872.9	24,420.5	4,739.0	5,357.3	15,641.0	2,871.7	6,221.0	19,490.0	3,338.3
High-income Affiliate Emp, Occupation	13,215.8	40,948.1	7,963.6	13,382.7	38,300.3	7,360.0	12,939.5	39,334.6	7,205.2
China Affiliate Emp	600.6	3,772.4	—	12.3	63.2	—	38.0	212.8	—
China Affiliate Emp, Occupation	732.4	2,104.4	472.5	13.7	40.4	7.3	40.8	128.4	21.8
India Affiliate Emp	156.2	980.9	—	22.8	117.3	—	26.4	147.9	—
India Affiliate Emp, Occupation	174.4	507.7	111.2	26.4	66.3	16.8	29.0	80.6	17.7
Mexico Affiliate Emp	2,481.6	15,587.7	—	1,847.1	9,489.0	—	2,539.5	14,228.6	—
Mexico Affiliate Emp, Occupation	2,739.8	8,884.1	1,576.2	1,925.7	5,792.8	991.1	2,752.4	8,799.9	1,438.6
Other Low-income Aff Emp	3,705.3	23,274.1	—	3,196.8	16,423.1	—	3,145.3	17,623.2	—
Other Low-income Aff Emp, Occupation	4,226.4	12,924.2	2,579.1	3,391.3	9,741.4	1,856.5	3,398.8	10,481.1	1,860.2
Import Penetration	0.0225	0.1416	—	0.0239	0.1228	—	0.0253	0.1420	—
Export Share	0.0400	0.2510	—	0.0353	0.1812	—	0.0348	0.1948	—
Import Penetration, Occupation	0.0261	0.0807	0.0158	0.0244	0.0701	0.0133	0.0271	0.0825	0.0151
Export Share, Occupation	0.0452	0.1285	0.0294	0.0374	0.1031	0.0215	0.0336	0.0997	0.0193
Import Penetration, low-income	0.0028	0.0175	—	0.0014	0.0070	—	0.0026	0.0145	—
Import Penetration, low-income, Occupation	0.0033	0.0103	0.0020	0.0013	0.0044	0.0006	0.0026	0.0087	0.0012
Import Share, China	0.0079	0.0497	—	0.0035	0.0178	—	0.0085	0.0477	—
Import Share, China, Occupation	0.0089	0.0271	0.0054	0.0033	0.0108	0.0015	0.0083	0.0273	0.0042
Import Penetration, China	0.0018	0.0116	—	0.0006	0.0032	—	0.0016	0.0090	—
Import Penetration, China, Occupation	0.0025	0.0074	0.0016	0.0006	0.0021	0.0003	0.0018	0.0059	0.0009

Panel 3: Technology Measures and Price Indices

	1998			2003			2006			2008		
	All	Manufa-cturing	Services	All	Manufa-cturing	Services	All	Manufa-cturing	Services	All	Manufa-cturing	Services
Real Price of Shipments	—	6,689.1	42,016.0	—	3,679.0	18,900.1	—	3,762.4	21,080.8	—		
Real Price of Shipments, Occupation	8,220.8	10,917.0	25,153.2	2,177.6	3,665.5	9,821.6		3,881.9	11,040.2	2,326.8		
Price of Investment Goods	—	0.2	1.1	—	0.2	1.0	—	0.2	1.1	—		
Price of Investment Goods, Occupation	0.1	0.2	0.6	0.1	0.2	0.6	0.1	0.2	0.6	0.1		
Total Factor Productivity	—	0.2	1.3	—	0.2	1.0	—	0.2	1.0	—		
Total Factor Productivity, Occupation	0.2	0.3	0.7	0.1	0.2	0.5	0.1	0.2	0.5	0.1		
Capital to Labour Ratio	—	25.1	157.4	—	23.7	121.7	—	25.9	145.2	—		
Capital to Labour Ratio, Occupation	22.2	32.1	84.6	25.0	63.7	15.6		28.9	77.4	18.4		
Computer Use Rates	0.45	0.44	0.38	0.32	0.31	0.28	0.40	0.40	0.37	0.41		
	163,286	26,402	136,884	191,073	25,605	165,468	185,476	22,848	162,628	182,535	21,772	160,763
	38.0	39.6	37.7	39.3	41.5	38.9	39.6	41.9	39.3	39.9	42.1	39.6
	0.5	0.3	0.5	0.5	0.3	0.5	0.5	0.3	0.5	0.5	0.3	0.5
	13.3	12.9	13.4	13.5	13.0	13.5	13.5	13.1	13.5	13.6	13.1	13.6
	17.2	18.7	16.9	18.0	19.5	17.7	20.4	23.4	21.5	20.4	22.0	20.2
	2981.7	3131.7	2952.8	2720.5	2824.2	2704.4	2890.6	2990.1	2876.7	2951.8	3033.8	2940.6
	0.51	0.59	0.49	0.51	0.59	0.50	0.5	0.6	0.5	0.50	0.58	0.49
	8,600.4	53,190.2	—	8,842.9	65,988.8	—	9,849.6	79,957.6	·	10,699.5	88,810.6	—
	12,861.4	79,542.5	—	12,372.0	92,323.9	—	11,303.7	91,761.6	—	12,025.2	99,814.8	—
	9,796.4	31,703.5	5,571.0	9,268.7	31,065.2	5,895.8	11,021.5	37,983.8	7,233.4	12,387.7	42,887.6	8,209.9
	14,218.3	45,372.8	8,209.1	12,610.3	41,721.0	8,105.6	11,893.0	40,770.0	7,836.0	12,991.2	44,908.4	8,619.3

(continued)

Table 8.A1 Continued

	1998			2003			2006			2008		
	All	Manufacturing	Services	All	Manufacturing	Services	All	Manufacturing	Services	All	Manufacturing	Services
	810.9	5,015.4	—	1,138.5	8,496.1	—	1,732.3	14,062.6	—	2,166.8	17,985.2	—
	964.4	3,156.9	541.5	1,345.4	4,525.9	853.3	2,101.5	7,183.2	1,387.5	2,582.5	8,873.4	1,720.8
	183.2	1,133.0	—	220.1	1,642.4	—	289.0	2,346.2	—	499.4	4,145.4	—
	197.3	669.1	106.3	224.2	740.8	144.2	303.6	1,034.0	201.0	536.4	1,849.1	356.6
	3,416.4	21,129.2	—	3,284.5	24,510.2	—	2,942.8	23,888.9	—	2,982.7	24,757.6	—
	3,810.5	12,738.2	2,088.5	3,342.1	11,378.1	2,098.6	3,150.4	11,093.2	2,034.5	3,395.9	12,018.5	2,214.8
	4,189.8	25,912.5	—	4,199.8	31,340.1	—	4,885.5	39,660.0	—	5,050.6	41,922.4	—
	4,824.3	15,139.2	2,834.7	4,356.9	14,420.3	2,799.7	5,466.0	18,673.5	3,610.4	5,873.0	20,146.7	3,917.8
	0.0269	0.1663	—	0.0272	0.2028	—	0.0279	0.2264	—	0.0234	0.1941	—
	0.0401	0.2478	—	0.0350	0.2609	—	0.0143	0.1158	—	0.0121	0.1002	—
	0.0306	0.0968	0.0178	0.0343	0.1088	0.0228	0.0378	0.1235	0.0258	0.0290	0.0995	0.0193
	0.0423	0.1245	0.0265	0.0414	0.1330	0.0272	0.0187	0.0592	0.0130	0.0144	0.0477	0.0098
	0.0036	0.0223	—	0.0052	0.0388	—	0.0068	0.0552	—	0.0059	0.0491	—
	0.0039	0.0131	0.0022	0.0066	0.0215	0.0043	0.0101	0.0328	0.0069	0.0077	0.0275	0.0050
	0.0104	0.0642	—	0.0142	0.1062	—	0.0178	0.1443	—	0.0191	0.1585	—
	0.0107	0.0343	0.0062	0.0162	0.0525	0.0106	0.0225	0.0748	0.0152	0.0256	0.0867	0.0172
	0.0023	0.0145	—	0.0038	0.0281	—	0.0052	0.0421	—	0.0043	0.0357	—
	0.0029	0.0094	0.0016	0.0053	0.0169	0.0035	0.0085	0.0271	0.0059	0.0062	0.0219	0.0040
	6,052.3	37,431.0	—	10,207.1	76,168.4	—	12,028.6	97,645.7	—	13,885.9	115,259.5	—
	7,739.9	21,769.6	5,033.8	16,223.5	42,575.0	12,145.7	24,273.9	62,453.4	18,909.9	30,974.3	76,599.3	24,724.6
	0.2	1.1	—	0.1	1.1	—	0.1	1.1	—	0.1	1.2	—
	0.2	0.6	0.1	0.2	0.5	0.1	0.2	0.5	0.1	0.2	0.6	0.1
	0.2	1.2	—	0.2	1.6	—	0.2	1.9	—	0.3	2.1	—
	0.2	0.7	0.1	0.3	0.8	0.2	0.4	1.1	0.3	0.5	1.3	0.4
	24.2	149.8	—	29.3	218.6	—	28.6	232.3	—	26.7	221.3	—
	29.8	82.9	19.5	41.6	117.2	29.9	44.7	128.4	32.9	41.7	120.7	30.9
	0.50	0.46	0.51	0.58	0.53	0.58	0.58	0.53	0.58	0.58	0.53	0.58

Source: sample consists of Current Population Surveys Merged Outgoing Rotation Group Workers for 1983–2008. Affiliate (or offshore) Employment data are taken from the Bureau of Economic Analysis annual survey of US firms with multinational affiliates for the same period. Low-income countries are defined according to the World Bank income categories. Import penetration and export share are taken from Bernard, Jensen, and Schott (2006). Computer use rates are taken from October CPS supplements during the sample period and kept at 2002 rates for the subsequent years. Investment good prices, total factor productivity measures, capital to labour ratios, and the real price of shipments are taken from the NBER productivity database. Services includes agricultural workers.

Bibliography

Artuc, Erhan, Shubham Chaudhuri, and John McLaren (2010). Trade Shocks and Labor Adjustment: A Structural Empirical Approach, *American Economic Review*, 100(3): 1008–45.

Autor, David H., Lawrence F. Katz, and Alan B. Krueger (1998). Computing Inequality: Have Computers Changed the Labor Market? *Quarterly Journal of Economics*, 113: 1169–213.

Autor, David H., Frank Levy, and Richard Murnane (2003). The Skill Content of Recent Technological Change: An Empirical Exploration, *Quarterly Journal of Economics*, 118: 1279–334.

Autor, David H., F. Katz, and Melissa S. Kearney (2008). Trends in US Wage Inequality: Revising the Revisionists, *Review of Economics and Statistics*, 90: 300–23.

Autor, David H., David Dorn, and Gordon H. Hanson (2013). The China Syndrome: Local Labor Market Impacts of Import Competition in the United States, *American Economic Review*, 103(6): 2121–68.

Bernard, Andrew, J. Bradford Jensen, and Peter Schott (2006). Survival of the Best Fit: Exposure to Low-Wage Countries and the (Uneven) Growth of US Manufacturing, *Journal of International Economics*, 68: 219–37.

Cosar, A. Kerem (2010). Adjusting to Trade Liberalization: Reallocation and Labor Market Policies. University of Chicago Booth School of Business, unpublished manuscript.

Desai, Mihir, C. Fritz Foley, and James R. Hines (2009). Domestic Effects of the Foreign Activities of US Multinationals, *American Economic Journal: Economic Policy*, 1(1): 181–203.

Ebenstein, Avraham, Ann Harrison, Margaret McMillan, and Shannon Phillips (2014). Estimating the Impact of Trade and Offshoring on American Workers Using the Current Population Surveys, *Review of Economics and Statistics*, 96(4): 581–95.

Feenstra, Robert C. (2008). Offshoring in the Global Economy. Presented at the Stockholm School of Economics, September 17–18 as the *Ohlin Lecture*. Available for download at the author's website.

Feenstra, Robert C. and Gordon H. Hanson (1999). The Impact of Outsourcing and High-Technology Capital on Wages: Estimates for the US, 1972–1990, *Quarterly Journal of Economics*, 114(3): 907–40.

Freeman, Richard (1995). Are Your Wages Set in Beijing? *Journal of Economic Perspectives*, 9(3): 15–32.

Grossman, Gene M. and Esteban Rossi-Hansberg (2008). Trading Tasks: A Simple Theory of Offshoring, *American Economic Review*, 98(5): 1978–97.

Harrison, Ann and Margaret McMillan (2011). Offshoring Jobs? Multinationals and U.S. Manufacturing Emploment, *The Review of Economics and Statistics*, 93(3): 857–75.

Hummels, David, Rasmus Jørgensen, Jakob R. Munch, and Chong Xiang (2011). The Wage Effects of Offshoring: Evidence from Danish Matched Worker-Firm Data, NBER working paper 17496.

Jensen, Bradford and Lori G. Kletzer (2005). Tradable Services: Understanding the Scope and Impact of Services Offshoring. Working Paper Series Number WP 05-9.

Kambourov, Gueorgui and Iourii Manovskii (2008). Rising Occupational and Industry Mobility in the United States: 1968–97, *International Economic Review*, 49(1): 41–79.

Kambourov, Gueorgui and Iourii Manovskii (2009a). Occupational Specificity of Human Capital, *International Economic Review*, 50(1): 63–115.

Kambourov, Gueorgui and Iourii Manovskii (2009b). Occupational Mobility and Wage Inequality, *Review of Economic Studies*, 76: 731–59.

Katz, Lawrence F. and Lawrence H. Summers (1989). Industry Rents: Evidence and Implications, *Brooking Papers on Economic Activity, Microeconomics* 1989: 209–90. Spring, 103–54.

Krueger, Alan B. and Lawrence H. Summers (1988). Efficiency Wages and Inter-Industry Wage Structure, *Econometrica*, 56(2): 259–93.

Krugman, Paul (2008). Trade and Wages, Reconsidered. Brookings Papers on Economic Activity, Spring, 103–54.

Lemieux, T. (2006). Increasing Residual Wage Inequality: Composition Effects, Noisy Data, or Rising Demand for Skill? *The American Economic Review*, 96 (3): 461–98.

Pierce, Justin and Peter Schott (2012). The Surprisingly Swift Decline of U.S. Manufacturing Employment, NBER working paper 18655.

Trefler, Daniel and Runjuan Liu (2011). A Sorted Tale of Globalization: White Collar Jobs and the Rise of Service Offshoring. NBER working paper, 17559.

United States Department of Labor, Employment and Training Administration. 1977. *Dictionary of Occupational Titles*, 4th edn., Washington, DC: US Government Printing Office.

9

Offshoring, Wages, and Employment: Evidence from Data Matching Imports, Firms, and Workers

Francis Kramarz

9.1 Introduction

The media have expressed the popular feeling that global competition from low-wage countries has induced a race to the bottom: low-skilled manufacturing jobs should be compensated less or else disappear from OECD countries. The issue is well summarized by Richard Freeman: 'Put crudely, to what extent has, or will, the pay of low-skilled Americans or French or Germans be set in Beijing, Delhi or Djakkarta rather than in New York, Paris or Frankfurt?' (Freeman 1995, p. 16).

Imports from developing countries into the USA or Western Europe were not huge at the end of the 1980s. However, the Single Market Program (SMP), an attempt to implement the internal market of the European Community (EC), was conceived in 1985, launched in 1988, with the hope of being achieved around 1992. It entailed decreased tariffs and barriers within the EC. Hence, imports from the EC increased at a very rapid pace in France during the second half of the 1980s.[1] In this context, the mere existence of new sourcing options was a

---

[1] French National accounts show that imports increased at a very fast rate over the years 1986 to 1992: above 6 per cent per year in the first five years with a decrease to 3 per cent in 1991 and 2 per cent in the final year. In fact, whereas import growth was at best mild between 1981 and 1985, our sample period appears to be the beginning of a period of rapid growth of French imports, that continued most of the ensuing years. http://www.insee. fr/fr/indicateur/cnat_annu/Series/t_1501p_25_4.xls (accessed 5 April 2005). In addition, Biscourp and Kramarz (2007) show that imports from low-wage countries were—and remained—a minor, albeit increasing, component of imports of goods over the analysis period. However, when measuring imports of manufacturing goods as a fraction of GDP,

signal that foreign outsourcing was a potential threat, particularly for industries or firms in which high wages were due to the presence of strong unions and the absence of product market competition. At the same time, and for the same reasons, because European firms could export to France more easily, French firms faced increased market pressures, not from Beijing but from other European countries.

Similarly, in the USA, union plants or firms started to lose employment in the 1980s. Many such plants were located in the north and new plants started to open in the non-union south. Foreign-owned car plants opened in particular around Interstate 85 starting in the second half of the 1980s.[2] This move to the south also took place in other industries (see the example of RCA in its various guises described in Cowie 1999). Of course, for the USA, 'imports' is not the right word and the evidence that unions caused job losses and the associated outsourcing, be it local or foreign, is missing. But France is a small country when compared to the USA and what is local outsourcing in the USA would be foreign in France (to the East though, rather than to the South at least during the period under analysis).

Hence, the two questions that I examine in this chapter derive from Chapter 8: in a context of increased competitive pressures and expanded opportunities due to the SMP, was foreign outsourcing, in particular the foreign outsourcing of final goods (offshoring) a possible response to high wages and strong unions, particularly in those years that followed the election of the French socialist government? And, indeed, what was the impact of increased outsourcing on wages and employment?[3]

Even though macroeconomists have examined these questions both theoretically and empirically, at the country or the industry level, there is virtually no microeconometric analysis, no empirical examination of the precise mechanisms at work using micro data sources. I will look at the effects that can be identified in the French context using differences across and within firms rather than across industries. More precisely, because I have access to administrative data on the nature (final good versus intermediates) as well as on the amount of imports and exports measured at the level of each French firm, I observe all

---

the ratio was 14 per cent in 1986 (as well as in the preceding years, 1981 to 1985). It increased to 17 per cent in 1989–1990 and 16 per cent in 1992. (http://www.insee.fr/fr/indicateur/cnat_annu/base_95/principaux_resultats/commerce_ext.htm/t_1501bis_95.xls and t_1105_95.xls (accessed 26 February 2008).

[2] See for instance http://www.csmonitor.com/2008/1205/p01s04-usec.html or http://www.usatoday.com/money/economy/2008-07-08-1004622626_x.htm among many other press reports.

[3] In this text, I will equate *outsourcing* with *outsourcing from foreign origin*.

firms that outsource intermediates or final goods and I can compute the firm's competitors, importing behaviour. Because I have access to administrative data on balance sheets and employment, I can compute the firms' value added or employment. I have access to a survey on union behaviour, therefore I can compute the strength of unions in most firms. Finally, because I use administrative longitudinal matched employer–employee data on wages, I can measure the changes in individual, not aggregate, wages.

A clear answer to Richard Freeman's question (albeit, slightly transformed) as well as mine would contribute to at least two strands of the literature. First, it would inform the wage inequality debate.[4] Second, because product market competition is a potential underlying mechanism causing some of the changes affecting the labour market, an answer would also contribute to the literature that examines the relationship between wages, bargaining institutions, and profits.[5]

To understand the identification strategy that I pursue, the following thought experiment is helpful. French manufacturing was relatively protected from international competition at the beginning of the 1980s. In addition, a relatively large fraction of firms (as compared to other similar Western European countries) was state owned, in particular after the election of president François Mitterrand. This lack of competition induced the creation of rents (a result documented in Abowd, Kramarz, Lengermann, and Roux 2007). Due to these rents, as well as because of the bargaining institutions, many French firms bargained with their workers, but not all. These bargaining regimes varied from firm to firm. Some unions were better placed to seize the potential rents. However, all firms were hit by exogenous foreign competition shocks. In particular, all French firms were hit by the SMP at the end of the 1980s and therefore faced increased foreign competition and increased opportunities for outsourcing. Biscourp and Kramarz (2007), based on the same data for trade (imports as well as

[4] On one hand, Lawrence (1994), Lawrence and Slaughter (1993), and Krugman (1995) have argued that recent changes cannot be accounted for by increased trade with low-wage countries. On the other hand, Wood (1995) has accused trade of being responsible for the deteriorated position of unskilled workers while Leamer (1994, 1996) and Freeman (1995) appear to stand in the middle. Unfortunately, the evidence is not compelling and mostly relies on import penetration measured at the aggregate or at the sectoral level (for instance Revenga (1992), see, however, Bernard and Jensen (1997) or the book edited by Robert Feenstra (2000)).

[5] Abowd and Lemieux (1993) examine the relation between product market competition and wages in a bargaining framework whereas Blanchflower, Oswald, and Sanfey (1996) look at the more general relation between profits and wages. Goldberg and Tracy (2001) as well as Bertrand (2004) focus on recent changes induced by increased import competition and movements in exchange rates. Unfortunately, these last authors used industry-level measures of imports because of the lack of firm-level data.

exports) and for firms and the same period that I use in the present chapter, have shown that *import growth (of final goods) was strongly associated with employment losses.* They show an association but no causal relationship. But, the increased competitors' imports or increased firm's sourcing strategies had the potential to affect the bargaining process because they were likely to change the firm's ability to pay the workers—the size of the quasi-rent—as well as the firm's and the workers' threat points. What happened to wages and employment in these different firms and under these different bargaining regimes? How did unions react? If I show that, both theoretically and empirically, strong unions caused offshoring which in turn caused employment and wage losses, I have a causal mechanism for Biscourp and Kramarz's result.

With these thought experiments at the back of our mind, I now present the structure of this chapter.

9.1.1 *The Road Map*

- To capture the influence of outsourcing threats on bargaining, I start by presenting a simple *model*, particularly well-suited to the French institutional setup studied here, which will help to capture the mechanisms by which a firm's outsourcing of final goods can directly affect wages and employment. In particular, the model shows that, with imperfect competition in the product market, firms facing strong unions are likely to use offshoring more intensively than firms facing weaker unions because increased offshoring reduces the size of the rent that the union and the firm bargain over. Indeed, offshoring acts as a threat point in the bargaining process and disciplines workers. Furthermore, in this context, employment decreases when offshoring increases. But, wages do not necessarily decrease in the same situation.

- My empirical analysis starts by showing how foreign outsourcing and, more generally, trade competition are related to the size of the rents at the end of the 1980s in French manufacturing. In particular, using a size-of-the-firm discontinuity present within French institutions, I show that bargaining institutions are likely to *cause* the structure of this relation.

- Because bargaining institutions matter and, in particular, unions' strength matters, I identify which firms face strong unions, that is, unions with a strong bargaining power, and which firms face weaker unions. To do this, I estimate a structural wage equation that directly identifies unions' bargaining power. I explain how matched employer–employee data sources allow me to directly measure the various components of this structural equation. My estimates then demonstrate that there are essentially two types of firms, depending on their bargaining regime: firms facing strong unions in which workers capture half of the rents and firms facing weaker unions where workers are paid their opportunity wage.

• Workers are negatively affected by import competition.

• Finally, I show that the former group of firms indeed increased outsourcing and, simultaneously, reduced employment over the 1986–1992 period, as predicted by the model while the latter group did exactly the opposite.

The chapter is organized as follows. Section 9.2 presents the theoretical model that I estimate in the following sections. In Section 9.3, I present the data that are used in the empirical analysis as well as the elements necessary for the empirical implementation of my model. In Section 9.4, estimation results are presented and potential interpretations are discussed. A brief conclusion ends the chapter. There are three Appendices at the end of the chapter. Appendix A derives elements for the theoretical model of Section 9.2. Appendix B describes the data sources in detail. Appendix C presents the estimation strategy for the structural wage equation in detail.

9.2 Wages, Employment, and Outsourcing: A Simple Bargaining Framework

Product market competition and wage bargaining are intimately related through the financial situation of the firms, their ability to pay their workers, as measured, for example, by rents (Abowd and Lemieux 1993). In the remainder of this section, I briefly present a simplified representation of the bargaining process that takes place between a union and a firm, using an extension of a classic bargaining model (McDonald and Solow 1981; Brown and Ashenfelter 1986) when firms can outsource part of their production.

The model that I use articulates stages of bargaining, with a first stage where the firm decides if and how much it outsources through imports (of intermediates or of final goods). The bargaining model relies on so-called strongly efficient bargaining, where workers and firms bargain over employment and wages,[6] because French institutions, as embedded in the French Labour Laws, and particularly the so-called Auroux Laws described in Section 9.3.1 and used in this chapter's empirical analysis, clearly favour annual discussion of many issues including wages, hours of work, working conditions, and employment between the firm and the workers' delegates or workers' union representatives. Let us study the second stage first.

9.2.1 Wages and Employment Determination (Second Stage)

In the strongly efficient bargaining framework, the union is rent-maximizing with objective function wl where w denotes the workers' wage and l denotes the firm's employment (in France, all workers employed in the firm are represented by the unions or the personnel representatives). These representatives negotiate with a profit-maximizing firm with profit denoted by $\tilde{\pi}$. The bargaining is over wages and employment. The threat points for the unions and for the firm are respectively $w_0 l$ and π_0.

To summarize, the Nash solution (w_N, l_N) to the bargaining problem solves the following equation:

$$(w_N, l_N) = \arg\max_{w,l}\{(1 - \theta)\ln[\tilde{\pi} - \pi_0] + \theta\ln[(w - w_0)l]\} \quad (9.1)$$

subject to $\tilde{\pi} = R(I, l) - wl$

where θ represents the workers' bargaining power, and, as before, I denotes firm's imports and $R(I, l)$ denotes the firm's revenue function.[7]

9.2.2 Outsourcing-Imports Determination (First Stage)

I can now write the firm's profit conditional on the above levels of wage and employment (w_N, l_N). Therefore, if I define $G(I) = R(I, l_N) - w_N l_N$, firms determine their outsourcing level by finding

$$I_N = \arg\max_I G(I) - c(I) \quad (9.2)$$

in which $c(I)$ denotes the cost of outsourced production, both at the *extensive* and the *intensive* margin. It can therefore include a fixed

---

[6] Rather than the right-to-manage model, where negotiation is restricted to wages. See again Brown and Ashenfelter (1986) or Abowd and Lemieux (1993).

[7] Koskela and Stenbacka (2009) use the right to manage model (with bargaining on wages and firm making the employment decision) in a similar context. Their results have a very similar set of implications to those I obtain here.

cost component paid at the moment of the import decision (hence for I to be positive, profits have to cover the fixed cost). Notice that this cost function, c, does not enter the second stage profit. Imports, being made in advance (first-stage), are subject to the usual hold-up problem (see Grout 1984, among others). In addition, at this stage, I do not distinguish between imports of intermediates (outsourcing) and imports of final goods (offshoring). In my modelling approach, I follow Chaney (2008) or Eaton, Kortum, and Kramarz (2009) in having a fixed cost paid at the decision stage rather than Melitz (2003) who introduces a fixed cost (of exporting, rather than importing as here) paid even before entry. Because there are many potential routes for imports, my theoretical analysis will mostly focus on a single form of heterogeneity, even though heterogeneous fixed costs could be allowed easily. Heterogeneous firms will come in the form of *heterogeneous bargaining powers*. Such bargaining powers can be shown to be related with size, productivity, and profitability. Hence, my approach takes a different tack, and uses bargaining as an outcome reflecting elements of firm's productivity and profitability. In addition, my analysis— empirical as well as theoretical—will remain *partial equilibrium*. A Melitz (or Eaton, Kortum, and Kramarz) type analysis of importing firms is clearly an important task that will be tackled in another paper.

9.2.3 Threat Points

Because the threat points are central to my problem, I discuss their exact interpretation now. First, notice that π_0 has often been set to 0 in previous empirical research (Abowd and Lemieux 1993, for instance).[8] Malcomson (1997) suggests that π_0 should measure the profits when the negotiations are inconclusive due to a delay or a breakdown. Hence, it should reflect market alternatives and pressures. In particular, the firm threat point may potentially vary with imports of competitors since they capture effective trade competition. This idea is explicitly incorporated in various theoretical papers relating trade and wages. Mezzetti and Dinopoulos (1991) or more recently Gaston (1998) explicitly interpret π_0 as the value of the option to switch production abroad. 'That is, π_0 varies positively with a credible outsourcing alternative for the firm' (Gaston 1998). Furthermore, 'During any dispute, the domestic firm supplies the market from abroad' (ibid.). However, these

---

[8] Their explicit introduction within my framework is a clear departure from virtually all of the previous empirical research.

papers provide no formal proof of these intuitions. Two papers, though, present game-theoretic justifications for this.

In Leach (1997), an infinitely repeated bargaining game is played between a union and a firm producing a storable good. The firm has the option of accumulating inventories. Hence, during a strike, the firm can sell these inventories. In equilibrium, this accumulation lowers wages by reducing the rents from further production. Unions can strike. They do so, also along the equilibrium path, in order to limit the firm's inventories and, therefore, raise wages.

Coles and Hildreth (2000) use a related framework, with a single episode of bargaining of potentially infinite duration between a firm and a union with random alternating wage offers. Again, inventories held by the firm during the negotiation process play a central strategic role. Furthermore, they show (Coles and Hildreth 2000, p.278, Theorem 1) that their (dynamic) problem can be rewritten as a Nash bargaining problem in which the firm's expected discounted profits, using the optimal sales strategy should the strike never end, is exactly π_0. After identifying the optimal sales strategy during the strike, they demonstrate that inventories are used as a threat to 'force lower wages' (Coles and Hildreth 2000, p.280, Theorem 3).[9]

Outsourcing in my approach plays the same role as inventories in Leach's or Coles and Hildreth's. Outsourcing is obviously a way to externalize the building of inventories, potentially without the need of any local worker. This strategy is all the more effective since outsourcing and, in particular, imports of finished goods are most often programmed in advance.[10] Because outsourced production has been put in place before bargaining, firms are able to use a sales strategy that does not rely on local workers (or at least not on all local workers, a fraction of them will still be available for certain tasks). Such strategies can obviously be implemented in various manufacturing industries either through foreign direct investments (FDI) or by using producers in relatively low-wage countries.

---

[9] In addition, they show that, because the firm's threat point increases faster than expected discounted revenues in inventories, wages are decreasing in inventories (Theorem 3). Finally, they use this model to evaluate empirically changes in bargaining institutions in the UK.

[10] For instance, in the clothing industry in France (and more generally in Europe), all sourcing strategies that involve delocalization of the production process imply defining the product at least one year before selling it. See the discussions in Linge (1991) or Sadler (1994) for examples of other industries. Competing strategies are more short term and allow the firm to produce locally in the so-called Sentier area, within Paris, that is, close to the customers. However, such strategies are almost exclusively used for restocking of small quantities based on the most recent information (Zara, a leading European clothing company, is another example of a firm using this constant restocking strategy).

I follow Coles and Hildreth in that I do not specify the exact mechanism that helps the firm build its 'inventories of imports'. I just adapt their results to my problem. And, based on their results and following the rest of the literature, I pose my problem in the form of a Nash bargaining problem in which the firm's and the workers' threat point potentially depend on the sourcing strategies. Consistent with Coles and Hildreth's theoretical results, I model the firm's threat point, $\pi_0(I) = R(I, 0)$, as the profit function when no worker is employed (hence the wage bill disappears). It is a function of outsourced goods, through imports.

The game is solved by backward induction. The bargaining problem (9.1) is solved first. Given imports I, at the solution, the marginal product of labour is given by

$$R_I(I, l_N) = w_0,$$

explaining why the bargaining is called 'strongly efficient'. And, the resulting wage is given by

$$w_N = w_0 + \frac{\theta}{1 - \theta} \frac{\tilde{\pi} - \pi_0(I)}{l_N}$$

or, equivalently,

$$w_N = w_0 + \theta \frac{\tilde{\pi}^0 - \pi_0(I)}{l_N}, \qquad (9.3)$$

with $\pi_0(I) = R(I, 0)$ and $\tilde{\pi}^0$ the profit when the wage is evaluated at w_0:

$$\tilde{\pi}^0 = R(I, l_N) - w_0 l_N.$$

Therefore,

$$
\begin{aligned}
w_N &= w(w_0, \theta, I, l) = w_0 + \theta \frac{R(I, l_N) - w_0 l_N - R(I, 0)}{l_N} \\
l_N &= l(w_0, I) = R_I^{-1}(I, w_0)
\end{aligned}
\qquad (9.4)
$$

are the first-order conditions for the bargaining game.

Then, the firm optimizes its outsourcing level I by maximizing $G(I) - c(I)$ with $G(I) = R(I, l_N) - w_N l_N$.

To gain a better intuition of the effects at play, let us consider the following CES functional form for $R(I, l)$: $R(I, l) = \left[I^{\frac{\sigma-1}{\sigma}} + l^{\frac{\sigma-1}{\sigma}} \right]^{\alpha \frac{\sigma}{\sigma-1}}$ with σ the elasticity of substitution. Rewriting $R(I, l) = p(y)y$ with

$y = \left[I^{\frac{\sigma-1}{\sigma}} + l^{\frac{\sigma-1}{\sigma}} \right]^{\frac{\sigma}{\sigma-1}}$, and $p(y) = y^{-\frac{1}{\eta}}$ with η the demand elasticity, the parameter α in the revenue function $R(I, l)$ is $\alpha = \frac{\eta-1}{\eta}$.

After some manipulation, the following result summarizes this section (see Appendix A for the general derivation):

Result: *whenever* $\frac{\eta-1}{\eta} < \frac{\sigma-1}{\sigma}$, *that is, the demand elasticity is strictly smaller than the elasticity of substitution between imports and labour, outsourcing (imports) is increasing in workers' bargaining power, θ. Under the same condition, employment is decreasing in the firm's imports. However, wages can be either increasing or decreasing in the firm's imports; on the one hand, decreased rents depress wages but the hold-up problem, on the other hand, may have the opposite effect.*

Proof: see Appendix A.

Therefore, under the above condition, a firm, facing a union with a large bargaining power, θ, will outsource a larger share of its production than a firm facing a relatively weak union.[11] Because I do not jointly model a firm's bargaining power and its fixed cost of importing, all the reasoning is made conditional on this fixed cost: the results hold for firms with similar fixed costs but facing unions with different bargaining powers. Now, the CES functional form gives a clear intuition of how firms use outsourcing to manipulate the size of the pie that they bargain over with their unions. Increasing production essentially decreases the output price. Hence, offshoring creates a threat point that reduces the size of the rent to be shared after bargaining. This pushes firms facing strong unions to outsource. Through these changes of the quasi-rent, this effect depresses wages. But, because of the potential hold-up effect—outsourcing being decided at first-stage, the cost of outsourcing is subtracted from revenues to compute the first stage profit of the game, $G(I) - c(I)$, but does not enter the second stage profit $\tilde{\pi} = R(I, l) - wl$ (bargaining)—the final effect of outsourcing on wages can be positive or negative (in contrast to Leach 1997, for instance, in which there was no potential for hold-up). Finally, under similar conditions, outsourcing leads to lower employment.

Intuitively, *the elasticity of substitution σ should be larger for imports of final goods than for imports of intermediates*. Hence, all these effects should be **stronger** for the former (offshoring) than for the latter type of imports (pure foreign outsourcing of intermediates).

---

[11] To see this, notice that the first-order condition for the outsourcing problem is $c'(I) = (1 - \theta)[R_I(I, l_N) - R_I(I, 0)] + R_I(I, 0)$, where $R_I(I, l_N) - R_I(I, 0)$ is a measure in the change of the size of the rent, $(1 - \theta)$ shows the hold-up effect, and $R_I(I, 0)$ captures the change in the threat point. And a greater θ entails a larger outsourcing I if the cross-derivative $R_{I,I}(I, l)$ is negative.

Indeed, the above discussion shows that *offshoring acts as a worker's discipline device* when there is imperfect competition on the product market. Let us contrast the outcomes under autarky with those under opening of trade. Under autarky with imperfect competition, prices are above marginal costs and supply of goods is reduced. Employment, under efficient bargaining, is independent of the bargaining power θ. However, this bargaining power affects the sharing of the rent between workers and firms. Hence, consumer welfare is not affected by θ (but is clearly decreased because of imperfect competition). Now, when markets open in this context of imperfect competition, two effects will positively affect consumer welfare. First, because firms are able to import goods and intermediates, the set of potential technologies available to the firms expands, with the associated (likely) increase in production. Second, firms facing strong unions will 'over-offshore' to discipline their employees, through an altered threat point. This effect also increases production and consumer surplus. Interestingly, opening is more beneficial to consumers when unions are strong than when unions are weak, in a context where employers have market power. [12]

In summary, we now have a structural model of employment and wage determination with clear game-theoretic foundations and clear predictions. And I show in the remaining sections that it has strong empirical support.

9.3 Data and Empirical Implementation

In order to examine the relation between offshoring, foreign outsourcing of intermediates, employment, and the size of quasi-rents as well as structurally estimate the wage equation (9.3) as derived in Section 9.2, it is useful to list all the components that are necessary to perform this task. It will help the reader understand the main differences between this chapter and its predecessor, as well as some of its contributions.

First, I need to relate a worker's wage with her employing firm's measure of outsourcing, quasi-rents, employment, competitive environment, and union activity. To measure quasi-rent, I also need to measure each worker's opportunity wage. All these variables are *directly* measured in this chapter, in sharp contrast with the rest of the literature. To examine *wages*, I use person-level measures together with observable

---

[12] I would like to thank Emmanuel Jessua and Cyril Nouveau for pointing out this consequence of my model.

personal characteristics (in contrast with Abowd and Lemieux (1993) or Blanchflower et al. (1996) who use firm-level sources). To measure workers' *opportunity wage*, I estimate for each individual her alternative wage on the market (taking stock of recent developments in the analysis of matched employer–employee data, used in my analysis). To measure *outsourcing* (offshoring of final goods and outsourcing of intermediates), I use firm-level measures of foreign outsourcing of the two kinds (in contrast with Bertrand (2004) who only uses industry-level import data) and to measure the size of rents that workers and firms share, I construct firm-level measures of quasi-rent (because they do not measure workers' opportunity wage, Abowd and Lemieux (1993) use an equivalent with potential measurement error whereas Blanchflower et al. (1996) use profits). In addition, I am the first to use exhaustive information on all imports (and exports) in France, measured both at the firm-level and at the product level (to directly measure trade competition). To measure *union activity* and *bargaining outcomes*, I use firm and establishment measures of bargaining agreements at the end of my sample period, 1992. Finally, because outsourcing decisions or quasi-rents are likely to be endogenous and OLS estimates biased when estimating my wage equation, I use a strategy similar to my predecessors and use instruments (Abowd and Lemieux (1993) for the quasi-rent; Bertrand (2004) for industry-level imports). Because measurement and endogeneity issues are directly related, I will show that by providing solutions to the former I solve (part of) the latter.

9.3.1 Measurement of the Variables in the Estimating Equation

DATA ON WORKERS' WAGES, AND THEIR FIRM'S
IMPORTS AND OTHER ECONOMIC OUTCOMES
The estimating equation relates a worker's wage to her employing firm's imports, quasi-rent, etc. Obviously, employee-level data sources and firm-level data sources must be simultaneously accessible. And the individual-level source must contain the employer's identifier. Indeed, I use data from four different ongoing administrative data sources or statistical surveys that allow me to match workers to firms.[13] The first of these data sources is the DADS (Déclarations Annuelles de Données Sociales), which is an administrative file based on mandatory reports of employees' earnings by French employers to the Fiscal administration. Hence, it matches information on workers and on their employing firm.

---

[13] These surveys were conducted by the Institut National de la Statistique et des Etudes Economiques (INSEE, the French national statistical agency), by the Ministry of Labour, or by Customs.

This dataset is longitudinal and covers the period 1976–1996 for all workers employed in the private and semi-public sector and born in October of an even year. In addition, for all workers born in the first four days of October of an even year, information from the EDP (Echantillon Démographique Permanent) (our second data source) is also available. The EDP comprises education and demographic information. These are my two worker-level sources. Using the firm identifier they can be directly matched to my firm-level sources, described now. The Customs data come from an administrative file based on mandatory declarations of all trade in goods. They are available for all years from 1986 to 1992.[14] Following Biscourp and Kramarz (2007), I contrast imports of finished goods and imports of intermediates. To define the two, I compare the three-digit industry of the imported good with the three-digit industry of the importing firm. If they match, I call this import a 'finished good'. If not, I call this import an 'intermediary consumption'. The first gives my measure of offshoring whereas the second gives my measure of outsourcing (of intermediates). The fourth data source is the BAL-SUSE file. It gives me balance-sheet information (value added, sales, intermediary consumptions in particular) and employment. It includes most French firms, subject to the fiscal report called the Bénéfices Industriels et Commerciaux (BIC). All sectors, except the public sector, are covered. Data are available for the period 1984–1992. Matching all these sources together yields (approximately) 112,000 worker-level observations. These sources are described in more detail in Appendix B.

DATA ON UNION ACTIVITY AND BARGAINING AGREEMENTS

To measure firm and establishment level bargaining activity, I use the so-called Enquête Structure des Salaires (ESS, hereafter) for 1992 (the final year of my analysis period). This survey collects information on firm- or establishment-level bargaining under the Lois Auroux. The Lois Auroux stipulate that bargaining must take place every year in an establishment or a firm which has more than fifty employees. But, crucial for the analysis, even though bargaining is mandatory, firms can refuse to bargain on some subjects, employment for instance, and firms are not forced to sign an agreement at the end of the bargaining process.[15] The data tell me whether a round of bargaining took place in that year. In addition, I know the topic of the negotiation: wages, employment, other. Finally, for each topic of the negotiation, I know if

---

[14] After 1992, data are less exhaustive: small transactions are not recorded any more.

[15] Even though bargaining is supposedly mandatory, some establishments do not start a round of negotiation every year.

an agreement was signed in that year. Unfortunately, because the ESS samples establishments using a frame based on establishment or firm size, I lose a fraction of my observations, mostly in smaller units. The resulting file has 37,698 (worker-firm-year) observations, a third of the original file.

MEASURING WORKERS' OPPORTUNITY WAGE AND FIRMS' QUASI-RENT

Opportunity wage: workers' alternative wage captures what workers can receive in case of a strike, that is, their value outside the firm. I first rewrite this alternative wage, w_0, as the sum of two components: $w_0 = w^a + w_0(\bar{I})$. The first component, w^a, captures the unconditional opportunity cost of time, which only depends on workers' characteristics, both observed and unobserved, with value in every industry. The second component, $w_0(\bar{I})$, tries to capture workers' value in firms that produce the same product as the original workers' employing firm.[16]

To directly measure each worker's opportunity wage, w^a, I *first estimate* the following basic statistical model

$$\ln w_{it} = x_{it}\beta + \alpha_i + \psi_{J(i,t)} + \varepsilon_{it} \tag{9.5}$$

in which w_{it} is the measured annualized earnings for the individual $i = 1, \ldots, N$ at date $t = 1, \ldots T$; x_{it} is a vector of P time-varying exogenous characteristics of individual i; α_i is a pure person effect; $\psi_{J(i,t)}$ is a pure firm effect for the firm $J(i,t)$ at which worker i is employed at date t, and ε_{it} is a statistical residual. For this, I use the full DADS sample over the 1976–1996 period, as described above (13 million observations, 1 million individuals, more than 500,000 firms).[17]

Based on equation (9.5) and its estimation results, I now explain how to derive each worker's opportunity wage. Assume that a simple random sample of N individuals is observed for T years. The external

[16] $w_0(\bar{I})$ is directly related to the declining employment opportunities in the worker's industry due to import substitution away from the labour input. To measure this component, I use various statistics on imports of the *same good* made by the firm's competitors and made by the wholesale or retail trade industry (see Appendix B). Potential effects of unemployment are captured directly by introducing the local unemployment rate in the control variables.

[17] Identification and estimation of this type of equation is discussed at length in Abowd, Kramarz, and Margolis (1999) as well as in Abowd, Creecy, and Kramarz (2002). In the latter, the full least-squares solution is implemented. These papers show that estimation of the person- and firm-effects requires very large data sets and a sufficient number of years for the person-effects to be precisely estimated. So, I estimate the previous equation using the full DADS dataset (13 million observations for the period 1976–1996).

(opportunity) wage rate for person i is the expected value of her wage conditional on her characteristics and identity, that is, not knowing the employer's identity. In my estimating framework, equation (9.5) gives a measure of this external (opportunity) wage rate, defined as $w_{it}^a = E\left(w_{it}\,|x_{it}, i\right)$.[18] Hence:

$$\ln w_{it}^a \approx x_{it}\beta + \alpha_i \qquad (9.6)$$

in words, the (log of) worker's opportunity wage is the sum of returns to her observed, time-varying, personal characteristics with her observed and unobserved time-invariant personal characteristics. Hence, $\psi_{J(i,t)}$ is a measure of the systematic premium paid to worker i by firm $J(i, t)$ over her opportunity wage.

Quasi-rent: to measure the firm's quasi-rent, I use the following strategy. First, as just explained, I posit that the workers' threat point (see 9.3) can be decomposed in $w_0 = w^a + w_0(\bar{I})$. This allows me to rewrite wage equation (9.3) as

$$w_N = w^a + \theta\frac{\tilde{\pi}^a - \pi_0(I_N)}{I_N} + (1 - \theta)w_0(\bar{I}) \qquad (9.7)$$

where $\tilde{\pi}^a$ is the quasi-rent evaluated at worker's alternative wage, w^a:

$$\tilde{\pi}^a = R(I_N, l_N) - w^a l_N$$

Now, assuming for simplicity that all workers have the same alternative wage w^a, we see that $w_N = w^a \exp\psi \exp\varepsilon$ (using both 9.5 and 9.6). Hence,

$$\tilde{\pi}^a = R(I_N, l_N) - E[\frac{w_N}{\exp\psi \times \exp\varepsilon}l_N]$$

where E denotes the expectation taken in the firm of the relevant random variable. First, note that the firm effect is constant in the

---

[18] Notice that $\ln w_{it}^a = \ln E\left(w_{it}\,|x_{it}, i\right) = (x_{it}\beta + \alpha_i) + \ln E(\exp(\psi_{J(i,t)} + \varepsilon_{it}\,|x_{it}, i)$. Then, because the pure firm effect $\psi_{J(i,t)}$ and ε both have mean 0, and variance σ_ψ^2 and σ_ε^2 respectively, we have $E[\exp(\psi + \varepsilon)] = \exp\frac{\sigma_\psi^2 + \sigma_\varepsilon^2}{2} \approx 1$, assuming that both ψ and ε are normal as they appear to be, and because, in the economy, σ_ψ^2 and σ_ε^2 are small (0.08 and 0.04 respectively, for all these results see Abowd, Creecy, and Kramarz, 2002) and can be taken as independent of the person observed or unobserved characteristics.

firm. Then, by the same reasoning as above, the equation can be rewritten as:[19]

$$\tilde{\pi}^a = R(I_N, l_N) - \frac{w_N l_N}{\exp \psi} \qquad (9.8)$$

Therefore, to measure the quasi-rent $\tilde{\pi}^a$, I use a measure of labour costs, $\frac{w_N l_N}{\exp \psi}$, that eliminates the costs due to the pure firm effects. Finally, to measure $\pi_0(I_N)$, I use a function of the firm's own imports.

To summarize, in equation (9.7) I am now in a position to directly measure each worker's *opportunity wage* w^a (from previous estimation), each manufacturing firm's *quasi-rent* $\tilde{\pi}^a$ (from balance-sheet data, see data description earlier in this subsection, and previous estimation for an estimate of ψ), l_N (from balance-sheet data), $\pi_0(I_N)$ (from Customs data at the firm level), and $w_0(\bar{I})$ (from the import data of competitors).

9.3.2 Endogeneity and Other Potential Econometric Problems

Apart from measurement problems discussed in Section 9.3.1, there are multiple potential econometric pitfalls in estimating equation (9.7):

(i) When the splitting parameter θ varies by firm, and when this parameter is correlated with the size of the quasi-rent, estimates of θ will be biased upward (downward) if this correlation is positive (resp. negative) (see Abowd and Lemieux 1993). Our discussion in Section 9.2 suggests that the correlation should be positive because large rents are likely to induce strong unions.

(ii) When the contract is not strongly efficient, then wages, quasi-rent, and employment are determined jointly. This standard endogeneity bias makes OLS estimates inconsistent. Abowd and Lemieux (1993) as well as Abowd and Kramarz (1993) show that proper estimates of (9.7), using instrumental variables, yield a lower bound for the bargaining parameter when the contract is not strongly efficient (see in particular the discussion in Abowd and Lemieux 1993, pp.988–90).

(iii) Because I want to separately identify the bargaining parameter θ from the threat point $\pi_0(I_N) = R(I_N, 0)$ and from import competition that affects $w_0(\bar{I})$, I must assume that θ does not

---

[19] Assuming that ε is normal with mean 0, and variance σ_ε^2, we have $E[\exp \varepsilon] = \exp \frac{\sigma_\varepsilon^2}{2} \approx 1$, since σ_ε^2 is small (0.04, see Abowd, Creecy, and Kramarz 2002) and is independent of the person and the firm observed or unobserved characteristics, as derived previously.

depend on imports of the firm nor on imports of competitors. Put differently, $\theta(I_N, \bar{I})$ is *not separately identifiable from* $\pi_0(I_N)$ *and* $w_0(\bar{I})$ *in equation (9.7). Hence, I assume that* θ *is fixed over the analysis period.*

In all cases, *in order to identify this bargaining parameter* θ, movements reflecting changes in product market competition should translate into movements of the quasi-rent. To understand the issue, Appendix C of Kramarz (2007) presents a model that explains the various problems. A first consequence of his model is the following. If the measure of the workers' opportunity wage is precise enough, the quasi-rent should not be endogenous in a **person-level** wage equation, as is estimated here. Use the argument from Abowd and Lemieux (1993, p.984).

However, an empirical strategy still has to be set-up *if* the quasi-rent is found to be endogenous despite all measurement efforts. I follow the literature in using instrumental variables. My choice of instruments is discussed later when I present estimates of equation (9.7).

9.4 Offshoring, Quasi-rent, and Employment

For years, many French firms enjoyed the protection of various regulations, subsidies, tariffs, and entry restrictions. In addition, because of collective agreements (first signed by large firms and then extended in the 1970s by the Ministry of Labour to virtually every firm and every worker in the manufacturing sector), firms faced unions with strong power and minimum wages were high. Small firms, which typically depend on lower labour costs, found it difficult to compete against larger companies. The entry and growth of potential competitors was reduced. In addition, the first years of the Mitterrand presidency witnessed a thorough nationalization process of large private companies. All these facts generated rents in many industries, most particularly manufacturing. These rents were directly reflected in wages, particularly in large firms.[20] In addition, the Lois Auroux were introduced in 1981 just after François Mitterrand's presidential election. These laws enhanced workers' bargaining power at the level of the firm.[21]

---

[20] See Abowd, Kramarz, and Margolis (1999) for evidence on France. More recently Abowd, Kramarz, Lengermann, and Roux (2007) analyse inter-industry wage differences in France and in the USA and show that the firm-specific component of these differentials is associated both with monopoly power on the firms' side and union power on the workers' side, in France and during the 1970s and 1980s, at least.

[21] The Lois Auroux explicitly include the obligation to negotiate for the establishment or firms meeting certain conditions (size, among others). See Cahuc and Kramarz (1997),

However, in the ensuing years, market reforms were implemented (see Bertrand, Schoar, and Thesmar (2007), for the financial side of the reforms in the mid-1980s) and foreign competitors entered the French scene. Simultaneously, new markets opened. In response, some of those large French firms increased their imports of intermediates and launched offshoring strategies. And, indeed, competition became fiercer. The early 'equilibrium' started to unravel. More precisely, in the so-called White Paper from the Commission, the Single Market Program was announced in 1985.[22] The SMP was launched in 1988 with the stated goal of achieving a single internal market for goods in 1992. This programme included a lowering of tariffs and trade barriers within the EC. As already explained in Hoeller and Louppe (1994), it took more time to reach the goal than initially thought. However, the period under study is one of great changes in trade. European firms could both import and export more easily, at least within the EC. And numbers show that, indeed, trade increased dramatically.

In the rest of this section, and before turning to more structural results, I want to present simple evidence describing the consequences of the above facts.

My first piece of evidence is presented in Table 9.1. The table shows the results of the following regression of quasi-rent (per employee), $\frac{QR_{j,t}}{I_{j,t}}$, on measures of imports by firm j at date t:[23]

$$\frac{QR_{j,t}}{I_{j,t}} = \delta \frac{I_{j,t}}{R(I_{j,t}, I_{j,t})} + \alpha_j + \varepsilon_{j,t}$$

where α_j is a firm-fixed effect and $\varepsilon_{j,t}$ is a statistical residual. The measures of imports distinguish between imports of finished goods (my measure of offshoring) and imports of intermediates (outsourcing). The regression controls for firm-fixed effects.[24] Hence, I capture the impact of within-firm variations over the sample period (1986–1992) of the import measures on the size of the rent.

Results in the first column show that more intense offshoring as a fraction of sales (imports of goods divided by total sales) deteriorates the size of the quasi-rent (per worker) that the workers and the firm

for a description of their principles, see also Abowd and Allain (1996), who provide some evidence supporting this claim. See my analysis in Section 9.6.

[22] See the text in http://aei.pitt.edu/archive/00001113/, accessed 21 November 2005.

[23] The observations are individuals matched to their firm. Larger firms have more individual observations, in proportion to their size. Hence, these regressions are identical to doing firm-level regressions weighted by employment.

[24] Most regressions discussed in the following paragraphs include firm fixed effects. If firm effects are not included, this will be explicitly mentioned in the text.

Table 9.1 Rents and outsourcing

	Quasi-rent	Quasi-rent (>50)	Quasi-rent (≤50)	Quasi-rent (80≥emp>50)	Quasi-rent (30<emp≤50)
(Imports of goods)/production	−35.2563	−39.0082	3.7053	−31.8886	−7.7315
	(1.6400)	(1.6880)	(5.8838)	(6.7691)	(9.5802)
	[8.2040]	[8.9514]	[11.2350]	[11.9582]	[9.5981]
(Imports of IC)/(local purchases)	7.2746	8.7769	−2.4706	−0.0820	−2.9929
	(0.8318)	(0.8906)	(2.2513)	(3.1878)	(2.9235)
	[7.0055]	[8.0317]	[3.4125]	[3.8067]	[2.9396]
Intercept	74.0972	82.4073	47.7757	47.7891	55.6862
	(0.1435)	(0.1745)	(0.2144)	(1.6362)	(1.6756)
	[0.6004]	[0.8081]	[0.2374]	[2.1056]	[1.9794]
R-square	0.8435	0.8533	0.7855	0.9104	0.9174
Number of observations	119,860	91,070	28,790	6,282	8,920

Notes: each regression includes firm indicators (16,078, for the regression with 119,860 observations). One observation is a person–firm–year. Standard errors in parentheses. Standard errors adjusting for clustering at the firm level in brackets. The quasi-rent is measured per employee. Regressions include time indicators and controls for import competition at the industry (3-digit) level.
Source: DADS-EDP matched with BAL-SUSE (BRN).

will have to divide if they bargain. Imports of intermediates (divided by total purchases) have no such effect. Interestingly, results in the next two columns show that offshoring affects the size of the rent only in relatively large firms (above fifty employees; the Auroux laws threshold) and does not have an impact on smaller firms where quasi-rents appear to be much smaller (see the coefficient on the constant).[25]

Now, this last fact might just be a reflection of size: larger firms might behave differently. To see if this threshold really matters, I perform a simple test based on this *discontinuity*. Presented in the last two columns of Table 9.1, it examines the same regression as before restricting attention in the first of the two columns to firms with thirty-one to fifty employees, and in the second of the two columns to firms with fifty-one to eighty employees. Results show a clear and sharp difference in the association between quasi-rents and imports of finished goods (offshoring) on the two sides of the threshold.[26] To give a sense of the magnitude of this effect, a 1-point increase in the share of offshoring in sales converts into a decrease of the quasi-rent of 350 French Francs per worker (or of 0.5 points of the QR per employee, see Table 9.A1).

Now, in the introduction, I mentioned that Biscourp and Kramarz (2007) have shown that employment losses for the same period were strongly associated with offshoring. The data used here mix the data on firms used in Biscourp and Kramarz (2007) with data on their workers. Because the selection may well differ due to matching of the different data sources, I also ask whether outsourcing similarly affects firms' employment. Table 9.2 helps answer this question. And the simple answer is positive, at least in large firms. But the smaller firms are not affected by more intense offshoring (see the next two columns of Table 9.2). And, in line with these results and with the model, the importing of intermediates has no clear impact on employment nor on quasi-rent (see Tables 9.1 and 9.2). In addition, to assess the robustness of these results, I introduced measures of trade competition (imports of finished goods by competitors). None of these results were affected.[27] To further

---

[25] In unreported regressions, I checked that, *as predicted by the theory*, quasi-rent per person is positively related to offshoring (results can be obtained from the author). Here, the negative relation comes from measuring offshoring as a fraction of sales.

[26] Importantly, the fifty employees discontinuity is not as sharp as in other economic examples. First, there are different ways to count the number of employees. For the Law, the exact limit is fifty, but all employees are not 'equal' in the computation (part-time part-year vs full-time full-year, for instance). Hence, I use fifty-one rather than fifty (results are unchanged if I use thirty-one to forty-nine and fifty to eighty groupings). In addition, the presence of union delegates or personnel delegates is another central element in the precise application of the Auroux Laws. To simplify the analysis, I will focus on the size threshold as measured above.

[27] Estimates are available from the author.

Table 9.2 Employment and outsourcing

	Employment (in logs)	Employment (in logs, >50)	Employment (in logs, ≤ 50)	Employment (in logs)
(Imports of goods)/production	−0.1286	−0.1333	−0.0660	−0.1286
	(0.0110)	(0.0099)	(0.0464)	(0.0110)
	[0.0509]	[0.0545]	[0.0732]	[0.0509]
(Imports of IC)/(local purchases)	−0.0796	−0.0923	0.0286	−0.0796
	(0.0056)	(0.0052)	(0.0176)	(0.0056)
	[0.0829]	[0.0962]	[0.0293]	[0.0829]
(Total exports)/(sales in France)				0.0017
				(0.0217)
				[0.0204]
Intercept	5.9291	6.9529	2.7385	5.9291
	(0.0010)	(0.0010)	(0.0017)	(0.0010)
	[0.0096]	[0.0130]	[0.0017]	[0.0096]
R-square	0.9943	0.9930	0.9421	0.9943
Number of observations	121,260	91,808	29,452	121,260

Notes: each regression includes firm indicators (16,078, for the regression with 119,860 observations). One observation is a person–firm–year. Standard errors in parentheses. Standard errors adjusting for clustering at the firm level in brackets. Regressions include time indicators and controls for import competition at the industry (3-digit) level.
Sources: DADS-EDP matched with BAL-SUSE (BRN).

assess robustness, the results in the last column of Table 9.2 show that exports are not associated with movements in employment.[28] Hence, there is something specific to the firms' offshoring (imports of finished goods).[29] Large firms decrease employment when their own offshoring increases; in the mean time, the relative size of the rent to share with workers decreases. Again, to give a sense of the magnitude of the effects, a 10-point increase in the share of offshoring in sales is associated with a 1.3-point decrease in employment.

To conclude this section, offshoring seems to be a strategy that affects quasi-rent and employment, for reasons that appear (*proving causality in this setting is virtually impossible since the discontinuity in the institutional setting is based on employment, a highly manipulable variable*) to be related to French bargaining institutions (the Auroux Laws). In Section 9.5 I focus on these bargaining institutions. More precisely, and in line with the theoretical model, I try to measure the strength of unions across firms and bargaining regimes and relate this strength to firms' importing behaviour.

9.5 Estimating Unions' Bargaining Power

9.5.1 *The Estimating Equation*

My model relates firms and unions with heterogeneous bargaining powers to their offshoring activity. But first, I must identify which firms face powerful unions and which firms do not. Therefore, I must connect my model with real-life institutions allowing me to understand the role of unions in the French bargaining process. To do so, I use the ESS survey for year 1992. Because the Auroux Laws stipulate that bargaining should take place every year in an establishment or a firm with more than fifty employees, the data tell me if a round of bargaining took place in that year. In addition, I know the topic of the negotiation: wages, employment, other. Finally, for each topic of the negotiation, I know if an agreement was signed in that year. Because the ESS samples establishments using a frame based on establishment or firm size, I lose a fraction of my observations, mostly in smaller units in comparison with results in Tables 9.1 and 9.2 (or those contained in Kramarz 2007). The resulting file has 37,698 (worker–firm–year) observations.

---

[28] All these results are in full agreement with those of Biscourp and Kramarz (2007), based on a larger set of firms.

[29] As a further test of robustness, the joint inclusion of the import competition variables (imports of competitors, of finished goods and of intermediates) and the firms' import variables does not alter any result of Tables 9.1 and 9.2.

Table 9.3 Workers' wages: workers' bargaining power and firm-level imports, controlling for competitors' imports

	The role of negotiations (Firms' quasi-rent and workers' seniority instrumented)	
		Wage level
Quasi-rent	(neg. on employment)	0.5387 (0.0533) [0.0660]
Quasi-rent	(neg. on wages, not emp.)	0.0570 (0.0455) [0.0528]
Quasi-rent	(no neg. on emp. or wages)	−0.1241 (0.0702) [0.0848]
(Imports of goods)/production	(neg. on employment)	23.3080 (17.5078) [31.5429]
(Imports of goods)/production	(neg. on wages. not emp.)	30.5606 (7.0047) [16.9916]
(Imports of goods)/production	(no neg. on emp. or wages)	15.2063 (5.3680) [17.9875]
(Imports of IC)/(local purchases)	(neg. on employment)	−55.2317 (16.2249) [42.3125]
(Imports of IC)/(local purchases)	(neg. on wages, not emp.)	4.3660 (5.3503) [13.9650]
(Imports of IC)/(local purchases)	(no neg. on emp. or wages)	4.9110 (6.1353) [13.7938]
Competitors' imports of goods (99th perc., sh. of production)	(neg. on employment)	−46.1815 (7.7865) [11.9360]
Competitors' imports of goods (99th perc., sh. of production)	(neg. on wages. not emp.)	−8.9339 (2.5897) [4.5533]
Competitors' imports of goods (99th perc., sh. of production)	(no neg. on emp. or wages)	7.1101 (3.2461) [4.9006]
Competitors' imports of IC (99th perc., sh. of local purchases)	(neg. on employment)	−20.6279 (5.0507) [17.7138]
Competitors' imports of IC (99th perc., sh. of local purchases)	(neg. on wages. not emp.)	3.0865 (1.7133) [3.0757]

(continued)

Table 9.3 Continued

Competitors' imports of IC (99th perc., sh. of local purchases)	(no neg. on emp. or wages)	9.5122 (2.9748) [5.4238]
Chi-square (df=37)		40.5432
Over-identfication test (p-value)		0.3169

Notes: 37,698 person-year observations. The sample period is 1986–1992. The regression uses a measure of quasi-rent that discounts assets. The regression includes the following variables (coefficients unreported): Competitors' imports of goods (99th perc., in level), Competitors' imports of IC (99th perc., in level) both interacted with three negotiations levels, Imports of goods from the trade ind. (sh. of total purchases), Imports of goods from the trade ind. (total purchases), seniority and seniority-squared, experience (quartic), marital status, indicators for having children below 3, children between 3 and 6, for living in Ile de France, for working part time, year dummies, experience in France (for the immigrants), the boat unemployment rate, 3-digit industry indicators, the estimated person-effect, and a full interaction of the person-effect with all previous variables (except seniority and industry indicators). The Quasi-rent, Seniority, and Seniority-squared are instrumented by lagged export price indices of US firms to four destinations $ US 5 of the same industry as the employing firm. The chi-square tests the validity of the instruments. Robust standard errors are between parentheses. Robust standard errors allowing for clustering at the industry-level are between brackets.

Sources: BAL-SUSE for firm-level variables. DADS-EDP for individual variables, Customs tile for import measures, OECD for the export prices. ESS for bargaining outcomes.

Descriptive statistics show that 26 per cent of workers were employed in a firm where negotiations on employment took place in 1992. For most of them, 82 per cent, an agreement was signed after the negotiation. Virtually all these firms also negotiated wages with their employees. Only 4 per cent of the workers are employed in firms that negotiated on employment without negotiating on wages. Furthermore, 81 per cent of the workers were employed in firms that negotiated on wages; with 65 per cent among them eventually signing an agreement. Even though the different bargaining regimes are not perfectly aligned with the theory, I focus on a limited number of bargaining regimes. Hence, for each individual observation, I classify the employing firm as one which:

(i) bargained with unions (or personnel delegates) on employment (and wages);

(ii) bargained with unions (or personnel delegates) on wages;

(iii) did not bargain with unions or personnel delegates.

In what follows, in line with the efficient bargaining model with imports that I adopted, I mostly contrast these three types of firms and I will try to estimate the bargaining strength of the unions in each of the above regimes. I also show that results are robust to different groupings. In particular, the first category widely differs from the rest of the firms. To distinguish between firms with heterogeneous bargaining regimes,

I estimate a variant of equation (9.3) in which θ can take three values, θ_e, θ_w, θ_n depending on the bargaining regime:

$$w_N = w^a + \theta_i \frac{\tilde{\pi}^a - R(I_N, 0)}{I_N} + (1 - \theta_i)w_0(\bar{I})$$

$$\text{where } i = e, \, w, \, n \text{ and } \tilde{\pi}^a = R(I_N, I_N) - w^a I_N \qquad (9.9)$$

My goal is to estimate the θ_is, the bargaining parameters. They will allow me to assess which firms face strong unions and which firms do not. Then, Section 9.6 will check how unions' bargaining power is related to outsourcing and employment.

As explained in Section 9.4, there are many reasons to believe that quasi-rent, $\tilde{\pi}^a$, is endogenous in equation (9.9). Hence, I must use, if necessary, an instrumental variable strategy. It is described in Section 9.5.2.

9.5.2 Instruments: Export Prices of US Firms to Measure French Product Market Conditions

Valid instruments must reflect changes in product market conditions inducing movements in the *quasi-rent* or in the *offshoring and outsourcing (import)* decisions of the firms, but they must be uncorrelated with the error terms in the wage equation.

Product market conditions are determined by local conditions as well as by global factors. Many among these local factors can be affected by the local firms' behaviour. But, most often, the global factors are beyond the reach of the French firms that I examine. Among these global factors, exchange rates naturally come to mind. Business conditions, costs, and productivity shocks that take place in countries that trade in the world market are likely to affect many local decisions of French firms. For instance, a positive productivity shock in the textile industries of some Asian economies might affect outsourcing decisions of French firms, hence their imports and their employment. An increase in the price of oil might have an impact on the ability of Middle Eastern countries to consume and to import. A positive productivity shock in the American steel industry will negatively affect the French steel producers but they will positively affect the French automobile industry, a heavy user of steel. These shocks in different countries will have a differentiated impact on the different firms depending in particular on their exposures to these various global markets since some export whereas some do not, some import whereas some do not, some are global competitors whereas some are not.

In addition, as explained earlier, the period under consideration is one of implementation of the SMP within the EC. Competition increased drastically in virtually all manufacturing industries; accordingly the reaction of firms to shocks should also be easier to identify during this period.

To summarize, valid instruments should be correlated with the quasi-rent, seniority, and other endogenous variables such as a firm's imports. In line with Abowd and Lemieux (1993), Abowd and Allain (1996), and Bertrand (2004), I am trying to capture variations in the firms' *ability to pay*, as measured by the $\frac{R(I_N, I_N)}{I_N}$. This ability to pay is particularly determined by supply conditions on the product market. And, to trace the supply (of goods) curve, I must find measures of exogenous demand shocks affecting product market competition. Therefore, I use international market prices, in US Dollars, to instrument both firm- and person-level variables. More precisely I use industry-specific export prices of US manufacturing firms in four destinations. These variables meet the various requirements presented above. Because they are export prices, they are determined on the world market and are therefore likely to be relatively unaffected by French producers. In addition, because they are export prices as set by US firms, they reflect world competition as perceived by a large player. In particular, *they may incorporate the shocks induced by the SMP*. Furthermore, as these price indices are in fact unit value indices computed in US Dollars, they also reflect exogenous variations in the exchange rate of the US Dollar vis à vis different destination countries. These prices are measured at the three-digit industry level. Therefore, I should be able to capture multiple variations, *differently* affecting firms according to their *specific exposures* to the various markets.[30]

Evidence that these export prices represent pure demand shocks is presented in Appendix C, first paragraph. One can conclude from this exercise that past variations in US export prices reflect *demand* shocks affecting French firms. These prices allow me to estimate valid *supply* equations: when prices go up, production increases. Hence, there are good economic reasons to believe that such instruments are well-suited to the present needs of my statistical analysis. More evidence is presented in what follows.

---

[30] Abowd and Lemieux (1993) used ideas related to this procedure when studying Canadian firms, Abowd and Allain (1996) also used a similar idea when instrumenting French firms' quasi-rents, Bertrand (2004) used a related strategy when instrumenting industry-level import penetration ratios by source-weighted industry exchange rates, and Gourinchas (1999) shows how exchange rates affect job flows.

9.5.3 *Estimation Results*

Following my previous discussion, and Kramarz (2007), I estimate the resulting equation exactly derived from equation (9.9) for worker i, employed at date t by firm $j = J(i, t)$ where J is a function that associates a firm j to a worker date pair (i, t):

$$w_{i,t} = \theta_{b(j)} \frac{\tilde{\pi}_{j,t}^{a}}{l_{j,t}} + \phi_{b(j)} \frac{I_{j,t}}{S_{j,t}} + \tau_{b(j)} \frac{IC_{j,t}}{P_{j,t}} + \lambda_{b(j)} f(\bar{I}_{j,t}) + h(x_{i,t}, \alpha_i) + \upsilon_{i,t}$$

where

- $w_{i,t}$ is worker i's total labour costs for year t, in levels (not in logs).
- $\frac{\tilde{\pi}_{j,t}^{a}}{l_{j,t}}$ is firm j quasi-rent at date t, measured using equation (9.8) described in Section 9.3.1.
- $\frac{I_{j,t}}{S_{j,t}}$ is my measure of offshoring at firm j at date t. It is the share of imports of goods in sales.
- $\frac{IC_{j,t}}{P_{j,t}}$ is my measure of foreign outsourcing at firm j at date t. It is the share of imports of intermediates in total purchases.
- $f(\bar{I}_{j,t})$ is a control function capturing the imports of competitors of firm j, $\bar{I}$. It includes measures of imports of goods, of intermediates by firms from the same industry as j; measures of imports of goods similar to those produced by firm j made by wholesale firms. These measures are both in levels and expressed as shares of respectively sales (for imports of goods) and purchases (for imports of intermediates). For the shares, the 99th percentiles of the respective distributions within each four-digit industry are used in the preferred specification (see Appendix B for a detailed description).
- $h(x_{i,t}, \alpha_i)$ is a control function of observables, $x_{i,t}$, and unobservables, α_i, of worker i for year t. It is estimated as a second-order polynomial of these variables. α_i is estimated using equation (9.5) based on the full data with 13 million observations, as described in the measurement section, in levels (not in logs). Because the estimated person effect is included, the equation controls for person effects.
- $b(j)$ is the bargaining regime of firm j (bargaining on both employment and wages, on wages, no bargaining). Because of the data and because of my identification assumption, it is time invariant.
- finally, $\upsilon_{i,t}$ is a statistical residual.

For the reasons discussed already (endogeneity, measurement error, etc.), this equation is estimated by instrumental variables (IV), with quasi-rent (interacted with the bargaining regime $b(j)$), seniority and its square instrumented using my measures of product market conditions—export prices (industry-level unit values measured in US Dollars of American firms to four destinations)—and the other control variables, duly interacted with the bargaining regime as required. Appendix C presents a fairly detailed presentation of the various elements of the estimation methodology.[31] Estimation results are presented in Table 9.3. For each estimated coefficient, I provide two sets of standard errors. Robust standard errors are given in parentheses. Standard errors that, in addition, account for clustering at the three-digit industry level are given in brackets. These results tell a clear story.

In firms that did not negotiate on employment with their unions, $\theta_w = 0$ and $\theta_n = 0$ (hence, for those firms that bargained on wages and for those that did not bargain at all, respectively). Because workers' bargaining power is essentially zero, workers receive their opportunity cost of time, w^a, plus their negotiation threat point, $w_0(\bar{I})$. In other words, in firms where unions were too weak to impose negotiations on employment, workers were compensated at the market rate. More precisely, estimates show that, in firms that negotiated on wages but not on employment, the threat point is marginally increasing with the firms' own imports of finished goods (offshoring). But, in those firms, import competition—as measured by the 99th percentile of competitors imports of finished goods—slightly lowers workers' threat point.[32] In firms in which no negotiation took place, be they on wages or employment, we see that w_0 is essentially equal to the opportunity cost of time, w^a.

Now, if negotiating on employment with their unions, firms have to share half of their quasi-rents with their workers. In other words, in those firms, unions were strong enough to extract half of the quasi-rent. Hence, because $\theta_e = 1/2$, wages should also depend equally on $\frac{R(I_N,0)}{I_N}$ and $w_0(\bar{I})$ (see equation (9.9)). First, there is no significant impact from a firm's own imports. But, the most striking result is the strong and robust negative impact of the firm's competitors' imports of finished

---

[31] Kramarz (2007) gives an even fuller account of these details.

[32] Hence, it seems that w_0 is also a function of the firm's own imports and should be noted $w_0(I, \bar{I})$. This result can be seen either as a simple extension of the theoretical model and just makes the optimal level of employment dependent on the firm's own imports, making the ensuing computations more complex, without changing the main conclusions. It can also be interpreted as a manifestation of a hold-up problem, because imports are made in advance (first stage of the game).

goods, and (not significantly so) competitors' imports of intermediates on workers' wages. Hence, workers benefit from the sharing of the rent, even though this quasi-rent appears to be under attack because of increased competition (see Tables 9.1 and 9.2), but import competition strongly decreases wages in firms that negotiated (or were forced to negotiate) on employment.

We checked these results by regrouping the two categories of firms for which $\theta_w = 0$ and $\theta_n = 0$. No previous conclusion is altered by this grouping. Other robustness tests were performed, including exports at the firm-level and estimated firm-effects, using the 95th percentile of the competitors' imports distribution rather than the 99th. None of the conclusions is altered. It is important at this point to remind the reader that, as shown by Abowd, Kramarz, Lengermann, and Roux (2007), France was, in those years, a country where high-wages were often the result of a lack of product market competition (virtual monopoly rents), giving unions incentives to bargain hard. Indeed, large firms mostly benefited from these rents. As stated earlier, the Lois Auroux force firms with more than fifty employees to negotiate with their workers but the topic is left to the parties. Indeed, most firms negotiate on something. However, not all firms agree to bargain on wages and even fewer bargain on employment (and wages, in fact). In that respect, because firms must negotiate but need not sign an agreement, the signature of an agreement, on wages for instance, is is also evidence of strong unions, as (unreported) results show: in firms that sign an agreement, the bargaining power is $\theta_s = 0.37$.

9.6 Union Bargaining Power, Offshoring, and Employment

To complete the story and test my model, I will now examine the causal impact of strong unions in an era of increased globalization and trade. I know which firms have strong unions and which firms do not. I now examine the effect of the bargaining regime on offshoring and employment. To do this, I adopt a simple linear framework where I regress my variables of interest *in first difference over the sample period 1986–1992* on indicators of the bargaining regime using my firm-level variables. I do this without and with instrumental variables for the bargaining regime. These instruments are inspired by my theoretical framework and express the competitive environment of each firm at the beginning of the sample period, in 1986. More precisely, I use firm-level variables: the quasi-rent per person—a measure of the size of the rent to be shared between workers and the firm—the labour costs per person, and employment and industry-level variables that capture the strength of the competitive environment of the firm: offshoring and imports of competitors, measured as a fraction of production or sales, respectively, and in levels. These industry-level variables capture the 99th percentile of the within three-digit industry measure of the relevant variable.

The results are presented in Table 9.4 and Table 9.A1. The first-stage shows, consistently with the theoretical framework, that high costs, high rents, and large firms at the beginning of the period are strong union firms (i.e. signed an agreement on employment and wages at the end of the sample period).

Firms that agreed (or were forced) to negotiate on employment with their unions at the end of the sample period had lower employment growth (in contrast to those firms that negotiated only on wages, the reference group, and much lower than those that did not negotiate). In complete opposition, these firms notably increased their offshoring (measured by imports of finished goods) more than

Table 9.4 Negotiation in 1992 and firm-level changes in the preceding period (1986–1992)

	No negotiation, either on wages or employment		Negotiation on employment and wages	
	Coef.	Std. Err.	Coef.	Std. Err.
Change in labour costs (per person, in logs)	1.2803	0.3207	2.9370	0.3430
Change in employment (in logs)	0.5041	0.1351	−0.7447	0.1556
Change in imports of goods (as a fraction of production)	−1.4728	0.3077	1.7646	0.3230
Change in imports of IC (as a fraction of local purchases)	0.1312	0.1183	−0.6472	0.1273
Change in the quasi-rent (per person)	0.0007	0.0005	0.0023	0.0004
Change in the competitors' imports of IC (99th perc., sh. of local purchases)	0.4842	0.1093	−0.4260	0.1209
Change in the competitors' imports of goods (99th perc., sh. of production)	0.7731	0.1742	0.5312	0.1754
Pseudo-R_2	0.1818			
Number of observations	7,210			

Notes: estimated by Maximum Likelihood. The reference group comprises firms that only negotiated on wages.

Sources: BAL-SUSE for firm-level variables, DADS-EDP for individual variables, Customs file for import measures, OECD for the export prices. ESS for bargaining outcomes.

firms that negotiated only on wages and even more so with firms that did not negotiate (the opposite holds for imports of intermediates, outsourcing). They also faced tougher competition, a higher growth in labour costs per person, and a higher growth of the quasi-rent per person over the sample period.

Using the model to give an interpretation, those firms facing strong unions improved their bargaining position (threat point) over the period by increasing offshoring before or while bargaining. Hence, these firms appear to have been substituting imports of finished goods for employment because of strong unions that forced them to share a very large fraction, $\theta_e = 1/2$, of their quasi-rent. The mere fact that unions were able to force firms to negotiate on employment suggests that they have been able to resist some changes, a reflection of their very strong bargaining power. As predicted by the model, strong union strength was associated with increased outsourcing of finished goods, eventually leading to further declines in their employing firms' employment in this increasingly competitive environment.

9.7 Conclusion

In this chapter, I present the first direct microeconometric evidence of the relation between unions' bargaining power, firms' response by outsourcing (of finished goods or intermediates), and the impact on workers' wages and employment (see Bertrand (2004) and Goldberg and Tracy (2001), for evidence on trade and wages in the USA, based on industry-level measures of import competition). The story that I evaluate relates firms' outsourcing strategies with their wages and employment behaviour in an imperfectly competitive labour market where unions and firms have to bargain. To accomplish this task, I first derived employment and wage equations from a bargaining model that allows the analyst to examine outsourcing and its impact on workers' outcomes. The model shows that firms facing strong unions should use offshoring more intensively in order to squeeze the size of the quasi-rent that is bargained over, and to discipline workers. To estimate this model, I have used a unique matched employer–employee data source that contains information on firms' inputs, including imports by type of product, unions' presence in those firms, as well as individual characteristics of a representative sample of workers employed at those firms. I show that the size of the quasi-rent is directly affected—decreased—by outsourcing, because of French bargaining institutions, in often formerly protected industries. Employment in these firms also decreased (see also Biscourp and Kramarz 2007). When I estimate the structural person-level equation induced by the bargaining model, I show that for firms that bargained on both employment and wages with their unions, workers captured half of the quasi-rent. Workers in other firms were not able to capture a significant share of the rents. As predicted by the model, the firms that faced strong unions increased offshoring and decreased employment over the analysis period while the rest of the firms saw their relative employment increase and appeared to have used outsourcing much less intensively. Unions' strength may well have backfired.

Appendix A: Proof

Let us denote by $\phi^\ell(I, l) = 0$ the first-order condition on employment $R'_\ell(I, l) = \omega_0$; by $\phi^\omega(I, l, \theta, \omega) = 0$, the condition on wage: $\omega = \omega_0 + \theta \left[\frac{R(I,l) - \omega_0 l - \pi_0(l)}{l} \right]$

Finally, let us denote by $\phi^R(I, l, \theta, \omega) = 0$, the first stage condition that maximizes revenue as a function of imports:

$$\frac{\partial R}{\partial I} - c'(I) - \theta \left[\frac{\partial R}{\partial I} - \pi'_0(I) \right] = 0.$$

From these three sets of equations, total derivation yields:

$$\phi'^l_I(I, l)dI + \phi'^l_\ell(I, l)dl = 0$$

$$\phi'^\omega_\omega d\omega + \phi'^\omega_I + \phi'^\omega_l dl + \phi'^\omega_\theta d\theta = 0$$

$$\phi'^R_\omega d\omega + \phi'^R_I dI + \phi'^R_l dl + \phi'^R_\theta d\theta = 0$$

The first equation yields $\frac{dl}{dI} = -\frac{\phi'^l_I(I,l)}{\phi'^l_\ell(I,l)} = -\frac{\frac{\partial^2 R}{\partial I \partial l}}{\frac{\partial^2 R}{\partial l^2}}$

$\frac{dl}{dI}$ is of the sign of $\frac{\partial^2 R}{\partial I \partial l}$ since $\frac{\partial^2 R}{\partial l^2} < 0$. Now, using the above expression:

$$\phi'^\omega_\omega d\omega + \left(\phi'^\omega_I - \phi'^\omega_l \frac{\phi'^l_I}{\phi'^l_l} \right) dI + \phi'^\omega_\theta d\theta = 0$$

$$\phi^R_\omega d\omega + \left(\phi'^R_I - \phi'^R_\ell \frac{\phi'^l_I}{\phi'^l_I} \right) dI + \phi'^R_\theta d\theta = 0.$$

We can directly compute the different elements of these expressions:

$$\phi'^\omega_\omega = -1$$

$$\phi'^\omega_\theta = \left(\frac{R(I, l) - \omega_0 l - \pi_0(l)}{l} \right)$$

$$\phi'^R_\omega = 0$$

$\phi_\theta'^R = -\frac{\partial R}{\partial I} + \pi_0'(I)$. Taken together, this yields

$$\frac{dI}{d\theta} = -\left(\pi_0'(I) - \frac{\partial R}{\partial I}\right) \Big/ \left(\phi_I'^R + \phi_I'^R \times \frac{\partial^2 R/\partial I \partial l}{\frac{\partial^2 R}{\partial I^2}}\right)$$

But, $\phi_I'^R = (1-\theta)\frac{\partial^2 R}{\partial I^2} - c''(I) + \theta\pi_0''(I) < 0$ given the concavity of R and π_0 in I and the convexity of c in I.

In addition, $\phi_I'^R = (1-\theta)\frac{\partial^2 R}{\partial I \partial l}$ then $\phi_I'^R + \phi_I'^R \times \frac{\frac{\partial^2 R}{\partial I \partial l}}{\frac{\partial^2 R}{\partial I^2}} = \phi_I'^R + (1-\theta)\frac{\left(\frac{\partial^2 R}{\partial I \partial l}\right)^2}{\frac{\partial^2 R}{\partial I^2}} < 0$.

Therefore, this shows that $\frac{dI}{d\theta}$ is always of the sign of $\left[\pi_0'(I) - \frac{\partial R}{\partial I}\right]$.

Now, $\frac{d\omega}{dI} = \left(\phi_I'^\omega - \phi_I'^\omega \frac{\frac{\partial^2 R}{\partial I \partial l}}{\frac{\partial^2 R}{\partial I^2}}\right) + \frac{\phi_\theta'^\omega}{\left[\frac{\partial R}{\partial I} - \pi_0'(I)\right]} \times \left[\phi_I'^R + \phi_I'^R \frac{\partial^2 R/\partial I \partial l}{\frac{\partial^2 R}{\partial I^2}}\right]$ with:

$\phi_I'^\omega = \frac{\theta}{l}\left[\frac{\partial R}{\partial I} - \pi_0'(I)\right]$

$\phi_I'^\omega = -\frac{\theta}{l^2}\left[R(I,l) - \omega_0 l - \pi_0(I)\right] + \frac{\theta}{l}\left[\frac{\partial R}{\partial I} - \omega_0\right] = -\frac{\theta}{l^2}\left[R(I,l) - \pi_0(I) - l\frac{\partial R}{\partial l}\right]$

$= -\frac{\theta}{l^2}\left[R(I,l) - \omega_0 l - \pi_0(I)\right] < 0$.

Assuming that $\pi_0'(I) - \frac{\partial R}{\partial I} > 0$ we deduce that $\phi_I'^\omega < 0$. Since $\phi_I'^\omega < 0$ there are two cases.

(a) If $\frac{\partial^2 R}{\partial I \partial l} > 0$ then the first part of $\frac{d\omega}{dI}$ is negative and the second part is of the sign of $\phi_\theta'^\omega$ but $\phi_\theta'^\omega > 0$ and the sign of

then the sign of $\frac{d\omega}{dI}$ is not determined.

(b) If $\frac{\partial^2 R}{\partial I \partial l} < 0$ the sign of $\frac{d\omega}{dI}$ is also undetermined since $\phi_I'^\omega < 0$ but

$-\phi_\ell'^\omega \frac{\frac{\partial^2 R}{\partial I \partial l}}{\frac{\partial^2 \ell}{\partial I^2}} > 0$.

Now, if one writes $R(y) = p(y)y$ and y being a CES production function, $p(y) = y^{-\frac{1}{\eta}}$ (see main text), it is straightforward to show that $\pi_0'(I) - \frac{\partial R}{\partial I} > 0$ with $\pi_0(I) = R(I,0)$ is equivalent to $\frac{\eta-1}{\eta} < \frac{\sigma-1}{\sigma}$. It suffices to note that $\frac{\partial R}{\partial I} = \alpha\left[1 + (\frac{l}{I})^{\frac{\sigma}{\sigma-1}}\right]^{\frac{\alpha\sigma-\sigma+1}{\sigma-1}} I^{\alpha-1}$. Furthermore, because $\frac{dI}{d\theta}$ is of the sign of $\frac{\partial^2 R}{\partial I \partial l}$ (see above), employment decreases in I whenever $\frac{\eta-1}{\eta} < \frac{\sigma-1}{\sigma}$.

289

Appendix B: Data Description

The Customs File: All movements of traded goods that enter or leave France are declared to the customs either by their owner or by the authorized customs commissioners. These declarations constitute the basis of all French trade statistics. Each movement—an operation—generates a record. All records are aggregated first at the monthly level. In the analysis file, these records are only available on an annual basis. They were aggregated at the firm level using the firm identification number, the SIREN. Even though each individual movement is present in the base files, the resulting files are not tractable. Hence, the analysis file contains, for all exporting or importing firms and for all years, the amount of their total transactions in each year between 1986 and 1992 for each product of the NAP 100 classification (3-digit equivalent of the SIC code). Transactions are recorded in French Francs and measure the amount paid by the firm (i.e. including discounts, rebates, etc.). Even though our file is exhaustive—all goods exports or imports are present—direct aggregation of all movements differ from published trade statistics, the latter being based on list prices. Furthermore, amounts are disaggregated by destinations for the exports and origins for the imports and by products (at the 3-digit classification level). The geographic classification is the most detailed possible since we know the exact country of origin or destination. In a previous analysis, I aggregated the data up to the following country classification:

(a) Germany, (b) Spain and Portugal, (c) United Kingdom and Ireland, (d) Italy, (e) Benelux, (f) Other EC countries, (g) Switzerland, (h) Eastern Europe countries, (i) Turkey, (j) Maghreb countries, (k) Middle East countries, (l) Other African countries, (m) USA and Canada, (n) Other American contries, (o) India, (p) China, (q) Asian 'Tigers' (Malaysia, Thailand, Taiwan), (r) Japan, (s) Other countries. These groups of countries have been further aggregated for this particular study into four categories: European Community, Other OECD countries, Low-wage countries close to France (Eastern Europe and Maghreb), Other low-wage countries (referred to in the tables as far-away low-wage countries) such as India, China, etc.

In addition, I define two groups of imported products. I compare the 3-digit industry of the imported good with the 3-digit industry of the importing firm. If they match, I call this import a 'good'. It gives my measure of offshoring. If not, I call this import an 'intermediary consumption' (IC, as already defined).

The original file has 4,159,208 observations for the period 1986–1992. An observation contains the firm identifier, the year, the transaction value, the product, the origin or the destination. However, I do not know the price of the transaction. To deflate our measures of firm-level trade, I use 4-digit import and export prices computed for three geographic zones (EC, OECD outside EC, outside OECD) by the statisticians from the French National Accounts.

OECD export prices: I also use the export prices of US manufacturing firms. These price indices are based on OECD computations based on US Customs declarations. They are unitary values indices computed as a weighted average of the ratio of either transaction values or list values to quantities declared by American exporters. All these values are expressed in US Dollars. These indices were aggregated at INSEE from the CTCI classification to the 3-digit level used in the French NAP (nomenclature d'activités et de produits, 1973) and are available for four destinations: developed countries including in particular OECD countries; countries from eastern Europe; countries from OPEC; and developing countries. These series are available for the years 1961–1992 even though I will restrict the analysis to the years 1981–1986 (INSEE, 1993).

BAL-SUSE: the BAL-SUSE database is constructed from the mandatory reports of French firms to the fiscal administration. These reports are then transmitted to INSEE where controls and confrontation with various other data sources (such as the EAE, Enquête Annuelle d'Entreprises) are made. All firms subject to the Bénéfices Industriels et Commerciaux regime (a fiscal regime mandatory for all firms with a turnover above 3,000,000FF in 1990 and 1,000,000FF in 1990 in the service industries) are included. Roughly 2,000,000 firms are present each year in the database. In 1990, these firms comprised more than 60 per cent of the total number of firms in France whereas their turnover comprised more than 94 per cent of total turnover of firms in France. The analysis period is 1984–1992. Hence, the BAL-SUSE is dynamically representative of French enterprises in all sectors except the public sector. From this source, we use balance sheet information (total sales, total labour costs, total wage bill, sales, value added, total purchases, total assets, full-time employment, and, finally, the dates of creation and of demise, if any). The total number of observations is greater than 13,000,000. To deflate those variables, I use various industry-level prices, production, value added, and wages. All these prices come from French National Accounts using a two-digit level of aggregation (twenty-four manufacturing industries, in the NAP classification).

Since the Customs file contains information on the trade of goods only—nothing on services—we will essentially focus on firms from the manufacturing sectors as well as on firms of the trade (retail or wholesale) sectors that may import goods in place of manufacturing firms and, therefore, act as competitors of these manufacturing firms.

The data on workers come from two data sources, the Déclarations Annuelles de Données Sociales (DADS) and the Echantillon Démographique Permanent (EDP) that are matched. The DADS is a longitudinal dataset based on firm declarations of individual wages to the fiscal administration. An extract of the original information is sent to the French statistical institute (INSEE) for statistical purposes. It consists of a 1/25th sample of the individuals based on their date of birth (October of an even year). Information is available whenever these individuals are employed by a firm in the private or the semi-public sector in any given year. Our sample period is 1976–1996. Data were not computerized in 1981, 1983, and 1990. The EDP is a collection of sociodemographic information on individuals and their families. It comes from the various Censuses (1968, 1975, 1982, and 1990) and from the registers of the Civil Status which collect data on births, deaths, and marriages.

The DADS dataset: Our main data source is the DADS, a large collection of matched employer–employee information collected by INSEE (Institut National de la Statistique et des Etudes Economiques) and maintained in the Division des revenus. The data are based upon mandatory employer reports of the gross earnings of each employee subject to French payroll taxes. These taxes apply to all 'declared' employees and to all self-employed persons, essentially all employed persons in the economy.

The Division des revenus prepares an extract of the DADS for scientific analysis, covering all individuals employed in French enterprises who were born in October of even-numbered years, with civil servants excluded.[33] Our extract runs from 1976 through 1996, with 1981, 1983, and 1990 excluded because the underlying administrative data were not sampled in those years. Starting in 1976, the division revenus kept information on the employing firm using the newly created SIREN number from the SIRENE system. However, before this date, there was no available identifier of the employing firm. Each observation of the initial dataset corresponds to a unique individual–year–establishment combination. The observation in this initial DADS file includes an identifier that corresponds to the employee (called ID below) and an identifier that corresponds to the establishment (SIRET) and an identifier that corresponds to the parent enterprise of the establishment (SIREN). For each observation, we have information on the number of days during the calendar year the individual worked in the establishment and the full-time/part-time status of the employee. For each observation, in addition to the variables mentioned above, we have information on the individual's sex, date and place of birth, occupation, total net nominal earnings during the year, and annualized net nominal earnings during the year for the individual, as well as the location and industry of the employing establishment. The resulting dataset has 13,770,082 observations.

The Echantillon Démographique Permanent: The division of Etudes Démographiques at INSEE maintains a large longitudinal dataset containing information on many sociodemographic variables of French individuals. All individuals born in the first four days of the month of October of an even year are included in this sample. All questionaires for these individuals from the 1968, 1975, 1982, and 1990 Censuses are gathered into the EDP. Since the exhaustive long-forms of the various Censuses were entered in digital format for only a fraction of the population living in France (1/4 or 1/5 depending on the date), the division des Etudes Démographiques had to find all the Census questionaires for these individuals. The INSEE regional agencies were in charge of this task. But, not all the information from these forms were entered. The most important sociodemographic variables are however available.[34]

---

[33] Meron (1988) shows that individuals employed in the civil service move almost exclusively to other positions within the civil service. Thus the exclusion of civil servants should not affect our estimation of a worker's market wage equation.

[34] Notice that no earnings or income variables have ever been sought in the French Censuses.

For every individual, education measured as the highest diploma and the age at the end of school are collected. Since the categories differ in the three Censuses, we first created eight education groups (identical to those used in Abowd, Kramarz, and Margolis 1999) that are later aggregated in three education groups, labelled low-, medium-, and high-education. The following other variables are collected: nationality (including possible naturalization to French citizenship), country of birth, year of arrival in France, marital status, number of children, employment status (wage-earner in the private sector, civil servant, self-employed, unemployed, inactive, apprentice), spouse's employment status, information on the equipment in the house or appartment, type of city, location of the residence (region and department). For some of the Censuses, data on the parents' education or social status are collected.

In addition to the Census information, all French town halls in charge of Civil Status registers and ceremonies transmit information to INSEE for the same individuals. Indeed, any birth, death, wedding, and divorce involving an individual of the EDP is recorded. For each of the above events, additional information on the date as well as the occupation of the persons concerned by the events are collected.

Finally, both Censuses and Civil Status information contain the personal identifier (ID) of the individual.

Creation of the Matched Data File: Based on the personal identifier, which is identical in the two datasets (EDP and DADS), it is possible to create a file containing approximately one-tenth of the original 1/25th of the population born in October of an even year, that is, those born in the first four days of the month. Notice that we do not have wages data for the civil servants (even though Census information allows us to know if someone has been or has become one), or the income of self-employed individuals. Then, this individual-level information is matched with the firm-level information. Because we focus on the imports of various goods, we keep all observations of individuals employed in a manufacturing firm at some point during the period 1986–1992. The resulting and final number of observations is 112,682 (when the first measure of quasi-rent is used) and 111,380 (when the quasi-rent with assets discounted) for whom all time-varying person and firm-level characteristics are non-missing.[35] Descriptive statistics are given in Table 9.A1

Creation of Competition Statistics: More precisely, for each firm, I compute a ratio of imports of intermediates over local purchases and a ratio of imports of finished goods over total production. To measure the import competition that each firm faces in its industry, I aggregate the imports using the 3-digit classification of the imported good. To measure the import behaviour of the industry competitors, for each firm I compute the ratio of imports of finished goods over production and the ratio of imports of intermediates over local purchases. Then, I compute percentiles of the resulting statistics by industry

---

[35] And outliers eliminated. Notice that less than a hundred observations have missing information on education. All programs are available from the author.

Table 9.A1 Descriptive statistics

	Mean	Std Dev
Earnings	94.9813	94.8287
Quasi-rent	83.1629	76.7386
Quasi-rent (assets discounted)	72.9103	71.5158
(Imports of goods)/production	0.0559	0.1213
(Imports of IC)/(local purchases)	0.1090	0.2058
(Imports of goods from Europe)/production	0.0412	0.0979
(Imports of goods from other OECD)/production	0.0069	0.0331
(Imports of goods from close low-wage countries)/production	0.0035	0.0253
(Imports of goods from far-away low-wage countries)/production	0.0043	0.0253
(Imports of IC from Europe)/local purchases	0.0842	0.1699
(Imports of IC from other OECD)/local purchases	0.0133	0.0556
(Imports of IC from close low-wage countries)/local purchases	0.0044	0.0311
(Imports of IC from far-away low-wage countries)/local purchases	0.0072	0.0379
Competitors' imports of goods (99th perc., sh. of production)	0.4180	0.2972
Competitors' imports of IC (99th perc., sh. of local purchases)	0.4806	0.3003
Competitors' imports of goods (99th perc., in level)	442594.4	1555874.0
Competitors' imports of IC (99th perc., in level)	147449.3	442278.9
Imports of goods from the trade ind. (sh. of total purchases)	6.3927	5.5426
Imports of goods from the trade industry (total level)	2.4014	10.8722
Person-effect	0.8119	0.4610
Firm-effect	1.5363	1.1317
Experience	19.5901	11.4992
Seniority	8.3349	8.3874
Experience in France	0.6552	4.0437
Married	0.6010	0.4897
Leaves in couple	0.0628	0.2427
A child between 0 and 3	0.0957	0.2942
A child between 3 and 6	0.0877	0.2829
Lives in Paris region	0.1228	0.3283
Part-time	0.0822	0.2747
Local unemployment rate	9.7351	2.2694
Male	0.6842	0.4649

Notes: number of observations: 112,682 for quasi-rent; 111,380 for quasi-rent with assets discounted and other firm-level variables; 112,682 for person-level variables.

Sources: DADS. EDP, Customs file and BAL. 1986–1992.

affiliation of the importing firm (4-digit). These percentiles measure the extent of import competition in each industry.[36],[37] I use the 99th percentiles of the distributions of these statistics within each manufacturing industry.[38] I also

[36] Because the initial data sources are virtually exhaustive (since they are of administrative origins), most firms within each 4-digit industry are small and do not import. The resulting distributions are therefore very skewed. To reflect the amount of imports in any given industry, one needs to use the 95th or the 99th percentiles of these distributions (see Biscourp and Kramarz (2007), who give a full description all these facts).

[37] Black and Brainerd (2004) has a somewhat similar setting but their focus is inequality and discrimination.

[38] To assess the robustness of my results, I also compute the 90th and the 95th percentiles of these distributions. As mentioned previously, the use of such extreme percentiles is justified by the extreme skewness of the distribution. The median, for instance, is almost always zero.

compute total imports of intermediates and total imports of finished goods for each manufacturing industry. Finally, I compute total imports of each good by trade firms (using the industry classification of the importing firm). Hence, any particular imported good that might affect directly a firm's competitive environment is accounted for. However, because of a lack of adequate data, I cannot keep track of the behaviour of a firm's suppliers that do not belong to the firm's industry.

Appendix C: Endogeneity and Instruments

US export prices as pure demand shocks: I follow exactly Abowd and Lemieux (1993) in estimating a supply equation. Hence, I regress the sales of French firms on industry-level ouput prices and industry-level wages. First, I estimate the relation between firm-level sales (deflated by industry-level output prices) and industry-level value-added prices, industry-level wages, and time indicators in the cross-section dimension. Then, I control for firm fixed effects. Finally, I instrument value-added prices using lagged US export prices (1981–1986, when my estimation period is 1986–1992). The results are presented in Table 9.A2. In column 1, the relation between industry-level prices is estimated by OLS. The least squares estimate is negative reflecting the fact that, in the cross-section, supply shocks dominate demand shocks. However, when firm fixed effects are introduced the coefficient becomes positive and is marginally significant (column 2). Finally, when value-added prices are instrumented by US export prices the relation becomes strongly positive (column 3).[39] The elasticity is equal to 0.458, slightly above the one estimated by Abowd and Lemieux for Canada whereas the impact of wage on sales is very comparable to theirs.

Table 9.A2 Using US export prices to instrument the price of value added in French manufacturing

	Firm-level real sales		
	(1) OLS	(2) Firm fixed effects	(3) IV (in 1st difference)
Price of value added (industry-level)	−0.5015	0.1555	0.4580
	(0.1046)	(0.0443)	(0.1756)
Wage (industry-level)	2.3416	0.1664	0.4714
	(0.0535)	(0.0772)	(0.0811)
R-square	0.0377	0.9673	0.0077
Number of observations	60,197	42,402	

Notes: each observation is a firm–year. The prices and wages are measured at the 2-digit level (forty industries). The sample period is 1986–1992. Instruments for the industry-level price of value added are export prices in US $ for the years 1981–1986 of US firms to four destinations.

Sources: BAL-SUSE, French National Accounts; OECD.

---

[39] The estimation is done in first difference as in Abowd and Lemieux (1993).

The instrumentation strategy (principle and tests): To understand the results of Table 9.3, several points must be discussed. First, all my regressions control for the person-specific unobserved heterogeneity using the estimated person effect. More precisely, all estimates, in this table as well as in those that follow, include an estimated person effect that results from estimating equation (9.5) using OLS in which log-earnings are regressed on a quartic in experience, a time-varying indicator for living in the Paris region, and an indicator for working full-time, these three variables being fully cross-referenced with sex indicators, and, more importantly here, a person fixed effect and a firm fixed effect. The full least squares solution for equation (9.5) is obtained using the full sample of more than 13 million observations and a conjugate gradient algorithm.[40] These last two effects are then used in the restricted sample that is analysed here. The estimated person effect is directly used in the regression as an additional control variable whereas the firm effect is used to compute the quasi-rent using equation (9.8). More precisely, each regression includes the following variables: experience(quartic), marital status, indicators for having children below the age of 3, children between the ages of 3 and 6, for living in Ile de France, for working part-time, year dummies, experience in France (for the immigrants), the local unemployment rate, 3-digit industry indicators, the estimated person-effect, and a full interaction of the estimated person-effect with all previous variables (except seniority and the industry indicators). Most of these variables are not available in the full DADS sample but only in the match between DADS and EDP.

In Table 9.3, I use a measure of the quasi-rent that subtracts a measure of the real opportunity cost of capital of 3 per cent per annum from the measure presented in the theory section (as in Abowd and Allain (1996); wages are expressed in 1,000 French Francs). As argued in Section 9.3, because OLS estimates are likely to be affected by endogeneity biases, I tested for endogeneity of the main variables of my wage model: firm-level quasi-rent, firm-level imports of goods (as a fraction of production), firm-level imports of intermediates (as a ratio of local purchases), the competitors import behaviour (the 99th percentile of the distribution of imports of goods as a fraction of production in the same 4-digit sector and the 99th percentile of the distribution of imports of intermediates as a fraction of local purchases in the same 4-digit sector), worker's seniority, and seniority-square. The test strategy that I use is very simple. I regress each potentially endogenous variable on the set of instruments (lagged export price indices of US firms to four destinations by 3-digit industries) and the wage equation exogenous variables. I compute the residuals of these regressions and augment the wage equation with these residuals. The exogeneity test amounts to a zero coefficient on the residual in this last equation for the variable of interest. For robustness purposes, I use the two measures of the quasi-rent. Results point to similar conclusions. All variables except quasi-rent and seniority

---

[40] See Abowd, Creecy, and Kramarz (2002). Notice that I do not correct for the fact that this person effect is estimated. Since I know the asymptotic variance of this effect as well as the covariance with other explanatory variables, I could push in this direction. However, first attempts at doing so show that this correction would be trivial.

are exogenous in this person-level wage equation. This result is presented in Kramarz (2007, Appendix C, Table 9.10). In addition, treating seniority as exogenous does not affect any of the results presented in this chapter.[41] Quasi-rent and seniority are the only variables that have to be instrumented. As explained previously, this quasi-rent is instrumented with lagged export prices of US firms to four destinations: OECD countries, eastern European countries, oil producers, and developing countries by manufacturing industry (by 3-digit industry). The detailed estimates for each instrumenting regression are available from the author, but those for the quasi-rent variable in firms where negotiation on employment takes place are summarized in Table 9.A3. In Table 9.A4, for each instrumenting regression, I present the F-statistics of the nullity of the instruments (the export prices). Because export prices should be set on the global market, export prices for US firms should be correlated with export prices for French firms. Abowd and Allain (1996) provide such evidence although the correlation is not perfect. If it were, most coefficients should be positive in this regression: an increase in price for US firms means better profit conditions for French firms. As can be seen in Table 9.A3, this is not always so. When the export

Table 9.A3 Summary of the signs and significance of the coefficients in the regression of quasi-rent (for firms negotiating on employment) on US export prices to various destinations

Year	Destination			
	Eastern countries	OECD countries	Petroleum producers	Developing countries
1985	Always negative	Always positive	Always negative	Always negative
1986	Most negative, once positive	Most positive, once negative	Most positive, once negative	Most positive, once negative
1987	Always negative	Always positive	Most negative, once positive	n.s.
1988	Always positive	Always positive	n.s.	n.s.
1989	n.s.	Positive	Positive	Negative

Notes: this table reports the signs and significance of the instrumenting regression of quasi-rent, in firms negotiating on employment, on US export prices. n.s. means that the coefficients in that cell (country–year) are never significantly different from zero in the regression. Similarly for the other cells country–year. Always positive means that the coefficients for that cell are often positive, significantly so, and sometimes not significantly different from zero. Positive means that they are sometimes positive, significantly so, and often not significantly different from zero. Similarly for negative signs. The regression also includes measures of the workers' employing firms imports, of the competitors' imports, and experience (quartic), marital status, indicators for having children below 3, children between 3 and 6, for living in Ile de France, for working part-time, year dummies, experience in France (for the immigrants), the local unemployment rate. the estimated person-effect, industry indicators (3-digit), and a full interaction of the person-effect with all previous variables (except seniority, import variables, and industry indicators). 37,698 person–year observations. The sample period is 1986–1992.

[41] I also estimated wage equations with competitors' behaviour treated as endogenous variables with no impact on my results. All these results are available from the author.

297

Table 9.A4 Strength of the instrumenting regressions

	F-statistics
Quasi-rent for firms negotiating on employment	32.79
Quasi-rent for firms negotiating on wages, not employment	23.99
Quasi-rent for firms not negotiating on employment or wages	16.92
Seniority	10.82

Notes: this table reports the strength of the instrumenting regression of quasi-rent, for firms in various bargaining regimes, and of seniority, on US export prices. The regression also includes measures of the workers' employing firms imports, of the competitors' imports (both interacted with the negotiation regime), and experience (quartic), marital status, indicators for having children below 3, children between 3 and 6, for living in Ile de France, for working part-time, year dummies, experience in France (for the immigrants), the local unemployment rate, the estimated person-effect, industry indicators (3-digit), and a full interaction of the person-effect with all previous variables (except seniority, import variables, and industry indicators). 37,698 person-year observations. The sample period is 1986–1992.

prices of US firms to OECD countries increase, the quasi-rent in French firms that negotiate on employment with their unions indeed increases most of the time; French firms apparently benefit from these higher prices. On the other hand, when export prices to eastern European countries increase, the quasi-rent of these French firms often decreases, possibly indicating increased import competition between French and US firms. An increase in export prices to oil-producing countries is likely to reflect an increase in oil prices. Two effects are at play, a direct one affecting (negatively) profits in France, a positive one due to increased imports from oil producers. Finally, Table 9.A4 presents F-tests for the nullity of the instruments—export prices of US firms—and provides a measure of the quality of the four instrumenting regressions: quasi-rent in the three regimes and seniority.

Bibliography

Abowd, J. and L. Allain (1996). Compensation Structure and Product Market Competition, *Annales d'Economie et de Statistique*, 41/42, 207–17.

Abowd, J., Creecy, R., and F. Kramarz (2002). Computing Person and Firm Effects Using Linked Longitudinal Employer-Employee Data, Cornell University working paper.

Abowd, J. and F. Kramarz (1993). A test of negotiation and incentive compensation models using longitudinal French enterprise data. In J. Van Ours et al. (eds), *Labor Demand and Equilibrium Wage Formation*, Amsterdam: North-Holland.

Abowd, J., Kramarz, F., Lengermann, D., and S. Roux (2007). Persistent Inter-Industry Wage Differences: Rent Sharing and Opportunity Costs, Crest working paper.

Abowd, J., Kramarz, F., and D. Margolis (1999). High-Wage Workers and High-Wage Firms, *Econometrica*, 67(2): 251–333.

Abowd, J. and T. Lemieux (1993). The Effect of Product Market Competition on Collective Bargaining Agreements: the Case of Foreign Competition in Canada, *Quarterly Journal of Economics*, 983–1014.

Bernard, A.B. and B. Jensen (1997). Exporters, Skill Upgrading, and the Wage Gap, *Journal of International Economics*, 42: 3–31.

Bertrand, M. (2004). From the Invisible Handshake to the Invisible Hand? How Import Competition Changes the Employment Relationship, *Journal of Labor Economics*, 22(4): 723–66.

Bertrand, M., Schoar, A., and D. Thesmar (2007). Banking Deregulation and Industry Structure: Evidence from the 1985 Banking Act, *Journal of Finance*, 62: 597–628.

Biscourp, P. and F. Kramarz (2003). Internationalisation des entreprises industrielles et emploi, 1986–1992, *Economie et Statistique*, 69–91.

Biscourp, P. and F. Kramarz (2007). Employment, Skill-Structure, and International Trade: Firm-Level Evidence for France, *Journal of International Economics*, 72(1): 22–51.

Black, S. and E. Brainerd (2004). Importing Equality? The Effects of Globalization on Gender Discrimination, *Industrial and Labor Relations Review*, 57(4): 540–59.

Blanchflower, D., Oswald, A., and P. Sanfey (1996). Wages, Profits, and Rent-Sharing, *Quarterly Journal of Economics*, 111, 227–51.

Bound, J., Jaeger, D.A., and R. Baker (1995). Problems with Instrumental Variables Estimation When the Correlation Between the Instruments and the Endogenous Explanatory Variable is Weak, *Journal of the American Statistical Association*, 90: 443–50.

Brown, J. and O. Ashenfelter (1986). Testing the Efficiency of Employment Contracts, *Journal of Political Economy*, XCIV, S40–S87.

Cahuc, P. and F. Kramarz (1997). Voice and Loyalty as a Delegation of Authority: A Model and a Test on a Matched Worker-Firm Panel, *Journal of Labor Economics*, 15(4): 658–88.

Chaney, Thomas (2008). Distorted Gravity: Heterogeneous Firms, Market Structure, and the Geography of International Trade, *American Economic Review*, 98: 1707–21.

Coles, M. and A. Hildreth (2000). Wage Bargaining, Inventories, and Union Legislation, *Review of Economic Studies*, 67(2): 273–93.

Cowie, J.R. (1999). *Capital Moves: RCA's 70-year Quest for Cheap Labor*. Ithaca, NY: Cornell University Press.

Eaton, Jonathan, Samuel Kortum, and Francis Kramarz (2011). An Anatomy of International Trade: Evidence from French Firms, *Econometrica*, 79: 1453–98.

Farber, H.S. (1999). Mobility and stability: the dynamics of job change in labor, Markets. In O. Ashenfelter and D. Card (eds), *Handbook of Labor Economics*, Volume 3B, Amsterdam: North-Holland, 2439–83.

Feenstra, R.C. (2000). *The Impact of International Trade on Wages*. Chicago: The University of Chicago Press for the NBER.

Freeman, R. (1995). Are your Wages Set in Beijing? *Journal of Economic Perspectives*, 9: 15–32.

Gaston, N. (1998). Outsourcing Jobs and Enterprise-Level Bargaining: 'Cheshire Cat' Unions Revisited? CIES working paper.

Goldberg, L. and J. Tracy (2001). Exchange Rates and Wages, Federal Reserve Bank working paper.

Gourinchas, P.O. (1999). Exchange Rates Do Matter: French Job Realloca-tion and Exchange Rate Turbulence, 1984–1992 *European Economic Review*, 43(7): June.

Grout, P. (1984). Investment and Wages in the Absence of Binding Contracts: A Nash Bargaining Approach, *Econometrica*, 52, 449–60.

Hoeller, P. and M.O. Louppe (1994). The EC's Internal Market: Implementation, Economic Consequences, Unfinished Business OECD working paper 194.

Kramarz, F. (2007). Estimating a Bargaining Model with Longitudinal Matched Employer-Employee Data, CREST working paper.

Kramarz, F. and T. Philippon (2001). The Impact of Differential Payroll Tax Subsidies on Minimum Wage Employment, *Journal of Public Economics*, 82, 115–46.

Krugman, P. (1995). Growing World Trade: Causes and Consequences, *Brookings Papers on Economic Activity, Microeconomics*, 1: 327–77.

Lawrence, R.Z. (1994). Trade, Multinationals, and Labor, NBER working paper 4836.

Lawrence, R.Z. and M. Slaughter (1993). International Trade and American Wages in the 1980s: Giant Sucking Sound or Small Hiccup? *Brookings Papers on Economic Activity, Microeconomics*, 2: 161–226.

Leach, J. (1997). Inventories and Wage Bargaining, *Journal of Economic Theory*, 75, 433–63.

Leamer, E. (1994). Trade, Wages, and Revolving Door Ideas, NBER working paper 4716.

Leamer, E. (1996). In Search of Stolper-Samuelson Effects in U.S. Wages, NBER working paper 5427.

Linge, G. J. R. (1991). Just-in-Time: More or Less Flexible? *Economic Geography*, 67(4): 316–32.

Mac Donald, I. and R. Solow (1981). Wage Bargaining and Employment, *American Economic Review*, 71(5): 896–908.

Malcomson, J.M. (1997). Contracts, Hold-Up, and Labor Markets, *Journal of Economic Literature*, XXXV(4): 1916–57.

Margolis, D. and K. Salvanaes (2002). Wages in France and in Norway, results from matched employer-employee data. *mimeo* CREST.

Melitz, Marc J. (2003). The Impact of Trade on Intra-Industry Reallocations and Aggregate Industry Productivity, *Econometrica*, 71: 1695–25.

Mezzetti, C. and E. Dinopoulos (1991). Domestic Unionization and Import Competition, *Journal of International Economics*, 31: 79–100.

Méron, M. (1988). Les migrations des salariés de l'Etat: plus loin de Paris, plus près du soleil, *Economie et Statistique*, 214: 3–18.

Osborne, M.J. and A. Rubinstein (1990). *Bargaining and Markets*. San Diego: Academic Press.

Revenga, A. (1992). Exporting Jobs? The Impact of Import Competition on Employment and Wages in U.S. Manufacturing, *Quarterly Journal of Economics*, 107: 255–82.

Sadler, D. (1994). The Geographies of Just-in-Time: Japanese Investment and the Automotive Components Industry in Western Europe, *Economic Geography*, 70(1): 41–59.

Staiger, D. and J. H. Stock (1997). Instrumental Variables Regression with Weak Instruments, *Econometrica*, 65, 557–86.

Van Reenen, J. (1996). The Creation and Capture of Economic Rents: Wages and Innovation in a Panel of UK Companies, *Quarterly Journal of Economics*, CXI(443): 195–226.

Wood, A. (1995). How Trade Hurt Unskilled Workers, *Journal of Economic Perspectives*, 9: 57–80.

10

Globalization and Structural Change: Upheaval in the Nineties or in the Noughties?

Matteo Fiorini, Marion Jansen, and Weisi Xie

10.1 Introduction

Recent years have witnessed a renewed interested in the phenomenon of structural change.[1] One side of the debate focuses on structural change in the context of development and has probably been triggered by the strong performance of a number of emerging economies. At the forefront of the relevant academic and policy discussions are questions regarding the role of different sectors for successful development (e.g. *The Economist* 2011; Pisano and Shih 2012; Szirmai 2012), the question of whether success is determined by productivity growth within sectors or by countries' capacity to move labour from low-productivity to high-productivity sectors (Kucera and Roncolato 2012; McMillan and Rodrik 2011), and questions regarding the role of government in driving the process of structural change (e.g. Lin 2012).

Another side of the debate focuses on structural change in industrialized economies and this debate is heavily influenced by significant employment losses in manufacturing in the USA, notably during the past decade. The most frequently discussed reasons for the strong decline in manufacturing in a number of developed economies are the offshoring of manufacturing jobs to emerging economies and technological change that is labour saving. Another phenomenon that may be behind the observed decline in manufacturing employment is

---

[1] Views expressed in this chapter are those of the authors and do not necessarily coincide with those of the ITC, UN, or WTO.

the increased use of outsourcing also within countries. With tasks being outsourced, numerous jobs that were previously counted as jobs in the manufacturing sector will appear as jobs in the services sector (e.g. in information technology or accounting). The nature of the job hasn't necessarily changed, but the employer has.

Although the two above-mentioned sides of the debate take place separately, the phenomena of structural change in developing countries and in the developed world are potentially linked. If structural change observed in industrialized countries is the result of offshoring, structural change in the industrialized world should go hand in hand with structural change in the developing world, for instance, because manufacturing jobs in the industrialized world are replaced by manufacturing jobs in the developing world.

It has been argued that technological progress and the reduction in trade and FDI barriers have made it possible to cut the production process into pieces and to create global value chains. Global value chains are being hailed as a new phenomenon and increasingly as a phenomenon mainly involving industrialized countries and emerging countries in Asia. An analysis of the time and geographical dimension of structural change could therefore give useful hints as to the drivers of observed structural change. If the existence of global value chains affects the main structure of economies, we would expect significant movements in the relative weight of sectors in developed countries and in the Asian region and this in particular in the most recent decade that saw the emergence of China as a major global trader.

Another aspect that the two above-mentioned debates have in common is their emphasis on the relative role of manufacturing and services. It is a stylized fact that the relative importance of the services sector increases as economies develop. The typical pattern that has been observed is one where developing countries are characterized by a heavy reliance on agriculture during the early stages of development. Growth has typically been associated with a shrinking of the agricultural sector and a parallel increase of the manufacturing sector. As countries grow further, the relative importance of manufacturing shrinks and the services sector gains in importance. Two questions are currently being debated. One debate focuses on the question whether developing economies can embark on a sustainable growth path driven by the services sector. The other asks the question whether the shrinking of the manufacturing sector in some industrialized countries may have gone too far and whether the preponderance of the services sector is becoming a burden for growth. These debates illustrate that any analysis of structural change cannot focus on manufacturing only.

It also leads to the question whether structural change is automatically associated with growth.

Another point worth highlighting is that structural change can be discussed in terms of changes in a sector's contribution to a country's value added or changes in its contribution to a country's employment. In terms of the growth debate, the emphasis is typically put on the former. In the current debate around structural change in industrialized countries, the employment side is typically emphasized. In this chapter we will look at both variables.

This chapter seeks to contribute to the ongoing debate by examining structural change in both developing and industrialized countries in an attempt to distinguish parallels or differences in observed trends. In particular we ask whether structural change in the most recent decade is significantly higher than structural change in previous decades and whether this phenomenon is observed across the globe. If it is, structural change in the developing and the developed worlds may be linked through the phenomenon of globalization. We also ask whether structural change is systematically associated with economic growth. Our discussion focuses on the extent of structural change, that is, on the amount of economic reshuffling across sectors, rather than on the direction of structural change.

10.2 Changes in the Economic Importance of Different Sectors

10.2.1 *Changes in the Economic Importance of Different Sectors: The Case of the USA*

The significant decline of manufacturing in the USA has been receiving a lot of attention in public and academic debates in recent years. Indeed, in absolute numbers, manufacturing employment has declined by around 3 million since the 2001 recession (Pierce and Schott 2012). However, when looking at the relative role of the manufacturing sector in the US economy and its longer run evolution, the changes in recent years do not appear to be that dramatic. Manufacturing employment has been declining at a relatively constant rhythm over the past three decades, as reflected in Table 10.1. The sector's share in total employment shrank by over 4 percentage points in the 1980s and by over 3 percentage points in the 1990s. In the period preceding the recent financial crisis, manufacturing employment shrank by around 3.8 percentage points. The information in Table 10.1 suggests that the speed of decline in manufacturing employment observed in the 2000s

Table 10.1 Percentage point changes of sectors' contribution to the US economy

	Employment			Value added			
	1980s	1990s	2000–08	1970s	1980s	1990s	2000–08
Agriculture, hunting, forestry, and fishing	-0.70	-0.30	-1.07	-0.49	-0.52	-0.96	0.17
Mining and utilities	-0.46	-0.49	-0.05	2.55	-2.03	-1.99	1.06
Manufacturing	-4.13	-3.22	-3.81	-3.16	-3.06	-2.87	-2.68
Construction	0.28	0.44	0.57	-0.31	-0.38	0.37	-0.27
Wholesale, retail, trade, restaurants, and hotels	0.39	-0.14	0.32	-0.79	-0.75	-1.41	-1.46
Transport, storage, and communication	0.39	0.59	-1.66	-0.03	-0.62	-0.12	-0.62
Business activities, finance, housing, personal and public sector services	4.22	3.12	5.70	2.24	7.37	6.98	3.80

Source: authors' calculation using data from the UN National Accounts Main Aggregates Database.

has been high but not necessarily higher than in previous decades, notably the 1980s. It also suggests that the first decade of the 2000s has been characterized by a significant reshuffling of employment across services subsectors and also that agriculture employment shrank more significantly than in the other decades.

When looking at the manufacturing sector in terms of value added, a somewhat different picture arises. In all decades, the sector's role in terms of value added declined less than in terms of employment. This implies that labour productivity increases in the manufacturing sector were more important than in other sectors of the economy. In terms of the overall composition of the economy, the 1980s and the 1990s appear to have been characterized by more significant change than the 2000s.

Overall, therefore, the data in Table 10.1 suggest that the pattern of long-run structural change has not been particularly interrupted in recent years. Instead, the impression arises that the US economy is continuing on a path it had already taken in the 1980s and that entails a continuing relative decline of the manufacturing sector accompanied by an increased weight of the services industry.

10.2.2 Changes in the Economic Importance of Different Sectors: The Global Level

In many industrialized countries, including the USA, the decline of the manufacturing sector has gone hand in hand with increased imports from the developing world. This has led to the popular belief that manufacturing jobs in industrialized economies are being replaced by manufacturing jobs in the developing world—and in particular in China—as part of the development process taking place in the latter. Although this is probably partly true, Table 10.2 and the Appendix tables illustrate that observed changes in the sectoral composition of economic activity are far more complex than what would be expected from a pure offshoring story. Table 10.2 reflects changes in the sectoral distribution of value added and employment in the four main exporting economies in the early 2010s: China, Japan, Germany, and the USA. Appendix Tables 10.A1 and 10.A2 reflect the same information for the remaining G-20 countries, which notably includes the other BRICS (Brazil, Russian Federation, India, and South Africa) and three of the four so-called MINTs (Mexico, Indonesia, and Turkey).[2]

---

[2] The N stands for Nigeria, that is not a member of the G-20.

Table 10.2 Percentage point changes of sectors' contribution to selected major exporting economies, decades

Country	Decade	Sec 1	Sec 2	Sec 3	Sec 4	Sec 5	Sec 6	Sec 7
		Value added						
China	1970s	−5.13	0.69	6.71	0.59	−2.00	−0.54	−0.33
	1980s	−3.35	0.79	−8.03	0.09	3.60	1.87	5.04
	1990s	−11.76	3.76	−0.08	1.17	1.48	−0.35	5.78
	2000s	−4.29	0.45	0.79	0.19	−0.42	−0.72	4.01
Germany	1980s	−0.79	−0.54	−1.45	−1.52	−0.56	−0.27	5.14
	1990s	−0.21	−0.81	−4.85	−0.88	1.11	−0.20	5.83
	2000s	−0.15	0.77	−0.07	−1.07	−0.71	0.27	0.97
Japan	1970s	−2.10	0.36	−6.84	1.42	0.51	−0.60	7.25
	1980s	−0.93	−0.41	−1.01	0.79	−1.69	0.29	2.96
	1990s	−0.61	0.01	−4.39	−2.37	0.77	0.30	6.28
	2000s	−0.36	−0.73	−1.64	−1.35	2.72	1.28	0.07
United States	1970s	−0.49	2.55	−3.16	−0.31	−0.79	−0.03	2.24
	1980s	−0.52	−2.03	−3.06	−0.38	−0.75	−0.62	7.37
	1990s	−0.96	−1.99	−2.87	0.37	−1.41	−0.12	6.98
	2000s	0.17	1.06	−2.68	−0.27	−1.46	−0.62	3.80
		Employment						
China	1990s	−4.24		−2.22	1.85	3.12	0.71	0.78
Germany	1990s	−1.50	−0.93	−7.71	1.48	3.35	−0.67	5.98
	2000s	−0.45	−0.03	−1.35	−2.01	−0.09	0.06	3.88
Japan	1980s	−3.20	−0.16	−0.55	−0.47	0.16	−0.31	4.53
	1990s	−2.16	0.03	−3.59	0.74	0.25	0.43	4.31
	2000s	−0.84	−0.05	−2.01	−1.68	0.82	−0.26	4.03
United States	1980s	−0.70	−0.46	−4.13	0.28	0.39	0.39	4.22
	1990s	−0.30	−0.49	−3.22	0.44	−0.14	0.59	3.12
	2000s	−1.07	−0.05	−3.81	0.57	0.32	−1.66	5.70

Note: the last year of information used for the decade of the 2000s is 2008 reflecting restrictions in the dataset for employment.
Sec 1: agriculture, hunting, forestry, and fishing.
Sec 2: mining and utilities.
Sec 3: manufacturing.
Sec 4: construction.
Sec 5: wholesale, retail, trade, restaurants, and hotels.
Sec 6: transport, storage, and communication.
Sec 7: business activities, finance, housing, personal and public sector services.
Source: authors' calculations using data from the UN National Accounts Main Aggregates Database and World Development Indicators (World Bank).

With respect to sectoral allocations, the tables reflect a general trend of shrinking agricultural and manufacturing sectors both in terms of value added and employment, while the economic weight of service sectors tends to increase.[3] But within this overall picture, a number

[3] See also Naude et al. (2013) on patterns of structural change in the BRICS.

of notable differences arise across countries. Within the BRICS group the relative shift towards 'business services, finance, and public sector services' has been much more significant in China, the Russian Federation, and South Africa than in Brazil and India. Brazil stands out for the relatively timid decline in the weight of its agricultural sector.

When focusing on manufacturing, it is interesting to note that China, the 'world's factory',[4] has experienced a decline in the relative weight of manufacturing employment in the 1990s. The sector's weight in GDP was relatively stable over the past decades. In Indonesia—a country with a labour market size similar to the USA—the sector's weight has increased both in terms of value added and employment. The Korean case is truly exceptional, as it is the only industrialized country that experienced an important increase in the manufacturing sector's weight in GDP accompanied by a significant decrease of the sector's weight in terms of employment.

It may come as a surprise that the weight of manufacturing in China's economy has declined both in terms of employment and—to a lesser extent—in terms of value added during the 1990s. However, this is a commonly observed empirical fact which is specific to China. When looking at total manufacturing output as a share of GDP, most Southeast Asian countries such as Indonesia, Malaysia, and Thailand have experienced constant growth since the 1960s. But for China, such a trend was not observed until the late 1970s and early 1980s, and in fact it has been declining since (Haraguchi and Rezonja 2009). Also, in terms of employment the share of manufacturing in total employment has remained rather stable in China in recent years (Chen and Hou 2008).

In this chapter, though, we are interested in the extent of structural change rather than in direction of structural change. We are particularly interested in knowing whether the rise of China as an exporter has coincided with a significant reshuffling of economic activity and production factors across sectors. In this context, let us recall some figures: China's exports represented around 2 per cent of world exports in 1990, 4 per cent in 2000, and close to 12 per cent in 2010. The country became a full WTO member in 2001. China's rise as a global trader, therefore mainly took place in the noughties (2000s). If other economies merely adjusted to the rise of China, we would expect to see a significant amount of reshuffling of economic activity in the 2000s.

When it comes to levels of change in economic activity, however, it is not the case that industrialized countries have systematically experienced higher declines in manufacturing employment in the 2000s than

---

[4] METI White Paper Year 2001, p.27.

in other decades. Among the countries for which sufficient data are available, only India, Mexico, and possibly the USA (the data in Table 10.2 do not include the years 2009 and 2010) experienced their highest decline in employment in the 2000s. Interestingly, the third NAFTA country—Canada—also experienced higher declines in manufacturing employment in the 2000s than in the 1990s. Japan, Germany, and Korea, instead, went through significant labour shedding in manufacturing in the 1990s. All three countries have trade surpluses with China and are considered to be successful manufacturing exporters.[5]

As for China itself, the country appears to have gone through significant reshuffling (in terms of value added) in the 1980s and 1990s and a relatively calm period in the 2000s. The main shift observed in the 1990s was a shift away from agriculture and towards services. Other countries are also characterized by decades in which activity in manufacturing remained relatively stable but major shifts took place between the agricultural sector and services (see, for instance, employment shifts in Japan in the 1980s). Focusing on activity in the manufacturing sector alone, would therefore lead to an incomplete picture of structural change.

10.3 Measuring Structural Change

One of the phenomena emphasized in policy discussion around the recent waves of globalization is the phenomenon of increased speed of change. Among trade economists the term 'kaleidoscopic changes in comparative advantage' is frequently used (e.g. Bhagwati 2005). In order to analyse the speed of change in the composition of employment or value added, a measure needs to be used that includes information on all sectors and that is comparable across countries.

10.3.1 The Structural Change Index

In this chapter, we measure structural change in a country by the so-called Structural Change Index (SCI) defined as follows:

$$\text{SCI}_t = \frac{1}{2} \sum_i \left| \overline{x}_{i,t} - \underline{x}_{i,t} \right|$$

---

[5] Based on trade data from UN Comtrade for the year 2011 and in line with WTO (2013). South Korea, Japan, and Germany also appear to be front runners when it comes to modernizing production processes. In 2012, the number of industrial robots per employee used in manufacturing in Germany was close to double the number used in the USA (*The Economist* 2013). The number of robots per employee used in Japan and South Korea was significantly higher.

Matteo Fiorini, Marion Jansen, and Weisi Xie

where:

$$\bar{x}_{i,t} = \frac{1}{N} \sum_{n=1}^{N} x_{i,t+1-n} \quad \text{and} \quad \underline{x}_{i,t} = \frac{1}{N} \sum_{n=1}^{N} x_{i,t-T+n}$$

$x_{i,t}$ reflects the share of sector i value added in total value added at time t. T reflects the length of the period over which structural change is measured. In this chapter we will focus on structural change over a ten-year period and T will take the value 10. Averages at the end and at the beginning of any decade have been used in order to smoothen out year-specific effects. We use five-year averages in this chapter ($N = 5$) but the results presented here are robust to smaller values of N.[6] The SCI has previously been used in Productivity Commission (1998) and in Bacchetta and Jansen (2003).[7]

The factor of one half in front of the summation sign normalizes the index to a range from 0 to 1. To see this intuitively, consider an economy consisting of only two industries ($i = 1, 2$). Assume that during the first half of the decade ending at t all the economic activities are concentrated in industry 1, so $\underline{x}_{1,t} = 100\%$ and $\underline{x}_{2,t} = 0$. One extreme case is that there is no structural change at all over the time period specified and things also remain the same in the last five years of the decade ($\bar{x}_{1,t} = 100\%$ and $\bar{x}_{2,t} = 0$). Using the definition we get $SCI_t = 0$. On the other hand, if the structure of the economy completely reverses such that all economy activities switch from industry 1 to industry 2 ($\bar{x}_{1,t} = 0$ and $\bar{x}_{2,t} = 100\%$), we will have maximum structural change. Given the definition we will get $SCI_t = 1$.

The SCI represents a measure of the extent of structural change that has taken place over the period under analysis. Expressed in percentages, it reflects which share of the economy has shifted sectoral allocation, that is, to what extent economic activity has changed its focus. The SCI does not indicate the direction of change, that is, it does not say whether economic activity has moved away from manufacturing towards services or vice versa. It merely indicates how much reshuffling has taken place. One of the advantages of using the SCI is that it is a measure that can easily be compared across countries. Another advantage is that it captures reshuffling across all sectors of the economy rather than focusing on the decline or rise of individual sectors.

To construct the SCI we use data on sectoral and total value added, and total exports and imports of goods and services in current national

[6] Results for $N = 3$ are available upon request.
[7] Francois et al. (2011) also refer to the measure without calling it SCI.

currency price from the UN National Accounts Main Aggregates Database. Some of the data on China come from the World Bank Database. The employment data we use follow Kucera and Roncolato (2012), and are collected from the ILO Laborstat Database. Our goal is to cover most economies for each year under the constraint of data availability. Our final dataset is an unbalanced panel of eighty countries, over the period from 1970 to 2010.

The level of disaggregation chosen to measure structural change is based on the one-digit ISIC Rev. 3 classification and thus uses data for seven economic sectors given the disaggregation of the UN data: (i) agriculture, hunting, forestry, and fishing (ISIC Rev. 3 A & B); (ii) mining and utilities (ISIC Rev. 3 C & E); (iii) manufacturing (ISIC Rev. 3 D); (iv) construction (ISIC Rev. 3 F); (v) wholesale, retail trade, restaurants, and hotels (ISIC Rev. 3 G & H); (vi) transport, storage, and communication (ISIC Rev. 3 I); and (vii) other activities (ISIC Rev. 3 J-P). This last group includes 'business activities', a grouping that in turn captures the majority of IT service activities. Other activities included in this grouping are finance, housing services, personal services, and public sector services.

We calculate the main SCI using sectoral value added data. Since the change in industry structure within a country is inevitably accompanied by the movement of labour across industries, we also calculate SCI using employment data to measure the aggregate adjustment of the work force. Note that the value-added SCI reflects the sectoral changes in employment, as well as changes in labour productivity at the sectoral level.

10.3.2 *Structural Change over the Past Three Decades*

When looking at the SCI for the USA, a similar picture arises as from the earlier sectoral discussions: structural change in terms of value added has not increased over the past three decades. In terms of employment, however, there seems to have been an acceleration in the most recent decade, an acceleration that appears more clearly when examining the evolution of the SCI than when focusing merely on changes in the size of manufacturing in Table 10.3.

This pattern does not necessarily hold for other developed countries, as indicated in Table 10.4. On average, structural change in terms of employment has been no higher in the 2000s than in the previous decades. The SCI for the 2000s only includes data until 2007 and the value may therefore end up being higher once the final years of the decade are included. It is nevertheless the case that the difference

Table 10.3 Structural change (SCI) in
the USA, decades

Employment		Value added	
		1970s	0.0272
1980s	0.0534	1980s	0.0685
1990s	0.0431	1990s	0.0672
2000–08	0.0634	2000–10	0.0539

Table 10.4 Summary statistics of 10-year SCI (value added)

Years	Mean	Min	Max
Developed countries			
1980s	0.0682	0.0353	0.1219
1990s	0.0652	0.0246	0.1464
2000s	0.0696	0.0160	0.1541
Other European countries			
1980s	0.0910	0.0495	0.1372
1990s	0.1657	0.0947	0.2456
2000s	0.0953	0.0207	0.2185
Asian countries			
1980s	0.0939	0.0475	0.1674
1990s	0.0891	0.0215	0.2233
2000s	0.0838	0.0434	0.2436
Latin American countries			
1980s	0.0943	0.0102	0.2391
1990s	0.0828	0.0389	0.1427
2000s	0.0762	0.0236	0.1373
Other countries			
1980s	0.1261	0.0544	0.2633
1990s	0.0834	0.0522	0.1051
2000s	0.0874	0.0518	0.1428

between change in the most recent decade and previous decades is clearly more pronounced in the US case.

A number of other points in Table 10.4 are worth highlighting. The one region that clearly stands out in terms of the SCI is the 'other European countries' region that mainly consists of former communist

countries.[8] These countries went through a fundamental regime change in the 1990s, the economic consequences of which are clearly reflected in the SCI, both in terms of value added and in terms of employment. Also 'Asian' and 'other countries' went through significant change in terms of employment in the 1990s with both the 1980s and the 2000s being calmer periods. This is in line with findings in other literature emphasizing that the 1990s has been a period of significant change in the Asian region.

More generally, structural change seems to be lower in the developed country group than in other country groupings, which could reflect that more mature economies are less prone to change. In the case of Latin America, though, it is interesting to note that levels of change in labour markets (Table 10.5) are more similar to those in the developed world than those in other developing or emerging regions.

A point worth mentioning is that international trade literature has documented the response of industrial structure within developed

Table 10.5 Summary statistics of 10-year SCI (employment)

Years	Mean	Min	Max
Developed countries			
1980s	0.0755	0.0449	0.1213
1990s	0.0675	0.0254	0.1269
2000s	0.0659	0.0429	0.1078
Other European countries			
1980s	0.0842	0.0571	0.1113
1990s	0.1651	0.0949	0.2356
2000s	0.1079	0.0431	0.2357
Asian countries			
1980s	0.0810	0.0301	0.1709
1990s	0.1107	0.0404	0.1805
2000s	0.0846	0.0334	0.1401
Latin American countries			
1980s	0.0626	0.0361	0.0998
1990s	0.0756	0.0406	0.1104
2000s	0.0718	0.0486	0.1086

Notes: data up to 2008 were used to compute values for the 2000s.
We do not consider the group 'Other countries' because of reduced data availability.

[8] See Appendix A for detailed information on the country groupings.

countries to the rise of the developing world. Notably, Pierce and Schott (2012) investigate the causal relationship between the decline in the US manufacturing employment in the early 2000s and the rise of China as a major trading partner based on a tariff policy change where by the USA granted to China Permanent Normal Trade Relations (PNTR). While our findings agree with theirs in that the US manufacturing industry has experienced consistent decline both in employment and productivity starting in 2001, our results also suggest that manufacturing employment in China has also shrunk during the 2000s, and the reshuffling of labour across sectors in Asia, including China in the 2000s, is relatively moderate compared to the 1990s, which seems to contradict with the theory of Pierce and Schott that China became a major manufacturing exporter to the USA after its accession to the WTO in 2001. However, our analysis indicates that the Chinese manufacturing industries exhibited a significant increase in terms of value added, implying large productivity gains. Therefore, we would argue that China's rise in manufacturing in the early 2000s was to a large extent due to higher sectoral productivity, instead of a simple expansion in size.

10.3.3 Is All Structural Change Good for Growth?

In order to get a first sense of the relationship between structural change and growth, we plotted structural change indices against average growth for individual countries within the country groupings applied in Tables 10.1–10.5. The scatter plots in Figures 10.1–10.3 reflect SCIs in terms of value added for three regions: developed, Asian, and Latin America. Markers' shapes indicate values for different decades. At first sight, no general pattern seems to arise regarding the relationship between structural change and growth. Indeed, different patterns arise across regions.

In the developed world, the values taken by the SCI are similar across decades. Average growth rates, instead, tended to be lower in the 2000s than in the previous decades. If structural change is costly, then the 2000s may have been characterized by change representing a higher burden on economies, as the cost of change had to be borne with lower economic growth.

The picture arising in Asia is slightly different. In that region, growth rates have remained relatively stable across the decades, but structural change has differed. In terms of value added, more reshuffling appears to have been taking place in the 1980s than in the succeeding two decades. Figure 10.2 would therefore also suggest that there is no stable

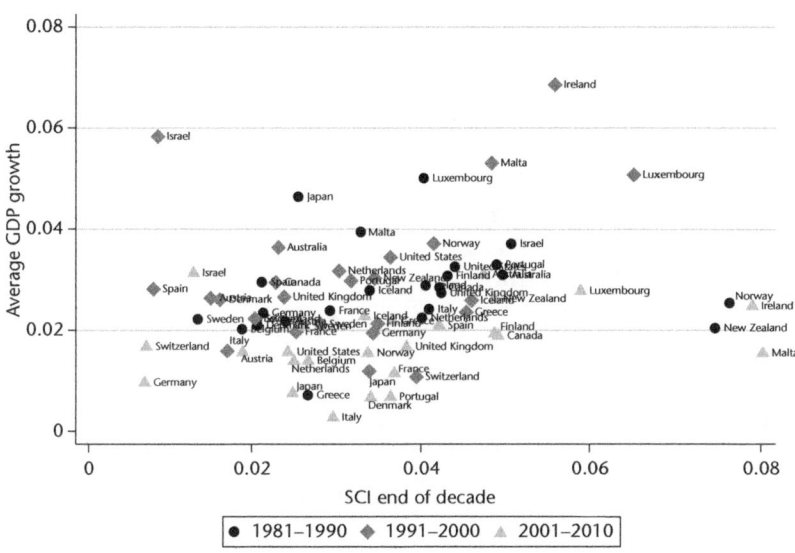

Figure 10.1 SCI (value added) and GDP per capita growth in industrialized countries

Note: average GDP growth is based on the author's calculation from World Bank GDP data.

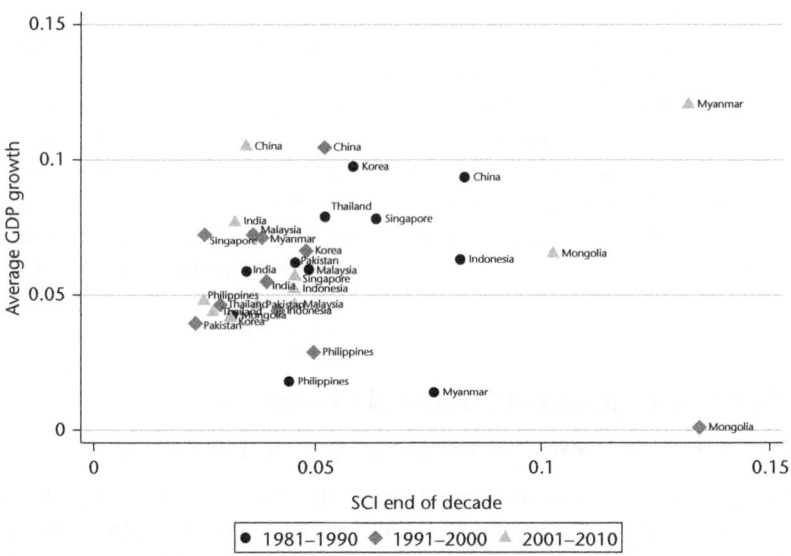

Figure 10.2 SCI (value added) and GDP per capita growth in (other) Asian economies

Note: average GDP growth is based on the author's calculation from World Bank GDP data.

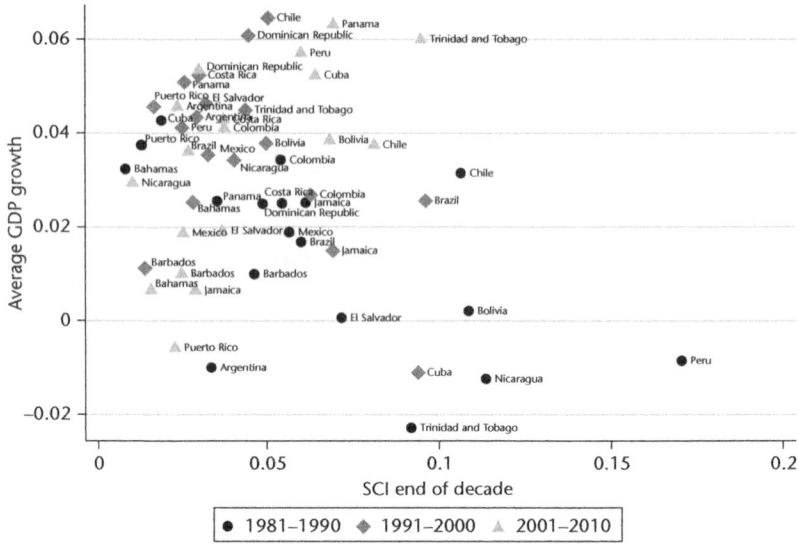

Figure 10.3 SCI (value added) and GDP per capita growth in Latin American economies

Note: average GDP growth is based on the author's calculation from World Bank GDP data.

relationship between structural change and growth, albeit for different reasons than in developed economies.

The scatter plot for Latin America (Figure 10.3) suggests that there may be a negative relationship between growth and structural change. In Latin America, the 1980s were marked by high levels of structural change. At the same time, growth levels were relatively low. In Eastern Europe—not depicted in the figure—a similar phenomenon took place in the 1990s, when high levels of change where accompanied by low growth.

10.4 Determinants of Structural Change

10.4.1 *Periods and Regions with Significant Structural Change*

The above discussion indicates that levels of structural change differ across periods and across regions. Although no general pattern seems to emerge regarding the relationship between growth and structural change, in some regions high levels of change may have been associated with low growth. In the following, we test the significance of these relationships in a simple econometric exercise in which the SCI is the dependent variable. We include decade dummies in the exercise to see whether specific decades were characterized by higher structural change. We also include regional dummies to see whether individual regions are prone to more change. We control for GDP per capita as we expect there to be a negative relationship between GDP per capita and structural change.

We conduct a first set of regressions using the value added SCI as a dependent variable. The first two regressions in Table 10.6 are meant to provide an indication as to whether regional differences or periods of observation matter more for structural change. It turns out that the decade dummies are not significant in regression (1), whereas the dummy for the 'Europe other region' clearly is in regression (2).[9] The R-square is significantly higher when regional dummies rather than decade dummies are included. It is also interesting to note that GDP per capita has the expected negative sign and is only significant in the regression with decade dummies. The variable loses significance when regional dummies are included.

These first findings suggest that structural change has not happened in parallel across the globe, but that different regions have been characterized by different patterns of change. The structural change that took place in the former communist European countries in the 1990s appears to have been the single major event in terms of structural change in recent decades when structural change is measured in terms of value added.

This finding is confirmed when region-decade dummies are included in the regression. The results reported in column (3) reconfirm that structural change in the 'other Europe' region was particularly high in the 1990s. Column (3) also reveals that the Latin American region has, on average, gone through more structural change than the developed world.[10] This is the case for the 1980s and—to a lesser extent—the 1990s, while the 2000s have been marked by a slowdown in change, as indicated by the negative and significant coefficient for the interaction between the region and decade dummy in regression (3).

When replicating the exercise using employment data, the findings reported in column (4) suggest that the 1990s and 2000s were charac- terized by a somewhat higher degree of reshuffling than the 1980s. The

---

[9] The 'Europe other' group includes Azerbaijan, Bulgaria, Croatia, Cyprus, Estonia, Georgia, Hungary, Kazakhstan, Kyrgyzstan, Latvia, Lithuania, Moldova, Poland, Romania, Russian Federation, and Turkey.

[10] No dummy for developed countries is included in the regressions. The coefficients for the other regional dummies therefore provide information on deviations from developed country performance.

Table 10.6 Explaining structural change in terms of value added

	SCI value added			SCI employment		
	(1)	(2)	(3)	(4)	(5)	(6)
1990s	0.0049		−0.0030	0.00896*		−0.0053
2000s	0.0006		0.0049	0.00846*		0.0004
Asia		0.0067	0.0103		0.0056	−0.0079
LAC		0.0063	0.0195*		−0.0013	−0.0026
Europe other		0.0382***	−0.0037		0.0197**	−0.0091
Other		0.0125	0.0289			
1990s×Asia			−0.0058			0.0249*
2000s×Asia			−0.0092			0.0171
1990s×LAC			−0.0173			0.0073
2000s×LAC			−0.0261**			−0.0021
1990s×Europe other			0.0731***			0.0602***
2000s×Europe other			0.0219			0.0252*
1990s×Other			−0.0322			
2000s×Other			−0.0208			
GDP per capita	−0.0082***	−0.0039	−0.0044	−0.00581***	−0.00315*	−0.0029
Constant	0.0603***	0.0460***	0.0469***	0.0453***	0.0438***	0.0449***
Observations	217	217	217	128	127	127
R-squared	0.096	0.200	0.324	0.136	0.196	0.339

*** $p<0.01$, ** $p<0.05$, * $p<0.1$
Note: we exclude from models (4) and (5) the only observation available for the other countries category, i.e. Egypt.
Source: GDP data: World Bank.

findings reported in column (6) suggest that this result is mainly driven by major labour market reshuffling in the other European countries in the 1990s and also (albeit to a lesser extent) in the 2000s. Interestingly, this regression also reveals that the Asian region went through major labour market reshuffling in the 1990s, in the decade preceding China's accession to the WTO.[11]

10.4.2 Growth and Structural Change

In order to assess the relationship between growth and structural change, we include a growth variable in the regressions, where growth is measured as the average GDP growth in the decade for which structural change is measured. The decades or regional dummies included in the dummy help us to control to a certain extent for possible problems of endogeneity within this rather simple econometric exercise.

GDP per capita systematically has the expected negative sign and is significant in the regressions reported in Table 10.7. The results for the other variables (already reported in Table 10.6) remain stable when the growth variable is included. We find that the growth variable alone is insignificant in most of our regressions. This confirms the intuition arising from the scatter plots presented in Figures 10.1–10.3 that there is no significant relationship between structural change and growth. Structural change can take place in a context of positive, none, or negative growth. If the latter is the case, this may be rather burdensome for the populations concerned.

Including regional interaction terms with growth stretches the ability of our dataset to capture variations rather far, but we nevertheless report the findings of the relevant regressions in columns (3) and (6) respectively. In all regressions, the former communist European countries are found to have undergone more significant structural change than developed and other regions. When examining structural change in terms of employment, the interaction term with growth is significant and negative for those countries, while it is weakly significant (at the 15% level) and positive for Asian economies. In Latin America, in contrast, it is structural change in terms of value added that is negatively associated with growth. The findings for Asia are in line with the findings of McMillan and Rodrik (2011) that Asia has outshone other regions in terms of growth enhancing 'structural change', measured by employment reallocation effects in their paper.

---

[11] For the group 'other countries', data availability only allows us to include an interaction term for the last decade.

Table 10.7 Growth and structural change

	SCI value added				SCI employment	
	(1)	(2)	(3)	(4)	(5)	(6)
GDP per capita	−0.00970***	−0.00483*	−0.0042	−0.0063***	−0.00321*	−0.0038**
GDP Growth	−0.3620**	−0.302	0.1490	−0.1540	−0.1220	0.0603
1990s	0.00312			0.00911*		
2000s	0.0035			0.0103**		
Asia		0.0147	0.0036		0.0079	−0.0200
LAC		0.0051	0.0233*		−0.0008	−0.0020
Europe other		0.0338***	0.0489***		0.0200**	0.0314***
Other		0.0140	0.0250			
Asia×GDP growth			−0.0460			0.4610^
LAC×GDP growth			−0.6400**			−0.0293
Europe other×GDP growth			−0.5710			−0.4010*
Other×GDP growth			−0.3990			
Constant	0.0731***	0.0564***	0.0431***	0.0507***	0.0476***	0.0438***
Observations	217	217	217	128	127	127
R-squared	0.167	0.242	0.267	0.160	0.212	0.212

*** p<0.01, ** p<0.05, * p<0.1, ^ p<0.15

Note: we exclude from models (4) and (5) the only observation available for the other countries category, i.e. Egypt.

Source: GDP data: World Bank.

10.5 Conclusions and Policy Implications

In this chapter we have examined structural change in both developing and industrialized countries in an attempt to distinguish parallels or differences in observed trends. In particular we asked the question whether structural change has speeded up in the most recent decade— characterized by the rise of China as a global trader in the first decade of the 2000s—and whether this phenomenon is observed across the globe. We also ask whether structural change is systematically associated with economic growth. Our discussion has focused mostly on the extent of structural change rather than on the direction of structural change.

We measure structural change by the structural change index, which reflects the percentage of economic activity that is being reshuffled across sectors. Our data analysis reveals that in the USA structural change in terms of value added has followed a rather stable pattern in the later decades of the twentieth century and the early decades of the twenty-first. Structural change was low in the 1970s but then remained around 0.06 in each of the three following decades. When structural change is measured in terms of employment, however, change has been particularly high in the most recent 2000s, a phenomenon that has also been highlighted in other studies of the US labour market, including the seminal paper by Autor et al. (2013).

Increased labour reshuffling in the beginning of the twenty-first century is, however, not a global phenomenon. Periods of high structural change have differed across regions, but the 1990s tend to stand out as a period of high structural change. An econometric exercise spanning a period of three decades notably shows that the restructuring that took place in the former communist European countries during the 1990s by far outperforms change observed elsewhere. In addition, Asian economies have been characterized by a significant amount of reshuffling in terms of employment in the 1990s.

In this chapter we use aggregate data to distil a number of aggregate trends and to examine whether these trends have differed significantly across regions and time. Any policy conclusions drawn from such an exercise have to be taken with caution and should ideally be backed up with additional microeconometric analysis. Yet this 'big picture' may nevertheless provide useful guidance to the extent that it contributes to reflections on drivers of change and adjustment to change.

In the past three decades, the most important global change in economic policy has arguably been the opening up of communist countries to global trade and investment. These changes mainly took place in the late 1980s and the early 1990s. In a number of Central

European countries, processes of economic integration went hand in hand with changes in political regimes in the late 1980s or early 1990s. In China, instead, this change occurred to a large extent through unilateral changes in economic policy and through application to the WTO,[12] a process that started in the second half of the 1980s and culminated in China's accession to the WTO in December 2001. The decade following this accession was characterized by a dramatic increase of exports from China to the rest of the world. While Chinese exports boomed in the first decade following WTO accession, FDI inflows into the country had already increased significantly from an average of US$ 1.8 billion annually in the 1980s, to US$ 28 billion in 1993, US$ 53 billion in 2003, and US$ 114 billion in 2010.[13] Indeed, China's jump to becoming one of the main global recipients of FDI took place in the early 1990s, and it has kept this position ever since.

Taking into account the above described changes, the aggregate-level analysis carried out in this chapter suggest the following policy conclusions.

First, our finding that structural change is not automatically associated with productivity increases and growth suggests that 'managing change' is an important challenge for policy makers. While 'change management' is a standard concept in project or business management, it is not a theme commonly analysed in economics. Our findings suggest that it may be worthwhile to reconsider this.

Second, while much of the policy discussion regarding the effect of China on labour markets focuses on the first decade of the 2000s, the changes that have triggered these effects seem to have largely taken place in the 1990s. Globally, the 1990s were a period of major structural change, reflecting above all the economic changes that took place in Central Europe and Asia. The 1990s witnessed a significant surge in FDI to China and an increase in the long-term elasticity of trade with respect to income (Constantinescu et al. 2015). The structure of FDI flows stabilized in the 2000s and the long-term elasticity of trade went down again. This suggests that in order to see another phenomenon of the scale witnessed in the 1990s, the economic integration of other economies of significant size would be needed. Candidates for such a driver of change could be the African continent, or major economic shifts in large countries like Brazil or India.

---

[12] In 1986, China formally submitted to the GATT Secretariat a request for a resumption of China's status as a contracting party to the GATT and in 1995 China formally requested to accede to the WTO.

[13] Values taken from World Investment Report 1995, 2005, and 2014.

Third, among the main trading nations, Germany, Japan, and South Korea have systematically been running trade surpluses with China, while the USA has run trade deficits. Germany, Japan, and South Korea all went through major reshufflings in their labour markets in the 1990s, while in the USA this reshuffling has to a larger extent taken place in the 2000s. This suggests that it may be important to pre-empt change in order to remain competitive as an exporter.

Appendix

Country Groups

Developed: Australia, Austria, Belgium, Canada, Denmark, Finland, France, Germany, Greece, Iceland, Ireland, Israel, Italy, Japan, Luxembourg, Malta, Netherlands, New Zealand, Norway, Portugal, Spain, Sweden, Switzerland, United Kingdom, USA.

Asia: China, India, Indonesia, Korea, Malaysia, Mongolia, Myanmar, Pakistan, Philippines, Singapore, Thailand.

Europe other: Azerbaijan, Bulgaria, Croatia, Cyprus, Czech Republic, Estonia, Georgia, Hungary, Kazakhstan, Kyrgyzstan, Latvia, Lithuania, Moldova, Poland, Romania, Russia, Turkey.

LAC: Argentina, Bahamas, Barbados, Bolivia, Brazil, Chile, Colombia, Costa Rica, Cuba, Dominican Republic, El Salvador, Jamaica, Mexico, Nicaragua, Panama, Peru, Puerto Rico, Trinidad and Tobago.

Other: Egypt, Mauritius, Morocco, Saudi Arabia, South Africa.

Table 10.A1 Percentage point changes of sectors' contribution (value added) to selected G-20 economies, decades

Country	Decade	Sec 1	Sec 2	Sec 3	Sec 4	Sec 5	Sec 6	Sec 7
Argentina	1980s	1.70	1.64	−2.90	−4.22	−1.06	0.72	4.15
	1990s	−3.06	0.38	−8.97	0.58	0.99	3.84	6.24
	2000–05	4.43	2.46	5.63	−0.09	−2.09	−0.01	−10.33
Australia	1970s	−0.64	3.48	−5.30	−0.66	−1.52	−0.77	5.41
	1980s	−2.47	−1.29	−5.04	−0.88	3.16	1.25	5.27
	1990s	0.33	−1.06	−1.67	−1.63	0.00	−0.08	4.10
	2000–08	−1.34	3.86	−2.99	2.05	−1.36	−0.53	0.31
Brazil	1970s	−3.35	−3.02	5.91	2.85	−8.12	4.55	0.69
	1980s	1.87	4.35	−7.73	−1.19	−1.18	−3.35	7.68
	1990s	−4.53	0.64	−8.31	−1.55	11.26	3.56	−1.09
	2000–07	−0.04	0.93	−0.19	−0.66	1.38	0.16	−1.58
Canada	1970s	−0.42	4.42	−2.89	0.04	−1.08	−0.71	0.63
	1980s	−1.18	−3.92	−1.88	−0.57	1.24	−0.92	7.23
	1990s	−0.59	1.45	2.29	−1.84	−1.23	−0.14	0.06
	2000–08	−0.37	3.94	−7.27	2.16	0.22	−0.08	1.41

Table 10.A1 Continued

Country	Decade	Sec 1	Sec 2	Sec 3	Sec 4	Sec 5	Sec 6	Sec 7
France	1970s	−3.61	0.65	−1.91	−0.43	−0.37	0.35	5.32
	1980s	−0.56	−0.24	−3.01	−1.15	1.39	−0.57	4.15
	1990s	−1.26	−0.36	−2.41	−1.47	−0.12	0.10	5.51
	2000–08	−0.37	−0.40	−2.13	1.32	−0.76	0.21	2.14
India	1970s	−6.67	1.31	2.54	0.08	3.09	0.30	−0.66
	1980s	−6.82	1.57	0.94	0.89	0.92	2.22	0.29
	1990s	−6.74	−0.18	−1.46	0.44	1.98	1.21	4.75
	2000–08	−5.57	−0.45	−0.17	2.68	2.30	0.12	1.08
Indonesia	1970s	−22.33	18.51	3.04	2.35	−2.61	1.36	−0.33
	1980s	−5.92	−12.68	9.46	−0.19	2.35	1.73	5.24
	1990s	−1.95	1.77	4.75	0.43	−1.26	−1.33	−2.41
	2000–08	−1.12	−0.90	0.07	2.97	−2.18	1.63	−0.47
Italy	1970s	−2.75	−0.53	1.32	−2.12	1.77	0.68	1.63
	1980s	−2.54	0.74	−5.48	−1.06	0.28	0.07	7.99
	1990s	−0.70	−0.19	−2.44	−1.15	0.07	0.85	3.57
	2000–08	-0.77	0.19	−2.47	1.26	−1.60	0.20	3.20
Korea	1970s	−13.11	0.64	6.05	2.81	−1.65	1.39	3.88
	1980s	−7.32	−0.55	2.05	2.51	−0.22	−1.12	4.66
	1990s	−4.06	0.23	1.64	−3.45	−1.10	0.54	6.22
	2000–08	−1.95	−1.19	−0.40	0.08	−1.50	−0.13	5.09
Mexico	1970s	−3.51	7.67	−0.39	1.34	−2.35	1.72	−4.48
	1980s	−0.37	−2.00	1.25	−2.77	−1.32	0.90	4.30
	1990s	−3.19	−1.93	0.68	1.52	−0.80	1.40	2.31
	2000–08	−0.73	3.92	−3.25	0.87	−1.13	−0.74	1.06
Russian Federation	1990s	−10.99	−2.74	−4.26	−3.64	17.26	−1.33	5.69
	2000–08	−2.39	1.75	−4.76	−0.23	−2.58	0.17	8.04
Saudi Arabia	1970s	−3.29	12.54	−4.25	4.01	−0.56	−2.04	−6.40
	1980s	4.75	−26.11	4.50	−0.96	2.44	2.05	13.34
	1990s	−0.80	4.61	1.04	−0.63	0.31	−0.44	−4.08
	2000–08	−2.63	19.86	−1.35	−2.07	−2.19	−1.15	−10.47
South Africa	1970s	−0.97	12.32	−1.18	−0.94	−2.81	−0.91	−5.51
	1980s	−1.57	−10.38	2.01	0.10	2.64	−0.28	7.49
	1990s	−1.36	−2.89	−4.66	−0.76	0.37	1.45	7.85
	2000–08	−0.30	1.64	−2.23	1.03	−1.29	−0.31	1.45
Turkey	1970s	−9.77	0.25	1.48	−0.43	3.22	2.66	2.58
	1980s	−6.68	1.14	6.43	0.65	2.69	0.66	−4.90
	1990s	−2.65	−0.10	−7.66	−1.19	−0.89	2.71	9.78
	2000–08	−2.32	0.83	−3.45	−0.16	−0.06	2.79	2.38
United Kingdom	1970s	−0.77	4.93	−5.74	−0.18	−1.43	−1.55	4.74
	1980s	−0.28	−4.70	−2.79	0.69	1.46	1.30	4.32
	1990s	−0.78	−0.09	−4.75	−1.47	1.97	0.17	4.95
	2000–08	−0.42	0.11	−4.95	1.41	−0.93	−1.14	5.92

Note: only individual G-20 countries not included in Table 10.2 have been included in this table. The EU is a G-20 member but not included in the table.
Sec 1: agriculture, hunting, forestry, and fishing.
Sec 2: mining and utilities.
Sec 3: manufacturing.
Sec 4: construction.
Sec 5: wholesale, retail, trade, restaurants, and hotels.
Sec 6: transport, storage, and communication.
Sec 7: business activities, finance, housing, personal and public sector services.

Source: authors' calculations using data from the UN National Accounts Main Aggregates Database and World Development Indicators (World Bank).

Sectors' Contributions to Selected G20 Economies

Table 10.A2 Percentage point changes of sectors' contribution (employment) to selected G-20 economies, decades

Country	Decade	Sec 1	Sec 2	Sec 3	Sec 4	Sec 5	Sec 6	Sec 7
Argentina	1980s	−1.49	−0.34	−3.55	−3.68	2.27	0.23	6.57
	1990s	−2.56	−0.02	−5.57	−1.50	0.57	1.94	7.15
	2000–08	−1.15	−0.26	−0.70	1.47	0.46	0.57	−0.39
Australia	1980s	−0.89	−0.90	−4.82	−0.19	1.00	−0.55	6.36
	1990s	−0.64	−1.01	−2.47	0.14	−0.07	−0.21	4.26
	2000–08	−1.65	0.68	−2.31	1.48	−0.95	−0.10	2.84
Brazil	2000-07	−0.40	−0.05	0.95	−0.31	0.14	−0.29	−0.04
	1980s	−1.35	−0.54	−4.36	0.41	1.67	0.10	4.07
Canada	1990s	−0.79	−0.59	−0.12	−0.80	−0.57	0.21	2.65
	2000–08	−0.96	0.56	−3.36	1.73	−0.20	−0.93	3.17
France	1980s	−2.80	−0.21	−4.40	−1.25	1.16	0.18	7.33
	2003–08	−1.17	−0.20	−1.83	0.57	−0.12	−0.05	2.81
	1980s	-5.51	0.21	0.73	0.68	2.33	0.32	1.24
India	1990s	−4.99	0.05	2.87	1.46	0.38	0.53	−0.30
	2000–04	0.36	0.06	−1.16	−0.20	0.85	−0.11	0.19
	1980s	−0.44	−0.01	1.13	−0.52	1.57	0.19	−1.93
Indonesia	1990s	−10.69	−0.29	2.80	1.17	5.96	2.02	−0.97
	2000–08	−4.93	0.66	−0.71	1.42	0.13	0.96	2.47
	1980s	−5.19	0.00	−4.14	−1.21	2.78	−0.14	7.90
Italy	1990s	−3.55	0.02	1.02	−1.04	−1.38	0.27	4.66
	2000–08	−1.45	−0.32	−2.63	0.80	0.43	−0.07	3.24
	1980s	−16.12	−0.40	5.55	1.28	2.62	0.58	6.50
Korea	1990s	−7.28	−0.44	−6.83	0.04	5.41	0.86	8.24
	2000–08	−3.46	0.10	−3.49	0.21	−3.13	2.00	7.77
Mexico	1990s	−9.32	−0.31	3.81	0.30	6.51	0.79	−1.77
	2000–08	−4.44	−0.01	−3.04	1.90	2.66	0.12	2.80
Russian Federation	1990s	0.58	1.70	−7.87	−5.76	5.27	0.68	5.39
	2000–08	−5.85	0.30	−2.28	2.51	3.71	0.82	0.78
Saudi Arabia	2000-08	−1.31	−0.92	−1.32	0.34	0.65	0.30	2.27
South Africa	2000-08	−10.11	−2.67	1.30	2.69	2.51	0.80	5.47
Turkey	1990s	−10.90	−0.34	2.03	1.62	6.27	0.68	0.63
	2000–08	−12.34	0.17	3.12	−0.47	3.89	0.19	5.43
	1980s	−0.47	−1.05	−5.63	1.55	0.99	0.06	4.56
United Kingdom	1990s	−0.60	−1.01	−5.51	−0.86	−0.47	0.44	8.01
	2000–08	−0.07	0.00	−4.84	0.96	−0.61	−0.13	4.70

Note: only individual G-20 countries not included in Table 10.2 have been included in this table. The EU is a G-20 member but not included in the table. For Mexico, employment data used for the 1990s cover the years 1991–2000.
Sec 1: agriculture, hunting, forestry, and fishing.
Sec 2: mining and utilities.
Sec 3: manufacturing.
Sec 4: construction.
Sec 5: wholesale, retail, trade, restaurants, and hotels.
Sec 6: transport, storage, and communication.
Sec 7: business activities, finance, housing, personal and public sector services.

Source: authors' calculations using data from the UN National Accounts Main Aggregates Database and World Development Indicators (World Bank).

Bibliography

Autor, David H., David Dorn, and Gordon H. Hanson (2013). The China Syndrome: Local Labor Market Effects of Import Competition in the United States, *American Economic Review*, 103(6): 2121–68.

Bacchetta, M. and M. Jansen (2003). Adjusting to trade liberalization: The role of policy, institutions and WTO disciplines. Geneva, World Trade Organization, Special Studies 7.

Bhagwati, Jagdish (2005). A New Vocabulary for Trade, *Wall Street Journal* COMMENTARY, 4 August 2005, p. A12.

Chen, L. and B. Hou (2008). China: Economic Transition, employment flexibility and security. In Sangheon Lee and Francois Eyraud (eds), *Globalization, Flexibilization and Working Conditions in Asia and the Pacific*, International Labour Office and Chandos Publishing.

Constantinescu, Cristina, Aaditya Mattoo, and Michele Ruta (2015). The Global Trade Slowdown Cyclical or Structural? Policy Research working paper 7158, The World Bank.

Economist, The (2011). 'Manufacturing' Statements, 'Opening Statements' and 'Manufacturing: Statements, Rebuttal Statements' 28 June–28 July 2011.

Economist, The (2013). Robots, Special Reports in edition of 29 March 2013.

Francois, J., M. Jansen, and R. Peters (2011). Trade adjustment costs and assistance: the labour market dynamics. In M. Jansen, R. Peters, and J. M. Salazar-Xirinachs (eds), *Trade and Employment: From Myths to Facts*, ILO, 213–52.

Fuglie, K.O. (2010). Total Factor Productivity in the Global Agricultural Economy: Evidence from FAO Data, *The Shifting Patterns of Agricultural Production and Productivity World Wide*, The Midwest Agribusiness Trade Research and Information Center, Ames, Iowa: Iowa State University.

Haraguchi, Nobuya and Gorazd Rezonja (2009). Structural Change and Sectoral Growth in Selected East Asian Countries, working paper 18/2009, United Nations Industrial Development Organization.

Kucera, D. and L. Roncolato (2012). Structure Matters: Sectoral Drivers of Growth and the Labour Productivity–Employment Relationship, ILO Research Paper No. 3, Geneva: International Labour Office.

Lin, J. (2012). *New Structural Economics: A Framework for Rethinking Development and Policy*. Washington: World Bank.

McMillan, M. and D. Rodrik (2011). Globalization, structural change and productivity growth. In M. Bacchetta and M. Jansen (eds), *Making Globalization Socially Sustainable*, Geneva, World Trade Organization and International Labour Office, 49–84.

Naude, W., A. Szirmai, and A. Lavopa (2013). Industrialization Lessons from BRICS: a Comparative Analysis, IZA discussion paper 7543.

Ocampo, J.A., C. Rada, and L. Taylor (2009). *Growth and Policy in Developing Countries: A Structuralist Approach*. New York: Columbia University Press.

Pierce, Justin R. and Peter K. Schott (2012). The Surprisingly Swift Decline of U.S. Manufacturing Employment, NBER working paper 18655.

Pisano, G.P. and W.C. Shih (2012). *Producing Prosperity: Why America Needs a Manufacturing Renaissance*. Boston, MA: Harvard Business Review Press.

Productivity Commission (1998). *Aspects of Structural Change in Australia*, Canberra: Research Report, AusInfo.

Szirmai, A. (2012). Industrialisation as an Engine of Growth in Developing Countries, 1950–2005, *Structrual Change and Economic Dynamics*, 23: 406–20.

World Trade Organization (WTO) (2013). *World Trade Report 2013: Factors Shaping the Future of World Trade*. Geneva: World Trade Organization.

11

Are Clusters More Resilient in Crises? Evidence from French Exporters in 2008–2009

Philippe Martin, Thierry Mayer, and Florian Mayneris

11.1 Introduction

During the 2008–2009 financial crisis, manufacturing was hit severely in many countries. The collapse of international trade in particular led many firms to exit export markets, or even to cease activities. In this chapter we analyse the factors behind the resilience of exporters during the crisis. Using French firms as a case study, we ask the data why some exporters were less severely affected than others during the trade collapse.

Let us first return to the alternative explanations that have been provided to explain the collapse of trade during financial crises. Chor and Manova (2012) analyse the effect that credit conditions had on international trade during the recent global crisis by examining the evolution of monthly US imports over the November 2006 to October 2009 period, and compare trade patterns before and during the crisis. They find that during the crisis period, countries with tighter credit availability exported less to the USA, relative to other countries. Amiti and Weinstein (2011) show that Japanese banks transmitted financial shocks to exporters during the systemic crisis in Japan that took place in the 1990s. Ahn et al. (2011) review the evidence that financial factors may have resulted in a greater decline in exports than were predicted in models without financial frictions. In the same vein, Bricongne et al. (2012) find that the exports of French firms in more external finance-dependent sectors were more adversely hit during the recent global crisis. Finally, Berman et al. (2012) found that the fall in trade caused by financial crises is magnified by the time-to-ship goods between the origin and the destination country. Because the risk of default increases with the time to ship, this aggregate and firm-level evidence points to the existence of financial frictions that are exacerbated during a financial crisis.

However, some economists have downplayed the role of financial frictions when explaining the drop in international trade. Levchenko et al. (2010) emphasize the disruption of global production lines and the reduction in trade in intermediate goods during the recent financial crisis to explain that the fall in trade was larger than the fall in output, and therefore conclude that trade finance played a minor role in the trade collapse of 2008–2009. Eaton et al. (2011) quantify the relative contributions of changes in demand versus changes in trade frictions, using a general equilibrium model of production and trade. They also conclude that the fall in demand was more important.

Whatever the exact mechanisms behind the trade collapse may be, some firms have been more resilient than others, which is our topic of interest. It is well-known that larger and more productive firms are more resilient to shocks than others. However, we know little about how the local environment of firms and how public policies affect this resilience. In this chapter, we focus on a specific dimension of the local environment of firms and on a specific type of public policy, namely clusters and cluster policies, as determinants of a specific type of resilience, namely the resilience of the export markets. To document the resilience of clusters and firms that benefit from cluster policies, we use data on French exporters from 2004 to 2009.

Since the end of the 1980s, agglomeration economies have been used to justify cluster policies by national and local governments. This has been the case in Germany, Brazil, Japan, Southern Korea, Spanish Basque country, or more recently in France (see Duranton et al. 2010). The economic literature on the empirical evaluation of these cluster policies is relatively scarce, as noted by Neumark and Simpson (2014) in their recent literature review on place-based policies, when compared in particular to the numerous studies conducted by government agencies and consulting firms. Most of these use qualitative methodologies and are quite descriptive in nature (for a recent survey of evidence, see Duranton 2011).

In two previous papers (Martin et al. 2011a, 2011b), we find mixed evidence on the effect of clusters and cluster policies. In Martin et al. (2011a), we use firm and plant panel data to measure the strength and the shape of agglomeration externalities in France, very closely to the micro theories. The sample covers the whole manufacturing sector. The estimation relies on GMM, and thus on short-run (yearly) variations of the variables. We find that in the short-run, taking into account several possible biases, localization economies are the only significant agglomeration externalities in the French economy. Hence, the starting point of those who favour cluster policies is right: there are productivity gains associated with clusters. However, the elasticity of firm-level TFP to the size of its own sector at the local level is rather low, equal to 5 per cent (in line with measures obtained in other contexts, see Rosenthal and Strange 2004), not because agglomeration economies are weak, but because those gains seem to be well internalized by firms in their location decisions. Indeed, we show that localization economies are bell-shaped, and the comparison between an estimated geographical distribution of plants that would maximize productivity and one that is actually observed suggests that there is no large gap, at least in the French case. It points neither to a situation where geography is too concentrated and specialized, nor to a geography that needs more clustering. In the same vein, note that many papers studying firm location decisions show that the presence of other firms in a region increases significantly the probability that a plant chooses to locate in this region (see, e.g. Head et al. 1999; Crozet et al. 2004; Devereux et al. 2007). Consequently, since firms internalize agglomeration economies quite well in their location decisions, the gains we can expect from more clustering are, at least in the short run, relatively small. Of course, this result is 'only' about productivity and is not about welfare, which agglomeration could affect through channels other than productivity. However, this suggests that even though the starting point of cluster policy advocates is right, their conclusion advocating costly public intervention to favour agglomeration is dubious, at least in France. Moreover, in Martin et al. (2011b), we use the same dataset to evaluate the first cluster policy implemented in France at the end of the 1990s, the 'Systèmes Productifs Locaux' policy. This policy aimed to boost collaborations between firms located in the same region and operating in the same sector, in order to enhance Marshallian externalities and increase firm-level performance. A modest subsidy (40,000 euros on average) was offered to various groups of firms willing to fund a collective action (creation of a common brand, participation to an international fair, etc.). Based on difference-in-differences and matching techniques, we find that the policy, contrary to its official goal, helped declining firms operating in declining sectors and areas, and had no measurable impact on firm-level productivity, employment, or exports.

This does not necessarily mean that all cluster policies are inefficient at improving firm-level performance. Falck et al. (2010) study a Bavarian cluster policy that is more specifically oriented towards high-tech industries, and find a positive effect on firm-level innovation and on R&D collaborations between firms and labs. Bellégo and Dortet-Bernadet (2014) evaluate the effect of the French competitiveness cluster policy on firm-level R&D expenses. They focus on small and medium sized firms. They find a positive effect of the participation to French competitiveness clusters (in a context of contemporaneous expansion of the R&D 'pôles de compétitivité' or tax credit offered to French firms, the *Crédit Impôt Recherche*), equivalent in size to the amount of subsidies the firms receive. There is thus neither a windfall effect nor a multiplier effect of the policy. They also find an increase in the number of R&D employees in treated firms. Finally, Viladecans and Arauzo-Carod (2012) show that the public incentives offered to develop a cluster of knowledge-intensive activities in a specific district of Barcelona had a small positive effect on the decision of high-tech firms to locate to the targeted district.

These conflicting results suggest that the effect of cluster policies might depend heavily on the context and the design of these policies: the nature of the incentives (R&D, location, infrastructure subsidies), their size, the type of industries, and the type of regions are certainly important determinants of the effectiveness of this specific type of industrial policy. Indeed, not all firms, sectors, or regions may need some help to innovate, some clusters may already have reached their optimal size while others may not; profitable collaborations might sometimes involve nearby firms or labs while in some other cases the adequate partners might be located further away, etc.

Another strand of the literature related to this chapter focuses on export spillovers, that is, on the role of surrounding exporters on firm-level export activities. The underlying idea is that the presence of other exporters might reduce the fixed and/or the variable export costs firms have to pay to serve foreign markets, through the exchange of information or the mutualization of some of these costs. In a pioneer work, Aitken et al. (1997) show, for example, that the probability that Mexican plants export in a given year is positively related to the presence of multinationals. More recently, Koenig (2009) and Koenig et al. (2010) show with French data that the presence of other exporters (whatever their nationality) increases the probability that French firms start exporting a given product to a given country; however, these spillovers occur at a very fine level in terms of activity, being stronger when specific to the product and the destination country that are considered. Moreover, existing studies suggest that export spillovers mainly affect the firm-level extensive margin of trade (export status or export entry), rather than the intensive margin (value of exports).

While the positive impact of agglomeration on firm-level productivity, exports, or innovation is now well documented, little is known about the potential effect of clusters on firm resilience. In the present chapter, we deal with this issue and ask whether the probability of remaining in an export market and, conditional on staying, the growth rate of firm-level exports are correlated to the presence of other exporters, and to the fact that firms benefit from cluster policies. We are specifically interested in how this correlation behaves during the financial crisis of 2008–2009. Such an issue is particularly important for developed economies in a context of structural change, where more and more industrial activities are offshored; indeed, if the presence of other producers and exporters positively affects firm-level resistance to shocks, the 'desindustrialization' process could be reinforced in a context of crisis due to weaker spillovers.

In our analysis, we distinguish the effect on surrounding exporters from the specific behaviour of French firms that are part of clusters benefiting from public support. We are more specifically interested in a cluster policy, the 'poles de competitivité (competitiveness clusters)' policy, which was launched in 2005. This policy is based on calls for tender leading to financial subsidies for innovative projects which are managed collectively by firms, research departments, and universities. The map of these clusters shows that they are quite dispersed on French territory. Most commentators have analysed this geography (which does not correspond fully to the industrial geography of France) as the result of political constraints that obliged policy makers to 'give' a cluster to each of the large regions of the country. Regarding the effect of the competitiveness cluster policy, we do not want to interpret the correlations we observe as causal, since many unobservable characteristics of the firms could make them good candidates both to be selected in publicly subsidized clusters and to be more resilient. We therefore want to stay cautious in terms of causal interpretation, even though we control for many characteristics of the firms and of their local environment in our analysis.

Our results show that the agglomeration of exporters positively affects the survival probability of firms on export markets, and conditional on their survival, the growth rate of their exports. These spillover effects are not stronger during the crisis; if anything, the opposite is true. Moreover, we find that on average exporters that belong to

Figure 11.1 Map of competitiveness clusters
Source: DGCIS/DATAR (April 2013).

competitiveness clusters are more likely to survive on export markets, and, conditional on survival, their exports increase more rapidly. However, this premium was considerably reduced during the 2008–2009 crisis. We then show that this weaker resilience of competitiveness cluster firms is probably due to the fact that firms in clusters are more dependent on the fate of the 'leader', that is, the largest exporter in the cluster. Section 11.2 details our empirical strategy and Section 11.3 presents our results. Section 11.4 concludes.

11.2 Determinants of Firm-level Resilience on Export Markets: Estimation Strategy

We use the French customs dataset that is now well-known and has been extensively used in other studies (see Berman et al. 2012, for example). We exploit the information available on firm-level export values from 2004 to 2009 at the firm-sector (hs2)-destination country level. The information on the municipality where firms are located is taken from the SIRENE database, which records various data for all plants operating in France.

11.2.1 *Estimating Equation*

We study two dimensions of firm-level resistance on export markets: the probability to survive, and conditional on surviving, the growth rate of exports. We conduct the analysis at the firm-sector (hs2)-destination country level. Firm-level export activities are subject to a lot of annual entries and exits which are linked to experimentations or occasional transactions for firms (see, e.g. Eaton et al. 2007; Albornoz et al. 2012). These movements do not necessarily reflect deep patterns of firm-level exports; in order to smooth the possible noise introduced by these multiple entries and exits, we focus on survival and export growth over periods of two years. Since we analyse customs data from 2004 to 2009, we have in the end a sample composed of four waves (from 2004–2006 to 2007–2009).

The main equation we estimate has the following form:

$$y_{idsct} = \alpha cc_i + \beta cc_i \times \text{crisis}_t + \delta X_{i(sc)t-2} + \gamma X_{i(sc)t-2} \times \text{crisis}_t$$

$$+ \eta Y_{d(sc)t-2} + \nu Y_{d(sc)t-2} \times \text{crisis}_t + u_{sct} + \epsilon_{idsct}, \qquad (11.1)$$

where, on the left-hand side, we are interested by either the probability of remaining on an export market or, conditional on survival, by the growth rate of exports for firm i, located in département d[1], exporting in hs2 sector s, to country c, at time t.[2] cc_i is a dummy that equals 1 if firm i is in a competitiveness cluster, whatever the year. Since the competitiveness clusters are labelled in 2005 and the first subsidies are

---

[1] Départements are administrative entities; there are just less than 100 départements in France.

[2] Note that following Davis et al. (1998), the growth rate of exports is computed taking the average size of exports in t and $t-2$ as the denominator, so as to reduce noise and regression to the mean issues. As a consequence, the growth rate of exports is bounded by -2 for disappearing flows and $+2$ for new trade flows.

allocated in 2006, there is no before/after analysis for the estimation of α in our regressions. This is why we do not claim to provide an evaluation of the impact of the French competitiveness cluster policy on firm-level resilience on export markets. We rather document a possible gap in terms of survival between firms selected in these clusters and other firms, this gap being possibly different during the crisis, as captured by the coefficient β. Indeed, $crisis_t$ is a dummy that equals 1 if the observation is during the crisis period (2008 and 2009). $X_{i(sc)t-2}$ correspond to firm-level controls at the beginning of the two-year period considered. These are the number of sectors and countries the firm exports to, and the value of its total exports by sector and/or destination. Hence, we take into account the fact that bigger exporters or exporters with a larger portfolio in terms of sectors and/or destinations are probably more resilient to negative shocks. Note that since we use customs data only, and not balance sheet data, these variables proxy for firm-level TFP, more productive firms being also bigger exporters. We also include $Y_{d(sc)t-2}$ which are département-level controls: these are the number of exporters by sector and/or destination, to measure potential externalities from surrounding exporters on firm-level resistance on export markets, and the Balassa index of the specialization of exports at département-sector and département-country level, to control for local comparative advantage.[3] Finally, we include u_{sct} which are sector–country–year fixed effects. They control for all time-varying characteristics that are specific to both the sector and the destination country: these fixed effects capture in particular both supply and demand shocks that are sector and destination specific. Firm and département controls are also interacted with the dummy identifying the years of the crisis.

Given this specification, our estimation is based on repeated cross-sections: the coefficient on the competitiveness cluster dummy is obtained by comparing competitiveness cluster firms to other firms exporting to the same market (sector-destination country) in a given year, while spillovers are estimated comparing firms exporting to the same market but located in different départements.[4]

The interaction terms capture the difference in the impact of these variables during crisis as compared to normal times.

---

[3] Which might explain both the agglomeration of exporters for certain types of sectors and destinations and firm-level export performance.

[4] We do not take into account potential spatial correlation in the explanatory variables or in the residuals. However, other papers studying export spillovers on firm entry, such as Koenig et al. (2010) or Mayneris and Poncet (2015), show that taking agglomeration into account in surrounding regions does not affect substantially the results.

Finally, information on exports is available at the firm level, and not at the plant level. For multi-plant firms which are active in different départements, all the département-level variables are thus subject to measurement error.[5] Our baseline results restrict the sample to single-plant firms to minimize those measurement issues. However, we have checked that the results are the same when we use all firms, considering in that case that multi-plant firms are located in the département of their headquarters (Tables 11.A2 and 11.A3).

11.2.2 Descriptive Statistics

We first provide descriptive statistics on the survival rate and the growth rate of exports (conditional on survival) separately for competitiveness cluster firms and for the other firms. 'Normal times' corresponds to the periods 2004–2006 and 2005–2007, and 'Crisis' to the periods 2006–2008 and 2007–2009; indeed, as shown by Bricongne et al. (2012), the collapse of French exports associated with the crisis starts in September 2008.

Table 11.1 reveals that competitiveness cluster firms are much bigger than the others: they export more and have a wider export portfolio, both in terms of sectors and destinations, resulting in a higher number of observations at the firm–sector–destination country level. This is in line with the results obtained by Fontagné et al. (2013), who analyse the characteristics of the exporting firms selected in the French competitiveness clusters. Their survival rate on export markets and the growth rate of their exports are also higher. Competitiveness cluster firms are thus bigger and more resistant exporters in comparison to other firms, both in normal times and during the crisis. However, given the results of Fontagné et al. (2013) a clear selection effect may be at work here in the sense that better performing and more resilient exporters may have been selected to be part of competitiveness clusters. Hence, we will be careful not to draw causality interpretations from our regressions relating performance or resilience and the competitiveness cluster status.

However, the evolution of the gap between competitiveness cluster firms and other exporters provides a slightly different picture. Both the survival rate and the growth rate of total exports decreases during the crisis for competitiveness cluster firms: 63 per cent of their export flows survive during the crisis on average, versus 66 per cent in normal

[5] Since a firm is 'located' in the département of its headquarters, which might be different from where its actual production for export is situated.

336

Table 11.1 Firm-level descriptive statistics

	Exp. value total	# hs2	# dest.	# obs. Firm×hs2×des.	Surviv. rate Firm-hs2-dest	Exp. growth Firm-hs2-dest	Exp. growth total
				Competitiveness cluster firms			
Normal times	49.12	5.7	16.3	37.4	0.66	0.10	0.12
Crisis	47.17	5.7	16.4	37.8	0.63	-0.04	-0.07
				Other firms			
Normal times	2.63	2.6	5.2	9.1	0.53	0.06	0.03
Crisis	2.66	2.6	5.3	9.4	0.53	-0.06	-0.09

Note: all figures are averages for the considered cell. Export values are in million euros. Survival rates and export growth rates are calculated from $t-2$ to t.

time, and their total exports decrease by 7 per cent during the crisis, while they are increasing by 12 per cent on average in normal times. Hence, the survival rate of their transactions decreases by 3 percentage points, and the growth rate of their overall exports by 19 percentage points. For the other exporters, the survival rate remains the same, equal to 53 per cent, while the growth rate of their exports decreases by 12 percentage points only, from 3 per cent to −9 per cent. Quite surprisingly, when comparing normal to crisis times, it therefore seems that competitiveness cluster firms suffered more during the crisis.

These patterns could be due to the fact that big firms were more affected by the crisis. Figure 11.2 presents the predicted survival probability at the firm–sector (hs2)–destination country level, estimated from a linear probability model[6] that controls for the initial size of the export flow and time trends. It is clear that, on average, firms in competitiveness clusters are more resistant in export markets. But while non-cluster firms exhibit a very similar probability of survival in normal and in crisis times, those in competitiveness clusters see their survival probability decrease during the crisis. This is true for the entire sample

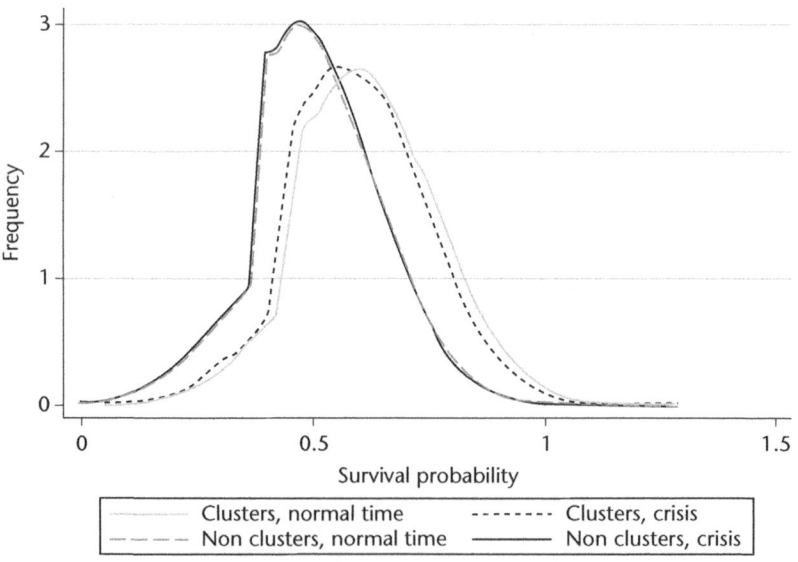

Figure 11.2 Survival probability (firm—sector—destination country export flow)

[6] Graphs are very similar when the predicted probabilities are computed with a logit estimation.

of firms and for single plant firms only. Hence, controlling for the size of the initial export flow does not affect the picture provided by Table 11.1.

Other firm-level characteristics, such as the sector of activity and the width of the export portfolio, or local characteristics such as the number of surrounding exporters and local comparative advantages, could be correlated to both the presence in competitiveness clusters and survival on export markets during the crisis. We address these issues in the econometric analysis.

11.3 Empirical Results

11.3.1 *Baseline Results*

We first estimate the determinants of the probability that firms exporting in a given sector to a given country at time $t - 2$ remain active on that market in t. We use a linear probability model, which has the decisive advantage of making the interpretation of interaction terms much easier. We moreover investigate whether these determinants vary during crisis times, as compared to normal times.

Regression (1) in Table 11.2 shows that when we do not control for firm performance indicators, exporters that belong to competitiveness clusters there is a much higher probability of them staying in a given export market: their survival probability is higher by 10 percentage points. However, this is less the case during the crisis period, as the interaction term with the two years of crisis (2008–2009) turns out to be negative and significant (even though it is small): during the crisis, their survival probability is higher by only 8.3 percentage points. Hence, in line with previous descriptive statistics, firms belonging to competitiveness clusters appear to be *less* resilient, even when the sector and the destination of exports are controlled for.

In regression (2) we control for some of the characteristics of the environment of the firm. We control in particular for the number of exporters located in the same département. We distinguish four types of surrounding firms: those that export to the exact same market (same sector–same destination) as the one considered on the left-hand side, firms exporting in other sectors but to the same country, firms exporting in the same sector but to other countries, and firms exporting to completely different export markets. These variables can be interpreted as a measure of 'natural' clusters. Note first that this measure is also correlated to the survival of firms in export markets. In particular, being surrounded by firms exporting to the exact same market positively affects firm-level survival probability on that market. This is interesting

Table 11.2 Survival probability: linear probability model (single-plant firms)

Dep. variable	Prob. to stay. in t			
	(1)	(2)	(3)	(4)
Cluster dummies				
Competitiveness cluster firm	0.099***	0.094***	0.031***	0.031***
	(0.003)	(0.003)	(0.002)	(0.002)
Competitiveness cluster firm × crisis	-0.017***	-0.017***	-0.016***	-0.016***
	(0.004)	(0.004)	(0.003)	(0.003)
Export cluster variables				
Log (# exp., same hs2-country-dep+1)		0.021***	0.018***	0.018***
		(0.001)	(0.001)	(0.001)
Log (# exp., same hs2-country-dep+1) × crisis		-0.005***	-0.003**	-0.003**
		(0.001)	(0.001)	(0.001)
Log (# exp., same hs2-other country, same dep+1)		0.014***	-0.010***	-0.009***
		(0.001)	(0.001)	(0.001)
Log (# exp., same hs2-other country, same dep+1) × crisis		-0.002	-0.003*	-0.003*
		(0.002)	(0.002)	(0.002)
Log (# exp., other hs2-same country, same dep+1)		-0.007***	0.013***	0.009***
		(0.001)	(0.001)	(0.001)
Log (# exp., other hs2-same country, same dep+1) × crisis		0.007**	0.005***	0.005***
		(0.002)	(0.002)	(0.002)
Log (# exp., other hs2-other country, same dep+1)		-0.036***	-0.024***	-0.023***
		(0.002)	(0.001)	(0.002)
Log (# exp., other hs2-other country, same dep+1) × crisis		-0.002	0.000	0.000
		(0.002)	(0.002)	(0.002)
Observations	1941836	1941836	1941836	1941836
Avg prob.		0.51		
Country-hs2-year fixed effect	yes	yes	yes	yes
Firm-level controls	no	no	yes	yes
Local comparative advantages	no	no	no	yes

Note: all explanatory variables taken in t–2. All regressions clustered at the country-hs2-dep-year level.

and to our knowledge this is a first time that firm resilience has been shown to be related to clustering. However, these spillovers are not stronger during the crisis; if anything, the opposite is true. Controlling for the size and the composition of the pool of surrounding exporters barely changes the gap between competitiveness cluster firms and the others in terms of their probability of survival, either in normal times or during the crisis.

In regression (3), we control for some firm-level observable performance characteristics, such as the size and the composition of exports (following the same decomposition as the one adopted for the pool of surrounding exporters) and the number of sectors and countries in the export portfolio of the firm; the 'average' premium of competitiveness cluster firms in terms of survival rate falls a lot, and is now equal to only 3.1 percentage points: this suggests that a selection effect exists in these competitiveness clusters. To save space, the coefficients on firm-level characteristics are not detailed, but, by and large, bigger firms have higher survival rates.[7] Hence, around two-thirds of the survival premium of competitiveness cluster firms in normal times can be attributed to their bigger size. However, the weakening of this correlation during the crisis persists, with a coefficient that remains equal to -0.016. The introduction of local comparative advantage measures in regression (4) does not change the results. Hence, even when sector, destination, firm-level, and local characteristics are controlled for, competitiveness clusters appear less resilient, that is, they suffer more during a crisis. The picture is even reinforced in relative terms, since in the end, their survival premium is reduced by more than half during the crisis, from 3.1 percentage points to 1.5 percentage points.

In unreported regressions, we have conducted several robustness checks. Results remain similar when we focus on the sectors that are most relevant for exporting firms, that is, when we eliminate the sectors representing less than 5 per cent of overall firm-level exports, when we distinguish intra-EU and extra-EU exports, when we control for the fact that firms have benefited from the first cluster policy implemented in France at the end of the 1990s,[8] or when we control for the value of exports of surrounding exporters instead of their count.

Table 11.A1 in the end of chapter Appendix presents the same regression as column (4) of Table 11.2, but at the sectoral level. We see that the survival premium for competitiveness cluster firms is largest for the transport sector. It is positive and significant for all sectors

---

[7] And this correlation tends to be reinforced during the crisis.
[8] The 'Systèmes Productifs Locaux' policy that we evaluate in Martin et al. (2011b).

except for mineral products. Note also that the negative coefficient on the interaction term between competitiveness cluster and times of crisis mainly comes from three sectors: agrifood, machinery, and miscellaneous, which together represent around 40 per cent of the observations in the entire sample. The weaker resilience of competitiveness cluster firms is thus not a general feature of French exporters; it mainly concerns a few sectors that are still quite important in overall French exports.

Finally, Table 11.3 shows that the results on survival probability extend to the growth rate of exports, conditional on survival. Firms in competitiveness clusters experience on average higher growth rates of exports, but did not do so during the financial crisis, which seems to have hit them more strongly. When firm-level and local characteristics are taken into account, their average premium on a given market in terms of export growth rate decreases by more than one-third, from 8.6 percentage points in normal times to 5.6 percentage points.

11.3.2 *The Role of the Leader*

After having shown that competitiveness cluster firms suffer more than others during the crisis period, even when individual and local characteristics are controlled for, we dig deeper to understand the reasons explaining this weaker resilience. One explanation could be that the survival of competitiveness cluster firms on export markets depends heavily on the export performance of a leader firm. Indeed, clusters are often viewed as a network of firms with strong relations, whether these relations go through market mechanisms (between input and output suppliers, for example) or non-market ones (technology spillovers or cooperation on specific projects). These strong relations may generate local dependence, and this local dependence may be hierarchical in that the largest firms/exporters may have more influence than others. This is certainly the case for input suppliers. Think of Airbus in Toulouse, for example, and its network of local partners, suppliers, and subcontractors. Due to the tight relationships between them, we can imagine that the export performance of Airbus strongly affects the performance of the other local firms active in the aerospace industry. If this is the case, part of the weaker resilience of competitiveness cluster firms during the crisis might be related to an amplification of the shock, due to their stronger dependence on one leading exporter in the region, when it is itself strongly hit by the crisis. A related literature (Crespo et al. 2014, is a recent example) has formulated several hypotheses linking the resilience of the cluster to key statistics of the

Table 11.3 Growth-rate between t−2 and t−1 firm/hs2/country (single-plant firms)

Dep. variable	Δ log(firm-hs2-country exports)			
	(1)	(2)	(3)	(4)
Cluster dummies				
Competitiveness cluster firm	0.054***	0.054***	0.090***	0.086***
	(0.007)	(0.007)	(0.006)	(0.006)
Competitiveness cluster firm × crisis	−0.029***	−0.029***	−0.031***	−0.030***
	(0.010)	(0.010)	(0.009)	(0.009)
Export spillover variables				
Log (# exp., same hs2-country-dep+1)		−0.013***	0.010***	−0.011***
		(0.003)	(0.002)	(0.003)
Log (# exp., same hs2-country-dep+1) × crisis		0.004	0.002	0.001
		(0.004)	(0.004)	(0.004)
Log (# exp., same hs2-other country, same dep+1)		0.006*	−0.009***	−0.036***
		(0.003)	(0.003)	(0.003)
Log (# exp., same hs2-other country, same dep+1) × crisis		−0.008*	−0.005	−0.009*
		(0.005)	(0.004)	(0.005)
Log (# exp., other hs2-same country, same dep+1)		0.014***	0.052***	0.058***
		(0.004)	(0.004)	(0.004)
Log (# exp., other hs2-same country, same dep+1) × crisis		−0.017***	−0.016***	−0.003
		(0.005)	(0.005)	(0.006)
Log (# exp., other hs2-other country, same dep+1)		−0.014***	−0.058***	−0.021***
		(0.004)	(0.004)	(0.005)
Log (# exp., other hs2-other country, same dep+1) × crisis		0.024***	0.021***	0.013**
		(0.006)	(0.006)	(0.006)
Observations	995251	995251	995251	995251
Country-hs2-year fixed effect	yes	yes	yes	yes
Firm-level controls	no	no	yes	yes
Local comparative advantages	no	no	no	yes

Note: all explanatory variables taken in t−2. All regressions clustered at the country-hs2-dep-year level.

network structure linking firms. The definition of cluster resilience in this literature is both larger and richer than in our study and is analysed within a framework of evolutionary economic geography. Our test for the impact of dependence on a leader can be interpreted as a test of whether linkages to the main node of the network matter in terms of resilience to shocks.

In this section, given the focus of our analysis, we restrict the sample to exporters that are active in sectors and départements in which there are also competitiveness cluster firms. We define the leader as the largest competitiveness cluster exporter in a given sector (hs2) and a given département at time $t - 2$.

Since we have restricted our sample, the coefficient on the dummy identifying competitiveness cluster firms is now estimated comparing competitiveness cluster firms to non-cluster firms which are active in the same sector–départements as competitiveness cluster firms. In column (1) of Table 11.4, we verify that we are still measuring weaker resilience for competitiveness cluster firms. The 'raw' survival premium in normal times is now reduced (from 10 percentage points to 3.8 percentage points), in line with Fontagné et al. (2013) who show that, within sectors, the French competitiveness clusters have been labelled in the best performing départements. However, we still observe a strong reduction of this premium during the crisis. In regression (2), we control for the survival (or not) of the leader. We find that in normal times, the fact that the leader survives on export markets increases the survival probability of firms exporting in the same sector–département. This is indicated by the positive coefficient on the dummy 'cluster leader stays'.[9] Next, we see that this dependence effect is even stronger when the firm belongs to a competitiveness cluster, as indicated by the positive coefficient on the interaction term 'cluster leader stays' × 'Comp. cluster'. These two results remain very robust in the following regressions, where we add firm-level controls or local (département) controls. This shows that survival in export markets depends more strongly on the performance of the leader for competitiveness cluster firms than for other firms.

How this dependence behaves during the crisis is less clear and robust. We see that the crisis reduces the role of the leader, but this effect disappears once local controls are added. For firms in competitiveness clusters there is no specific dependence on the leader during the crisis. However, it seems now that once firm-level characteristics are controlled for (regressions (3) and (4) of Table 11.4), the survival rates

---

[9] This dummy is equal to 1 for around 72 per cent of the observations.

Table 11.4 The role of the leader (single-plant firms)

Dep. variable	Prob. to stay. in t (linear probability model)				
	(1)	(2)	(3)	(4)	(5)
Cluster dummies					
Competitiveness cluster firm	0.038***	−0.116***	−0.107***	−0.022*	−0.031**
	(0.004)	(0.011)	(0.015)	(0.013)	(0.012)
Competitiveness cluster firm × crisis	−0.021***	−0.026***	−0.047**	−0.000	−0.000
	(0.006)	(0.006)	(0.021)	(0.018)	(0.018)
Dummy 'cluster leader stays'		0.014***	0.018***	0.006***	0.006***
		(0.001)	(0.002)	(0.002)	(0.002)
Dummy 'cluster leader stays' × comp. cluster firm		0.168***	0.156***	0.056***	0.061***
		(0.011)	(0.016)	(0.013)	(0.013)
Dummy 'cluster leader stays' × crisis			−0.007***	−0.006**	−0.003
			(0.002)	(0.002)	(0.002)
Dummy 'cluster leader stays' × comp. cluster firm × crisis			0.026	−0.023	−0.024
			(0.022)	(0.019)	(0.019)
Cluster leader exp. growth		−0.001	−0.003***	−0.001	−0.000
		(0.000)	(0.001)	(0.001)	(0.001)
Cluster leader exp. growth× comp. cluster firm		0.001	−0.001	−0.005	−0.003
		(0.003)	(0.004)	(0.004)	(0.004)
Cluster leader exp. growth× crisis			0.004***	0.000	−0.001
			(0.001)	(0.001)	(0.001)
Cluster leader exp. growth× crisis× comp. cluster firm			0.002	0.010**	0.009*
			(0.005)	(0.005)	(0.005)
Observations	1172526	1172526	1172526	1172526	1172526
Avg prob.			0.51		
Country-hs2-year fixed effect	yes	yes	yes	yes	yes
Firm-level controls	no	no	no	yes	yes
Local controls (spillovers and comparative advantage)	no	no	no	no	yes

Note: all explanatory variables taken in t–2. All regressions clustered at the country-hs2-dep-year level.

of competitiveness firms during the crisis and in normal times are not significantly different. These results consequently suggest that the weaker resilience measured so far was due to a stronger dependence of competitiveness cluster firms on the export activity of the local leading firm, both in normal and in crisis times.

11.4 Conclusion

Clusters are popular among policy makers. There are good reasons for this: geographical concentration of firms operating in the same industry has been extensively shown to favour firm-level economic performance (productivity, exports, innovation, etc.). However, the previous literature has also shown that the gains to be expected from public policies that provide incentives for more clustering are relatively modest, since agglomeration gains are already partly internalized by firms in their location choices. While previous literature has investigated the effect of spatial agglomeration and clusters on the level of firms' economic performance, little is known on how firms in clusters behave over the business cycle. We tried to fill this gap by investigating whether firms in clusters are better able to resist economic shocks than others. In this chapter, we use French customs data to document how an agglomeration of exporters is correlated to the export performance of French manufacturing firms during the 2008–2009 crisis. On average, exporters that belong to competitiveness clusters are more resilient in that their probability to continue exporting on a market is higher than for other firms. However, this premium decreases sharply during the 2008–2009 crisis. We show that this can be explained by the fact that firms in competitiveness clusters are more dependent on the fate of the 'leader', the largest exporter in the cluster. These 'stylized facts' should be interpreted with caution given that causality regarding the effect of the policy itself cannot be fully assessed. However, they highlight an interesting feature of clusters that has been ignored so far: by reinforcing the relationships and the interdependencies between firms, clusters might amplify the transmission of shocks, and thus increase the volatility of the activity at the local level. This might be advantageous in the case of economic booms, but disadvantageous during crises. Policy makers interested in promoting clusters need to bear this in mind when evaluating the costs and benefits of implementing a cluster policy. Hence, the gains of clustering (in terms of productivity and therefore competitiveness) should be balanced with the risks of too much specialization and reliance on one sector or one leading firm.

Large metropolitan agglomerations are able to reap the productivity gains of clusters but also the benefits of risk diversification given that they are typically not specialized on one sector or one firm. This is certainly a reason for their continuing success. The constraints on these large agglomerations are typically congestion constraints such as public transport, housing, or pollution. An alternative to public policies that aim to artificially increase the size of clusters is to aim to increase the gains from existing clusters especially in large metropolitan areas. Public research infrastructures or education policies may certainly help to do this. Public policies can therefore help reduce congestion costs that are a clear brake on the expansion of clusters. The congestion of networks and of public infrastructures and the reduction of quality of life are well-known examples. In the case of France, public transport infrastructure in large metropolitan areas (such as Ile-de-France around Paris) has, for example, been largely neglected. This type of public policy is certainly less exciting than an attempt to create a cluster in bio-technologies or a new Silicon Valley, but the knowledge accumulated by economists on the subject suggest that it is more reasonable.

Appendix

Table 11.A1 Survival probability by sector

Dep. variable	Prob. to stay. in t (linear probability model)							
	Agrifood	Min. Prod.	Chem./Plastics	Leath./Text/App.	Stone/Glass/Met.	Machin.	Transp.	Misc.
Cluster dummies								
Competitiveness cluster firm	0.0435***	0.0228	0.0402***	0.0528***	0.0155**	0.0341***	0.0727***	0.00624
	(0.00721)	(0.0255)	(0.00516)	(0.00889)	(0.00621)	(0.00486)	(0.0124)	(0.00690)
Competitiveness cluster firm × crisis	−0.0167*	−0.0396	−0.00263	−0.00501	−0.000507	−0.0427***	−0.00235	−0.0255***
	(0.00985)	(0.0368)	(0.00712)	(0.0127)	(0.00873)	(0.00682)	(0.0169)	(0.00950)
Observations	205486	13710	300026	282229	271977	409663	91587	228479
R2	0.1439	0.1361	0.1433	0.1550	0.1637	0.1679	0.1651	0.1729
Avg prob.	0.63	0.55	0.55	0.48	0.51	0.50	0.41	0.49
Country-hs2-year fixed effect	yes	yes	yes	yes	yes	yes	yes	yes
Firm-level controls	yes	yes	yes	yes	yes	yes	yes	yes
Local controls (spillovers and comparative advantage)	yes	yes	yes	yes	yes	yes	yes	yes

Note: all firm-level and local characteristics taken into account but not reported. All explanatory variables taken in t–2. All regressions clustered at the country-hs2-dep-year level.

Table 11.A2 Survival probability: linear probability model (all firms)

Dep. variable	Prob. to stay. in t			
	(1)	(2)	(3)	(4)
Cluster dummies				
Competitiveness cluster firm	0.129***	0.129***	0.024***	0.024***
	(0.001)	(0.001)	(0.001)	(0.001)
Competitiveness cluster firm × crisis	-0.024***	-0.024***	-0.025***	-0.025***
	(0.002)	(0.002)	(0.002)	(0.002)
Export cluster variables				
Log (# exp., same hs2-country-dep+1)		0.020***	0.018***	0.018***
		(0.001)	(0.001)	(0.001)
Log (# exp., same hs2-country-dep+1) × crisis		-0.002*	-0.001	-0.002*
		(0.001)	(0.001)	(0.001)
Log (# exp., same hs2-other country, same dep+1)		0.012***	-0.014***	-0.011***
		(0.001)	(0.001)	(0.001)
Log (# exp., same hs2-other country, same dep+1) × crisis		-0.001	-0.001	-0.002*
		(0.001)	(0.001)	(0.001)
Log (# exp., other hs2-same country, same dep+1)		-0.007***	0.005***	-0.004***
		(0.001)	(0.001)	(0.001)
Log (# exp., other hs2-same country, same dep+1) × crisis		0.003**	0.002	0.006***
		(0.001)	(0.001)	(0.002)
Log (# exp., other hs2-other country, same dep+1)		-0.027***	-0.014***	-0.010***
		(0.001)	(0.001)	(0.001)
Log (# exp., other hs2-other country, same dep+1) × crisis		-0.001	-0.000	-0.002
		(0.002)	(0.002)	(0.002)
Observations	3739953	3739953	3739953	3739953
Country-hs2-year fixed effect	yes	yes	yes	yes
Firm-level controls	no	no	yes	yes
Local comparative advantages	no	no	no	yes

Note: all explanatory variables taken in t–2. All regressions clustered at the country-hs2-dep-year level.

Table 11.A3 Growth-rate between $t-2$ and $t-1$ firm/hs2/country (all firms)

Dep. variable	Δ log (firm-hs2-country exports)			
	(1)	(2)	(3)	(4)
Cluster dummies				
Competitiveness cluster firm	0.034***	0.034***	0.081***	0.077***
	(0.003)	(0.003)	(0.003)	(0.003)
Competitiveness cluster firm × crisis	-0.024***	-0.024***	-0.023***	-0.023***
	(0.005)	(0.005)	(0.005)	(0.005)
Export spillover variables				
Log (# exp., same hs2-country-dep+1)		-0.010***	0.015***	-0.004**
		(0.002)	(0.002)	(0.002)
Log (# exp., same hs2-country-dep+1) × crisis		0.005*	0.006**	0.008***
		(0.003)	(0.003)	(0.003)
Log (# exp., same hs2-other country, same dep+1)		0.003	-0.014***	-0.034***
		(0.002)	(0.002)	(0.003)
Log (# exp., same hs2-other country, same dep+1) × crisis		-0.003	-0.001	-0.001
		(0.004)	(0.003)	(0.004)
Log (# exp., other hs2-same country, same dep+1)		0.008***	0.047***	0.057***
		(0.003)	(0.003)	(0.003)
Log (# exp., other hs2-same country, same dep+1) × crisis		-0.020***	-0.016***	-0.010 **
		(0.004)	(0.004)	(0.004)
Log (# exp., other hs2-other country, same dep+1)		-0.007**	-0.052***	-0.026***
		(0.003)	(0.003)	(0.003)
Log (# exp., other hs2-other country, same dep+1) × crisis		0.021***	0.013***	0.006
		(0.004)	(0.004)	(0.005)
Observations	2041154	2041154	2041154	2041154
Country-hs2-year fixed effect	yes	yes	yes	yes
Firm-level controls	no	no	yes	yes
Local comparative advantages	no	no	no	yes

Note: all explanatory variables taken in t-2. All regressions clustered at the country-hs2-dep-year level.

Bibliography

Ahn, J., M. Amiti, and D. E. Weinstein (2011). Trade Finance and the Great Trade Collapse, *American Economic Review P&P*, 101(3), 298–302.

Aitken, B., G. H. Hanson, and A. E. Harrison (1997). Spillovers, Foreign Investment, and Export Behavior, *Journal of International Economics*, 43(1–2): 103–32.

Albornoz, F., H. F. Calvo Pardo, G. Corcos, and E. Ornelas (2012). Sequential Exporting, *Journal of International Economics*, 88(1): 17–31.

Amiti, M. and D. E. Weinstein (2011). Exports and Financial Shocks, *Quarterly Journal of Economics*, 126(4): 1841–77.

Bellégo, C. and V. Dortet-Bernadet (2014). L'impact de la participation aux pôles de compétitivité sur les PME et les ETI, *Economie et Statistique*, 471; 65–83.

Berman, N., J. de Sousa, P. Martin, and T. Mayer (2012). Time to Ship During Financial Crises, NBER working paper 18274.

Bricongne, J.-C., L. Fontagné, G. Gaulier, D. Taglioni, and V. Vicard (2012). Firms and the Global Crisis: French Exports in the Turmoil, *Journal of International Economics*, 87(1), 134–46.

Chor, D. and K. Manova (2012). Off the Cliff and Back? Credit Conditions and International Trade During the Global Financial Crisis, *Journal of International Economics*, 87(1), 117–33.

Crespo, J., R. Suire, and J. Vicente (2014). Lock-in or Lock-out? How Structural Properties of Knowledge Networks Affect Regional Resilience? *Journal of Economic Geography*, 14(1): 179–98.

Crozet, M., T. Mayer, and J.-L. Mucchielli (2004). How do Firms Agglomerate? A Study of FDI in France, *Regional Science and Urban Economics*, 34(1): 27–54.

Davis, S.J., J.C. Haltiwanger, and S. Schuh (1998). *Job Creation and Destruction*, Volume 1 of MIT Press Books. Cambridge, MA: The MIT Press.

Devereux, M.P., R. Griffith, and H. Simpson (2007). Firm Location Decisions, Regional Grants and Agglomeration Externalities, *Journal of Public Economics*, 91(3–4): 413–35.

Duranton, G. (2011). California Dreamin': The Feeble Case for Cluster Policies, *Review of Economic Analysis*, 3(1), 3–45.

Duranton, G., P. Martin, T. Mayer, and F. Mayneris (2010). *The Economics of Clusters: Lessons from the French Experience*. Oxford: Oxford University Press.

Eaton, J., M. Eslava, M. Kugler, and J. Tybout (2007). Export Dynamics in Colombia: Firm-level Evidence, NBER working papers 13531, National Bureau of Economic Research, Inc.

Eaton, J., S. Kortum, B. Neiman, and J. Romalis (2011). Trade and the Global Recession, working paper 16666, National Bureau of Economic Research.

Falck, O., S. Kipar, and S. Heblich (2010). Industrial Innovation: Direct Evidence from a Cluster-oriented Policy, *Regional Science and Urban Economics*, 40(6): 574–82.

Fontagné, L., P. Koenig, F. Mayneris, and S. Poncet (2013). Cluster Policies and Firm Selection: Evidence from France, *Journal of Regional Science*, 53(5): 897–922.

Head, C. K., J. C. Ries, and D. L. Swenson (1999). Attracting Foreign Manufacturing: Investment Promotion and Agglomeration, *Regional Science and Urban Economics*, 29(2): 197–218.

Koenig, P. (2009). Agglomeration and the Export Decisions of French Firms, *Journal of Urban Economics*, 66(3): 186–95.

Koenig, P., F. Mayneris, and S. Poncet (2010). Local Export Spillovers in France, *European Economic Review*, 54: 622–41.

Levchenko, A., L. Lewis, and L. Tesar (2010). The Collapse of International Trade During the 2008–2009 Crisis: In Search of the Smoking Gun, *IMF Economic Review*, 58(2): 214–53.

Martin, P., T. Mayer, and F. Mayneris (2011a). Public Support to Clusters: A Firm Level Study of French 'Local Productive Systems', *Regional Science and Urban Economics*, 41: 108–23.

Martin, P., T. Mayer, and F. Mayneris (2011b). Spatial Concentration and Plant-level Productivity in France, *Journal of Urban Economics*, 69(2), 182–95.

Mayneris, F. and S. Poncet (2015). Chinese Firms' Entry to Export Markets: The Role of Foreign Export Spillovers, *World Bank Economic Review*, 29(1): 150–79.

Neumark, D. and H. Simpson (2015). Place-based policies. In Gilles Duranton, J. Vernon Henderson, and William C. Strange (eds), *Handbook of Regional and Urban Economics, Vol. 5*, Amsterdam: Elsevier, 1197–287.

Rosenthal, S. S. and W. C. Strange (2004). Evidence on the nature and sources of agglomeration economies. In J. V. Henderson and J. F. Thisse (eds), *Handbook of Regional and Urban Economics*, Volume 4 of *Handbook of Regional and Urban Economics*, Amsterdam: Elsevier, 2119–71.

Viladecans, E. and J. M. Arauzo-Carod (2012). Can a Knowledge-based Cluster be Created? The Case of the Barcelona 22@district, *Papers in Regional Science*, 91: 377–400.

Author Index

Subject Index